Accidental Ukrainians

Parts One to Three

Written from the Russian-Ukrainian War

Helion & Company Limited

Dedicated to the Men and Women of the Armed Forces of Ukraine (AFU).

Helion & Company Limited
Unit 8 Amherst Business Centre
Budbrooke Road
Warwick
CV34 5WE
England
Tel. 01926 499619
Email: info@helion.co.uk
Website: www.helion.co.uk
X (formerly Twitter): @Helionbooks
Facebook: @HelionBooks
Visit our blog at http://blog.helion.co.uk/

Published by Helion & Company 2025
Designed and typeset by Mach 3 Solutions (www.mach3solutions.co.uk)
Cover designed by Paul Hewitt, Battlefield Design (www.battlefield-design.co.uk)

ISBN 978-1-806721-56-6

British Library Cataloguing-in-Publication Data.
A catalogue record for this book is available from the British Library.

For details of other military history titles published by Helion & Company Limited, contact the above address, or visit our website: http://www.helion.co.uk

We always welcome receiving book proposals from prospective authors.

Contents

Introduction to Accidental Ukrainians: Parts 1–3

27 October 2025. Day 1,342 of the full-scale Russo-Ukrainian War. Day 4,267 of the actual war that started when Russia took Crimea. It's an Indian Summer Day here in the woods of the formerly occupied Borodyanka-Bucha region. Natasha is in the Hague for a conference on education and hasn't had the best experience so far. That story won't appear until Part Four, when she shares her reflections from Year Four of full-scale war. Helion & Company signed us for four parts, and we never hoped or even thought that the war would be over by February 2026, which is when Part Four is due to end.

This three-part set is the first time that *Accidental Ukrainians* will be available as a physical book. You will walk through three years of war with us as we experienced it as non-combatants. You will meet briefly our neighbors, friends, clergy, partners and others. Some are still with us; some have moved on, and only a few have died (that we know of). Photographs included in all three parts show what, in some cases, looks like an ordinary life. Sometimes a picture says a thousand words, while at other times it does not. We have seen enough of the horror from the front by now to know that if you want to look at that, there are plenty of sources for it.

Our dog, Philly, is still with us and that's why are now staying in the forest between Borodyanka and Bucha. He has a stress-related disease (Addison's Disease) from the missile and drone attacks in Kyiv. Philly can no longer climb the four flights to our flat in the centre of Kyiv. We humans carry our own scars but don't show them. Animals also carry scars, and ours shows them. For Natasha and me, our scars have made us stronger, but Philly suffers physically. He is holding his own and snores on his bed as I write this introduction. The disease steals the strength from his hindquarters, so he needs some assistance. Philly is our War Dog. We are a War Family. We Are War.

We refuse to gloss over the fact that living through this war will ever be forgotten or that we will completely heal from whatever spiritual, moral or psychological wounds we may have. Luckily, we have not suffered any physical wounds so far. You are essentially being given a glimpse into some of our experiences. What you will find is strength, resilience, defiance and a dark sense of humor. Natasha uses her talents as an educator, and I am using my experience of writing through difficult events to try to help others heal. This is a program called 'Narrative Processing' which I am currently developing for English-speaking veterans, with the hope of converting it for Ukrainian veterans if enough revenue is generated. Natasha and I are lucky to be strong, and that's something we feel compelled to share.

This three-part set comes at an important time because we are now entering our third winter of war and again are experiencing attacks on the energy grid. Out here in the woods, we can always light a fire. We, like most who live in Ukraine, have become highly adaptable. In fact, many have become a self they never knew existed. Our mettle has been tested and forged into METAL.

We don't know what the future holds for us or Ukraine. No one knows how the war will end. We don't pay attention to predictions. What we do is Carpe Diem every day that we are alive. Even if it's something small. That goes for everyone we know and work with. Today, our partners (UA Ants) are welcoming Ukrainian veterans and their families for a 'Side-by-Side Retreat' in the Carpathian Mountains. Almost all of us in Ukraine will Charlie Mike.[1] We are fighters, Cossacks, delivery people, teachers, soldiers, doctors, nurses, volunteers, businesspeople, and every other role that exists worldwide, with the exception being that we do ours in a full-scale war. That doesn't make us better, it just makes us different.

Natasha and I hope that at least one sentence or chapter calls out to you as a reader. We hope that you catch a glimpse of reality from within the war that's not caught up in the need for 'Likes', self-promotion, misinformation, disinformation or propaganda. Neither of us has a political agenda, nor do we want one. We have seen the worthlessness of most in that sphere this far into the war. The best thing you can do is honor and appreciate your own fighting men and women. If you are in Europe, the other thing you can do is be prepared because no one knows what comes next. Most importantly, you can help Ukraine even in small ways and make a difference. We have seen the power of everyday people and what they can do. We hope *Accidental Ukrainians: Parts 1-3* inspires you, as that is the desired intention.

1 Charlie Mike means Continue Mission.

Part 1

Foreword

Accidents

I think these are God's pseudonyms. When He, for reasons unknown to us, hides His signature in the events of our lives. But it is still His creation. Not a random one. You understand this after time has passed. For His ways are not our ways.

You are holding in your hands a book that was born in the process of seemingly random events.

But that's not true.

Having met this wonderful family, John, and Natasha, I constantly see God's hand in their destiny. This book, at first, looks like a chronicle of the events and impressions of the life of a married couple in a new country for them. But with every line read, the depth and sincerity of their experiences, thoughts and actions are revealed. The wisdom of the old soldier, John, and the sincere kindness of the feminine Natasha captivates the reader in every event described.

I met John on Medium, where I also wandered, as if by accident. It turned out that having started to express my thoughts about the war in Ukraine in the written form, it became much easier for me to endure all the hardships of this difficult period. John turned out to be a grateful and wise reader. We probably both felt an invisible spiritual connection, which grew into friendship and brotherhood. God has a sense of humor. Only he could spiritually unite an Orthodox American and a Protestant Ukrainian. Although, it would be logical to do the opposite.

John and Natasha appeared in my life at a time when I, having been a volunteer since 2014, moved into the category of a 'full-time volunteer' with the outbreak of a full-scale war. John immediately took on the function of a communicator with European and American donors and charitable organizations. He's a great communicator. Knowing the mentality of Western people, John greatly helped to establish relations with them. And it wasn't easy. We rejoiced at the results together and were upset together when there were only words without deeds.

Thanks to this family, a river of humanitarian and military supplies flowed into Ukraine. I remember how in the winter, while on the front line, my boys and I put the soldiers in the winter boots of the British Army. I looked at those boots and thought about John.

And it all started with a simple comment on Medium. Accidentally?

I am sincerely grateful to these 'random Ukrainians' for communication, their constant donations for fuel and super-expensive army equipment, for wise advice, and moral support. This is very valuable for me and my country.

Now is a difficult time for the whole world.

Many have already understood this, but most still live in the paradigm of the past calm decades. The world has changed and will never be the same again.

Many Ukrainians have reached out to the West, now trying to become Americans, Poles, British, Canadians... Not at all by chance, but because of one wave of the hand of a crazy Russian dwarf...

Millions of migrants.

Some blend into the new society, simply living according to the home-work-home pattern. Others carry their Spirit, their soul, and benefit a new community.

War changes people and brings out their best and worst qualities. You can't hide it. You can immediately see who is who. There are Ukrainians living in the USA, and they are far from the War and the suffering of people. There are Americans living in Ukraine, and their hearts and souls hurt from what they see and feel... And they don't just watch. They are doing everything they can to help Ukraine fight Evil.

The paradox is that I don't see John and Natasha as immigrants. I see them as missionaries. Their mission is to love, help, support, share wisdom and joy. Bring the Light. Even when it's dark around. And War.

I see them as Ukrainians. It was no coincidence that they ended up in Ukraine. They understood and accepted the Spirit of this country. The spirit of this country accepted them. And I'm very happy about it.

God does not come to us in the clouds, answering our prayers. He sends people.

People who do not immediately understand that they have been sent. But God, knowing their hearts, is confident that the Mission will be completed, though it might seem accidental.

Andrii Getun

Introduction

Do you want to read about average Americans living through the largest land war in Europe since WWII? Do you want to read a book about the Russian-Ukrainian War without a political agenda? Do you want to experience the war through the eyes of Americans living in it? If you do, then read this book.

Nothing is ever perfect or complete. This book captures some of the essential experiences of an average American couple living in Kyiv who decided to stay when the Russians attacked on February 24, 2022. Kyiv has an ancient tradition of chroniclers going back to Nestor the Chronicler (1056–1114). This book is a chronicle of events as experienced from the beginning of the full-scale invasion until the second-year mark on February 24, 2024. Some of it is insight. Some of it is telling the truth of the experience. None of it is perfect.

Andrii Getun, a Ukrainian military volunteer begins the story with his Foreword. One cannot call oneself an 'Accidental Ukrainian' without an endorsement from an actual Ukrainian who has remained in Ukraine for the entire length of the war that started in 2014. Natasha Sennett continues the story with an explanation of why the couple were in Ukraine. She is a US citizen who grew up in the Soviet Union and has Ukrainian roots. John provides the rest of the story. Some of his entries are dated and 99% of his chapters were written in the order that they appear, as they happened. Tristan Ruark is a US Combat Veteran who lives in Odesa with his wife (Tanya), their stepson (Genya or Jay) and their infant daughter (Adelina), who was born while the war was raging. He provides his unique perspective in the Epilogue.

Some sentence, paragraph or experience in this book will affect you. It may be positive or negative, but it will resonate within you. All the stories here do not show the end of war because it still rages on. The long-term survival of the people in the book is not guaranteed. They all are grateful to those of you who read and understand. 'They who have ears, let them hear. Those who have eyes, let them see.'

We owe our lives to many Ukrainians and the different members of the International Legion and all of those operating under the Ukrainian Ministry of Defense.

Slava Ukraina!
Slava ZSU!

1

Decisions, Decisions...

I guess I should start at the beginning. The whole idea of 'moving back home' was not mine. My husband John planted the seed. It took a good two years to ripen in my own head and become the leap of faith we finally took in 2020.

Almost a year prior to that, I went to visit my family for Christmas in my native country, Belarus. I couldn't wait to break the news to them over the home baked goods and excellent wine that my dad spent a long time making, curing, and saving for almost two years especially for my visit. The whole family had been buzzing like a beehive for almost three weeks just getting ready. My mom went out of her way to prep meat, vegetables, more meat, a variety of traditional salads, cheese, baked buns, pierogies, and the main dish – a stuffed and roasted goose, who only recently was walking about so importantly in the shed. It was a special occasion indeed. It was not every year that their daughter, sister, godmother, sister-in-law, cousin, and good ole childhood friend (me) came for a visit from the US. In return, I came bearing gifts. As many as we could afford and put on the plane, overpaying the fee for two very big and heavy suitcases.

Voila! 12 hours and a few thousand miles later, there I was! The same airport I left almost twenty years ago and then came back to exactly four times. We've seen each other more than that. Both of my parents came for a visit to the States, and one time we all got together in Moscow, where my brother lived and worked at the time with my lovely sister-in-law. But all in all, family visits like these are rough on the budget and require vacation time, which is not as simple as it seems. Folks who have families on a different continent might relate to my situation.

The reality is that I left the nest when I was 16. I went to college away from the small Soviet military town I spent my childhood and finished high school in. I had always wanted to see the world outside of it, outside of 'now you need to get married and have babies, and, basically, stay married till death or your 19-year-old husband's drinking problem do us part.' I never quite fit there. I cringed at a skill of cleaning the guts of a dead pig and then stuffing those with meat for sausages. I couldn't properly clean the killed chicken, nor did I find it amusing running around the yard with its head chopped off. My poor mother could only respond with 'Oy, vei! There's not a man in town who will take you as a wife! How are you planning on feeding a family??' My response was quite snappy: 'I'm planning on having a vegetarian husband!!'

Back to my story. Stepping off that plane in December of 2019 felt like I had come back to the past. My eyes moved past the seats with duct tape on them (at the national airport!) searching for my dad and my brother. The joy of that moment was something I will always remember. Pure, sincere, deep, authentic, tearful moment that touches not only your soul, but puts an involuntary smile on everyone around you, complete strangers, who happen to be sharing the moment with you, unable to keep the customary (for that part of the world) unibrow on their faces.

During that visit we had a talk. I spoke about returning to Belarus, reuniting with my family, and being there for my aging folks. I didn't want to be that child, who left years ago and dropped things into my brother's lap as far as care for the parents was concerned. That's not how I was raised, so let's just leave it at that. The shock came and went (oh-dear-god-you-are-leaving-america-to-come-back-here) and the excitement found its way in. We all searched and found an awesome house 30 minutes ride from my folks. My husband okayed it via Skype. We negotiated and settled on the price. The owners were not in a hurry to sell, we needed the time to sell our place in Florida. Things looked like it was all meant to be. We put the deposit down, signed the contract, discussed the time frame, and started the process.

Everything went smoothly. We stayed in touch with the owners, kept them updated on things. In June of 2020 our house flew off the market in Florida and things were going according to the plan. We had a few things to wrap up, deposits to pay, pack up, make sure the dogs were up to code for the plane ride, and so on, and so forth. A lot! By the end of July, we were ready to transfer the money for the house in Belarus and made 'a dry run' with small amounts to make sure the banks of Belarus were able to hold up their end of the international transfer.

We knew the elections were about to take place in Belarus at the beginning of August. Media was having a field day with it. We kept a close eye on the situation because our movers were waiting for a green light from us at this point for an exact day, either in August or September. What happened after the so-called election was a disgrace, a shame, a tragedy, an eye opener of sorts for everyone who wasn't 'all that political' like me.

To think that I could possibly live in a place that is run by a blood thirsty liar who is holding on to his throne with fingers blue from the intensity of the effort gives me the creeps. Not that the majority of the nation wasn't aware of the fact prior to the 'election'. But the masses (and we would have become a part of them) have been living parallel to all that for over a quarter of a century. He babbled something on TV about the importance of potatoes and manure and it was kind of like watching Saturday Night Live – just grab your popcorn and laugh out loud. People have been patient enough. The whole post-soviet generation have grown and developed into a smart and quite capable kind. The kind who thinks and creates, enjoys everything the modern world has to offer, and wants nothing to do with growing potatoes for the rest of their lives. Not that there's anything wrong with good farming. But if cleaning up cows' manure and planting potatoes is offered as the only possible option to people with brains capable of so much more, then, inevitably, they start considering other options. Plus, greed of the 'leader' made it impossible to have a legitimately successful business. For example, tobacco shops in Belarus are pretty much a recession proof and failure proof kinda start up for anyone with a bit of cash to invest. Profits are guaranteed. Over time, the shops got 'nationalized', and the main profit holder became 'batska' (father in Belarusian, and a term sarcastically applied to the president). And that's just one little drop in the ocean of hypocrisy and lies of the regime, which lost its entertainment streak a long time ago. Over the years the government became bolder and bolder, got away with more and more, changed the law left and right to suit its needs to get rich and leave the regular folk powerless, moneyless, weak, and stripped of basic human rights. That growing boil came to a head in August of 2020. The pus is still pouring out and covering everyone in the perimeter with its foul stench.

2

Family Comes First

We waited and followed the news. Everyone: my movers, my family, my husband, my extended family. People I got close to in the States, people I left behind in Belarus, and people sitting on their couches in my home country numb with fear of going out and protesting with hundreds of thousands who risked their lives for a chance to be a free nation.

My parents:
– Just stay put for a couple of weeks. It'll all blow over soon enough and return to 'as before.'

My brother:
– Give it a month.

The seller:
– We all need to wait for calm waters. Money transfers might be considered 'support for the uprisings.'

The movers:
– ???

My husband:
– We can't go. We will not make it passed the airport in Minsk. 'Foreign spies' is our bright future in Belarus.

Me:
All of the above spinning viciously in my head. Nail biting stuff.

The closer we followed the situation on the ground the more convinced we were that Belarus was not the place for us or any individual in his or her right mind.

Of course, we waited. Mostly, to see if Putin was going to get involved and squash Lukashenko before Lu killed more peaceful protesters dressed in white carrying flowers. We hoped against hope that Putin would use the situation to his advantage and come out smelling like a rose and a humanitarian in the eyes of the whole world. He made no move. Belarusian people were being washed in the pool of their own blood, raped and tortured in prisons, violently beaten, grabbed in their own apartments by unknown men in ski masks waving balaclavas and guns in front of women and children. All hell broke loose because there was no accountability, no proper investigations, no need to identify themselves, to think for themselves, to remember the oath taken to protect the people or to just be human. Devil's messengers they were, devil's messengers they will always be. The shame of their mothers, and a criminal kind we observe right now 'liberating Ukraine.' See, the story is the same, the narrative is the same, the 'leaders' are made from the same cloth. The script is one. The actors are different. When millions of people rose up (Belarus has a population of a little over nine million) Putin did make a move: polite green men (the Crimean annexation in 2014 was quietly done with the same kind) showed up on the scene. The number of guns, violence and torture tripled or quadrupled. Which brings us to Belarus today: half the country is in prison, and the other half is guarding them.

This was that breaking moment of truth for me about Belarus and Russia alike. This is where my views and opinions on politics became very clear and concise, principled if you will. I was personally involved. The future of my family was on the line. The tragedies of thousands of Belarusians left me teared eyed, furious, frustrated, and sleep deprived. My faith was shaken. I wanted justice for all victims. I'm not talking about the judicial system, proceedings, the Hague… I mean 'Die Hard' and glorious American action, folks.

Belarus under its current regime is not a place for a free spirited, little hippie, little Jersey, little gypsy all combined in one and shaped over the years in America, the land of the free. John and I allowed a hypothetical 'ok, we went, and made it past the airport' scenario. In it we couldn't just sit quietly on the couch when the entire country is fighting for its right to exist without Lu. We would last until the next bloody protest, possibly a week, maybe two. We weren't planning a suicide but a family reunion. So, where to? Money is paid, the house is sold. We've been sitting on our suitcases since July. All the places in Europe seemed a bit too far for that category. I knew from experience what a plane flight means when you want to see your family more often. We might as well stay in the States…

'Have you considered Ukraine?'

My brother's suggestion was a ray of hope in that whole mess. Kyiv is a six-hour car ride from my folks' place. A straight shot, so to speak. We can see each other a few times a year, not just holidays. Trains go often, a few times a week. You get on a train at night, and you are in Ukraine in the early morning. Easy peazy lemon squeezy! Plus, my parents' house is a ten-minute walk to the train station. Does it get better than that?? Yes, it does. I am half Ukrainian.

3

My Beasties

If you are not a dog person, feel free to move on to the next chapter. This is strictly for dog lovers. I haven't always been one. It's too messy, too slobbery, too hairy, and to top it off, you need to pick up their poo (a right thing to do). Then we bought our first house in Florida and things changed. We adopted Sammi – my first ever, my best ever, my smartest ever, and the most beautiful English Pointer mix. She chose me at the shelter. Amidst loud barking, angry dogs, she was simply sitting quietly in her cage with a bewildered look in her eyes that said 'I don't belong here. Is it necessary to be so loud? What's going on? Can we all just calm down and figure this out in a positive quiet way?' And this is how she has always been: a pure bright sunshine, the sweetest thing to be around. You would never know we had a dog in the house unless you saw her. No barking, no nonsense, and, surprisingly, no slobber, just the occasional bubble on the side of her mouth. At the shelter they told us to watch her, 'She is a runner. We caught her in two different counties three times. Make sure you have a fence.'

When we brought her home, it was like she has always lived there and was a part of the family. My previously adopted parrot, Freida, immediately took to her, and even attempted to clean her ears (unsuccessfully) a few times. But they got along alright. Frieda would jump on Sammi's bed and squawk about when bored. Sammi had manners, properly bred behavior in her genes. It's not like we knew what we were doing at the time anyway, we simply got lucky. Sammi loved jogging with me, and, let's face it, was much better at it. But she didn't run away, she needed no fence, and made all things better just by being there. She lived with us, hiked with us, jogged with us, went on vacations to my beloved Georgia with us, and shared fully in the adventures of traveling.

Philly Cheesesteak is a different kind of dog. We adopted him a few years later for Christmas. Sammi took her sweet time to get used to a new addition and didn't care much for him in the first two weeks. She would ceremoniously and indignantly get up and leave the room when he was in it. Not that she was jealous, but she was a very intuitive dog and sensed a trouble coming. Philly was and is a troublemaker. Sammi took upon herself to protect the parrot and Philly would get a paw slap on his snout every time he even looked in Frieda's direction. The same followed if he held up the process of getting ready for a walk (leashes, commands, and following directions aren't his strong suit). As a matter of fact, Sammi was better at training him than both of us put together.

She kept him in check and became a mother hen to him as time went on. Kind of an older sister whose brother is a handful and needs a paw slap here and there to stay in line, but also a wound licking if he got into a fight with another dog.

Sammi couldn't keep Philly from killing Frieda. We went to a midnight liturgy for Christmas, closed and covered the cage, and placed it out of reach. When we came home that night Sammi ran out to greet us as she usually does, but this time, she kept her paws on my shoulders and wouldn't let me go into the house. We thought she was overexcited at first, but she jumped off my shoulders and blocked the way in. John had to physically help her move. Commands didn't work, which was strange, because for Sammi one look was enough, and she knew what needed doing. John went in first and told me to stay outside with Sammi. I never saw what happened but trusted my husband. He cleaned up my birdie who had been with us for almost eight years. We called it a Christmas Massacre due to the circumstances under which Frieda was ripped apart and eaten. I was devasted, and so was John, even though he wasn't especially attached to her. We decided to take Philly back to the shelter after the holidays. But he won us over against our will. We tried distancing ourselves from him, but it was a pointless exercise. Philly's affection and love for us all (except Frieda) was genuine. The dog simply wouldn't give up on 'apologizing' to everyone by showering us all with affection for three days straight. When the holidays were over, he took his rightful place in the family whether we doubted him or not. He simply settled in, adjusted his behavior (a little) and was showing all the signs of an animal who is very comfortable and loved. It was almost like he was waiting for us to realize that he belonged, and he has become a part of our family already.

So, when the big move to Belarus was under way, we were all going, dogs included. Leaving either one behind wasn't an option. If you have ever tried relocating your dog overseas, you know the process is gruesome. But we couldn't possibly leave them behind. So, the shots were up to date, cages prepared, money paid, forms filled…

4

The First Major Bump

My heart still skips a beat when I remember a phone call from the company we hired to relocate our dogs. It was after the country of choice was set upon, the dates were chosen, tickets were bought, and the nervous anticipation of a major life adventure was in the air for a couple of months. At that point it was just a waiting game, or so we thought. The young lady called to inform us in a very matter of fact way (sort of 'oh, I almost forgot, no big deal or anything') that Ukraine didn't accept the rabies shots that our furry friends had a few months before. You see, Belarus did, so they assumed Ukraine would also. To make the long story short, we had to do everything all over again to get them ready for international travel. Then, we had to wait for three months after the shots were complete to make sure Sammi and Philly had antibodies and other such things.

It meant we would have to leave the dogs behind until they went through that process. And one of us would have to stay to wrap up 'a couple of procedures' along with it.

I still choke up with the tears of frustration and sadness that phone call caused for both of us. So much time got wasted in between, when we thought we were done and had been sitting (literally) on our boxes/suitcases/carry-ons that got delivered to the house for the upcoming trip. If they had checked all the requirements necessary for transportation of dogs to Kyiv, as agreed upon two months before, my dogs would have been apart from us for two to three weeks, tops, instead of three months.

I had to physically hold my tongue and sweat profusely from the effort of not telling the young lady exactly what she didn't want to hear from me. First of all – to what end? Second of all –would things change miraculously if I let the load off my chest, would that make any difference? I couldn't believe how a human being could lack a simple compassion in delivering such atrocious news in a manner fit for a check-out clerk in a supermarket. Even there one often hears: 'Did you find everything ok? How are you today?'

On our end a ticket needed to be cancelled, a decent place for my dogs to stay had to be located, arrangements had to be made, extra money spent, the dates changed… And teary good-byes had to be lived through on a supposed 'family adventure.'

5
My Beloved South Jersey

The 'days of my life' began 22 years ago at the Jersey Shore. I spent four years in college back in Belarus studying and getting ready to major in World History and English. I had one year left to go to get my Masters, when I stumbled into a lecture auditorium by mistake trying to locate my class. Some guy was giving a spiel on 'practicing English in a native environment, a complete language immersion through getting a job, something about a student exchange program' or whatever. Suddenly, I felt like I had come to the right place! Everything he was saying started to make sense, plus, summer was on its way, and I had run out of exciting options to spend it a long time ago. My parents were going to think about it ($3,000 had to be either wisely spent or wasted) and decided in my favor (a good and responsible girl that I was) as far as my getting a job in the States for six months through the student exchange gig.

A few adventurous students I met on the plane headed to JFK were trying to convince me to ditch the contract I had with the Seashell Ice-Cream Parlor in Wildwood and try my luck in NYC instead. Their argument was that 'strength comes in numbers.' But my thought process kept sabotaging the idea with 'what kind of immersion are we talking about if I'm going to be hanging out with a bunch of you fools from my own country?' Plus, 'the good girl' in me was determined to see it through.

So, my first major 'coming into adulthood' experience started in New Jersey. I still remember sitting on a bus from NYC, trying to imagine what a glorious place the ocean must be and the town I was about to see, when North Wildwood Boulevard welcomed us with that special marsh fragrance. You know, the kind that makes one look around all indignant, suspecting a foul case of breakfast burritos from half the passengers on the bus. Little did I know that over time, the smell of the marshes would always bring me back to the summer of 2000 and the Jersey Shore no matter where I was on the planet or what I was doing.

To my surprise, I experienced none of the culture shock everyone was insisting upon. New Jersey welcomed me like I was coming home. People had an excellent sense of humor, openness, and general likeability about them. I felt like I could finally set my sarcasm free, curse a little, and fit right in along the way. A big NO in my own country for a lady. I felt a load off my chest because the culturally imposed 'standards' of behavior for a woman didn't strangle my desire to live. 'A damsel in distress who doesn't curse and obediently follows her alcoholic macho husband's instructions' was never my cup of tea.

I'm too sarcastic to accept that with no comment. So, imagine you are a kid in a candy store… That's how the Jersey Shore felt like to me. Live and let live, mind your own business, get your English up to par, and keep it short and sweet – no one lives forever, time is money, hon. And, of course, there was the ocean, which made everything better, bestowing a sense of 'being in the right place', seeing the true beauty in the world with everyone else who was lucky enough to share in it.

That summer was a turning point in my life not only because of the new experiences, people, and glory days, but because I met my person, my lifelong partner, and the love of my life.

John worked across the street from Seashell and 'frequented' the joint due to his sweet tooth problem we are still dealing with. Let's just say it was not love at first sight for either one of us, but a strong sense of mutual dislike, which over a course of three months grew into friendship. Love came later, ultimately, when John came to visit me in Belarus the following year in February of 2001 (I returned in October of 2000 to finish college). After graduation, I came for another visit which led to marriage a few months later, on December 26th, 2001.

When you live by the shore you get to know all the little towns along the coastline. Each has its own charm and personality. My favorite was Cape May Point. There's something about the place that touches the soul. I got to know it and initially saw it through my husband's eyes. I felt like I was let in on a secret of sorts. A little gem away from the beaten path, away from loud tourists and bright casino lights, boardwalks, and modern condos. It has an unadulterated feel of purity and nature still to be found in its original design, unspoiled by human efforts to 'fix the world around'. It is easy to love and useless to resist its charm. Cape May Point became a place to recharge, reset, forget the worries, and cherish the memories we made together.

I think of the Jersey Shore from time to time walking the streets of Kyiv, my mind brings me back to the little village by the sea, with the 'diamonds' in the sand, slippery rocks, the salty smell of the ocean, a light breeze and soothing waves gently greeting the shore. This is what I hold on to when the sinister sound of the air raids begins its dreaded song about death and destruction.

6

A New Home?

You can't call our move 'a smooth sail.' The bumpy wooden roller coaster at Morey's Piers in Wildwood comes to mind. Great White, I think it was called. The one with all the thrills and a severe back pain episode afterwards, all the wooden pieces counted by your spine every time it goes up or down. Exciting? Yes! Do you feel every bit of it rolling? Absolutely. I'm glad I tried it, but don't think I will repeat the experience voluntarily again.

I flew to Kyiv first. Papers needed to be filed in person, the apartment needed to be set up and the lease signed. I needed to adjust first and be ready to help John transition. He, in turn, needed to take the dogs for additional shots, visit them a few times at a dog hotel to help them adjust better, and wrap up a few things before the flight.

Separation was hard on everyone. My husband and I are best friends, and my dogs had never been separated from either of us for longer than a day in years. The sense of bewilderment in their eyes was more than either of us could bear. It's not like you can sit down and explain the situation to them: 'Hey, we love you and will see you again in three months, after you go on a plane for 12 hours and land on a different continent. Then you both are going to board another plane that will finally take you to the Kyiv area. Then you are going to go on a ride with people you don't know. Sound good? I know it was supposed to be all of us going together, but remember that lady on the phone? Well, she messed up. Now we deal with that. I know, sweety, humans can be awful.'

I flew with my heart heavy. Still dealing with an agent on the phone regarding additional 'small issues' that came up with the dog relocation. I literally finished the 'conversation' and made the last boarding call on the plane to Amsterdam. The flight was mostly empty due to the pandemic that had been abusing the planet for almost a year. I had plenty of time to rest and prepare for the unknown as much as I could.

The taxi driver by Borispyl International Airport outside of Kyiv settled on a good price to take me to the Solomenskiy district, where we had found a three-bedroom flat that would allow for two large dogs. I was dead tired from the flight and the customs, and the shots, and the self-isolation prospect that was waiting on me – potentially two weeks or so until the results of the test showed negative for COVID. The usual blah, blah for anyone facing international flights during the pandemic.

I remember seeing the outskirts of the city on the way and thinking to myself: Well, this is not pretty at all. It's overbuilt, overpopulated, dirty, and large. I hope the district we are going to live in will be somehow 'better'. It wasn't. When he pulled up the car to the multistory atrocity dating from the Soviet times, the driver looked at me suspiciously and asked: 'Are you sure this is the place you wanted?'

I couldn't answer that question. We knew it wasn't going to be a high-end building (they didn't allow pets) but, dang, what a sad looking structure. It had a stench of USSR 'style' all over it. The photos made it look better than it really was, and the wallpaper in most rooms threatened an epileptic shock if stared at directly for too long. To make matters worse, it lacked a dryer, a boiler, and a heater. I realized the importance of having all three in a tragic way, through having neither in a cold environment that has hot water turned off randomly for prolonged periods of time, as well as communal heat that only functions November through March. Alright, I thought, this is temporary, until the situation in Belarus resolves itself, or this place goes either way.

The neighborhood park nearby was the only worthy place to hang out and find beauty in a district desperately lacking pretty things to look at. Well, that, and a Georgian bakery within a walking distance to load you up on some carbs when the depression mode got the better of you.

We've come across some major 'snot blowing' problems amongst the residents of the above-mentioned district. The male and female population found it quite alright emptying their nostrils right on the sidewalk in front of them while running their errands. Over time I managed to maneuver around it as to not step into it or receive it on my person in passing. Couth, anyone? Thankfully my natural desire to observe made me hopeful: the snot blowers were primarily the Sovietski type. You know, the kind sporting a perpetual unibrow on their swollen-with-hatred face, ready to jump ahead of you in line anywhere, disregarding the manners expected in civil society. This is the type to watch out for if you are a dog owner and happen to share a walkup with that sort of an ape. Rat poison is laid about intermittently in the yard in hopes for your puppy to lick it and die in agony. Those are a few general characteristics of the undeveloped, uneducated, unworldly Soviet population who still reside throughout the former USSR territories, ready to tear into pieces any trace of independent thought and innovation that keeps the rest of the planet 10 steps ahead in relevance and human evolution. Thankfully, that kind of folk is a miserable minority compared to the younger, gentle, creative, and free-spirited Ukrainians we came across in Kyiv, away from Solomenskiy district.

John didn't complain much about the 'perks' of our current living arrangements and handled it better in some cases than I did. When the old water pipes burst in the building during a cold season, he filled up the buckets from the truck provided by the district admin that parked by the building for a few days with the best of them. I was amazed at how quickly he adjusted and figured what needed doing while I was away running errands and wasn't even aware of the issue.

Similar problems would happen with electricity and heating. You wake up to some type of 'surprise' every couple of weeks or so, squeeze your teeth, roll your eyes, and deal with it.

The fact that our dogs weren't with us to make everything seem better in life was sad and teary at times. I kept wondering if they would forget us in three months, be angry at us, or simply get depressed and wait for us at the dog hotel to come and get them immediately. I would wait for the short videos and pictures every couple of days to see their faces. It gave me the strength to count down the days left until we hugged them and were in their presence again. Everything else seemed unimportant and small. John and I had each other to get through those times on this continent. Sammi and Philly were together also. That counted for a lot.

I remember February 11th, 2021 vividly. My beasties were to be delivered to the building. The snow on the ground was up to your knees, the temperature outside-in the teens Fahrenheit. The sprinter van finally made it late in the evening. We ran downstairs, my heart pounding in my ears from the excitement. The guy opened the back door of the vehicle. Sammi recognized my voice and was shaking the cage from side to side, unable to contain herself. Philly was tense and still. Maybe he's forgotten me already?? But, no. His priorities were twisted for a moment due to an immediate bathroom need. Once relieved, he gladly shared the joy of reunion.

The gratitude of having my beasties healthy and sound back with us made the problems seem futile and unimportant somehow. That feeling lasted for the rest of the year.

7

A New Home!

COVID took its toll on travelers and took away the desire or the ability to travel freely between the countries along with it. Our three-bedroom apartment served no purpose as we came to realize my family was unlikely to come for a visit any time soon. Belarus closed the border with Ukraine and getting out turned into a major hassle with special permits needed from the 'leader' himself or the 'government'. The political situation there hadn't changed either and had no signs of improving in the near future. Unidentified men in balaklavas continued roaming people's apartments, taking away 'the suspects of the 2020 election protests' in front of their families, labeling each one 'a terrorist' with no rights for attorneys or any such democratic nonsense, resulting in the unlawful imprisonment of almost a half its thinking population, or anyone with ability to think, and, God forbid, speak their mind. The other 'half' was either guarding the prisoners or shaking the guns in their hands like someone would their car keys to subdue the unruly thinking types into submission before the 'leader', but first, before the apes with guns and absence of any moral compass. Live and let live wasn't, isn't, and is not going to be on the Belarusian horizon until Lu and Pu are no longer alive or in power.

So, how about our lives? What are we to do in the meantime? The apartment, the district, and the whole 'renting' thing is ok for a few months at best. We needed a place to call home in Kyiv.

We started to fall in love with the city and its streets soaked in history and things to admire visually and intellectually as we walked for hours at a time gaping at everything it had to offer for such history lovers like us. Imagine to be able to see, touch, and appreciate something that was built in the ninth century? Kyiv is a living monument, graceful, gorgeous, and a tad grungy all at once. It interlaced centuries worth of stuff to ponder on, ancient and modern, glorious and ugly, clean and not so much, all trying to coexist together, and, surprisingly, making it work. Two years into it I still feel like a tourist every time I take a walk. I don't get tired of looking at architecture, people, parks, cathedrals, cafes, mysterious arks connecting the buildings, 500-year-old trees, and art galleries. Every walk is an adventure of sorts. Did you know that so-and-so's grandmother lived in the neighboring building?! Did you know that so-and-so got blown up on this street and 'the black widow' still lives here?! Fascinating is the best word to describe Kyiv.

The old city appealed to our senses the most, so we bought there, a flat they call it. The location and the building itself was 'perfect.' Built in 1902, it had survived a few wars, and was sporting original windows and frames in the walkup. I'm a sucker for things like that. Gimme a good story, just not the Soviet kind.

The flat was outdated, dilapidated, and in a state of needing urgent care. Ghastly wallpaper found us here as well, reminiscing times lived in the seventies and refusing to move on. We tore down the entire space back to its original structure and rebuilt everything, restoring the original charm of the space, so brutally wronged by lack of common sense, or taste for that matter. We took down the plaster covering everything and opened up some room to breathe and be. In the process we uncovered a long plastered over fireplace right in the middle of the living room wall. We lifted the nasty floor to find 80 centimeters of space under it, all stuffed with building debris, so faithfully left there by the Soviet renovators and inhaled over the course of the years by various occupants of the flat. In the process we located the original brick from the early 1900s with proud stamps of the brick makers of that era. I saved every single piece and incorporated it in the newly restored and freshly painted walls as part of the building's history. Some of the pieces had the small footprints of a dog or a cat running about on the factory premises, roughing up the smooth face of the freshly made brick. It felt like paying a tribute long overdue to a piece of architecture so neglected and underappreciated. Every corner of our apartment was rebuilt and renovated, smiling happily back at us, that gorgeous little thing!

I will gladly skip over the renovation process which took six months of the usual headaches, plus a certain naivete on our part of not quite understanding what an undertaking it would be to deal with a historic property in a communal building somewhere overseas. If I were to give advice on such a purchase, here it goes: first of all – No! Second of all – Don't!

8

Family Reunion

Finally, Solomenskiy was behind us and Shevchenckovskiy all around. What a difference in everything! We had spent a great deal of our time there ever since we moved to Ukraine. Lots of things to do, see, and enjoy being around. Now it was ours to explore in detail. We couldn't have chosen a better location for us and the dogs. Fomin Botanical Garden, Taras Shevchenko Park, and two smaller neighborhood parks sealed the deal.

The dogs were in heaven, and so were we.

– Can you believe we live here?
– OMG, still getting my head around it!

Moving into a place and bringing it up to your standards of living are two separate things. Boxes, suitcases, pictures, books… When all was unpacked and rightfully found its place in the flat, a new kitchen was delivered. The train station scenario went on for a few months. January came and we still missed the bathroom door and the bedroom door. COVID became a wonderful excuse for all sorts of delays, and the dates on the contract to deliver and install the above-mentioned doors became irrelevant, much to our dismay.

At the end of December of 2020, I got a phone call from my brother. They were working on coming to Kyiv for a visit. That meant a great deal of hassle and money paid to random tourist agencies who supplied the necessary papers for crossing the borders. Not for the Ukrainian side, but for Belarusian one. Just think how ridiculous that sounds. People of Belarus needed to come up with special permits and funds necessary to be let out of their own country. It begs a question: is it really their own? But my younger brother and his wife started the process with careful optimism. Kept their fingers crossed without getting our hopes too high. In Belarus anything can happen, and that's not a good thing. We wanted to get excited badly but kept our emotions in check regarding an actual visit. We waited impatiently for the word and, halleluiah!

Now we really needed those doors! Hours on the phone with twelve different managers didn't go to waste. Squeaky wheel I was and managed to set up the delivery and installation on the second day of my brother's stay with us.

We still couldn't believe we were going to see each other after a year and two months of our life in Ukraine. Belarus is only six-hour drive from Kyiv. A straight shot, no nonsense, but we might as well have been in America.

Having my brother and his wife with us for a short week was everything that we were hoping for – a pure wave of joy and happiness that only comes when you are placed in the presence of people who love you by the bond of blood, happy for you when you are doing well, and cry with you when life serves a fully loaded punch, just because it can. All that happiness is wrapped up in a nice circle of great food, wine, some whisky and an occasional cigar, that follow heart-to-heart communication that cannot hold a candle to social media posts and text messages, no matter how many little hearts and smilies are thrown into the mix.

For my bro, Kyiv was love at the first sight. His reasons mirrored ours, but for a person who still resided in the country of 'No! Not an option! Shut up! Never-gonna-happen!', Kyiv had an aura of freedom and authentic messiness that can only happen when self-expression is present everywhere because it is allowed, welcomed, and offered a stark alternative to Lysol sprayed on every original, forward thinking individual who spoke too much or dared to claim his place in the society desperately requiring development in every possible field in the twenty-first century, when the rest of the world has moved on to better conquests. Kyiv was a breath of fresh cold, liberating air, that seemed to raise its shoulders and say 'well, we are definitely not perfect, we have a long way to go, but, for now, it works this way, you can take it, leave it, or, or, well, you decide what you wanna do.' So, my brother and sister-in-law started an out loud plan for their next visit, in spring of 2023.

9

He What?!

The famous visit week came and went, the food eaten, the wine and spirits drunk, the sights explored, the shopping done, the gifts exchanged, the tears spilt, the good-byes said, the warm embraces offered, and our first with the family was over.

We all followed the 'Russian military exercises on the borders' with a tinge of eye-rolling and sarcasm. It smelled of bluff and muscle flexing, it seemed juvenile and loud. 'The loudest in the room, they say…' Ukrainians did not panic, neither were they surprised – after all, the country was at war since Crimea was occupied. The hot zone was the East, but the rest of Ukraine had operated in the 'business as usual mode', which inevitably affected every person who was not immediately present where the 'action' took place.

My knowledge of that war as a US citizen, too caught up in my own job to pay attention to anything else in the world, extended to 'they are fighting for Crimea, not sure who started/did not intend to give up/whose fault it is, the government, the president, of which country'? In a word: ignorance (is bliss).

It was not until we landed in the Solomenskiy district of soon to become our beloved Kyiv and started to meet people, walk the city streets, see the actual places of recent bloody history that took place while I was wrapped up in a cocoon of my own affairs, that my 'apolitical view' had died and was buried by the Saint Michael's Cathedral wall of heroes – those who died very young so the rest of the country could be free from the 'brotherly Russian love.' I was staring at the pictures of 25-year-olds, handsome, full of dignity, a full life ahead of them, just boys, and wondered: 'What was your reason for an ultimate sacrifice? What is really going on in the East? How come we never knew how serious this was? Why there were never any news in the West about it??'

Mostly, I wanted to get my facts straight about the history that has been stolen from Ukraine and sold to the West as 'Russian'. Our journey began. Searches were done. Eyewitnesses and participants of various glorious events spoken to (my neighbor is a native Kyivan, our former landlords, my contractors, my realtors, and anyone we came into contact with). The more you get to know Ukraine, the more you fall in love with the spirit of Ukrainians. I was fascinated, proud (Ukrainian blood runs through my veins also) and discovered a strange new sensation for myself in this world – a sense of belonging.

I will always feel American because that is where I came into adulthood and partial maturity as a human being. We are all, in a sense, products of our environment. America has shaped me to be an American, that's a fact. We have lived, collectively, in four different states, appreciated and learned from the experiences they had to offer, worked, loved, and prayed in each one of them, and somehow ended up in Ukraine for our next chapter. So, we are 'expats' in Ukraine. America will always be in us, with its magnificent logic and efficiency, appreciation for diversity and individuality in everything, cultural hodge-podge with opportunities, fallback options, money to be made or recovered, places to see, people to meet, accents to be heard, oceans to swim in, beaches to lounge on, and whatever your heart desires nostalgia. I am forever grateful to have experienced all of it. The leader of the world, the place where everyone wants to go at least once in their lifetime, I got to live there for twenty plus years and that is something amazing to me. I have brought my 'baggage' here with me, and, amazingly, somehow it worked out. Or so we thought.

On February 24th, 2022, we woke up in the middle of the night of some strange wailing in the air, that seemed far away and weird sounding. We did not think much of it at that moment. I remember thinking to myself that 'Ukraine has got to get more efficient garbage trucks or something, the sound is annoying', and fell back asleep. The sound came back after a while and disappeared again, and so did we, in the dawn hours of sweet slumber. John got up for work to check his emails on the phone, he stood in the middle of the room scratching his head intensely, mouth half open, eyes wide, grave expression on his face.

– Oh. My. God. (John)
… (John)
– John, you've got to finish your sentences!
– He invaded Ukraine!
– What do you mean?!
– Russia attacked Ukraine last night. They started the war.

How can one put into words what followed if you have never experienced a full-blown war firsthand but only learned about it in high school or college, and followed the news somewhere far away in the world where such idiocy could still be happening? One needs an attitude adjustment to face the new reality. Thankfully, we live in the world of technology. Things are on tap, at the reach of your fingertips, anytime anywhere. All I needed to do was to grab my phone. There had to be a mistake! Are we sure this is a full-scale war, or did they just shoot at us with something while 'training'?

Denial was quickly dispersed by the sound of aviation in the air, the news stating the obvious, and occasional 'booms' somewhere in the distance.

The US embassy has been flooding our inbox for a month with warning emails about 'leaving Ukraine' and 'eminent threats of invasion' and 'all US citizens are strongly advised', but we did not actually think the reality was going to be as stated above. Nobody did. But American authorities did not give up on us and started calling the phone numbers we had listed when we registered in Ukraine, politely asking if I was old enough to make the decision to stay in the country (awe, thank you! I am a bit over forty). However, after receiving a phone call or two, we decided to stock up on groceries, canned goods and such, just in case that hurricane was going to hit us as they were saying (even though the grocery stores were fully loaded on whatever your heart desires, plus, the mad supply of milk and toilet paper was not diminished in any way). I remember the cashier giving us a stare, and a person ahead of us in line curiously eyeballing my 'stash'. Either way, we were not planning on running, but I refused to do nothing at all when American intelligence advised of a shitstorm lurking around.

However violently moronic, delusional, and politically suicidal the Russian plan of attack was, there we were, in our little apartment in the city center, watching the sky, the news, eyes searching for something or someone who is going to shake us out of our stupor.

10

The First Time for Everything

The next hours were long, filled with uncertainty and frustration at the fact, that despite the digital world we live in today, all channels were simply stating the obvious, devoid of true emotion, speculation, prognosis, or reassurance. I NEEDED someone who was going to explain the situation beyond 'the Russian troops are at the…, the Ukrainian forces are…, the Mrya got destroyed, the enemy is attempting to seize Hostomel, the tanks are moving toward…' What does this all mean for us? Are we going to be killed? How long do we have left? Will they really be shooting at military targets only? How is Ukraine going to fight them? Do we have enough weapons? Isn't this village only 30 kilometers out?

Official channels updated events every few hours or so – seriously not often enough for the raging current of thoughts gushing through my head. Where is someone who will come out and tell everyone that everything worked out or is expected to within the next few weeks (it would be better by the end of this week of course, but let's be realistic here ,– at least a month…).

Feeling unsatisfied with the 24-hour live reports that simply repeated the events over and over, we searched for other means of updates, and a myriad of Telegram channels happily obliged. The information poured in every five minutes. Some was true, some was retracted, some was the hopeful speculation going through everyone's head at some point in time, and some were just memes to lift up the spirits. As time went on, we filtered out a bunch, including weird Russian propaganda that posed as Ukrainian news on the internet. Medvedchuk[1] was still in Ukraine doing what he was the best at – riling up and confusing many Ukrainians, driving his nasty wedge between the people, and then collecting dirty Kremlin money for a job 'well done'.

We learned quickly that Ukrainians collectively have a solid sense of humor. The more serious the situation got; the more opportunities were there for the locals to laugh at it. Once the shock settled down a bit, we could manage a chuckle here and there at the stories from the eyewitnesses, trending on social media. Very quickly a few of them circled the nation and turned into a hit. I remember feeling 'normal' when the video of one such hit was flooding the channels: some old and very kind looking babusyia (Ukrainian grandma) in her full Ukrainian attire came out of her village house to check

1 Viktor Medvedchuk is a pro-Kremlin Ukrainian politician.

out a few tanks parked unceremoniously in her garden. A few young Russian men in uniforms were fussing about confused. When they saw the babusia approaching them, they stopped and looked at her long and hard. She did not flinch (I am thinking WWII, considering her age). A young man of 20-something broke the morbid silence: 'We are lost. Can you tell us how to get to Kyiv from here?' The babusia took her hand to her face cheek, shook her head a bit as if disappointed, and responded in a calm wise tone: 'Sweet Lord… What a dumbass you made!'

There were other soul warming comments and actions of the locals, who even tried reasoning with the newcomers politely to no avail. Just like the babusyia stated in her infinite wisdom – dumb as a rock they were.

For us, these bits and pieces soothed our agonized and tortured heads with the unknown to be surrendered to our souls. Kyiv turned into a ghost town within a week. For the very first time I experienced living in a city without people in it. It was so quiet, like an old castle reverberating with every sound for a good mile, with a vicious silence filling the space. I could hear faint security system beeps inside the emptied-out stores when passing them on the block – sounds typically drowned in the city's energetic bustle. The air smelled of sulfur, gunfire, and smoke from explosions. A strange shift in the aura honestly announcing danger, uncertainty, and death- all in the mix of the morbid air raid ringing. Those who left, left. Those who stayed looked at each other in the streets with authentic gratitude as if to say, 'Thank you for being here, I will not die alone'. Maybe I am just projecting my own feelings, but I do know this: all of us in the perimeter were happy to see a familiar face in the neighborhood, the only resemblance of the true human connection that cannot be achieved through social media, as hard as we might rely on that elusive temptation. Those judgements we passed on one another pre-war seemed ridiculous and small-minded: 'you know that so-and-so, who never picks up after his dog? This one never says hello, this one laughs too loud, this one…', they evaporated in a quick snap of mutual sorrow, uniting everyone, taking social masks off, revealing 'dead men walking', holding on and hoping against all odds.

The first days and the days to come quickly turned into a single, long, exhausting, and dreadful day, with quick 'shut-eye' shifts in between the air raids, sudden runs to the multiple stores for water supplies, taking the dogs out for bathroom breaks and walks close to the buildings with bomb shelters or massive arches to go under when the bombings were on. Curfew was the new 'normal', 11 p.m. to 6 a.m. daily, extending sometimes to three days and nights of being stuck inside while collaborators, sleeping agents, and saboteurs were torturing the city until caught and handled.

One night I woke up from a screaming voice on the ground floor of our apartment building. Someone was either yelling for help or trying desperately to get a message across to those of us still here. I listened in, my instincts sharp, my elbows poking toward Philly and John. The tone did not resemble a drunken stupor. We were up and ready in seconds. A young male voice was moving in and out of reach again, like that of a person who runs, and his message runs with him. I just wanted him to stop for a split second, so I could pinpoint his message. He did. When I heard it, a chill went through my veins as it still does when I think to those first weeks: 'Wake up people! Rise! On your feet!!! Katsapy[2] are here!' The clock on my phone stated 3 a.m. John moved closer to the balcony, looking out quickly, and moved away from the glass. Within a few seconds, rapid gun fire announced that Ukrainians (we prayed they were) dealt with it because the answering gun fire continued for a while. The resolution came within an hour, as the ominous silence settled about once again, but the outcome was uncertain. Who lived? Who died?

We did not have a gun but slept with knives we had brought for a gun fight. Yet, we resolved to go out fighting, however that might look or seem to others, it mattered to us how we died in this. The new reality was not waiting on us to be ready to settle in and get used to it at our own pace. It invaded with no care for anyone's feelings, demanded coldness of heart, lack of emotion toward life or death, and complete presence of mind in the moments of total horror. The only way to deal with it was to live through it. Were we going to live through it? Did we want to? Why on earth did we stay?

I think I know what I am doing, but I don't think I can explain. I will try.

2 Katsaps is a Ukrainian derogatory word for Russians.

August 2020: Photo taken in Palm Coast, Florida. The T-shirts were in support of the Belarusian Opposition bought for Natasha's birthday.

May 2022: Photo taken in Kyiv in St. Michael's Square with destroyed Russian tanks from the Battle of Kyiv and local child wrapped in Ukrainian flag.

May 2022: Photo taken in Kyiv in St. Michael's Square with destroyed Russian tanks from the Battle of Kyiv.

August 2020: Palm Coast. Florida with Sammi and Philly on the beach while awaiting departure for Kyiv.

March 2021: Beginning the demolition of our Kyiv flat purchased in January 2021. Preparing for renovations.

April 2022: Anti-tank protection (Hedge Hogs) on the streets of Kyiv.

August 2020: John, Sammi and Philly playing in the surf of St. Augustine while waiting to leave for Kyiv.

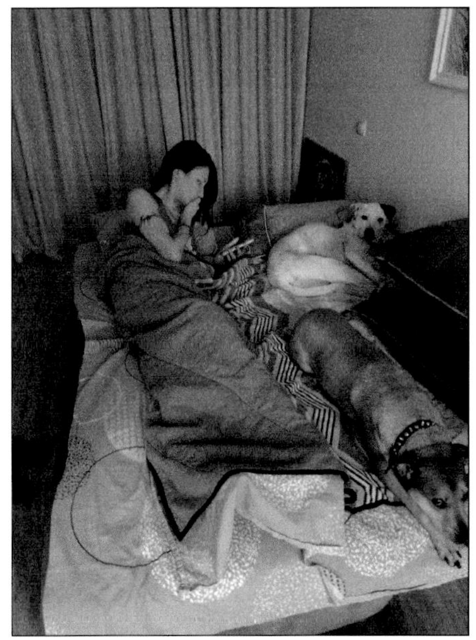

Natasha trying to find updates on the invasion and Battle of Kyiv at home in the Kyiv flat.

September 2021: Demolition completed in the flat and new walls constructed, almost ready for plastering. Natasha checking on renovation progress.

November 2021: Natasha arrived first in Kyiv to secure living space while COVID was still raging.

June 2022: Taking Philly for a walk in Kyiv and stopping at St. Michael's Square to see if any new destroyed equipment was on display.

Philly guarding the yard from Muscovite invaders.

June-July 2022: Missile attacks seemed aimed at cultural monuments, so all were protected by volunteers in Kyiv filling sandbags.

April 2022: St. Andrew's Church, Kyiv while out on a walk.

August 2021: Kreshchatyk Street, Kyiv with Ukraine Armed Forces equipment prepping for military parade.

11

So, Why on Earth Did We?

In the following months almost everyone we knew, saw, and exchanged pleasantries with pre-war, fled the city, ran, moved to the suburbs, or simply stopped answering their phones.

Our walkup in the building had three flats with occupants still in them, us included. To the right of us, there were Lena and Valik, an older couple, who we had a rough relationship with from the start. This was due to our loud renovations that lasted longer than expected and irritated everyone around in the immediate perimeter. I would also be that neighbor, irritated and indignant if the loud contractors settled in close by and terrorized the space with nonstop banging, drilling, and whatever else just as loud to hearing apparatus for the sake of a better flow and comfort of space. Lena and Valik were straight forward about their feelings as far as our project was concerned, and I did not delay with reciprocating as politely as I knew how to deliver to them the message that our apartment will continue to be a nuisance to everyone concerned as long as I had the will and determination to see through what I started. That being said, the acquaintance was off to a bumpy and resentful start on both sides.

I still remember seeing her at the top of the stairs one night, after we took the dogs out for a quick bathroom break and were coming up as quietly as we could in the dark (not to save electricity, but as to not draw attention to the building itself at night during curfew). Lena came out to see who was fussing in the building at such an hour. When she made out our faces, her expression changed into that of a loving mother, who hasn't seen her child in years, and the child has finally made it home. I never knew her smile could be so warm and welcoming. She spoke first. We learned from her (as she was the person in the know as far as everyone's affairs were concerned) that there were four families left for now. Her situation was as follows: Valik (the husband) could not come downstairs easily due to his hernia and a bad hip. She was not leaving him behind come what may.

'I am born and bred Kyivan', she said, 'I will die here, in my own bed.'

'What about Valentina next door?' I asked

'She is staying also. So, there are us three, and the guy on the second floor'.

I did not realize it at the time, but this was a turning point in our relationship.

The next morning, after the curfew was up, we were coming down with the dogs for our routine around-the-block attempt, to see the above-mentioned 'guy from the second floor' dragging his bags in a hurry downstairs, with some snacks and what-nots falling out as he ran leaving all sorts of trails to tempt my dogs with. So here we were, just the three of the flats occupied, out of seventeen.

Knowing that some were still there made things easier to bear. Strength is in numbers, they say. Ours were small numbers, but it was enough to plant a seed of hope for the upcoming days. Valik needed a man's strength to help him downstairs to the bomb shelter during bombings – that was a fact. John simply stated what was going through my mind at the time: 'I am going to have to carry him downstairs, there is no other way' (that was the first drawback to living in a 1901 building with no elevators).

Valentina, our neighbor to the right, was the quiet one. She kept to herself mostly and refused to be 'assisted': she took her time getting up on the top floor carrying her own groceries, and, walking her energetic puppy she had adopted a year prior to the war. I would stop on the stairs to greet her, check in with her, and talk about weather, utility bills, dogs, and the days long past. Her demeanor had not changed since the war had started. She would have the same pleasant smile to greet you, she never went to the bomb shelter or had any trace of anxiety on her typically glowing face. The smile of a person with a life well lived, with no regrets, that can only shine through the entire bullet-proof interior of the facial expression if, in fact, you are that person – deeply satisfied and ready to accept whatever comes your way. I remember thinking to myself: 'I want to be a woman with no regrets, acting from a place of deep inner satisfaction and comfort if I live that long'. I asked her if she felt comfortable getting downstairs during air raids and why didn't she camp out at the bomb shelter downstairs as the rest of the neighborhood does. Her answer was in the smile she wore: 'I am too old to be afraid, honey, I lived a very long life'. She had no relatives close by or children to care for her. But she did have friends visiting, once in a while. She also had us. If something dreadful were to happen to her, she would not be forgotten or abandoned in an empty walkup, not if John and I could help it.

Then, there was Sammi. My sweetest dog got diagnosed with stage IV cancer in November of 2021. Hemangiosarcoma, with no signs or symptoms – devastation that reveals itself only when there is nothing left to do about it, other than wait, and make sure the dog is comfortable. Three separate veterinarians on two continents missed it. It was discovered by accident, during a routine teeth cleaning procedure in Ukraine, but metastases had spread through her body by then. We went through denial, anger, bargaining, and few other stages of grief. It is the acceptance that is the hardest. I cannot begin to describe the stupor I felt when looking at her, still being her sweet self, eating, walking, occasional jogging, rolling in the comfy couch, and chastening Philly (Sammi was the alpha dog in the pack). I simply could not, would not accept the diagnosis without the biopsy. After a bunch of tests, vet clinic visits, and other procedures involved, we made the decision of going through with the surgery – metastasis in her lungs caused a fluid buildup and was the more dangerous and pressing matter, because she could die any time in agony at not being able to breathe. We fought for her life the best we knew how. The surgery was a success. It prolonged her life for a few more months with us, and I was grateful for not agreeing to put her down as soon as they diagnosed her. She seemed fine, why would I put her down without knowing for sure?

My answer was simple – surgery and biopsy. End of discussion! This was the denial. The bargaining stage was more of an inner struggle: I sensed the inevitable but was hoping against hope during sleepless nights that a surgery would prove to be miraculous, the dog would heal, and the retched sickness would leave her body if we do this and that, and I would pray more, praise God and all the saints that healed her, so that I would not have to deal with the unbearable outcome. Just looking at her face was piercing my heart with pain of inevitable grief that was to come.

God did have pity on us. He did not take her on Christmas, and she gladdened everyone, including my brother and his wife with her presence and a certain sweet and kind way about her that makes even the devoted cat lovers to question their attachments. Sammi made everything in our lives better. Life was more colorful with her around, she was generous with unconditional love for all of us.

She was still with us when the war broke out. Moving a bit slower, getting a bit sicker, with good and bad days in this big mess of human stupidity. Getting her downstairs from the top floor was a challenge, but she refused to do her business inside, the true lady that she was. When the explosions would settle and the gunfire would cease, we proceeded with the 'routine' the best we could. Going up and down the stairs was enough 'exercise', but she could still get on her favorite couch for some comfort.

The situation we found ourselves in was the answer to the question of staying or leaving Kyiv. Getting a ride for a family with two dogs, one of whom was in no shape or form to travel when there were families with children who evacuated in little sedans carrying 10 plus persons along with hamsters, parrots, cats, and tiny lap dogs? Not an option. Ours was a fate of staying. The news channels were flooded with photos of cars leaving town in droves and staying in traffic jams for hours at a time on the way out of the city. The borders of nearby Poland, Moldova, Slovakia, and Romania turned into a several days of waiting period to cross into the safety zone after a tremulous and uncertain commute. We could not possibly imagine leaving the dogs behind. We had left them once and I was not reliving that nightmare again. My dogs were staying with us, and if we were to die, we would be dying together. My heart was breaking when we walked the streets and saw random pups running around, still looking groomed, collars on their necks stating previous belonging to someone, looking through trash for scraps of food or following strangers with tiny hope they would take them home. I could not live with myself (and what a life would that be??) if I did that to my animals. And there we were…

When I say the city cleared of all former resemblance of normal existence in it, I do not just mean people left town. Hospitals and clinics were closed, private businesses had shut with shutters in the windows until further notice; cafes that used to tempt the walkers-by with their pastry and coffee aromas came to null; and the drugstores that we popped into for quick medicine refills were available no more.

But we had our dogs and each other. To be honest, my dogs were the very creatures that allowed my heated imagination of a worst-case scenario to cool down and face our new reality as the humans God designed us to be. They made everything more bearable, brought peace to our exhausted souls, and reminded us to smile once in a while, despite it all. That whole time I thought I was the one doing the right thing by my beasties, while it was the other way around: my dogs were the rescuers! I will forever be grateful to have had them by my side in the worst hours of my life.

12

Dear Ukraine

Natasha's brother, A., and his wife, T., had left and the shadows of war cast an ever expanding darkness on all of us in Ukraine. We only took it as saber-rattling with the thought in our heads that somehow the Muscovites would act rationally. The US Department of State kept emailing us that we should leave like NOW! Like YESTERDAY! Well, we took the panic in check just like we did back in the US for announcements about impending hurricanes and snowstorms. There was a mad rush to the stores which were emptied quickly of milk, eggs and toilet paper – like the Armageddon is coming and somehow having toilet paper will make a difference. Natasha and I just went about our business and didn't stock up on any of those items for the alleged impending war. We didn't stock up in the States when they made the storm announcements so why should we do it now? Americans love to panic buy. Maybe it's the nature of the uber-capitalist beast. Sometimes I wondered if all the retailers and toilet paper suppliers paid someone off to create the hype but that's neither here nor there.

Embassies were emptying. Foreigners were getting out. Most Ukrainians were going about their business. We decided to stick with the 'When in Rome' tactic. In order to express myself, I wrote the following letter on February 17, 2022, just one week before the full-scale invasion.

> *Dear Ukraine:*
> *We are still here with you. We are not the only ones as we see others on the streets who are not Ukrainian going about their business. Your people are our inspiration. A sense of calm and normalcy pervades our lives because we see it in yours at the grocery stores, cafes and in the parks as we walk our American dogs. Yes, our pets stand with you too. Even the one who has Stage Four cancer and will soon leave us. She'll leave all of us and we will suffer grief as many of you have over these last eight years and generations before you in the Great Patriotic War and the Holodomor3. Grief and suffering will soon enough be overcome with joy and triumph.*
>
> *We see that about you. Ukraine will prevail in the end. The problem is when is the end and what will it look like? You are already triumphing because your calm is*

3 The Soviet-inflicted Ukrainian famine of 1932–1933.

contagious. Had we listened to our government and media, we would have left weeks ago. But the situation on the ground tells another story. We laughed at the FEMEN protestor standing on the US Embassy sign in Kyiv painted with the words 'Don't Be A Pussy'! That appealed to the Jersey within us. Then, like Tony Soprano, We said well, the Russians are on the border and here we sit, whaddyagunnado?

When I say 'we', I mean my wife and well, the dogs as stated. My wife, my druzhina, she is my foxhole buddy and fits the Kyivan Rus military meaning of the word. We came here to be closer to her family in Belarus. We have seen a couple of them once because 'Uncle Sasha' has made travel in and out of Belarus next to impossible. We came to you, Ukraine, because of family and now you have embraced us and made us part of yours. Funny they are only five and half hours away which seems further than when we lived in the States. Now, I am an American mutt with no Ukrainian blood, but my wife is half Ukrainian. She regales me with stories of visiting her grandparents outside Vinnytsia as a child and the hope, joy and abundance those visits entailed. This is an abundant land in so many ways.

We are yours now, Ukraine, and you are ours. Most of our savings went into buying our property, so we aren't going anywhere. We can smell the blood that has drenched your soil over these last thousand years, and it smells like forbearance, loyalty, honor and independence. Maybe our blood will soon seep into your soil. Ukraine, we are ok with that and it is a good reason to stay. One of our visitors from Belarus said to us as we walked about Kyiv, 'It smells like freedom here.' That's a good smell to have when two of your neighbors reek of something else left unsaid.

We have barely even met you, Ukraine. Some day we hope to hike the Carpathians, walk among the sunflowers in the steppes, have a barbecue in the northern forest and slowly walk on the beach by the Black Sea. Maybe we will become fluent in your language (at the rate we are going, maybe we won't). We would love to read your great authors who have not yet been translated into English and visit sites of your vast history.

Are you perfect? No, but neither are we. That's one thing we love about you, Ukraine. Your problems and imperfections make you real and remind us that no one is. We can't speak for others who are staying that are not Ukrainian. Tonight, we will go to sleep and not be surprised to wake up to air raids or artillery fire, just like you. We'll drink some Ukrainian cognac (don't tell the French that yours is better!), listen to the Talking Heads play 'Life During Wartime' and maybe just wake up to another day. Normal is boring. We won't give into the panic set about by the Western talking heads. Maybe we'll just ignore them altogether.

Anyway, Ukraine, we are here, and we are with you in mind, body and spirit. Keep staying strong, you are good at it. Keep being calm and patient. Don't give into the provocations you have held back from so far. You are setting an example for the world in what seems to be a new paradigm of this century. History will remember you for it and we will be dust…

Glory to Ukraine!

On February 21, 2022, I wrote a poem that also reflected our feelings at the time. I had a hot date with Natasha on February 22nd and would be off from my remote gig. This is what I wrote the day before.

Sonnets of War

No drumbeats can be heard in the simmering distance across the steppe
Just satellite images of tanks, missiles and weapons of mass destruction
Yankee President screams like Chicken Little, a geriatric crying wolf
Will we wake up tomorrow or will our corpses lie in bombed out rubble?
Is the Kremlin now in the hands of a complete genocidal madman?
What will your legacy be, Vova? The one who launched World War Three?
Is that what you want? Because that's what you are going to get, brother
Orthodox on Orthodox war in a new century steeped in death
Diesel tanks stinking, rise like deadly turtles from the mire
Will you unleash their force upon your own brethren and the innocent?
Freedom is not another word for nothing left to lose to blue/yellow patriots
Cossack blood runs deep, they will stand and fight for their Motherland
Your own stood against Napolean and Hitler, outnumbered and outgunned
Will you be this century's first War Pig on a total and international scale?
Bodies burning in fields of sunflowers, wheat, corn and black soil abundance
Once you stood together against foes will you now slaughter your brothers?
How can one at this moment consider committing words to verse, Vova?
Wilt thou then send Great Khimki Wood to high Zamkova Hora?
Will thee be vanquished when Svyatoshinsky Wood come to Sparrow Hill?
A War Poet does not much of a great soothsayer make, doth he?
Many may wish your bloody demise, Vova, but not this poet
No condemnation but that instead you deeply consider your salvation
For rulers of men are called to judgement for the souls granted them to tend
Wilt thou be known for wars and rumors of wars, deaths of innocents?
The Sunday of the Prodigal Son has dawned here in the Heart of Ukraine
As it also has over the St. Basil's and upon the flowing waters of the Volga
Kyiv is not a prodigal to return to its wicked stepfather, the great Muscovy
No, brothers-in-arms, the Mother of All Rus shall not bow to its own offspring
Instead, shall you come, your Kyivan Mother will fill her deadly quiver
Open her Scythian soul, release her Amazons and fight those once she loved
No mother wishes to slay her distant children but would rather embrace them
Reconcile thee to the will of Our Father, do not release the death machines
Did you not more than once, fight side-by-side to protect a great Fatherland?
Would you destroy your kin because they seek that which you do not?
Are you not proud of how you all repelled great aggressors on your own soil?
Do you forget the fierceness of these Cossacks ready to die for their Motherland?
Beware, they will not quit as your war machines come, their wrath is mighty
If you commit this folly, it will be the end of all that is great about Russia

When you go down in the history books, whose faces will yours be next to?
Those of great Czars? More likely those of former enemies and despots
Spring flowers begin to rise here, Vova, and the land has become muddy
We all await your actions against this beautiful, abundant country
Some with fear, others with indifference and many with guns in their hands
Here we sit, waiting for the most Holy Fast in all of Orthodoxy, praying
For our lives will go on whether you come or not, for we know the Truth
You have no power against them unless it was given you from above
How will you use the power that has been granted you from above, Vova?
To bring lambs to slaughter or allow peace among the Slavic Brotherhood?
Would this be the eternal break of the Great Tripartite of Ancient Rus?
The grass begins to grow green as the weather warms on Volodymyrska Hill
St. Volodymyr stands strong, looking East to see if Vladimir's troops
Dare enter this sacred land to burn over a thousand years of Orthodox history
Ukraine's troops stand brave and strong, wait for the worst, hope for the best
Not to have to kill brothers and sisters who dare to cross that oh so thin line
Kyiv, she goes on as if nothing is coming, the sun glows, flowers grow
St Michael stands guard, watching the souls in the city under his guard
Knowing she has been through this before and she will survive yet again
And we wonder, will the Theotokos intercede and spread her veil over all of us?
Most Holy Theotokos, please save us. Amen.

13

February 22, 2022

Tuesday is my Saturday due to working in the hospitality industry (remotely) for a client in Atlantic City. That particular day in Kyiv was cold, slightly windy and there was still some snow and ice on the ground. Just a day or so before, little 'Snowdrop' flowers had bloomed on my street in the city center that I noticed as I walked our dog, Philly Cheesesteak. That day, February 22, 2022, did not feel like a spring day at all. Winter seemed to want to hold on a little while longer. Russian troops were still massing on the Ukrainian border, but we had grown used to that. The US Department of State kept emailing us to leave Ukraine as an attack was imminent. We either didn't believe that Russia would actually invade, or maybe we just didn't want to believe. Plus, we had a date.

My birthday had passed just a couple weeks back and Natasha had bought tickets for a ballet at the Kyiv Opera House. This magnificent structure is just a seven-minute walk from our flat in Kyiv. Philly likes to roll in the grass in front of it during spring when it is green and new. So, we walk by it all the time. The ballet that night was an interpretation of Nikolai Gogol's 'Evenings on a Farm Near Dikanka.' Natasha knows that I was a bit of a fan of Gogol ever since reading his dark tale 'Viy'. Twelve years ago, I had stood and taken a photograph at his grave in the Novodevichy Cemetery in Moscow. Yes, we had visited Moscow as a family back in those days and had enjoyed many museums, monasteries, churches, and sights. We had met up with her parents, brother and his wife and rented a flat big enough for all of us. We had not been all together for some years and it felt like it was time. I didn't do so well in a tight place with so many people, but they really had the time of their lives as a family and luckily, my occasional irritation didn't dampen it for them.

Natasha's brother (A.) and his wife (T.) had accompanied us one day to Moscow's Christ the Savior Cathedral where a baptism was taking place. Baptism in Orthodoxy is one of the seven sacraments, and it is said that if you say a prayer at a baptism, the Lord and His angels will be there and hear it. T said a prayer that day to have child. Later, after we returned to our home in Ventnor, New Jersey, T would call us and let us know she was pregnant. Now, I can't use their names because they live in a place that is controlled by the Kremlin. All those holy places we visited in Moscow don't seem holy but cursed now. We can't see any of Natasha's family due to the Russian invasion of Ukraine. She can't speak with her father about any of it because he has been programmed by the Kremlin propaganda machine and believes it all while missiles and rockets fall on his daughter and son-in-law.

Now back to that Tuesday, just two days before Russia attacked. I am not a fan of ballet or opera, in general. Give me Bruce Springsteen or Tom Waits any day. However, it was a gift, and I was willing to keep an open mind and enjoy myself. Natasha is more than just a wife. She is a partner, a friend, a counselor and now after almost a year of war, my foxhole buddy. I cannot describe in words how beautiful the production of 'Evenings on a Farm Near Dikanka' was. The whole performance moved me on the inside while dazzling my ears with its music, lighting my eyes with its sets, costumes, and ballet dancing. The whole shebang was just a stunning experience and masterpiece work of art all around. Inside, the Kyiv Opera House is even more elegant in its architecture than the outside and that just added to the whole experience. Despite the threat of war, the place was completely packed. The enemy was at the gates, and we were at the opera house. That's how it has been for over a year now.

These Ukrainians are indescribable. You can't really know them until you spend time on their home turf, within their culture, literature, food and all the things that make up a society. I hope when this war is over, that some of you readers will come and experience it for yourself. Natasha and I left the performance exhilarated, enlightened, and highly entertained. We strolled up Volodomorskya Street (1,000 years old as a street) as the wind blew down from St. Michael's Monastery. Many people had already left the city, so the traffic was lighter than normal. We climbed the small hill to Zoloti Vorota (Golden Gate). This piece of architecture (or at least part of it) has been standing for over a thousand years. Nothing beyond Native American burial grounds has stood that long in the US. There in the park before it, the original gate in Kyivan Rus, you breathe, smell, see and stand on ancient history. Natasha and I are lucky enough to live just minutes from this and so many other memories of Ukraine's place in history.

We dined that night at an Italian restaurant just across from Zoloti Vorota. After dinner, we strolled home to our two American dogs (Sammi and Philly). Sammi died of cancer just after the Battle of Kyiv and that was a very difficult loss for both of us. She was the first dog we had ever had in our lives, and she was so loving, intuitive, and special. War is loss. War is suffering, death, violence. All of us in Ukraine have lost something in this war even if it is small, it is still significant because it happened for no reason other than the ambitions of one man who heads a seemingly dying last empire along with those who just go along for the ride. Thousands of them now lay rotting and dead in Ukrainian steppes. For what? For whom?

Anyway, I smoked a Cuban cigar and drank some Ukrainian cognac after I had taken the dogs out for a nightly walk. Natasha relaxed and drank tea on her windowsill where she sits to watch Kyiv life float by. I sat on our balcony smoking and gazing at the cold winter moon. This is our home. We had bought the flat in a 'Tsar House' which is what they call pre-revolution buildings. Natasha had flawlessly designed and tended to the remodeling, arguing with contractors, picking tiles and choosing fixtures. Sure, I had participated but she had done the lion's share of the work. The end-product is very much 'us' in its style and layout. We have melded more together after twenty-one years of marriage, from our courtship at the Jersey Shore through when we decided we hated Florida and had to get out.

After the opera, we just sat there and enjoyed life, our dogs, flat and each other's company. Two days later, Russia attacked, and we stayed in Kyiv. But you know what? If I could wish it, we'd go back to where we were on that cold winter night on February 22, 2022.

14

Dear Kyiv

This chapter was written on February 23, 2022 and echoes some events from the previous day, but they have not been edited out because they take on a new relevance. This memoir is better shared with you, the reader, if most of the content is presented in chronological order. This way you get to experience most everything as it happened. This letter was written on the evening of the full-scale invasion.

Dear Kyiv,

Yesterday, all our truths so far away were revealed globally. We all knew what was coming, didn't we? There was no surprise for us as the West soiled its adult diapers. Nope. I walked through the Botanical Garden with my dogs and the old guy who plays guitar on the path from the Metro was playing 'Yesterday' by The Beatles. You know that guy, right, my fellow Kyivites? He is there all the time, strumming except in the dead of winter when it is too cold for his fingers to be nimble. Sometimes I see him in those months below the tunnel that leads to Symon Petliura Street. Anyway, his strumming made me smile, my fellow Kyivites. The sun was shining brightly, and it smelled like spring even though the news was bad. 'I heard the news today, oh boy.' I felt warm towards you, brothers and sisters, as I walked on past St. Volodymyr's Cathedral.

On my way home, I came upon Vitali Klitschko entering his brother's building on the street near the Velotrak. We looked each other in the eye. The tension showed in his expression and then we went about our business. That's what we do here in the face of all this bullshit, isn't it?

In the evening, the chilly air was bearable and life in Kyiv was going on as normal. My wife and I strolled down Bohdan Khmelnystsky Street to the National Opera. How's this for irony? We attended a ballet based on 'The Night Before Christmas' from Evenings on a Farm Near Dikanka by that great Russian writer, Nikolai Gogol. Oh, wait, there's the irony, you see it? Russian imperialism kind of steals your great history, writers and artists to this day. So as Russia rolled into Donbas, we attended a play by a stolen Ukrainian writer. We went out to dinner after the ballet, drank wine and I came home to some Kobelvo Cognac and a Cuban cigar. Life felt good, it still does, and it will no matter how bad it might get. It's those tiny moments that make it sweet.

Today, God woke me before dawn. I asked Him to. The morning air was colder today but I saw some snow flowers blooming on my street as I walked the dogs. God woke me early because I wanted to make Divine Liturgy at St. Volodymyr's Cathedral (I attend there because it is the closest church to my home and not for any Orthodox political reasons). There were not many faithful about on this Wednesday Fast Day before Meatfare Sunday. Maybe twenty-five of us or so. The priest remembered my name (they call me Ivan, there) even though I speak very little Ukrainian. I apologize for that as foreign languages don't come easy for me. So, I said my Confession in English and the priest forgave my sins in Ukrainian. Does it matter what language you use to try to reach salvation? Don't think so, nor will they ask who you voted for despite that seemingly being a way to damnation or salvation in certain spheres of American politics.

I don't miss all that crap, Kyiv. Being Orthodox in a majority Orthodox country feels good. That brings to mind something else, my city. I have no Slavic blood, yet you, Kyiv are a Holy city to me. Not 'The' Holy City. You are home to the ancient Christianization of the Slavic peoples. How can Muscovy forget that? How can they claim that they are the heart of the Rus peoples? Somehow, I hope you find a way to take that back from them. This city should be pilgrimage site for Slavic Orthodoxy. Frankly, I am surprised that none of you Ukrainians have turned that into a business. You're good at that sort of thing.

Anyway, Kyiv, the sun is sinking low outside my window and tomorrow I will work remotely from here for my small business in New Jersey. Today, I am thankful to be alive and to have partaken of the Holy Mysteries. Tomorrow, God willing, I will work my five days straight and will receive my wages next week. And I'll donate money I make from America to my church and spend it here in Kyiv. Trying to do my little part to keep this city and country afloat as all of you are. We will go on together and pray for peace.

May God bless Kyiv, Ukraine and all its people.

15

Dear World

The letter below titled 'Dear World' was written on February 28, 2022 out of rage and anger. Four full days of war and it seemed then as if the world had written us off in Ukraine and I mean anyone on Ukrainian soil regardless of nationality. We could hear small arms fire, artillery and missile strikes throughout the whole day and night. Air raid alarms were constant. On February 27th, I had waited for Natasha to get back from a quick supply run. Soon as she walked in the door, I told her I was leaving to go join Ukrainian Territorial Defense to protect Kyiv. We saw videos of Muscovite vehicles in Obolon just north of our district. Curfews were heavily enforced as there were Muscovite saboteurs everywhere on the streets. At that moment, it felt like 'do or die' time. I wanted to at least be able to protect my neighborhood when the enemy troops entered, and it certainly seemed they were going to be there within hours to a day or two.

I hustled down the main street to the center of the city where the recruitment center was allegedly based at 25 Kreshchatyk Street. A scared and skeptical woman in an official government office directed me toward the Kreshchatyk Metro Station where the Kyiv Military Administration was bunkered at the time. The streets were empty and everyone who was out was either military, police, people looking to sign up, or very nervous civilians. A very large Ukrainian soldier stood guard holding a modern assault rifle.

In broken Ukrainian I asked him, and he replied in broken English to catch up with three young men about five meters away who were also looking to sign up. These guys were nineteen or twenty-years old tops, maybe a little younger. One of them spoke a little English and the rest of the communication took place through Google Translate. Basically, they had been running around trying to sign up all morning. The big soldier at the metro had directed them back to 25 Kreshchatyk and I informed them that there was no recruitment center there. Of course, they didn't believe me, so I followed on with them figuring maybe they knew something I didn't.

We tried every entrance to no avail. As the four of us rounded the back of the building, I remember this memory vividly. Three or four middle aged folks were about to exit the building as we approached. The fear in their faces was striking as they all ran back into the building. I guess they figured we were saboteurs or something.

Finally, Yaroslav, who seemed to be the leader of the trio, got some reliable information. The actual recruiting center was about three kilometers away. Oh, and they were out of weapons already. Another thing, it would be at least two to three weeks before more would come. That is, if we weren't already slaughtered by the enemy by then. By now, I had been wandering around for hours trying to sign up, but the boys decided to plod on. I chalked it up to God's will and turned toward home.

Natasha was bewildered when I walked in the door.

'What just happened?'

'Um, I figured we were both bad at good-byes and it was better if I didn't give you time to think.'

So, I told her the story above and she gave me a hug. I gave her a good one before I left figuring it might be our last but not wanting to tell her that. She told me she was proud of me but was really glad it didn't work out. We both agreed it must have been God's providence. The fact that we were out of weapons and the Collective West seemed to be drinking Starbucks and waiting for us to be conquered and killed enraged me. How could we be out of small arms already? Hell, they knew we didn't have heavy weapons, good air defense, or much of anything that would deter the second greatest army in the world (that's what we thought of the Muscovites at the time). They couldn't at least have made sure we could go down in a blaze of glory? Weapons in hand, fighting for every meter is how we all imagined it would happen in the next couple days. So, the next day I wrote the letter below:

Dear World,

Well, here we are. Is it the end of the world as we know it and do we mind? I mind because my family and I are in the middle of the suck right now. Yea, we could have gotten out, but we don't have to live like refugees. Should I stay or should I go is too late to be asked. War, what is it good for? Lining somebody's pockets for sure. Sometimes you just have to stand and that is what we have decided to do alongside these heroic Ukrainians whose blood is as mixed as many. Like a rock.

So, world, here we are in what should be human evolution with millions of lives once again in the hands of a psychopath. Wait, wait, did you forget that we have been through this before and on the same continent? Oh yea, we see you with your posturing, your condemnation and hot air. We see you taking actions that will drive him further into a corner to possibly unleash even more murderous weapons against us in Ukraine. What the fuck do you care? You pretty much figure he won't cross that NATO line.

Meanwhile, a new hero among heroes is born among world leaders. None of you deserve to be in the same room with President Zelensky at this point. I doubt the vast majority of you would be willing to sacrifice your lives and your family's lives alongside your very own people. Yea, shit is going to change after this one. 'Give me liberty or give me death' has shifted continents and peoples.

You'll go on sipping your Starbucks or whatever, bemoaning your portfolio losses, whining about how much it takes to fill your tank and soon enough, how expensive bread is due to rising wheat costs. All this while children lie dying in the streets, old people starve and freeze to death due to war and young men and women stand bravely to die. Where is your evolution now?

That's ok. We'll fight, we'll die, we'll starve, we'll freeze, and we'll survive. Not all of us, but enough. Enough to call all of you to account as well as the aggressor. The guilty are easy to see. But many who feebly tried to help will be called for judgement. What form it will take, I don't know. A day of reckoning is coming for us all in one way or another. And you, world, are in for it if you don't do more now.

Out of this, the blue and gold shall rise. Many will perish before it does, but it is already on the ascendant. The true Sons and Daughters of Liberty live here now. If you don't personally do something right now for Ukraine, individually and collectively, then you are just as guilty as the Kremlin. I don't care what it is but do something that hurts even if it just hurts your bottom line. The real pain is here but if we know you are willing to feel some, it will make all of us in Ukraine even stronger.

Slava Ukraina!

16

Finding Home in a War

Home. Sometimes we take this word for granted or maybe really don't understand it. Today, on the eighth day (March 3, 2022) of the war in Ukraine, this word applies to the steppes, the Carpathians, the cobblestone streets of Kyiv and Lviv, the beaches on the Black Sea, the cliffs of Crimea, the forests in the north and every single inch of Ukrainian soil. Soil that is soaked with over fifteen hundred years of the blood of Tatars, Scythians, Amazons, Mongols, Roma, Slavs and now, modern Ukrainians. This soil did not ask for the blood that is now being soaked into it by a war between brothers and sisters. Maybe Ukraine's great fertility comes from all of those that have been willing to die for it. Yes, this is a most fertile land and full of natural abundance. But it did not need to be fertilized with blood yet again.

Ukrainian blood courses through my wife's veins as she decides to take a stand against the aggressor and stay here on this land. She is a Ukrainian woman and an honorary Jersey Girl. They don't make them much tougher and obstinate than that. Bombs are dropping, tanks are rolling, and young soldiers are dying needlessly. Ancient cities are being levelled, modern infrastructure is being decimated and leftover buildings from the Soviet era are crumbling beneath the onslaught of the country that gave them birth. Together, we are staying here in Kyiv on our little fifty four square meters of home. Will we be found dead in the rubble alongside our two dogs?

Whether that is the case or not, we will have died at home. We will have bled blue and gold just like so many others. And we would be proud to do it just like all the brave men and women that are standing and fighting for their homeland. If it is not the case and we survive, we will hold our heads high and stand with all the other survivors of this war. Ukraine will survive and Ukrainians will survive. This land will be a shining beacon of liberty that was once held high by my former homeland. New Jersey, and specifically, the area around Cape May County will always be my home as well. That is where my best memories are from and also where I met my wife.

However, now I am truly home simply because I was willing to stay and die. Words cannot describe how one feels when you experience this. Only those who live through it can truly understand it. I do not know if I will ever return to my homeland. If we survive this war, I want to be here with my new people and get my hands dirty rebuilding what the aggressor cannot destroy. We who survive will all have work to do. I will have to learn Ukrainian so I can communicate. Ukraine will have to finally and completely release the noose the oligarchs have around its neck. Many countries have pledged to help rebuild Ukraine when this is all over. We will need the world's help in so many different ways. Build back better will have a real and true meaning here in this land of Cossacks, Tatars, Hutsuls and so many others.

New memorials for those who have died in battle will leave those from World War II in the shadows. This is the Great Patriotic War now. Ukrainians are showing the world how much they love this land. Stories will need to be told. Hollywood and western media will screw it up as usual. Western media is already skewing the information coming out of the war. Ukraine now stands for the truth and their truth must be told by them, not somebody else.

Our story is one or two of over some forty plus million individual ones in this war zone and outside of it. Our story doesn't matter all that much compared to so many more who have died and are dying in the battlefields whether as soldiers, rescuers or humanitarians. My wife and I will bow our heads in our Orthodox Church and always be thankful if we are spared. One day, I hope we are old and living in a valley in the Carpathians. Me tending a few beehives and her looking after a small garden and cooking delicious food. That is for God to determine, we are all in His hands. I only hope we are there and buried peacefully in the ground with our local Orthodox Priest and fellow parishioners praying over our graves. For now, 'We're not gonna take it, anymore.'

17

The Battle of Kyiv

The Battle of Kyiv officially took place from February 25, 2022 through April 2, 2022. Some of the previous chapters were written during the Battle of Kyiv as will at least one of the following chapters. I will try to avoid any redundancy in this chapter which is primarily about how we survived during this time period. This chapter is being written after the fact where most others were written as they took place. The information is being drawn from memory and notes from that timeframe. During this part of the war, Kyiv was one of the frontlines. You could feel the war every day because you could smell, see, hear and touch it. Gunfire, tank and artillery battles, missiles, and rockets could be seen, heard, and that acrid smell lingered. This is a smell we will never forget as it hit us dead in the face when we left the flat to walk Sammi and Philly. A burning, acidic mix that invaded your nostrils.

Cold. Wind and snow whipped through the streets as the fighting began or at least that's how I remember it. March is a very unpredictable month in Ukraine. Weather can be warm with a sweatshirt to downright brittle. The first few weeks of the battle were very cold and snowy. Our flat lays at the bottom of a yar (ravine) near the old city. Wind comes off the Dnipro and must go around buildings before it reaches down into our lowlands. When Kyiv was young, our area was just outside the original city walls. Later, it would become a neighborhood for the middle level merchant class. Why am I telling you this? Wait for it.

The advantage we had and came to realize soon as the war started was location. We are separated from the building behind us by only four meters and it is slightly higher. About 50 meters behind that there is a new high-rise which stands about twenty-five stories. Both of those buildings face exactly due North toward Belarus and Russia where many rockets and missiles were launched from. We are at the bottom of the yar which means a missile shot at us has many targets to hit before it lands on us. East of us is covered by an old building from the Stalin era which is seven stories. Our building tops out at four stories which means we sit below everyone else. The direction of missiles shot from the Black Sea is also blocked by another larger building. We don't worry about the western exposure because they don't shoot missiles from that direction currently. Here, in this rather boring paragraph I am laying the foundations for some of the reasons we stayed.

Our disadvantage is that we live on the fourth floor and would be the first to get hit if something were not blocked. We are also only a few kilometers from the President's office and many other important offices that could be targets. Now on to the action, shall we?

We watched as the city emptied out rather quickly. Local news and social media were full of stories about people stuck at the border for days, abandoning cars and walking across. All I could think about at those times was the song by Tom Petty and the Heartbreakers 'You don't have to live like a refugee.' Sammi had Stage Four cancer and was unable to travel, so leaving was out. There weren't any veterinarians around where we could go and have her put to sleep. We love our dogs as Natasha has explained in previous chapters. So, we had to stay for family reasons.

Kyiv went from being a vibrant, bustling city to what seemed like a one-horse town within about forty-eight hours. Empty streets, closed cafes and retail stores, some hastily left behind, others with security gates, along with almost no traffic. You could go out for an errand or a walk and not see another human being. It felt like one of those zombie apocalypse movies only this time with frequent air raids accompanied by almost round-the-clock artillery fire. Night often brought small arms fire. Curfews were strictly enforced, and store shelves were quickly emptying. Funny thing, the garbage men were still working. So were most of the street sweepers. A few grocery stores remained open, but we had stocked up enough food in the first few days to last for a good month. Canned goods and carbs primarily along with plenty of drinking water. Lucky for us, we usually follow most of the fast rules for Orthodox Great Lent (No meat, dairy, eggs, fish, wine or olive oil). The full-scale invasion began just a few days before Great Lent started.

Speaking of no wine. Mayor Vitali Klitschko quickly banned the sale of all alcoholic beverages. This was ok for the first few days but within a week, the alcoholics began walking around with wild eyes. I felt pity for them, not disgust. Imagine what it was like for them going through withdrawal as an enemy attacked. We all expected the enemy troops to be in the city within days and most likely we would be killed, tortured, or captured unless we managed to hop on an outgoing train. Natasha and I felt like it would be better to have a weapon, but we might just hunker down and be quiet. Our door is thick, and you'd need a grenade to open it, so we figured maybe they'd just move on. One day I went over to Kolo, the local convenience store to grab whatever they might have in stock for junk food. The manager (Elena) was there and had showed up every day. She had covered the alcohol with black trash bags, but it was clearly visible. Two crazy-looking drunks were inside eyeballing her and the spirits. So, I lingered and took my time picking out a few snacks for the quickly depleting stocks. They bought smokes and seemed to reluctantly move on. Elena still works there and shows up every day she is scheduled. All of those who stayed and continued to function are the unsung heroes of this war.

Fighting seemed to be getting closer. Cars abandoned after accidents were just sitting on the side of the road like abandoned corpses. We knew that the fighting around Hostomel Airport was tough but that the local Ukrainian militias along with armed forces had blocked a major landing and staging space for the Muscovites. They had planned to helicopter in and fly in additional troops to take over Kyiv but that had failed. Saboteurs were marking spots for missile attacks. X marks the spot but that didn't work out too well for them as their alleged precision weapons were not, well..., precise. That didn't stop them from trying. We kept a wary eye on anyone who didn't look familiar. We learned and studied the faces we saw every day so as to be able to point out anyone who didn't belong. All of our senses were on high alert and ready for anything. When death is knocking, you feel so much more alive.

Curfews grew longer with the longest one lasting just over seventy-two hours. No long walks for the dogs. We pretty much stuck to within ten meters of the building. Walking the dogs was tough even without curfews as you always wanted to be close to a place to shelter when the missiles fell. In the early days, we sometimes only had a few minutes between an air raid and a missile strike. The dogs seemed ok. Sammi was sick and weak from the cancer, so she didn't like going very far anyway. Philly seemed to sense it and kept his energy in check as best he could. We managed to stock up on enough dog food also.

Our church, St. Volodymyr's Cathedral, stayed open most of the time. Evening services were cancelled, but Divine Liturgy was held daily around 09:30. We went as often as we could because there was sense of peace and solace there. I guess our thinking was to be ready for death and that it wouldn't be so bad to die while taking Communion or standing for the services. One day, we met some reporters from Agence France Presse while at church. They asked for an interview in the coming days and we agreed. They showed up on time in between air raids and we entertained guests during a war. Frankly, it was kind of weird but comforting at the same time. Our interview is out there floating in the web-sphere still.

The weather began to warm a bit by mid-March as the fighting continued. All the information we had seemed to show that Ukraine Territorial Defense, private citizens and the Ukraine Armed Forces were keeping the enemy from getting into Kyiv. They were doing it by the skin-of-their-teeth, but they were doing it. We were grateful and none of us yet had knowledge of the horrors that were committed in Irpin, Bucha, Hostomel and other places. Somehow despite all odds, we were alive and supplies to the stores were picking back up. We had checked out the bomb shelter early on and never ended up using it because it was packed with people and pets. We could see them come out to smoke and get fresh air on occasion from our balcony. One of the bomb shelters behind us had a commercial kitchen. They were cooking for the troops and delivering it on scooters. Resilience and bravery were everywhere.

The worst day of the whole war came for us on March 25th. Sammi lost her battle with cancer that day. I can't even write these sentences now without getting a lump in my throat so there will be no detail. She is at peace and we are still grieving well over a year later. What I can say is that Sammi taught me unconditional love, obedience, trust and so much more. She became for me, our symbol of loss in this war. Everyone in Ukraine has lost someone or something. We had to pay our dues and Sammi gracefully paid them for us.

March 23, 2022: Honchar Park, Kyiv on the first day the coffee stand (Grky) was open since the invasion began. Natasha ordering a latte.

March 12, 2022: An abandoned car that sat for weeks on Shevchenko Blvd. A suspicious vehicle used by possible Russians agents, collaborators or saboteurs. Gunfire was heard the night before it showed up.

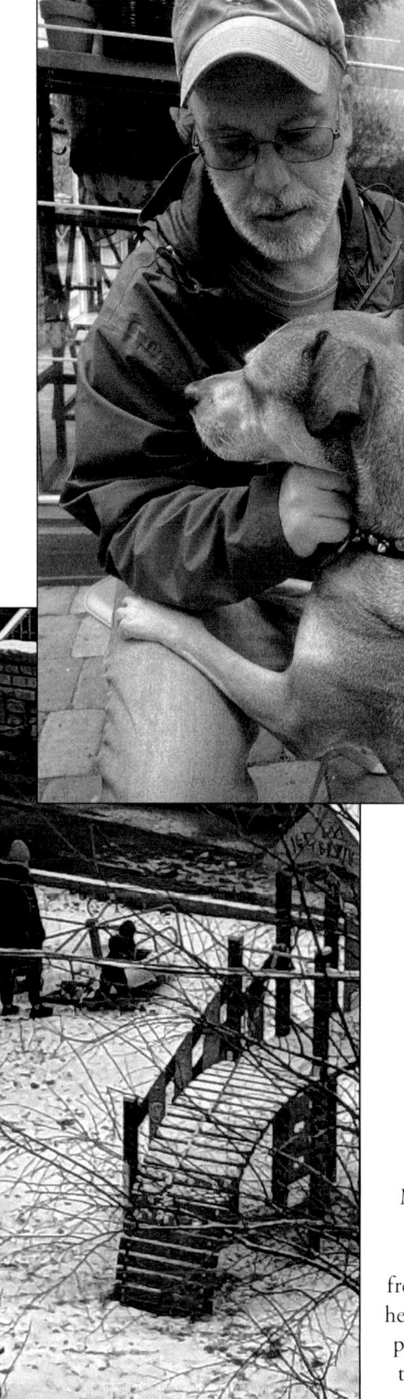

April 25, 2022: The official day that the Battle of Kyiv ended. John and Philly out for coffee in Fomin Botanical Garden, Kyiv City Center.

March 1, 2022: Curfews were long and regular. Missile attacks were frequent. Artillery could be heard in the distance as this parent brought their child to play at the playground below our flat in Kyiv.

March 2022: Missile attack concussion caused debris from building to fall on our street in Kyiv City Center.

March 1, 2022: Kyiv had mostly emptied out and went from a bustling metropolis to a one-horse town within a week.

March 3, 2022: Our empty street in Kyiv after the snow had melted.

March 3, 2022: 'Slava Ukraina!' in Ukrainian painted on the walkway of Fomin Botanical Garden just over a week into the invasion and Battle of Kyiv.

March 19, 2022: Honor (in Ukrainian) alongside Happyness in English written in graffiti on our Kyiv street as the battle still raged.

April 24, 2022: Our priest (Father Bohdan) defied the curfew and held midnight Pascha (Easter) services. The procession around the church prior to Easter Liturgy is an old Orthodox tradition.

February 27, 2022: Three days into the invasion only one (state-owned) pharmacy in the neighborhood was open. People stood in line as tank and artillery fire could be heard in the distance.

April 2022: Natasha standing and praying at the front of St. Volodymyr's Cathedral in Kyiv.

March 19, 2022: The statue of Oles Honchar (Ukrainian Soviet writer) covered in snow in the park named after him. Kyiv City Center.

This popular meme on Facebook appeared on February 27, 2022 showing the history of Kyiv vs Moscow.

March 9, 2022: A lone woman stops at the statue of Taras Shevchenko in the park named for him in the Kyiv City Center as if seeking guidance and inspiration during the Battle of Kyiv.

April 3, 2022: Orthodox Christians stand waiting to give their Confession at St. Volodymyr's Cathedral, Kyiv.

18

Thirty-Two Days

Thirty-two days since Russia attacked Ukraine and headed toward our city, Kyiv. Strange how one becomes used to air raid sirens after this much time. How you react depends on where you happen to be when their ominous wail begins. Say, you are walking where there is a government building, well, you immediately distance yourself from the potential target and take cover where you can. Then, you wait to determine where the rockets or missiles will fall. One can usually tell if it is safe to go on once they start to fall as usually, they fall in a concentrated area. Often, nothing falls, and you just have to decide whether to continue taking cover or start heading to whatever destination you originally set out for. If you are walking your dog in the Kyiv Botanical Garden, most of the time you just go about your business while they sing their song of very possibly impending death. Why? Well, it doesn't seem to make sense that Russia would attack a public park with no nearby targets of any significance. Then again, maybe when it comes to Russia at this point, you can't expect them to do anything that makes sense. Regardless, there is a certain resolve to just keep walking when the sirens scream. Sometimes, you should just head home because it is close.

The crash and boom of rockets, missiles and artillery in the distance also seems increasingly not to faze people. Yes, that's right, fighting is heard in the background as people stand in line for their latte from the coffee stand that recently reopened on about the thirtieth day of war. In church, we can hear the thuds but stand in line for Confession and Communion regardless. After all, if we die in church, well, that'd be ok. Rarely is small arms fire ever even heard in the city center anymore. Oh, we heard it in the first few weeks but that close-in fighting has died down. Just the heavy thuds in the distance, which is the new normal.

People with all manner of weapons on the streets in Kyiv also seems like the natural order of life. Now, if I was in the States, well, I'd be seriously concerned even if there was a war on. Here there is no fear of mass shooters, but maybe that one of the people carrying a weapon is not fighting for Ukraine. But then there is a trust that Ukraine's Armed Forces and Police will know if someone is not supposed to be walking around with an AK-47 or some other assault rifle. Yes, there is a certain confidence after thirty-two days of war that Ukraine knows what it is doing. Armed individuals in varying uniforms and convoys of soldiers are just the backdrop of this heavily fortified city.

More traffic and people have returned to Kyiv. Shops are reopening, old ones and new ones are even beginning to appear. Everyone is out in the warm spring air. Crocuses are blooming in the gardens. Leaves of tulips and hyacinths are beginning to poke through the soil. Walks are more pleasant because of the warming air. We know this thing is far from over, but there is a renewed sense of confidence. Ukraine is getting the job done. It's not an easy job and it's not one anyone wanted, but being an adult means doing the things you don't really want to do.

Of course, we, and I can only speak for us, have survivor's guilt, or not coming under full-attack guilt. We watch as those in Mariupol, Kherson, Chernihiv, Irpin, Bucha, other areas just north of us in Kyiv and throughout Ukraine come under constant bombardment. Life is not really that tough here in our part of Kyiv. In other parts of Kyiv that are within rocket and missile range, it is a horrible existence. We can now walk out our door and go to the bakery or hit the coffee stand for a latte while others barely have enough water to drink. Are we thankful that we are ok and do not live under those conditions? Yes, we feel blessed and protected. But we don't necessarily feel good about it. I am sure there are others in Kyiv who feel the same including President Zelensky and his team.

President Zelensky's office is within two miles of us. We can walk there from where we live. The reason we are doing ok is because we are in that Presidential Zone of Protection. He needs to be protected because he is leading and inspiring the whole of Ukraine and the world. We watch as US and European leadership dropped the ball over and over again. Sure, the US handed Ukraine something called a cheeseburger with a gourmet bun, fresh pickles, onions, lettuce, tomato. Then they topped it with government cheese. 'Where's the beef?'

Ukraine has already proven itself in these first thirty-two days of war. The job ahead in the capital will not be as dangerous, but it will require new methods and practices in this once fledgling democracy. Kyiv will continue to lead and run the country no matter what it looks like when this war is over. This is truly a capital city. It has earned that over fifteen hundred years and now must look to a future of transparency in all its dealings. Otherwise, what is everyone fighting and dying for? Not to return to what it was only thirty-three days ago.

Meanwhile, about that latte…

19

Unsung Heroes

Ukraine is full of heroes today and every day, every hour, every minute, every second, someone steps up to 'Git-R-Done'. We easily see the heroes on the killing fields from the soldiers of Ukraine's Armed Forces to the Rescuers from State Emergency Services to the Territorial Defense Forces to the Doctors, Nurses and Medical workers on the battlefield who are stepping up to take care of the sick and wounded to those who are driving, delivering and distributing humanitarian aid to those who need it. Who will sing the song of the Unsung Heroes?

I will sing it. I see you the Unsung Heroes on the streets and in the parks of Kyiv every day. I see you when I am walking my dogs or out on an errand while the air raid sirens are blaring as the thuds of munitions are heard.

It is you, the girl at the convenience store around the corner who is working alone while banned liquor is easily seen behind the counter. I see the fear in your eyes as those who look like alcoholics come in and eyeball it. Yet you go on ringing up purchases even though you are clearly scared.

It is you, the landscape and maintenance man at the University of Leontovicha St across from St. Volodymyr's Cathedral. Air raid sirens are going off and I watch as you neatly rake one of the gardens under your care. The other morning when dawn had just broken and night was still trying to cling to day, I saw the freshly trimmed branches on the tree on the garden you care for. I wish I could tell you how much that meant to me to see that the fresh cuts were a day old at most. Now, I pass by to see what work you might have done and look for the flowers that are grasping for the sun of impending spring. I see your compatriot in the Botanical Garden cleaning up, emptying the trash and actually singing as he does it while the missiles make their dull thuds in the distance.

It is you, the sanitation workers, I see as I walk one of the surrounding streets with my dogs. Riding on the back of your sanitation truck and collecting the garbage of those of us who have stayed in this ancient, beautiful and strong city. You are keeping our health and hygiene as a top priority and your garbage truck is your armored tank in this awful war.

It is you, the Priest, the Deacon, the choir and babushkas who extinguish the candles before the icons and keep the church clean at St. Volodymyr's Cathedral. You, the Priest, Deacon and choir who conduct the Divine Liturgy with such joy and enthusiasm even though the sirens are screaming against you and the missiles are trying to silence you. Even though only a handful of us faithful are there, you sing as if the cathedral is full. It is you, the Priest who remembers my name and hears my Confession, absolves me and makes the sign of the cross so I can take Communion even though you don't understand a word I say, and I understand little of what you say.

It is you, the ladies and girls who work at the local bakery making fresh bread, sweets and croissants. The best chocolate croissants I have ever had on this earth, and I thought that before the Russians attacked. Imagine how wonderful it is now for me to bite into one during the war and know that you probably stayed overnight to make them in the bakery because you couldn't travel during the curfew hours to or from work. How wonderful your bread tastes and how thankful we all are that you show up.

It is you, the cashiers, stockpersons and managers of the grocery stores that keep us fed, nourished and clean during this. You bravely come to work each day while all this violence disrupts our lives. Yet, you show up, open the doors and help us stay alive with your sacrifice. And we all thought COVID was bad. Kinda funny, huh?

I know there are many more Unsung Heroes out there that I have not recognized or seen. Forgive me for that. Please all of you that are out there and living in this war zone, remember to be polite and appreciate these people that we so easily take for granted. Without them, we could not go on with some semblance of normalcy in our lives. Viva the Unsung!

20

Holy Week and War

In the Orthodox East, April 17, 2022, is Palm Sunday. Today is also the 53rd day of the Russian-Ukraine War and the 41st day of the Spiritual Warfare and ending of Great Lent. Palm Sunday is for us Eastern Orthodox, a feast day. Not a full-blown feast, mind you, but a feast before the feast of feasts. You wonder what that means? Orthodox Christianity is more described as a way of life versus a religion by its practitioners or adherents, or whatever word you in the West wish to call them. In Ukrainian, we are called *pravoslavny christiyan*. Pravoslav means truth if translated. Not, however, truth in the western logical sense of the word. But truth in the mystical sense of the word. I am not here to convert or to go deep into what it means to be a practicing Orthodox Christian. Some explanation, however, is required.

First and foremost is, this is Palm Sunday and despite what the world might be doing or involved with, this is a Holy Day. Now, I can't speak for the Russians sitting in their tanks and armored personnel carriers just about a four-hour drive to the east. The situation seems to have made them forget that this day is one of the most important in our shared faith. Yes, our faith is very much similar whether we are Greek, Antiochian, Israeli, Bulgarian, Russian, Romanian, Georgian, Ukrainian, American or any other nationality. If you attend Divine Liturgy in any of these places, conducted in any of the languages, the service is about ninety percent the same. Ukrainian soldiers on the front lines would much rather be home for this holiday, celebrating with their families than fighting against their own Orthodox Christian brothers.

Conventional warfare has not stopped, and Spiritual Warfare never stops. Great Lent began just a few days after Russia attacked Ukraine. We attempt to focus totally and completely on Spiritual Warfare. Those who practice Orthodoxy try to curtail their popular entertainment intake, stay away from secular reading and other activities, read more of the Holy Fathers or Scriptures, attend church services more often, pray more, do prostrations and follow the fast rules laid out by the Church. Now, imagine trying to do this while bombs, missiles, and rockets fall from the sky; tanks run over cars, people and villages; soldiers rape, torture and execute everyday people on the street. Living within a conventional war zone while attempting Spiritual Warfare is probably impossible for some and just not on the minds of others.

Yet despite it all, some of us have managed to adhere somewhat to what the Church suggests we should do during Great Lent. Now, it must be said that the Church does not tell us we must do it or that it is even necessary for our salvation. No one says that if you eat meat during Great Lent that you will be condemned to an eternity in hell. Great Lent is more like attending military basic training once every year. The Church is encouraging us to be spiritual soldiers against the ultimate enemy of mankind. We are not conscript soldiers who are forced to join. We who wish to, do it voluntarily. Fighting an enemy takes discipline, strategy and organization. Ours begins with fasting. We have other fasts, but Great Lent is the most difficult one because it leads to the culmination of the Greatest of Feasts, Pascha (Easter). Thus, Great Lent came as a gift this year because we were entering the Great Fast as the war began and the shortage of goods just seemed to match the timing. That does not mean we were free of the demons though.

Remember that Jesus said that certain demons can only be expelled with prayer and fasting? (Matthew 17:21). Great Lent is about exorcising your own demons. What demons live within the Russian soldiers, leadership and heads of their churches right now? How do they even light a candle and stand in front of the icons during this war? Ukraine is doing its best to exorcise these physical demons from its territory even as I sit here and write from my flat in Kyiv. Will a Priest have to hear the Confession of those who raped, tortured and murdered innocents? Will that Priest be able to absolve them of that if they do confess? Probably those who did these things will not seek penance.

I cannot say that what is happening in Ukraine is God's will. No one can know the will of the Divine. What we are seeing in Ukraine is man's free will. Particularly, the free will of one man in the Kremlin. Soldiers who fight bravely and honorably as well as those who commit atrocities are all exercising their free will. This gift that God has given us of free will is ours to use and own. The Orthodox practitioner is merely attempting to align it with God's will. This is no easy task for a normal person and what most monastics aspire to. The Church gives us the fasts and disciplines so that we might find the path that leads to salvation. But we are also fighting within.

> *'The whole of our treatment and exertion is concerned with the hidden man of the heart, and our warfare is directed against that adversary and foe within us, who uses ourselves as his weapons against ourselves, and, most fearful of all, hands us over to the death of sin.'* – St. Gregory the Theologian

We can fight our physical enemies with weapons of war when they make war against us. A just war is one in which peoples are defending their lands, peoples and values. Ukraine is on the just side of this war. The outcome is still unknown as we will not know the outcome of our spiritual war until after we take our last breath.

Today, I will feast on a tuna steak, wine and a cigar. Tomorrow, we return to the strict fast of Holy Week. Many will be cowering in basements, dying in battlefields and running for their lives. Kyiv is quiet today but who knows what the week holds? Whatever it may hold, I will try to finish it out by focusing on the last week of Christ's earthly life and try to be stricter with myself. Whatever you believe, may you find peace and may all of us in Ukraine be free and victorious.

21

Easter at War

Tradition! Traaddition! These words sung by a fictional Ukrainian Jew named Tevye the Dairyman also applies to we Orthodox Christians. We put a lot of weight in them, sometimes too much. Natasha and I never really ever prepared the traditional Easter basket that features so prominent in the celebration. These baskets are blessed by the priest at the end of the Paschal (Easter) service. There are certain items that are included in all baskets, but I won't bore you with that minutia. Take my word for it, after about 50 days without eating meat, we were hungry! Any other items that aren't meat are just ancillary. This year we joined everyone and prepared a basket because we still felt like life might end at any moment. Once death seems so imminent, it becomes less scary or so that's what we tell ourselves. You tend not to lie to yourself much when a missile might just take you out on your way to church to celebrate Easter or some other daily routine.

A curfew had been set and we were informed by the Kyiv city administration that attending Easter services was banned. We were told this by the national Ukrainian authorities as well. The curfew was set for 23:00 until 06:00. Even though it was April, a cold wind was blowing through abandoned alleys and streets that night. Territorial Defense had checkpoints and guarded areas throughout the city. We carried our basket as we made our way toward the church that night and no one stopped us or said anything as we walked through the ancient part of Kyiv at around 22:30. Yes, we were going to break man's rules that night in order to be with God.

Our priest, Father Bohdan, along with our fellow parishioners had conspired to hold services anyway. We would have to spend the night in the church until the curfew broke. Paschal services are long anyway. They begin with the readings before the services and end with the blessing of the baskets. Traditionally, they begin about 23:30 and end between 02:30–03:00. The Battle of Kyiv was officially over and information about the atrocities committed just outside the city limits by the Russian soldiers was beginning to come to light. We chose to come to the Light. Jesus broke the rules all the time as related to secular and Pharisee society, so we felt no guilt or remorse as we climbed the stairs to the church.

Our little church (St. Yuri's) only has about a dozen people who attend regularly. It is a little wooden structure tucked away in an alley just a stone's throw from St. Michael's Monastery. We entered, lit our candles, said our hellos and prepared as the choir sang the verses and Father Bohdan responded in kind. The monks at St. Michael's were also doing the same. Floral incense from the loud Paschal censer with its many bells wafted about and filled our nostrils with a pleasant familiar smell. Bells from St. Michael's began to ring. Simultaneously, the air raid siren began to wail its mournful tune in the background. We expected the Russians would attack on Easter as their true colors had long been exposed. Again, it was better to die in church giving praise to the Father, Son and Holy Spirit than to die fearful in our beds or buried in a bomb shelter.

The sirens deadly song stopped nothing. Father Bohdan and the choir didn't even skip a beat. No one looked around fearfully or made to go to the closest bomb shelter. We all seemed of one mind to stay and celebrate the most Holy Day of all for those of us who adhere. Eventually, the air raid siren went quiet, but the bells of St. Michael's did not. It seemed as all of us were on the same page. The readings were over, and the Divine Liturgy began. All of us were tired and knew it was going to be a long night. We stood and listened to the words, sang the traditional songs and everyone took Communion without Confession as is the tradition on Pascha. This is the only day of the year in which all may partake. The hours passed rather quickly and soon enough the baskets were all blessed. A joyous spirit lived within all present. You could tell by the way their faces glowed and eyes lit up.

There, at around 03:15, we moved the chairs about and set up a small table. I had prepared the signature chicken dish from my family back in the States. Others had prepared the traditional sweet Easter bread (kulich). Some made a kulich for each of us. Others brought food and wine to share. That Easter night as we sat in church, eating, drinking and chatting until 06:00 is one of our most memorable Pascha experiences. A true sense of peace for the first time since the invasion began settled in and stayed through the whole day. Soon enough, the sun's rays broke through the stained-glass windows. Father Bohdan departed before the curfew was over. He knows police, military and SBU all around as he performs funerals for the fallen regularly. We said our good-byes and went our way.

Philly anxiously greeted us upon our return, and I mustered enough strength to take him for a walk around the block before coming home and sleeping until we awoke hungry. Ready to feast. The whole day felt blessed as we enjoyed our time and the hope of the Resurrection. It is one of the richest spiritual experiences of my life and I will always be grateful when I remember it.

22

Ukraine's Manifest Destiny

Humanity often thinks it knows and can determine the mind of God by stating that certain people or nations are pre-determined or pre-destined to accomplish a certain thing. In the United States, the belief that God determined that country's Manifest Destiny with the expansion of democracy and capitalism across the North American continent and beyond is built into our fabric. Whether it was true and determined by God is not important. What is important is that citizens, politicians, bureaucrats, organizations, the military and many other believed that it is true. When a nation believes that a higher power has endowed it with certain tasks or goals, that nation can also become unstoppable. This idea of Manifest Destiny came to be in the mid-1800's and drove the US forward for nearly a hundred years.

President Putin also believes in a Manifest Destiny for the Russian Federation to take back former lands once controlled by the Russian Empire. Propaganda in the RF has been pushing forth Putin's 'Make Russia Great Again' narrative since the 1990s. People have been forced to believe that this is Russia's Manifest Destiny, and the ideal is now ingrained in their minds. However, the difference between the US idea (expansionism for democracy and capitalism) and Russia's is that RF expansionism is merely vengeance for perceived past wrongs. Both the US and Russia adhere to the belief that it is God who has manifested their destiny. The brutal reality that the RF is now facing is that it has driven itself straight into Ukraine's Manifest Destiny.

Ukraine did not know it had a Manifest Destiny, nor did anyone really announce it within the government or anywhere else for the most part. Even in 2014 and the years after, there was no real mention of Ukraine having a Manifest Destiny. Peace had been broken, land had been taken, but nobody listened to what the Ukrainians had to say about the RF's further expansion plans. Ukraine's Armed Forces (UAF) held the line but could not do much due to a lack of weapons and resources. Ukraine's Manifest Destiny was laid in front of it when the RF started its full-scale invasion on February 24, 2022.

Is Ukraine's Manifest Destiny pre-determined by God? Only a fool would state they know the mind of God. However, Ukraine's Manifest Destiny is a true reality easily seen by a logical mind. Ukraine is the country to reveal the truth about Russia. The Ukrainians did not want this task or ask for it. They are free-spirited people who only have ever sought their own freedom and peace upon their lands. Like everyone else in history, they have made mistakes in the past including perhaps some misguided alliances. The past is to be learned from and then moved on from.

The present is what matters. Ukraine's present is the grim reality of 'It's a dirty job but someone's gotta do it.' Ukraine is revealing they are the true Rus people, and that the RF is really just Muscovy and always has been. The whole Ukrainian nation is fulfilling its Manifest Destiny by exposing a thousand years of lies and false history. The old mantra that history is written and told by the winners has held true by the Muscovites for that long of a period. Ukraine's Manifest Destiny is now showing the real truth and history. A nation of liars with power and massive amounts of weapons is now killing everyone in its path to try to stop these truths from being told. But it is already too late for the lies to be covered up. Years after the war ends, Ukraine will have the responsibility of continuing to expose and tell the truth about the false narrative of Muscovy's history.

Faculties of Russian studies in the West and elsewhere will have to totally reinvent their curriculum. New scholars of history, politics, economics, sociology, theology and psychology will have to be developed and take the reins of academia in the field. History will literally have to be rewritten so that it tells the truth. Libraries of books with false history will have to be cast aside and news ones will need to be written. Historical films will need to be made with accuracy of true history. Ukraine's Manifest Destiny is no easy task as the amount of resources and intelligence needed to accomplish it on a global scale is monumental. First, the war must be ended and that is only Step One in the fulfillment of Ukraine's Manifest Destiny.

Decades and maybe even a full century of hard work lies ahead for Ukraine. Ukraine's past must be revisited, and the truth told. Ukraine's present must be a victory for the nation. Ukraine's future is yet-to-be-determined. No matter what emerges, Ukraine is fulfilling a Manifest Destiny that it never really wanted or asked for. That seems to make all the more real and true because now the fulfillment of it is crucial for Europe and the world. Realistically, it is also of utmost importance for the RF because at some point a nation of roughly 190 million will have to completely reinvent itself from centuries of lies. First, they will have to stop the killing and face the truth that Ukraine is now proving to the whole planet.

23

Right to Exist

In Ukraine, we go to bed at night not knowing if we will exist in the morning. If we wake up in the morning, we wake up knowing we may not exist when it is time for us to slumber again. We walk out the door to run an errand not knowing if we will return. We here live daily with existential crisis. No, not the type of existentialism that bothers those not living under constant threat of death but the one where a whole nation denies our right to exist. Maybe Ukraine should be the new thinking movement that adds the 'Right to Exist' as an amendment to its constitution. That is, of course, if we continue to exist here in Ukraine and are not wiped off the face of the planet by an enemy that increasingly seems not to be human.

Psychologically and spiritually can you set your mind on how difficult it can be to exist in this existential reality of ours here in Ukraine? How we wake up every day and go on? Some do it for the belief in the country; others for the pursuit of freedom; many because of their faith in God; soldiers in uniform because they must and are ordered to do so while maybe still employing all or one of the above reasons. Do you have any idea of the daily human toll this takes upon us? We see either right before our eyes or on some sort of screen, dead children, mothers, grandmothers, and so many more slaughtered by an enemy that just pushes a button and never sees the innocent dead. Other enemy combatants seem to do it purposely with all manner of weapons, sometimes first employing torture. They have castrated male soldiers and civilians to stop these Ukrainian men from ever fathering a child and bringing it into existence.

Ukraine is trying and has been trying for many years to redefine itself as a nation. Now, they are doing it under fire and we who are here with them, only want them to succeed. Success depends on our continued collective existence. Wrap your mind around that. Individually and collectively, we must fight every day for the 'Right to Exist.' Existentialism is based on the idea that humankind determines its own destiny. Christian Existentialism posits that we follow the will of God in order to find meaning in our existence by trying to follow Him. Orthodox Christians are the majority in Ukraine, and we must balance our faith with a Christian Existentialism which doesn't necessarily mesh with the dogmas of the Orthodox Church.

Yet, we do, every second, every minute, every hour, week and month. We fight within ourselves as we fight the enemy each in our own unique ways. Do you have any idea of the stamina this takes for millions of people? Don't blame those who became alcoholics and drug addicts after February 24, 2022. The ones who were that before were already that. They are still that and wander zombie-eyed through the streets of Kyiv just like they always have. Their existential dilemma is long over as they already are what they are. Those of us who are not and realize it, well, we're kinda fucked, aren't we?

There is, of course, a portion here that exists as deniers who deny this is real despite their neighbors being killed. There are the ostriches with their heads in the sand. There are the collaborators who betray their people and nation. This is a small minority, which means the majority of us are having to deal with this whether we like it or not. We have to deal with the fact that what is attacking us no longer seems human, yet it is also not some supernatural being of lore. No, it is flesh and blood on a grand scale that is seeking to take away our existence. Even we faithful understand that not every person in Russia and Belarus is demon-possessed. Many there also support what is being done to Ukrainians and seem to revel in it. How do we see what they are doing and still see them as human?

We know we are human. Early in the war, the attacking forces were soon called 'orcs' from that of Tolkien fame. We can call them any name we want but the fact is that for the most part, they look like the rest of humanity. Pictures of Nazi atrocities to those of us who did not live through World War II were just awful black and white photographs of a time before. Now, we who are alive and in this have to face what the Jews and other persecuted peoples of the Third Reich had to face. Pure human evil that does not seem to be human at all. One can now understand how the Nazis were seen as monsters. People in the West just see pictures and videos of awful events but they have no feel for the dark energy and smell of sulfur that emanates from the enemy here. Maybe two whole Slavic nations are demon-possessed. No, the rational mind just can't wrap itself around that, can it? It would be easier if we could.

Ok, forget about Satan for a minute if you are not a believer. How do we explain this from a purely rational and scientific standpoint? Ok, so maybe they are a nation of complete sociopaths and psychopaths. Nah, that doesn't make sense either but what does in this situation? Our existence goes on and we focus on survival for ourselves and the Ukrainian nation because no one can really explain how we can continue to believe the enemy is human and also has the 'Right to Exist'. Historians, psychologists, lawyers, military strategists, spiritual leaders will ponder and study us for years after this war ends. It will end and we pray it doesn't end with our end. But none of that pondering will help us now. Now we need more powerful weapons in greater numbers since the world has left us to shoulder the responsibility of defeating one of the largest conventional armies on the planet. Killing them is not a problem, they are an infestation from somewhere we choose not to admit exists. Someday the killing will stop, and millions will still live in Russia and Belarus who condoned the torture, rape and murder. Rape and murder are no longer just a shot away for the Baltics and others in Europe or for that matter, anywhere else. How do we who have lived through this, ever forgive those who did not kill but sat watching it on their phones across the border and did nothing to stop it? We will not seek to end their existence even though what happily see ours. Right now, we are still here.

We have the Right to Exist, therefore, we are.

24

A Kyivan, but Not a Ukrainian

Written from Kyiv on September 16, 2022

I was busy volunteering from May through August and didn't write much during the summer other than the occasional poem. A chilled Autumn wind blows up the Svyatoslavsky ravine rising and turning its ascent on Afanasivskyy Yar to strike the protective walls of Medieval Kyiv where it again turns and flows its way down and through the Zoloti Vorota (Golden Gate) entering the heavily guarded city and blowing the cassock of a priest as he enters St. Sophia Cathedral for Vespers. The greens of August have given way to the yellows of late September as they have always done and as they will always do long after I am gone.

Kostyantyn Paustovsky, a Soviet writer unknown for the most part in the West, once lived near the Svyatoslavsky ravine and had this to say in the early 1900s:

> *'All day, trains of 'kalamashek' with clay were going past our house to Svyatoslavsky ravine. Carts for transporting earth were called kalamashka in Kyiv. Kalamashniks filled up ravines and leveled the ground for the construction of new houses.'*

This short tale is being written from the fourth floor of one of those 'new' houses constructed in 1901 for the mid-level merchant class before the Bolsheviks ruined the world for most of Eastern Europe. They call this type a building in Kyiv a 'Tsar house' because it was built while Imperial Russia still ruled the roost (or should that be the Rus?). Kostyantyn didn't care much for that ravine in those days, but he played in it with his friends as a boy. Although born in Moscow, he had Polish, Turkish and Ukrainian blood running in his veins. His great-grandfather was a Cossack of the Zaporozhian Sich. He wrote of Ukraine:

> *'I grew up in Ukraine. My relatives on my father's side spoke only Ukrainian. Since childhood, I fell in love with the singing, flexible, light, endlessly rich in images and intonations of the Ukrainian language.'*

Konstyantyn also lived on the old path of Afanasinskyy Yar which was named Nestorivska Street and is now known as Ivana Franka Street in Kyiv; 33 Ivana Franka

Street is now home to the Austrian Embassy. These are the streets where I now live and walk with my wife and almost every day with our American dog. This neighborhood would have originally been outside the city gates of Medieval Kyiv. Maybe they were inhabited by blacksmiths or other peasants who lived just outside the city that Volodymyr the Great and his son Yaroslav the Wise built.

A balmy mist now blows up Lypynskoho Street and turns at the corner of my building heading north up Ivana Franka Street, but the old city walls are now gone and the mist disperses on Yaroslav Val Street (same route as the first paragraph but with different names). The Scorpions sang 'Winds of Change' how many years ago now? The winds on the Moskva don't seem to have changed much but our wind in Kyiv and throughout Ukraine has. Walking the streets of Kyiv, the earth breathes its history, and the soil is still soaked and nourished with the blood of the dead over a course of fifteen hundred years. You feel it in your bones, and it goes even deeper to the spirit, the soul. Maybe some can ignore it, but I cannot.

I am a Kyivan but am not a Ukrainian. My heredity is just as mixed as much as Konstyantyn's was but there is no Slavic blood in my genetic cocktail. My link is through my wife who is half Ukrainian and half Belarusian, both victims of the Russian Imperialism that seems to be now on its deathbed. Now, the Ukrainians who we stand with throughout the full-scale invasion are bringing an end to that history and exposing the truth. But this tale is not about politics.

Kyiv has been a center for trade for well over a thousand of years. I can walk up my street and touch the original walls of the city at the Golden Gate. How many merchants, tradesmen, hucksters and religious pilgrims walked through those gates to enter this city before me? Some came seeking their fortunes, others came to the spiritual center of Slavic Orthodoxy. Many of them stayed, worked, became monks or nuns at one of the monasteries while others probably ended up as beggars along the ancient city walls. Many of them, like me, were not Ukrainians. All great cities attract foreigners of all shapes and sizes for many different reasons. Diplomacy is one that I failed to mention as it is relevant here in Kyiv and other capitals around the world.

My Uncle Joe left the small city in South Jersey where he grew up to escape the provincial outlooks and ideals of 1930s America toward his homosexuality. He assimilated and became a New Yorker barely ever venturing beyond his neighborhood in Hell's Kitchen and even less so beyond the borders of Manhattan. Uncle Joe taught me the beauty and diversity of cities and New York will ever remain my favorite city on the planet. But New York is not 'my' city, it was his. Kyiv is my city.

Kyiv was never the city that I dreamed of living in but the political situation in Belarus forced our hand. Once the decision was made and before coming, I reveled in learning about the history of Kyiv and Ukraine. Then, for me, as a convert to Orthodoxy Christianity, I began to see Kyiv as a Holy City. Saint Andrew-the-First-Called is purported to have planted a cross on a hill overlooking the Dnipro River in the first century A.D. and to have prophesized the coming glory of the city to be built on its shores. Prince Volodymyr who was establishing the foundation of the Rus culture forced the pagans of this land to be baptized in the Dnipro. Maybe forcing Christianity on them wasn't the best tactic but what came after resulted in the spiritual development of Slavic lands. The Bulgarians had been the first of the Slavs to convert in large numbers and many of the great missionaries and teachers came from Bulgaria to see the new kingdom of Kyivan Rus.

Bulgaria had fought a twenty-year war with Constantinople (the Byzantine Empire) and declared their own Patriarch in 919 with a peace treaty in 927. Byzantium recognized the right of Bulgaria to have its own Patriarch. This was the first Patriarchate to arise after the ancient ones to come into being. Prince Volodymyr of Kyiv would not be baptized until 988 at Chersonesos in Crimea for a political marriage to Princess Anna, the sister of Byzantine Emperor Basil II. His rise to power had been under paganism but his glory would be in Eastern Orthodoxy. The prince returned to Kyiv after his own baptism and tossed the pagan idols into the Dnipro while helping oversee one of the largest group baptisms in history on the shores of the Dnipro River at the foot of Kyiv's hills.

Now, even though there is no Slavic blood running in my veins, I cannot ignore the significance of this city from an Orthodox perspective nor its influence on Europe. Volodymyr's son and his successor, Yaroslav the Wise would eventually marry Ingegerd Olofsdotter, the daughter of the king of Sweden. Yaroslav's daughter, Anastasia of Kyiv would marry the future King Andrew I of Hungary and his other daughter, Anne of Kyiv would marry Henry I of France and eventually become Regent there.

Do you see now what I am getting at? Kyiv is the founding city of all of Rus and is inherently more European than it is...well, the other thing. Muscovy was a muddy back water while Kyiv was home to religion, literature, art, culture, trade and diplomacy. Technically, Kyivan Rus should have been granted the status of an Orthodox Patriarchy in the twelfth or thirteenth century. But the invading Mongols and the poor succession after the death of Yaroslav the Wise saw the decline of this great city and culture. Obviously, the details are richer than I have described.

I have never been anywhere in Ukraine other than Kyiv and that is not by choice. By the time we had settled in, the war began. I still remember how quiet and empty the streets were back in March of 2022. Despite the war, I loved walking in 'My' Kyiv and believe me, it felt like there were only a few of us in the city at that time. How beautiful, magnificent and calm it was in between the fighting. There was this sense of peace and holiness that swirled around me with the cold winter air and falling snow.

Sadly, I know that at some point not too far away, we may have to leave Kyiv. We are still foreigners here despite living through the war. There are only limited opportunities for us economically as we are just average working-class. Like Springsteen in the state of my youth, I may have to sing songs of leaving. When I run with Philly on Taras Shevchenko Boulevard, I can feel the carcinogens from the car exhaust entering my lungs like a heavy dark smoke. How I will miss Kyiv if the day comes when health or age force me to depart. She is my city, I love her and having survived the Battle of Kyiv with her, she will forever be with me.

June 15, 2022: Taking a break on the Dnipro River within Kyiv City limits for a few nights.

June 6, 2022: Collage photo with John and destroyed Russian equipment on St. Michael's Square, Kyiv.

June 6, 2022: Philly relaxing on the Dnipro River in Kyiv.

June 26, 2022: Posters mocking Putin on Lviv Square, Kyiv.

June 26, 2022: Poster mocking Putin on Lviv Square, Kyiv.

July 25, 2022: Death's head ice cubes reflecting the mood of war.

August 10, 2022: Rainbow over Kyiv.

Soviet Monument to Ukrainian Soviet Collaborator defaced on Shevchenko Blvd in Kyiv. Reads: Murderer. Traitor.

25

Ukrainians Saved Our Lives

This was written on October 14, 2022 just four days after a massive missile attack

People always ask why are you in Ukraine? Why are you staying there during a war? These may sound like simple questions, but they are not. There is something in my soul that kept me from running. My wife, Natasha, is Ukrainian in heart, soul, mind and blood so her story is different. Her mother may be from Belarus but here in the Slavic world, you follow your patristic bloodline. A small village outside Vinnystia is where her grandparents lived, and her patristic last name is linked to two very famous Ukrainians but I won't reveal it during wartime for security reasons. One of them is a famous theologian and another is a famous beekeeper. We don't know if she is related as we are not even sure that the records exist anymore. The Soviets may have destroyed them all. But the name is not a common one, so there is a good likelihood.

As a child in Belarus, Natasha was not the typical fair-haired, blonde of that nation. She has the dark features and raven hair of her Ukrainian ancestors. On the playgrounds of Belarus, in her Soviet Young Pioneers Club and in the summer camps of Crimea, they called her 'hohlushka' and her brother 'hohol'. These are essentially insulting names used for Ukrainians. Sticks and stones never broke their bones and names never hurt them. Now, she stands proud of her Ukrainian roots, although maybe Ukraine really doesn't want her because of where she grew up. That's understandable to her as well, she doesn't hold it against Ukraine seeing what their northern 'brotherly' neighbor has allowed to be done from its territory.

The important thing is that the Ukrainians have saved both of our lives. Today, October 14th, is Defenders Day in Ukraine. This day we honor all those who fight for Ukraine and those who have fought over hundreds of years to break the yoke of Russian Imperialism and any other invaders. The International Legion also deserves credit here as do the Georgians, Belarusians and Russians who are fighting for Ukraine. They are fighting and dying to keep us alive and so Ukraine can win. Many foreign fighters have been killed defending this country.

The missiles, rockets, artillery and small arms fire of the Battle of Kyiv in February–March of this year have long since passed. You can read a great article about that battle in the Wall Street Journal titled 'The Ragtag Army That Won the Battle of Kyiv and

Saved Ukraine.' Google it if you so desire. That article put names and faces to just some of the Ukrainians who saved our lives. We will probably never meet and have the opportunity to thank them, but they don't need or want that kind of recognition.

Missiles hit just six hundred meters from our flat only four days ago where we walk our dog, Philly named after the brawler city just across the river from where I grew up. The closest the Battle of Kyiv ever came was some small arms exchanges a few blocks from our house but nothing as large and destructive as a missile. A few were shot down during that battle not too far way but not quite close enough to be life-threatening. October 10, 2022, I got a late start on taking Philly which very likely saved my life. Had Natasha walked him, she would most likely have been killed by the missiles that fell on Taras Shevchenko Park as they both hit in places where she always took him. Natasha has changed her route since that day.

Faces, names, places, we don't know all of them. The people who died so we could live we can only honor by praying for them by lighting a candle before the icon in church or at home. These are not just soldiers, or the Ragtag Army that won the Battle of Kyiv, but innocent people living in villages and suburbs who have borne the brunt of the fighting. They saved our lives by sacrificing theirs in the name of freedom. Territorial Defense units who protected the entry and exits of the cities also saved us. In the early days of the war, many Russian saboteurs were on the loose throughout Kyiv and the region. The Kyiv city and military administration imposed curfews so they could root these lowly dangerous types out. Every person that worked to keep Kyiv running. Every person that baked bread or showed up at the stores for work amidst the onslaught. Every member of the state emergency services who treated injuries and put out fires. Every delivery driver who brought goods and other essentials under threat of death. Every volunteer who cooked and delivered food to the troops. Even the trash truck drivers kept working. All these Ukrainians saved our lives. Every single one of them made a sacrifice, took risks, so we could live in a civilized manner unlike the hordes that attack and kill in Ukraine every day.

There is a gratitude that we will never be able to express to all these wonderful people. Sure, we have helped where and when we can but not near the level they have done. We speak the truth to the war and the genocide committed by the Russian Federation. No, it is not just Putin who bears the blame. There are millions within Russia and Belarus who have direct or at least compliant responsibility. Those Russians who ran to escape mobilization? Guilty. They should have risen up not run like scared rabbits. Cowards run, blame others and launch missiles on civilians, shoot up humanitarian convoys, rape children, old folks and women. There's that song by The Doors called 'Five-to-One' whose lyrics say 'They got the guns, but we got the numbers. Gonna win, we're taking over.' Those hundreds of thousands of Russians who ran had the numbers but chose to be cowards. We chose to stay (so far) with the Ukrainians. The Ukrainians have chosen to stand, to be free, to not back down and to believe in what they are fighting for.

The Ukrainian PR Army is a non-profit that we volunteered for in the first six months of war. They do their part as do hundreds, maybe thousands of other organizations. Millions of people stay in Ukraine. Others help from abroad as best they can. But it's the people here, in country, in the suck as they say in the Marines, that saved our lives directly. We're just two. Who knows how many others they have saved through sacrifice and resistance? Ukrainians are saving your lives too, whether you know it or not. All of Free Europe is being protected by these brave people. All systems and governments that believe in freedom, work for justice and the rule of law are also being saved by these ancient Slavic people. Please don't forget that if it feels a little colder this winter, it costs a little more for that tank of gas or bottle of milk for your child. Freedom has costs. You're paying in currency. The Ukrainians are paying with their lives.

Today, along with being the Day of the Defenders of Ukraine is also the Orthodox Holy Day called Intercession of the Holy Mother of God (Theotokos) when She spread her veil over people suffering an onslaught from the pagan Rus and protected them from defeat. Rather fitting that today, an unholy Russian enemy is attempting to carry out the complete destruction of the Ukrainians who are the original Rus people. We ask the Theotokos this day to protect our Defenders, our innocents and all of Ukraine and for victory. Slava Ukraina! Glory to the Heroes!

26

War Train Ukraine

Part I

Written from Kyiv, May 17, 2023

Seven days after the missile hit the street on the path where we walk Philly, we would depart Kyiv for the first time since the full-scale invasion began. We talked about it for at least three days before making the decision. It was not an easy decision to make but tactical awareness was in full gear. Additionally, economic survival was at stake. Working remotely in a war zone requires reliable internet and electricity. Let me backtrack for a minute. I never stopped working throughout the whole thing. The first month, I scaled back my live duties and focused only on answering emails and scheduling trips for my client in Atlantic City. So, I worked through attacks because that's what we needed to maintain our life and to be able to donate to the Ukraine Armed Forces, humanitarian aid, and other areas. Frankly, working helped preserve my sanity along with writing. Now, our livelihood was threatened.

Natasha had signed up to take some online classes in September, so she was in the same boat. Ever since the missiles hit close, the bombardments continued, and she was sleeping on the heated floor in the bathroom as it is the safest room in the house. During these times, she continued to study. Clearly, the Muscovites were targeting heating and power sources to disrupt the everyday life. We had no choice but to leave but we didn't want to leave the territory of Ukraine unless we absolutely had to in order to survive. We did have to continue working and studying which meant relocating from Kyiv at least for the time being. Hours of research were conducted, and we settled on Chernivtsi.

Chernivtsi is just a short drive from the Romanian border in case we had to get out altogether. It is in the Carpathian foothills, has decent infrastructure and most importantly, at that point it had never been hit by any missiles. Prices for AirBnBs were affordable enough and train tickets could be bought online. We were waiting on our new Temporary Resident Cards (TPR's) which we had applied for just as the missiles started to fall. We chose to leave without picking them up since we had six months to get that done. Natasha and I thought it prudent as the missiles were increasing and so were power and internet outages. It was time to go.

A friend (Oleksandr) and his wife (Lesya) braved the threat and drove from the Left Bank to give us a ride to the train station. The train was due to depart about 22:10 so we left early. This was so Oleksandr and Lesya could get back home before the 23:00 curfew kicked in. Natasha had bought a mid-level full cabin so we could travel without Philly disturbing others. He can be a scary dog at times and has attempted to bite people he doesn't 'like' in the past. We endure it because the Jersey in us causes us to act the same at times.

The train station was packed, and Philly did not like the police dog on patrol. We stood in the waiting hall waiting to enter. A full train was headed for Kharkiv in the Northeast. Those people were brave. That's like driving straight into the fire. Ukrainians are like that. Home means something. Their city means something. It's a trait to be admired and respected.

Soon enough, it was our turn to board, and we were snug as a rug in the old Soviet style train car. Philly settled down quickly because it was late. Natasha felt nostalgic for her years growing up in the Soviet Union when they took trains to see her grandparents in Vinnytsia, or for a summer vacation in Odesa or Crimea. The lull of the train put us to sleep, and we were on our way. Three hours in, the train picked up so much speed that it was hard to sleep soundly. We made it safely and emerged into a completely new city and environment.

Part II

Written on the train from Chernivtsi to Kyiv, December 16–17, 2022

This part I started writing on the train from Chernivtsi to Kyiv. Missile attacks had slowed somewhat, and we felt we should return for a couple of days to check on our flat and pick up our TPRs. Our neighbors informed us that they were suffering through long periods without electricity but hey, the heat was still working!

No streetlights on the edge of Chernivtsi as we were exiting the rented flat. Cold air briskly enters the lungs, blows against faces, awake! The flashlight bounces with each step taken on uneven pavement. Headlights illuminate the curbs at times. The way to the station is all downhill, steep in the low hills at the beginning of the Carpathians. A wild dog barks on the approach to the station. Outside, people, war people, wait for the train to Kyiv, smoking, talking on phones, saying their good-byes. A painted girl trying to flash fashionable bags stands as an old man steps out blowing his nose on the ground, both disgusting in their own unique ways.

Inside, people mill about for the next war train to take them wherever they may be going. This train goes closer to being in range of Muscovite missiles and rockets, but they go anyway. Business must be attended to. Families must be fed. Studies must continue. Soldiers board, heading for the front. A smell of diesel on the tracks as the train pulls up, a bark of a dog further down the tracks as the conductors ready their cars for the passengers who travel in a war zone. No one hurries. They take their time boarding. An old couple says good-bye to their grandson in the next cabin sitting with him before the departure. Not long after, they wave through the window standing on the platform as the train begins to ease from the station. He is too young to be a soldier, maybe he is a student returning to university or holds a job in the great city of Kyiv.

How many stories ride in the other cabins? Stories of heartache, loss, suffering, bravery and even possibly treachery. War makes it easier to smell an enemy. It brings out the best and the worst. We are all now pulling away from the station in Chernivtsi heading closer to the front and not away from it. Our reasons are varied but we must go on despite what the enemy throws at us.

Slowly the train crosses the bridge over the Prut River and the lights of the city begin to fade away. In the rural areas, an occasional light is seen from the train window. Darkness soon gets even deeper but the moon breaks through the clouds. The grey-white light of the moon illuminates the trees as they pass by the window and makes the ground look snow-covered even though it is not. When the train passes groves of birch trees, they look like tree ghosts with their branches reaching out for a haunting.

Click-clack-click-clack, the train rolls down the track creating its lullaby. Eyes grow tired, limbs become weary from carrying luggage, the dog snores on the corner of the train bed and soon enough, a light sleep brings calmness and peace. Faint conversations from the other cabins sometimes get loud enough to awaken briefly but then the lull of the tracks takes over again. Soon enough, it is morning, and the faint light of pre-dawn forces the passengers to rub their eyes and prepare for arrival.

Disembarking, Philly does his business on the poles of the platform and a line forms to exit. Soldiers patiently and politely check documents and send the passengers on their way. Passengers enter the bustle of the busy Kyiv Railway Station. Ukrzaliznytsia (UZ-Ukrainian Railways) has done it job efficiently, politely and on time in a war zone. War weary soldiers wander about, maybe home for a visit or a short leave. Fresh troops in clean uniforms head to platforms where the trains will take them closer to the front. Students, businesspeople and average pedestrians all make their way to the station exit. There, the doors open wide to the continued bustle of wartime, a light snow falls, cold wind blows in the face and the travelers make their way to the comfort of home or wherever they may be going.

We arrive before the curfew is due to be lifted. The thought of waiting another hour and a half before going home seems a bit much. Most passengers choose to remain inside the railway station but a few venture out into the darkness. The sun is nowhere close to rising just yet, so it is Zero-Dark-Thirty. Natahsa, Philly and I are beat up and exhausted from the long train ride so we decide to test the waters to see if there is a way that we can get home which circumvents the curfew rules. Natasha cuts a deal with a taxi driver who has a permit to drive during the curfew and we are on our way to the city center at only a slightly higher price than normal. Our building welcomes us and yes, it's home whether the electric is on, the heat is working, and the water is running. It's always good to come home no matter what the conditions. That's all most Ukrainians want. To go home and live in peace.

Just a few days before Christmas, we returned to Chernivtsi on yet another overnight train on a thankfully quiet and uneventful journey away from our home in Kyiv.

27

Thanksgiving in Ukraine

I wrote this on Thanksgiving Day from Chernivtsi as Natasha prepared an American style meal for us to celebrate the holiday as best we could. It is more of an essay but bears certain memoir leanings. Thus, I have decided to include it because after reviewing it, I thought it appropriate.

Today in the US, people will gather around tables across the country to share a meal of thanks. Jokes will be made about the discomfort of being around certain family members, children will play with cousins they rarely see, wine will be drunk, maybe a little blood will be spilled, or feelings hurt, but smiles and good times will dominate, and throughout it all, for most people, will be the smell of the turkey in the oven. Oh, that glorious smell and anticipation! People will volunteer at soup kitchens, churches, and other venues to make sure to their best ability that every person who wants to, will have something to eat on this, the most 'American' of all feasts.

Thanksgiving has mostly moved beyond the realm of pilgrims and Native Americans. We as a nation have come to face the reality of our Manifest Destiny and the harm it has done to the indigenous peoples of our land. Americans never look at themselves as conquerors even though this is how our Republic came to be. Thanksgiving has moved beyond that to be something more because we also as a nation, tend to prefer to focus on the positive and move on from the sins of the past. Some sins we can move on from while others are simply too fresh to be let go of. Today, we give thanks regardless of all that. Today, we look to our God or whatever other symbol we choose and say, 'Thank you.' We say this whether we live in the hood or in a mansion. Collectively, we as a nation find something in our lives to be thankful for and most of us vocalize it around the Thanksgiving table, on social media and in many other places. This is one of the traditions of our nation that makes us unique.

Today, in Ukraine, in our AirBnB where we stay because of power, internet and water outages in our home in Kyiv, we will also have the smell of turkey, mashed potatoes and homemade cranberry sauce. We'll drink some wine and give thanks. We will give thanks today for having each other, our dog, and for surviving this war (so far) alongside the Ukrainians. We will give thanks to the soldiers, medical personnel, utility workers, administrators, and everyone else who fights to defend Ukraine and keep the country running. Most of them will never know we are doing it. Somewhere in Ukraine and maybe throughout the whole nation, there will be other US citizens who fill find a way to celebrate Thanksgiving. Maybe that's one way of colonizing that we should look upon in a positive light.

Perhaps it is time for us to gift the holiday of Thanksgiving to another nation. That doesn't mean giving it away but sharing it. Thanksgiving as a holiday is all about sharing and being thankful. I know no other nation that deserves it more than Ukraine right now.

You may wonder why and so I will merely give my opinion:

1. Freedom-Loving People – Ukrainians are by their very nature, lovers of freedom. This is not just in a modern context but goes back centuries, maybe even a millennium. The free-wheeling Cossacks to the Hutsuls in the Carpathians all have this in their blood and the way they look at life. Thanksgiving is now a tradition that celebrates our unique American style of freedom even though it also symbolizes the repression of another culture. We must bare/bear our collective guilt in this but we must also look at the bigger picture.
2. Persecuted Indigenous Peoples – The Ukrainians, like our own Native Americans, have borne the brunt of an oppressive system seeking to subjugate them on their own lands. This started about the same time as the US was beginning its onslaught against the Native Americans. The Zaporizhian Sich (the Cossack proto-state) was tribal in nature and may in certain ways resemble the Iroquois Confederacy as well as the Scottish clan system. This is a cultural gift of Thanksgiving to Ukraine because of that commonality.
3. The Spirit of Ukraine – This is not the 'Russian Soul' but something altogether different which it seems is just something else the Muscovites tried to expropriate from Kyivan Rus and the Ukrainians by calling it the 'Russian Soul'. Ukrainians have a noble, carefree, deeply spiritual, and creative nature unlike any that I have come across in this world. No, they do not have the monopoly but what they do have is a similar spirit to our own or at least what once was our own.
4. Food – Ukraine's agrarian richness and the variety of crops grown here show an abundant and fertile nation. The US was built on a highly productive agrarian economy even having patches of chernozem soil (the richest soil on Earth) which has now been ruined by the like of massive corporate farming. Ukraine still has most of it despite large American conglomerates being present here and foaming at the mouth to get their hands on it (sorry for the political digression but it is true). All the dishes we find on our Thanksgiving tables in the US are also grown or raised here in Ukraine. That means, all we must do is share the holiday, so they can cook and eat to their heart's delight.
5. The Spirit of America – Yes, we have our problems but what I see is that the US is one of the most generous nations and peoples on Earth. Our lives from childhood are built upon the idea of giving back and being thankful. Many may let that fall by the wayside but inside us as a people is that core value.

> This is a quality we all can be proud of and one that we can share with the Ukrainians.

This does not go to say that we cannot gift this most unique of American holidays to another nation. However, Ukraine is so very much like us in spirit that it is almost uncanny. No, you will not see it so much from videos or posts or even if you come visit as a tourist. It was not as apparent prior to the full-scale invasion to me either. However, it rose like a phoenix after the first shots were fired. We need to help the Ukrainians hold onto that once the war is over. Gratitude ingrained in hearts and minds is how we get to it. Ukraine will have much to be thankful for when this all ends. The spirit of giving gives birth to the spirit of thankfulness. This is something we can gift to Ukraine so that it can find its own way to celebrate.

Maybe one day, people in the US will hear Thanksgiving greetings from our friends in Ukraine who have already cooked and eaten their turkeys while someone at home is just putting theirs in the oven. That holiday smell of the turkey in the oven will drift across Europe and the Atlantic Ocean to waken people in the US who share the spirit of freedom, the spirit of giving, the spirit of thankfulness and the shared spirts of the USA and Ukraine. We here in Ukraine give thanks to you today, America. Now about those leftovers…

28

Christmas in Chernivtsi

Today, we celebrate the birth of a baby. Just about the whole world takes part in this celebration. This one birth has brought together trillions of people over the years to give thanks, make merry, stop the influence of the outside world and focus on joy, family, gratitude and giving. A baby who was born without electricity, running water, and heat, nestled among poor shepherds and animals. This child was homeless when He was born as well. Yet, billions of people today sit in their warm homes feasting on sumptuous meals, laughing, joking, opening gifts and sharing joy with the ones they love. A homeless, poor child is what brought this gift to the world. Today in Ukraine, we have so many of these children who also have lost their parents. The beauty of the children is that they do not see it the way we adults do. Gifts are being given that have been sent from abroad, as well as gifts from within Ukraine. Ukrainians are cooking whether in their own warm homes away from the front or in basements, yards under shell fire, and bomb shelters. Celebrations are taking place no matter what the circumstances. The children will laugh, play, eat and open gifts here as well.

The homeless baby had parents. These parents had a child that they knew was special as every parent feels about their child when it was first born. Mary and Joseph now had no home and had to flee their homeland. They had to flee because a murderous tyrant decided their child was a threat and had to be exterminated. Herod ordered all male children under two years old near Bethlehem to be slaughtered. Herod gave the order and soldiers carried it out. A murderous tyrant gave orders and unscrupulous soldiers carried out the order. This event would become known as the Massacre of the Innocents.

Right now, the murderous tyrant in Moscow is also giving these types of orders and this time, he doesn't care about gender, age or religion. However, he does care about geographical proximity, much like Herod did. Ukraine is now full of orphans. Millions do not have heat, water or power. These same people living under these conditions are determined to still celebrate the birth of a homeless baby. Tears roll down the faces of millions who like Mary and Joseph had to flee to a foreign land to escape the Chief Murderer and his minions who carry out his orders.

Yet today, we will eat borscht and other traditional dishes like you will in your homes. We will say prayers, open gifts and try to find a moment of joy to honor the Child who was born today. We will pray for our soldiers in the trenches who cannot celebrate and be thankful for their sacrifice on our behalf. We will think of all the orphans, internally displaced people and refugees who have to live like this. And we will go on to survive and fight another day in the hopes that next Christmas, we will be in warm homes with our families or out wandering one of the beautifully decorated city squares smelling the holiday smells and drinking mulled wine. Next year in St. Sophia's Square!

Lying in bed on Christmas morn, there are no presents under the tree. Oh wait, there is no tree, but there are lights on the plants in this AirBnB. We brought battery powered LED Christmas lights with us from Kyiv just in case we lost power. In the end, we used them for their created purpose of illumination for the holiday instead of emergency backup. Weeeahhh is the growing sound of the air raid siren as it rises whilst we are lazing in the bed with Philly this soft unseasonably warm morning on the day of the Nativity. It is more like a wail than a screech as the volume rises. Natasha checks her phone to see what the threat is, Philly yawns in tandem with the air raid. Belarus is where the bombers took off from and they rarely strike from there anymore it seems. This is the Muscovite's lame attempt at psychological warfare. They send planes into the sky to disrupt people's lives and daily routines. You get used to their patterns as the war goes on. Real threats versus empty ones.

So, this languid morning, we rolled over and Natasha drifted off along with Philly. I lay there on my back and visions of Christmas from my childhood home in Woodbury, New Jersey began to come to me. Those ghostly frames of Christmas Past while my parents were still married, and I got along with my brothers. First, it was like I could smell the old balsam tree we always had set up in the corner of the living room by the front window. The tiny colored lights reflecting on the silver tinsel would greet my brothers and I as we came down from the upstairs bedroom and that fresh, refreshing smell of evergreen. My dad always wore the same old blue and worn-out terrycloth robe, my mom in flannel pajamas.

Dad owned a flower shop and he always closed early on Christmas Eve, had a party for the employees and gave out cash Christmas bonuses to everyone even the people who only worked the holidays. It was the beginning of making merry for our family. All of us in the family had worked through these holidays with their ten-to-twelve hour days leading up to Christmas. These were the memories that were flooding in as I lay in bed on Christmas morning in the Ukraine War. After we opened the presents, dad would make a sumptuous Christmas breakfast of pancakes, or eggs and bacon. We would sit beneath the tree and play with our newfound treasures.

Later, that day, we would head to my dad's cousins (Sue Gail and Jim) house in Wenonah for time with family. We would laugh, we would sing, eat appetizers, play together and finally all sit together at a huge table in that old house to say a prayer, celebrate the birth of Jesus and eat ourselves into stuffed roly-poly revelers. We would be there for hours enjoying the company of family. The good memories of those innocent holidays flowed liked the wine at the wedding in Cana. Gratitude was what I woke to on Christmas morning in Ukraine. That's the Christmas Spirit.

Natasha was finally up, and I was working remotely on this holiday as my business runs 365 24/7. I only get Christmas Day off when it falls on my regularly scheduled day off. This doesn't trouble Natasha as she worked for years as a cocktail server at Resorts Casino in Atlantic City and often worked holidays. Soon, she was out the door with Philly, and I was going through emails for reservations, reviewing the schedule for January that had come through, then putting the trips in the reservations system. I was thankful to have work and to be able to continue to work remotely throughout the whole war. We found a very comfortable place in Chernivtsi and now enjoy the quiet here versus the constant threat of a missile or drone strike back home.

The day moved at a slow pace. Natasha ran out for some-last minute goodies since everything here is open on Christmas Day. Western Christmas hasn't really caught on in Ukraine just yet. Most here still celebrate the old way on January 7th. New Year's is held in higher regard because the Soviets had essentially banned Christmas, but the people needed a holiday. So New Year's Eve and Day became that for the atheist-based system. The borscht had been made the day before. Natasha had picked up New York Cheesecake from the Vienna style café and bakery for dessert. Today, she only had to make derheni (potato pancakes) which are a traditional Slavic dish at the holidays. She makes a mean yogurt sauce with garlic and parsley to be sloshed on the derheni. I sat in the kitchen and worked as Natasha cooked and listened to Christmas music on Pandora. Our ears always perk up when they play some version of the Ukrainian Shchedryk (Carol of the Bells in English).

We drank wine, ate a slow feast and talked about our twenty-two years together and our coming 'official' wedding anniversary the following day for twenty-one years of marriage. Natasha looked at me and told me all day she had felt gratitude for Christmas. She reflected on all the good things we had despite what Russia was doing. This news made my day even better. Natasha spoke about how much she loves the way Christmas is celebrated and revered in the US. We hoped that maybe Ukraine would one day learn that. The candle flames danced, we were cozy and warm and yes, the Christmas Spirit had won the day.

October 26, 2022: A mural showing patriotism in Chernivtsi.

December 24, 2022: Christmas decorations at our AirBnB in Chernivtsi.

December 25, 2022: No electric on Christmas Day. We cooked our meal on the gas stove top and celebrated by candlelight.

January 2023: Front of the bottle of Dovbush Cognac bought to have with a cigar.

January 2023: Back of the bottle of Dovbush Cognac bought to have with a cigar.

October 10, 2022: Fifteen minutes after the missile attack, John went to walk Philly. A car that was hit had its windows covered to hide the casualties – a common practice to respect the dead in Ukraine.

October 10, 2022: John visited the scene of the attack just minutes after it happened. Smoke from the fires and vehicles that were struck was still rising.

October 11, 2022: Natasha passed the spot where she usually walks Philly and found this crater in the children's playground at Shevchenko Park.

December 18, 2022: We had returned to Kyiv to sort out some papers and check on our flat then made our way by train back to Chernivtsi. Natasha and Philly watching the night pass by.

November 24, 2022: Natasha managed to rustle up an approximate full American style Thanksgiving Dinner.

December 2022: A man who lost his leg in the invasion hobbles on crutches through a park in the Chernivtsi City Center.

29

Entering the Second Year of War

Our guard never quite came completely down even when we were far removed from the battles that were raging. Christmas and New Year's had passed uneventfully in the quiet city of Chernivtsi. Long gone were the days where we suspected every stranger to be a possible saboteur or collaborator. Trust does not come easy in war. We stuck with people we knew and only allowed the occasional new addition to our circle. The long parade of grand standers, social media stars, opportunists and all the other filth that war attracts continued to march on. Survival requires a very heavy filter and ours was in place although occasionally some chaff somehow gets through. Our network was strengthening, and we were recruiting more donors and partners with the outlook of establishing long-term relationships. We started avoiding the fly-by-nighters who came for their fifteen minutes of fame and stolen glory. This applied to both foreigners and Ukrainians. Your sense and intuition sniffs out those who are not worthy to work with fairly quickly even if they manage to wriggle in a slight bit. Soon enough, true intentions become apparent. We must be brutal realists in order to continue living within the war and making sure we only spend time on those who can actually provide tangible help to the soldiers. Humanitarian aid was everywhere so we sharpened our focus to soldiers only. After all, they were the ones risking their lives to protect us, so it was our duty to make sure they had what they needed to do their job to include their self-preservation.

No one was particularly looking forward to or celebrating the first anniversary of the war. None of us wanted to think how easily it would roll into the second year of full-scale war. Our minds, our bodies, our spirits were still very strong as the ominous date approached. Hope, that is, realistic hope, continued to keep us forging ahead. We didn't hope for the end of the war but that certain weapons systems would be delivered on time. This was the reality as we rolled toward the first anniversary. New tranches of military supplies and technologies seemed to be announced almost daily. Knowing our soldiers would be supplied not only by us but by the multitude of Ukraine's partners kept a pep in our step.

Snow fell like a blanket of cleanliness in those winter days. We would walk to the pedestrian mall in Chernivtsi to a little Viennese café to have brunch or dinner. Their strudel topped with heavy whipped cream was a weakness for my sweet tooth. I smoked cigars and sipped Dovbush cognac on the balcony of our AirBnB as the snowflakes languidly laid down on the rooftops. We went about our lives as best we could far from our beloved Kyiv. Sometimes I would stand and watch the internally displaced persons line up for provisions from the charity across the street. There I would wonder about their stories. How their families survived. Where they had come from. What it felt like for them as native Ukrainians to have been forced from their homes. We knew what it felt like as expats, but we could never really get into the depth of their suffering. Suffering. That's the word we all know and something that comes no matter how much we try to avoid it. The levels of suffering are different, but they are there for all of us. Surviving suffering is best done by simply accepting it, embracing it, living with it and not focusing on it. That's one of the most important survival tools that we learned in the first year of the full-scale invasion. There is a book called 'The Sunflower' by St. John of Tobolsk which we read while in Chernivtsi and that work is what guided us through those turbulent seas as we approached a port we did not want to enter.

Epilogue

By Tristan Ruark

The buzzing sound of the Iranian-sourced Shahed suicide drone woke me from my sleep. I could hear it motoring loudly overhead. Shahed's sound like mopeds, with the exhaust removed, driving into a tunnel with the throttle half-cracked.

I tried to spring up to my feet to grab the baby. My body wasn't responding. 'Get the baby!' I screamed. I tried to scream. I screamed into my mind.

My body was gripped by sleep paralysis. I couldn't move my limbs or my mouth. I tried to yell; I tried to get any sound out of my mouth so that my wife would wake up and run with the baby, wake up the boy, and go to the corridor while I tried to force my body to wake up. I finally willed my body awake and sat up. The sound was gone. I grabbed my phone – 0430. It was just a night terror.

Thirty minutes earlier, we had just come upstairs from the safety of the parking garage beneath the building and laid back down. At 0200, I had been ripped out of my sleep by explosions in the city and the sound of air defense glowing through the fog that had settled over Odesa. I had slept through the air raid siren. The bloody siren had been going off all week but usually around 2300, followed by the sounds of war.

We went through the routine: grab the baby, put her in the stroller that had been prepped before going to bed with water for us, a thermos of warm water, an extra bottle, and two meals for the baby just in case. The boy grabbed the camp chairs staged by the stroller, and we went to the garage and gathered with the building dog and the rest of the red-eyed neighbors while our air defense destroyed Shaheds near the port.

Only a week ago, I was walking the streets of Kyiv for the first time with my son and my friends Natasha and John. They took me on a tour through the city they loved and shared their passion for it with me and the boy. I woke up on Saturday to a text from John asking me if my family was okay. A Shahed had hit a civilian apartment building in Odesa, my newly adopted city, and caused the USSR-era building to collapse. The first message I read from the Odessa-Info Telegram channel said that a mother and her baby had been killed. Though I knew my wife and my seven-month-old daughter were fine, my heart sank when I read the birthday of the baby. She was only four days younger than my daughter.

Five kids died that day. The kill count for children in Odesa, a city 300km from the front lines, is already at six for 2024. The Russians brought in the New Year, a celebration we share in Odesa where the family gathers for a nice big meal akin to Christmas or Thanksgiving, with the biggest ballistic and suicide drone strike that I had witnessed since moving back to Ukraine in July of 2023. They sent 90 suicide drones as their gift to Odesa. A city they claim is Russian. On New Year's Day, Odesa mourned the death of fifteen-year-old Alexey Marshak.

On the first day of Spring, two years after the full-scale invasion, the Russians celebrated by killing five children ages four months, seven months, three years, eight years, and ten years old.

The body of seven-month-old Liza was found cradled in her mother's arms as her mother tried to shield her from harm.

Two years into the war, and because the world has dragged its feet, children are still being murdered, and it will continue long after you read these words. Our hearts are heavy this week. Tomorrow is a new day. We will live in our new normal. We will rally behind our defenders. We will not hand these lands over to the invaders.

The resiliency of the Ukrainian people will continue to be on display for the world to see. As it was during the Bolshevik revolution, as it was when the Nazis invaded, as it was when Stalin tried to starve them, as it was when the negligence of the USSR polluted it with Chornobyl.

We will continue to live and hope.

Glory to the Defenders!

Slava Ukraine!

> 'To Ukraine call warmly, invite as a guest
> everyone you meet, random strangers even.
> When the war is over, we'll do our best
> to show our gratefulness for the peace of the children.'
>
> Pavlo Vyshebaba

Part 2

Introduction

by Andrii Getun

Once upon a time, a good man died. A moment later, standing in front of the Heavenly Gates, Apostle Peter met with him.

'We are not sure where to place you… You're not ready for Heaven, but Hell is not right for you either. Why don't you take a tour to both places and decide for yourself where you want to live?'

The man agreed.

It was wonderful in Paradise. Idyllic. People in white clothes. Heavenly music. Unbelievable beauty all around. Calm, peace, joy. After Paradise, he was brought to Hell.

It was as if the man had fallen back to Earth. Restaurants, parties, loud music, alcohol, fun, beautiful women.

'Well? What are you thinking?' asked Peter.

'You know, Apostle, Paradise is wonderful! I will never forget this! Incredible place! But I seem to be more familiar with Hell. I think I will be happy here. Send me to Hell!'

At that very second, the demons grabbed him, stripped him, beat him and threw him into a cauldron of boiling tar.

'You asked for it yourself!', terrible demons shouted.

'But how can this be? Where is everything I saw today, people having fun, parties?'

The demons laughed loudly in his face.

'You made a mistake, sinner! There is a great difference between tourism and permanent residence!'

My name is Grizzly

John came up with this call sign and it stuck firmly with me, despite many other names people called me since the war started. John was right on target. His ability to understand people, to see their hidden character traits, always surprised me. Let me tell you, to have such a partner in volunteering business is worth a lot.

Clear analytics, knowledge of the psychology of foreigners, an innate sense of tact and sensitivity towards people, helped us to avoid mistakes, and nurtured the development of business and human relationships.

A separate, but inseparable part of everything has been Natasha, the ever-burning flame that never goes out in the face of problems, depression and uncertainty. Together they are very strong. But strong people also need encouragement…

So, tourism and permanent living mean different things, radically.

During the war, I saw a lot of foreigners who came to Ukraine. One for a few days, the other for a few months. And those who have been here since the first day of a full-scale war.

My volunteer community and I have begun to divide these people into three types.

The Tourists

Lately, there have been so many of them.

These are the guys who painted in their heads a romantic and slightly mythical image of Ukraine and its people. They are coming to us with a burning desire to help, but they are not sure how exactly. Their motives are good, and they are good people. Unfortunately, they mostly become a burden for Ukrainians, wasting their time and resources. The term 'tourist' is not related to time. Tourists can stay in Ukraine for months. Everything ends for them, often with depression, dissatisfaction and leaving for home.

The Fighters

The name defines their essence. These people can come for one day, but they clearly know for what purpose. They don't necessarily come to Ukraine, but their contribution is magnificent. 'Fighters' collect money and cargo abroad and bring it to us. They communicate with the Ukrainians, ask for advice on how to most effectively utilize resources. John and my British and French friends are truly representatives of the tribe of fighters. And, of course, the soldiers who fight on the front lines and train Ukrainian soldiers.

Real

The third type of foreigners are the very same accidental Ukrainians – like John and Natasha.

Their soul is soaked with the Ukrainian spirit. They can no longer imagine a different life. They are a link between Ukraine and the outside world because they know and understand both worlds. I thank God for all these people.

* * *

Both of our families have dogs. Dog owners know something about having dogs, they become our life companions and full-fledged family members. But there's yet another kind of dog… uninvited, but there it is, chasing us like a shadow. A 'black dog', as Churchill named her.

Ours is not completely black. It is camouflaged, and the reason for its manifestation in our lives relates to the war. Our dog is not just sadness or despondency but a heavy burden that lies on our shoulders, forcing us to doubt every step and decision we make.

She sneaks up quietly, but when she is near, you feel her heaviness with every breath you take. She makes you feel helpless, but it is important to remember that this is not you, it's her. We support each other in those moments when the darkness seems too thick.

John reminded me, 'The main thing is not to give up. The sun always shines, even when it is not visible.' Sometimes, when we think about what we have lived through, we realize we are stronger than we seem. For me, the dog has become a symbol of what we all fight for in difficult times. She reminds us that everyone has his own weaknesses, but also strengths. And this strength is born in support, in courage, in not being afraid to share your pain.

* * *

To choose Hell for yourself by painting a beautiful picture on your head?

Or to consciously live in the Hell of war, risking your life every day?

The first choice makes you a 'Tourist'. The second choice is for people who have reasons to stay. They don't paint pictures in their heads. They live in reality. Hard reality. Because they are Real. They may have accidentally become Ukrainians, but they certainly don't accidentally shine goodness and light on people around them.

God chose you for this…

1

You Can Take the Girl Out of Ukraine, But You Can't Take Ukraine Out of the Girl

I am nine or ten. I am excited about the train ride. This is an event that brings the whole family together, and promises a real adventure, far away from where we live. I know this is going to be awesome because it has always been so. Every summer, my dad, my mom, and my little brother get on that train. Nobody fights, no chores are waiting for anyone, we are loaded up with snacks and lemonade to pass the time, staring out the train car window into the beautiful fields and villages. Strangers are selling vegetables and fruits from their gardens by the train tracks. Occasional raindrops fill the air with the smell of freshly cut grass and some wildflowers while I lounge about on the top shelf, unable to sleep or simply rest from all the excitement filling my body and heart, all the sugar I am allowed to have due to the special occasion, and, man, did I take advantage of that! My brother is on the top shelf across, letting the landscape of the passing scenery sing its lullaby to him. He is six, going on seven. All of us, 'khokhly' going to 'Khokhliandia'.[1]

The term is stark and a bit unpleasant to a child growing up in Belarus, where you are called that by pretty much everyone. You see, my dad is from Ukraine, born and raised, therefore-khokhol. My mom is from Belarus, born and raised, but that doesn't matter. She is married to khokhol, and the whole family, by extension, is 'khokhly'.

When you hear that from your friends or neighbors when you are young, you think the term itself could not possibly be offensive. After all, your closest neighbors would not offend you so on purpose, would they? Yet, somehow, if they call us that, but not each other, it shows you are not one of them, maybe different, maybe lacking something everyone else has? You start paying attention to your whole appearance and realize-this must be it! My dad, my bro, and I don't look like any Belarusians I know: our hair is not milky white but jet black, and my dad has an 'accent' and uses some weird words in between his otherwise normal 'Russian'. He sounds like my grandma, who I can't

1 Khokhly is plural for khokhol. Khokhol is a derogatory term for Ukrainians used by Russians and some Belarusians. Kokhliandia is the 'Land of the Khokhly' or the derogatory for Ukraine.

wait to see! So, in reality, we are not 'bulbashy'at all.[2] But why do they call us 'khokhly', dad? 'Because we are "khokhly", Yes, we are. So what?' That was my dad's response to the question I asked him only once. I felt better afterwards, making peace with it in my little curious mind that 'khokhly' must mean dark-haired and obstinate (because my mom told me so many times when I did something opposite to her strong urging: 'You are your father's daughter!'), and not quite Belarusian.

My dad's whole family is in Ukraine, hence the occasion, the train ride and all the fun following it, because that train is just a little preview of many memories to be made for all of us, my dad included. Above all, it has a strange feeling of coming home. I did not consciously think that as a child, I only felt warm, excited, on the edge of my seat to get to Ukraine and see my grandma. But I do know that now.

We get to Vinnytsia early in the morning, then take a long bus ride (or what seems to be a long bus ride to a child), followed by a long walk to my grandma's village. The walk has always been my favorite part because we got to see all the beauty surrounding the village. To get to our destination, we walked through gorgeous wheat and sunflower fields. I liked touching their rough stems and admired how tall and wonderful they were. I knew that once we got to the fields, we would see the village rooftops poking out here and there on the left, traditional Ukrainian homes beckoning with the abundance of their gardens all around them, everything drowning in the sunlight of early morning, lush, beautiful, serene. Those images are my happy place. Some of it is a bit faded by time, but the roots are implanted deeply, and all rush to the surface at the urgent need for a happy place all grown-ups rely on in the big wide world. Mine is left behind in that village, the gorgeous sunflower fields with a narrow dirt road going through them, and me, walking toward the sun, to my grandma's house, where everyone was asleep, not expecting us because my dad loved to see the surprise on everyone's face.

- How come they don't know we're coming?
- Because this is how I roll!

I see the face of my dad and realize he is barely containing his own emotions, smiling quietly, maybe whistling in between the wide steps he takes, making coughing sounds that seem to suppress an anticipation of mischief that soon will be released into the open, when we finally get to the front gate. My own heart is beating faster and faster, here is the village road, and only a few houses left before the iron gate, painted all blue, will be swung open by my dad's strong hand.

Instinctively my brother and I step behind, letting the creaking sound to do its job waking the household: my grandma Alexandra, my grandfather Victor, my auntie Halka, her husband Volodia, and their son, Sashko, who is only a year or two older than Alex. Plus, I wanted to see if my dad's anticipation will be everything, he was hoping for it to be.

2 Bulbashy means the people of Belarus which also Is sometimes derogatory as it refers to them as 'Potato People'.

I hear muffled voices, some fussing in the general perimeter, but realize quickly it is not coming from the outside kitchen to the left, where Sashko has been known to sleep occasionally, in the open air, but from the house ahead of us to the right. I hear a latch making a clicking noise, and right behind it my other family is rushing out, one by one, or all at once. I hear joy flooding the air all around us, authentic, gradually-becoming-loud joy that comes from surprises of this kind.

The smiles on my grandparents' faces, the hugs, the lifting us off the ground parts that seem surreal because I am not sure who is holding me at this point and where my brother is; he was just here a second ago, standing right behind me.

I still cannot recollect even the warmest embraces, excluding my dogs, so fierce in nature, as if the prodigal son himself appeared on the doorstep of his beloved father. So many years ago, yet not so distant, that I remember the smells and the sounds of pure joy all around us, that I cherish it in my heart to this day.

Here, I am the 'favorite' grandchild, or so it feels. My grandma used to call me by a lovely Ukrainian word, 'manunie', pronounced with a genuine smile, a warm touch, and soothing motherese energy. I felt an instant relief, pride, and gratitude all at once. I have never been anyone's favorite outside of her presence. Just an older sister. A responsible daughter. An excellent student… Like an earned badge for each category, I had to work for, do my best, and make good choices. We were not a touchy-feely family in Belarus, not too wordy about our personal family business. Being in Ukraine felt like a breath of healing air that suddenly filled your lungs to their full capacity with love. Exhale in peace and inhale some more. There's plenty for everyone to go around, you don't even need to be on your best behavior, it's free simply because you are here. The motto of my summer home had a theme, 'take it easy, go eat babusia's food and play-play-play, manunie'.

It's like we entered a different dimension once we stepped into the perimeter behind that blue-painted, double iron gate with no lock. A place run by old traditions and curious language, melodic and unpretentious, natural, organic, all-embracing and peaceful. This was my home also. Nobody needed to specify it for me with words. It was a feeling. I felt like we should have been there longer, not just for summer, but for always.

2

The Kitchen

Play we did. My brother and me. The best buds. Until we grew up and grew apart, by geographical distance to begin with. But that is another story for another time. For now, we are here, in the village of Gostynne, Nemyriv district, Vinnytska Region. We are starved for a good adventure and all things to see behind, within, under, and beyond. So much so that neither of us sleeps a full night. It's more of a 'I can't wait to get up and do stuff' for both of us because the stuff never involves the chores, responsibilities of helping around the house or the garden, or the kitchen. My brother is excited for me: I am officially off duty for the glorious days to come, therefore, an equal partner in crime and a friend in all possible exploration of the village and its inhabitants, half of which are apparently relatives of some godfather's uncle and an auntie who died a long time ago, but their cousins didn't, and they all know my grandma, and are, therefore, relatives.

I think I will be the first one up, and I will find something really cool, and bring my bro over to show it to him… I sleep with my grandma in one of those beds I only see in movies from the times long gone. It is an antique twin bed with a cast iron headboard, cushioned by goose feather pillows so large they cover most of my spine. My grandma whistles in her sleep. I am too excited to sleep. Is it morning yet? I will most definitely get up at the crack of dawn.

The faint smell of a wood-burning stove outside with some delicious contents on its top fill the house where I was still unforgivably asleep. I need to be out there, hearing all the stories that typically follow the tradition of cooking in the summer kitchen. I probably missed a bunch by now! Disappointed at my own sleeping mishap, I run as quickly as I can to the hearth. Face washing and such can all happen there, followed by a pre-breakfast snack in my hand, before the actual eating happens.

It's a delicious process, procedural, slow, devoid of fuss and nervous energy. For me cooking means storytelling. Not fictitious, some fairy tale for children to keep them entertained, but paced, real life plots, with problems and solutions, or the lack of the solutions and quiet brainstorming sessions instead, where questions and comments from all present around the hearth have weight and value, even from small children, like us. My brother has a clay bowl of sugared rice porridge laced with delicious-looking orange strands of fruit, smelling fragrant and welcoming, as I lean my unwashed morning face into it. My grandma is prepping another, intuitively sensing my presence and speaking to me without turning her head. I proceed with the cleanup routine, hungry for everything.

The kitchen is large. It spreads around the perimeter outside the house in almost an L shape, absorbing everyone under its cover like some promise of redemption. The hearth is in the corner to the left. Comes colder weather, one can lounge right on the side of it, keeping warm and cozy. The tables and the benches are some way off to the right, easily fitting 20 guests or distant family members, who can choose the side with the raspberry bushes behind them or the house side. I sit where my grandma sits in between her trips to the stove, kindling the fire.

A couple of visitors are hanging out at the kitchen, excluding my brother and me. There is a babusiya in a white kerchief, tied neatly about her head. She is wearing white everything, speaking quietly, sharing something or other about someone or another. My grandma listens mostly, offering occasional feedback in a very comforting way. Another visitor joins us, opening the gate, helping herself to the porridge to go around for everyone who wishes to have some. Meanwhile, the dough and the fillings are being prepared for the varenyky. There will be a feast for the village, to share the joy with everyone. We have the room. As I eat my porridge and drink fresh milk from the cow in the barn, I see people come and go, come again, sit down and rest from the heat, eating grandma's food (at this point, there are home fries with meat and freshly baked pampushkas on the stove), and enjoying each other's company. It feels like everyone lives here, in this house, in this outside kitchen, like it's a place where people meet and hang out, eat and drink, talk and cry, laugh and celebrate, and live their beautifully paced lives of simple joys and human affection. I am mostly mesmerized by the scenery unfolding in front of my eyes, being a part of this kitchen and its atmosphere. I am not shooed away to play by anyone so adults can talk, I am simply accepted as I am to be there, included, welcome, as if I have been there since my birth and this is where I belong, despite my still unwashed face, because I didn't want to miss a beat. I pick up the clean folded towel off the hearth, blinded by the babusia's all-white and fresh getup and the majesty of her appearance.

3

Cherries on Top

I have the image of the pear tree outside the main gate to the house, fifteen feet away, no more. A large, old, and luscious tree, full of shade, branches extending out in all directions, solid, tall, protective. It's our spot for spying on the perimeter. Our place, a fort comfortably located just close enough and high above eye level. It suits us well. We can stuff ourselves silly on the biggest, juiciest pears as we dream about the way our lives could be, talking nonsense, gossiping, trying to figure out the 'meaning of it all', but, mostly, pretending to be someone else, invisible and mischievous, like all the kids are at some point or other.

We are proud of our secret location, as it takes serious work to climb up and settle between just the right branches, making ourselves one with the tree, camouflaging our very presence to unsuspecting passersby. We can also claim that neither of us, ever, had the audacity to lose our balance or cool, diving noses down, bleeding or any other such nonsense. We took climbing the trees pretty seriously after the major incident back in Belarus, where I most definitely have learned my lesson to respect that climbing. Occasional pear core throwing is innocent enough, as long as the 'target' is far away and will not automatically lift up their head to suspect foul play coming from the tree. The hit had to be light enough to make it look natural, like an unfortunate harvest time moment for that particular pear falling and scaring the bejesus out of the villager. The sudden jumping, face twitching, or tripping made us giggle quietly in our fort and made it almost worth it. When I think back, I think Karma was waiting on us just around the corner. Which brings me to the most valuable lesson I learned in my life in Ukraine about the generosity of spirit, holding one's tongue, not allowing emotions rule in the face of injustice, and good 'ole 'kill them with kindness'in action.

So, here it goes…

Exploring the village after sitting in a tree for a couple of hours was a given. The feeling of adventure kept filling our spirits on any given day from the start. Maybe there is a reason we cherish our childhoods so much: that faraway place a long time ago, where basic and mundane seemed worth looking into, was full of promise, fun, discoveries, and magic.

As we walked along the single dirt road in that quaint village, we noticed a lot. It was like being in the middle of a Venn diagram, Belarus on one side, Ukraine on the other, and us, right smack in the middle of it, involuntarily comparing what we saw: the houses built, the front yards, the fruit trees that grow here but not there, the way the local people dressed and sounded…

- Why don't they harvest anything? Look, how many dark cherries are spilling out into the road! Do they even know it's time to get them out into the 'safe place', away from people walking by at night? They don't even have locks on the gates, or a fence.
- Who lives here? Isn't it that old lady, who always dresses in white? The one who stops by every morning to chit chat with grandma?
- Nah, it's just some other old lady, I dunno. Those cherries sure look good. I love cherries in Ukraine. They seem juicier. Look at the size of those bad boys! Is it even stealing if the branches are not behind the fence? The tree is, but, obviously, they don't even care! Otherwise, they would harvest the side by the road. I'm not sure if we have cherries at home. Do we?
- I think we do, it's in the back of the house, behind the graves.
- We have graves behind the house??! Who is buried there? Great grandfather?
- No. Those are ancient graves or something. I couldn't read the names right. Just the first two numbers. It said 16, the rest is covered with moss and worn off. There is a letter on the stone cross.
- Alright, we should check it out. Now, you are the look out! See if anyone's looking out from the window, or walking. Be cool! Roll up the bottom of your T-shirt, like that. And that's how you make a 'pocket'.
- We should get going, it feels weird! Maybe we should run?

And run we did, thinking ourselves 'street-smart, tough and funny'. That day my brother and I made a pact: no one gets in on the secret about the pear tree or the dark cherries. Not because we were afraid of spanking.

As we were debating about the moral side of our adventures later in the house, we heard grandma's voice outside, talking to someone, all surprised. We rushed to the open window, hearts pounding so hard, I could feel mine in my temples. That babusiya, who dresses in white did live in that house with cherries in the front yard! It was HER talking to grandma by the gate, and there was the big white bucket full of dark red cherries next to her!

I couldn't make out all the words as my heart sank into my stomach, and I patiently waited to be spanked shortly after someone would call our names out in that tone that says, 'oh you are in trouble!'. My brother felt the same. I could tell by his big round eyes he was getting ready to leave the secret pact behind and come clean with the truth: *We stole the cherries earlier from the babusiya, and before that we threw the pears at a grown man, well, three of them, actually.* I will get the brunt of it as the older sister. That was the deal. We heard the following:

- Want a plate of borscht? Should be ready by now, unless you're going someplace with those cherries?
- Those are for you.

- For us? Are you alright? I had no time to pick mine yet, but I'm thinking 'vyshnevka' and lots of preserves is the way to go. The harvest is good.
- I thought, maybe the ravens got yours this year? No? Sasha, please take those. Neighbor to neighbor. Your varenyky are to die for, I know you will find use for those.

There was more said in between, but as we stood there in the window, looking at those cherries and listening for the righteous complaint about the grandkids messing around the village to come up any minute now, followed by spanking (the worst case), or grounding, depending on how upset the white babusiya was, we realized it was not coming. This was it. We stole your cherries. You saw us, obviously. Not only did you not mention a word to anyone about it, but you brought an entire bucket full, just in case we wanted more. She saw us and waved, a pleasant, kind, 'you know I know' smile. We couldn't move, we were so mortified, both of us. The actual consequence was our lasting burning shame. Somehow, it no longer seemed so 'funny'.

Much time has passed since then. The incident was never brought up or discussed with us simply because the lady in white never mentioned it. I do know that if we were to get caught by a neighbor in Belarus, our bottoms would feel it. There would be a long lecture, and apologies would be required, public remorse would be demanded, preceded by judging looks, curt words, and a steel demeanor from the suffering party. I had my fair share of bad judgements as a child, even though I knew right from wrong, and many consequences followed. I do not quite remember their specifics, though, other than I messed up somewhere, somehow and got grounded. But this one… I still vividly remember what I did wrong and to whom, and this is why I would never ask for what ought to be offered ever again.

4

Let's Be Real

Time went by, and with it, the energy of the city transformed from ominous into hopeful, pivoted to furious and courageous, lingered there, and came back audacious but exhausted. People have accepted the new normal. People like us. The phrase 'a new Israel' was popping up in the media, promising a very unfortunate fate prepared for Ukraine in the nearest future.

Everyone and their grandmother had an opinion, a forecast of sorts on the duration and the outcomes of the war. Experts were selling five types of potential scenarios, one 'better' than the next, depending on where in the world you were reading the news. At some point, I had a shift. I realized that all of it and none of it could happen. I had no faith in the sons of men blabbering about the fate of the world if Ukraine wins or loses, if Putin croaks, if Trump wins, if America gives weapons, if the UN has the nerve to kick Russia out… The world was taking their sweet time talking about everything. Too much noise. Noise on the news, noise in my head, noise in the city… The reality is different for everyone involved, based on their geographical location. The reality of Kyiv is not the same as the reality of Kharkiv, Kherson or Dnipro. The reality of the Ukrainian diaspora in any given part of the world does not compare to Ukraine on the ground. The reality of Mariupol is my theoretical knowledge, no matter how many survivor stories I have translated into English, crying at every paragraph, going through an entire box of Kleenex by the time I was finished. I still cannot possibly say, 'we know the same war, we suffer together'. There is a distinction. There is a clear separation of our war realities, no matter how much empathy we might feel. The reality of our soldiers is another beast altogether.

The dread of the bombings, the cacophony of it, the shaking of bookshelves and buildings, and the ringing of the windows still intact might feel different to all of us. My personal agony had to do with the fact that I have had my 'last suppers' since the beginning of the war. I have come to accept I was going to die soon. Our chances were not good. When you carry that feeling for a while but live for some unknown reason, it takes a toll on the psyche. I would rather be done with it all, because it is exhausting. God, if this is my time, please make it quick and painless. Please do not let me suffer with my limbs torn off or flying about; do not make me a burden to John or anyone around. Every time a sinister siren pierces the air and wails that awful sound, every person in the perimeter grabs their cell phones trying to see how to proceed. Is it some *Mig*? Is it actual ballistics or a threat of ballistics? Two separate events. Shaheds above your heads may sound manageable to someone who heard ballistics explode in the perimeter. The noise is harder to bear, the earth booms in your chest, and my dog stresses out by throwing up bile. Unless the drones are in hordes, mixed in with ballistics.

One time, when the Russians had a case of uncontrollable shahed diarrhea coming to Kyiv, I was following Telegram channels in the bathroom (retaining walls, the safest place in the flat) for specific locations. It ups the chances of survival and makes you feel in the loop. As I was scrolling frantically through, jumping at the air defense firing close by, a live video of the drone flying above our building made me feel nauseous. You have to extend your exhales to get through it, a kind of tactical breathing. And the only way to get through it is to live through it.

Year two into it and the skies were wide open still. Question: what the heck were we still doing here? Donations, volunteering, connecting generous people with the right crowd on the ground, keeping the economy rolling. A very small part indeed. Not fighting on the front lines, that's for sure. But, if this is going to be a long haul, like a five-year stretch, can we seriously say we are going to 'tough it out'?? What life is that when you live anticipating your own death day in and day out? Can we handle it and still come out sane on the other side? How long can I hack sleeping on the bathroom floor all night? Is this OUR war? We don't even have permanent residency, for Christ's sake! We are basically just visitors.

With that 'winning' attitude we mentally started the process of packing up and going back to the States. All the logic pointed to it. We are logical, reasonable people, right? Yet, somehow, neither of us felt a sense of relief or anticipation for things left behind in America a few years ago. Occasional nostalgia about the speed and convenience. No one can dare call America inefficient, slow, rude, or lacking systems. America is the most relevant and business-like country that ever existed. America *is* business. Then how come we felt no particular joy about going back 'home'? It was more of an obstacle to overcome in the messy process of life. Now I needed to figure out the state I wanted to live in, possibly the one that doesn't break your will to live after you pay property taxes (sorry, NJ), or a sweltering, drippy, humid climate (no offense, FL). I also know how to play the game after I've spent my life in the States, clawing my place in the sun, appreciating the comfort of my lifestyle when I finally got there and the paycheck that allowed for it. I will need a solid job, not some freelance crap, to reestablish all that, and I was too burned out from teaching in public schools or any other types of educational establishments. I wanted to pivot my teaching career into something else, not entirely different, not exactly the same.

Speech Language Pathology was the answer. I enrolled into an American university online to get all my pre-reqs in order and get that process rolling. Once on the ground, I would put in two and a half years in one of the colleges (hello student loans) and possibly have a part-time job in between. *There is no rest for the wicked, money don't grow on trees…* I know that too.

5

A Blessing in Disguise

Rolling into a college in your forties online can be quite stressful on its own. First of all, I am not from the tech-savvy generation, this kinda stuff isn't just naturally clicking in my brain, I need to work at it, cursing under my breath a lot. To some spring chicken this might seem like a breezy walk in the park, but for me, I associate a lot of modern technology with stress or anxiety. It takes a lot of attitude adjustment on my part. However, it is a necessary evil in our world that makes it spin at lightning speed. There is comfort in that. I mean, think about it: I can sit in my flat in Kyiv and attend classes in the US. So, there's that.

After the initial unsettling feeling of the unknown and a nagging fear of 'looking and sounding stupid' in the eyes of my professors and fellow students, I went for it. It was a welcome frustration that provided a distraction from the war. A housewife with plenty of time available to accomplish household duties and who is addicted to checking the horror show on the news and thinking *war war war bastards bastards bastards die die die* looks at life differently than a student with deadlines. My consciousness shifted from running the household into anatomy, phonetics, language development from birth to adulthood, audiology, physics, and pathologies of all kinds. It was a lot, come to think of it, but I began my new journey. It gave me a sense of pride and achievement as the time went on, but most importantly, it gave me a longed-for sense of normalcy, filling my existence with a purpose besides surviving the war or increasing my chances for it. It sheltered me from a state of permanent rage stewing just below the surface, ready to explode at the sight of another atrocity of the 'loving neighbor'. Essentially, going to college forced me out of the war zone and out of my head.

Things were exactly the same as the year before: occasional quiet spells, as the enemy was saving up for the terror tactics to employ on some unsuspecting children's hospital or a maternity ward in the country. On those days, I caught myself wondering how 'easy' it was to get used to the war after the initial shock settled in. If occasional breaks are experienced, we exhale deeply and step into our fantasy reality with coffee shops, ballets and exhibits, mani-pedi, and a relaxing massage, because your body bounces back with tension when someone taps your shoulder. It almost felt like the war itself was not real. The spell runs a few days until ballistics hit again before the air raid had the chance to warn you, and you are below the rock bottom of the 21st century living once again. Emotional seesaw.

The difference for me personally was that now I had papers and projects due in the midst of it. The natural chain reaction of thoughts leads you to believe that you were not in the right state of mind, making the decision to pay for the courses and start a term. I knew from experience about the power outages and how 'fun' they were for John who works remotely, live US time. I also considered how he managed to pull through or run to a café around the corner with a generator working, and therefore wi-fi available, to get the job done. At this point in the war, our building did not have a fiber optic internet provider servicing the area.

The way I dealt with it was simple. I typed, researched, and submitted between the bombings, always ahead of the game, not waiting for the deadlines. If it wasn't early, it was late. My psyche could not handle the added pressure any other way. I gave it my full attention and felt alive again. My brain was stimulated; I did not even realize how much I craved that! The studies became the priority above all.

- Ballistics?
- I need ten minutes… Alright, John, I'm coming, Jeez!

My bathroom served me well. There were those days… You pick up on the energy of the day, catching on quickly on what to expect. It is going to be nasty, so you might as well bring the pillows and the blankets under your bum to the 'safest place' in the house. The shelter downstairs was packed to the gills with pets and people. I couldn't work like that. Plus, the time it takes to run there when ballistics have been shot does not equal a smart choice. I would be wide open in the street right about the time it lands. You gotta do the math: if they shot it from the Odesa region, we've got three minutes at best.

When the skies were falling on a day like that, I was sitting in the bathroom working on my 3D project of the human ear: the outer, the middle with three tiny bones – the hammer, the stirrup, the anvil, and the inner ear itself, with cochlea showing. I could still buy playdough, thank God, and make it as intricate as it needed to be! It is true what they say about remembering better/learning faster if a strong emotional response is directly connected to the experience of learning. Who says it needs to be a positive emotional experience? Mine was breathtakingly negative, hands shaking in between the attachments of various pieces of that human ear puzzle! Look at me now, I know and distinctly remember the anatomic names and the nicknames of every tiny part of that unique hearing instrument.

Looking back on it, I realize that getting my pre-reqs was an absolute necessary distraction and a confidence booster in the middle of the war that kept my sanity intact. The distraction part is self-explanatory. A confidence booster, though it took some reflection and other people pointing that out to me before it became obvious: yes, I enrolled and successfully finished three college semesters in the second year of this war. Stuff that in your pipe and smoke it, Putin, Lukashenko, and that North Korean dickhead.

6

The Displaced

The Muscovites have driven us from our homes. Some of us are Ukrainian; others are not. Ukraine is our home because our families have been here for their entire existence as early as Kyivan Rus, or someone migrated from Greece, the Republic of Georgia or some other former Soviet State to make a new life in the past few generations, or work brought us here, or life's journey for some reason led us to this fertile and ancient land. The reasons matter individually to us, and they are varied. Our truth now is that all of us have been displaced. We cross the border, and they call us refugees. We stay within the borders of Ukraine, and they call us internally displaced. We don't care what they call us; we just want to go home.

Home no longer physically exists for some of us; it's just a pile of rubble, unlivable. Yet, many of us would rather set up a tent on our little pile of rubble and begin to rebuild what was once ours because that ground which may be soaked with blood, contaminated by spilled fuel from destroyed tanks, empty casings from machine guns or the debris from missiles, artillery shells or drones or worse, the decomposed corpses of dead Russians, is still the place we call home. Many of our neighbors, friends and relatives are dead, and we cannot mourn them in the places where we all used to live and to love, laugh, argue, get drunk and just do those everyday things.

We do everyday things wherever we now live, but they don't feel the same. The food doesn't taste quite as good; the drink doesn't drown the sorrows quite as deep. We sleep, or sometimes we don't. We wake, and sometimes, we barely can lift ourselves out of bed to go on. We do not complain. We do not make a show of our suffering because we know our soldiers in the trenches are suffering more. We know those who refused to become displaced in the places we left behind struggle for survival, heat, water, food, medicines, and all other daily comforts every minute, every hour, every day. We try to send them things if we can because we know they are holding the place many of us call home. Some are brave, while others just don't have any choice but to stay.

Our guilt for leaving it all behind eats at us. We argue within ourselves that we did it to survive, but we always lose that argument. We hide our pain, and we stand tall, strong, yet the tempest inside eats away at our bodies, minds, and spirits. Some of us may never go home because the wounds run too deep or we simply don't have the energy to rebuild. Yet, we know that home will always call us even when we don't want to answer.

Those of us whose homes are still intact pine away to return. We imagine our flats, our houses, cottages, whatever form our home has. We remember exactly how we left them, where everything was when we walked out the door with only what we could carry. Did we turn off the electric? Did a missile blow out the windows and ruin everything? Will the pipes freeze? We wish for the familiarity of our home streets, paths, shortcuts, and our grocery stores, cafes, and other places nearby, like the park where we walk our dogs. These things seem mundane to those who live their lives every day and are not directly affected by the death and destruction of our reality. Small everyday treasures are something that we have also lost in this mayhem. Little pieces of our lives that we all took for granted. Now we ask, when can we go home? How long before the enemy just gives up and realizes they can't win? Why would God let this happen? Why won't NATO do more?

We get tired of trying to answer the big questions. We grow weary of watching every tidbit of information about the fighting: the empty promises of politicians and allies; the speculation about how and when the war will end. Nobody knows, and we don't care what they think anymore. We are a year into this invasion, and some have been displaced since February 24th, 2022, while others just left today because of the shelling, missiles, and drones. Like the workers who were paid equal wages no matter what time they came for the harvest, the displaced who come early or late suffer equally.

God is not to blame, we know that, but we want someone or something to be responsible beyond the obvious enemy. We seek those that are compliant or have given a meager response. Anger, frustration, impatience, sadness and, eventually, that numbness that pervades our very existence begins to rule. There is no comfortably numb for us no matter where we are. Existence becomes a struggle. How many have already taken their own lives in this state? How many more will? How many are just thinking about it? These are not thoughts most of us would have if the war had not stolen our lives from us. Maybe some of us will get our lives back, but they will never be the same. Some of us will return, and the reality will be too difficult to deal with and face as we look at our homes that are just pieces of brick, twisted metal and debris on a piece of contaminated earth. How does the earth beneath us feel after being devastated by this violence?

Many of us dreamed of traveling before we were forced to leave. Now, we are involuntary gypsies who have not been given a choice if we want to prosper or just survive. The enemy forced us to take our suitcases, backpacks, pets, laptops, and a few memories on a road we didn't want to go down. This is not a vacation. Sure, we try to take advantage of our new digs when we can. That helps a little. Even if we sit in a café and enjoy a good meal, it still makes the food a little dull. If we go to a church, we feel God there, but it is still not our church, not our Father Confessor. If we are lucky enough to have other family members or a pet with us, our comfort is only found in them. Photographs from home before we left only bring the blues. If we go home, will we ever want to leave or to travel? Will we have dreams we choose to pursue?

Displaced is just one word, one meaning for who we are. Our lives, like millions more in Ukraine, have been stunted. How many years will the healing take? How many years will we live like this if we make it through? Even if we sued Russia and got millions in compensation, you can't buy more time. Once time is stolen, it cannot be returned, redeemed, or fixed. That wound will always be open, will always bleed or give pain. Some of us who are strong will bear it, but what of those who cannot? What will become of them? We, the strong, will be there for them and try to support their tragedy, but we can't do it all. They will look for others who went through this for consolation. Outsiders will try to help, but they will never really understand.

In the end, many of us will become healers to those whose wounds are taking longer to heal than our own. Some of us will become builders to raise a new Ukraine from the rubble. Others will become the storytellers of all that has happened on a human, political or military level. Those who held their faith may become spiritual leaders. Right now, who among us would even want to enter politics? Yet, we know, more than anyone else, that many of our brothers and sisters will not make it. They will destroy themselves with drugs or alcohol or some other risky lifestyle, and we will have to be understanding. There is no salve for some wounds, and some people never heal. We know many will take their own lives even if we try to help. We will not abandon them in their darkest hours because we have walked there, too.

These are the long-term results of deep spiritual and psychological wounds that cannot be seen on the surface. We know we cannot show them yet because our soldiers need their time to heal and grieve. Those who stayed in the occupied territories are more of a priority than us. We know we have to ride in the backseat for now and keep our mouths shut. We know we can't keep asking 'Are we there, yet?' to our drivers and front seat passengers. We must suffer silently, with dignity, with strength and let Ukraine achieve victory.

Brothers and sisters, we will do our best out here in our lives as the displaced so as not to get in your way. We support you and know we do not suffer as much as many others. We are trying to keep it together and send money or whatever help we can. We are tired also, but we know we cannot rest as you sit on guard duty or once again go on the offensive or merely just stand strong and hold your defensive positions. We are grateful in the midst of our sadness because only you can bring us home.

7

Ukrainian Patriots Forged from American Metal

The smithy lit his fire, and something began to be forged. Hotter and hotter as it grew stronger with each blast of the enemy. A weapon within began to take shape made from American metal. Fear of death always lingered but did not rule. Steely resolve as the Ukrainians repelled an overwhelming enemy. Air raid sirens wailed, yet we went on. The ground reverberated with missile strikes. A constant boom of fighting not so far away. The weapon grew stronger, but it is one that, once forged, must be sharpened and kept clean constantly. Battles sometimes come about, and it gets nicked but does not break.

Blue and yellow began to flow through our veins. If we were going to bleed, these are the colors that would pour forth from our wounds or death blows. We sang 'Oh, the Red Viburnum in the Meadow' whether we knew the meaning of the words or not. We stood in the Cathedral of St. Volodymyr as the air raids continued and lit our candles, said our prayers, made our Confessions, took Communion, and bowed our heads to the icons and holy men that fed our spirits, kept our souls clean and ready for death. But death has not come. The weapon within stays powerful and strong. Our bodies, minds, and souls – all are wounded, but strength, resolve, fortitude, perseverance, and faith drive us on.

The Battle of Kyiv was only the first test. We stood our ground then, along with so many others. We did not waiver, we did not falter, we did not run, and we never lost faith. Soon enough, that battle was over. Spring flowers gave way to the heat of summer. We went to the banya (steam room and Finnish sauna) and barbecued on the Dnipro River as the sun warmed our bodies. Soon enough, the winds of Autumn came, and so did the missile attacks. This time, we lost power and Internet. Our means of income was interrupted, and we had to leave our beloved Kyiv but not our Ukraine. A long train ride to an unknown city where now we roam the streets and cafes.

Ah, my raven-haired one, my Peace-Renown of Zakhar Berkut fame. How gorgeous she is with her sinewy arms and green eyes – a dark-browed woman of Ukrainian roots. Now I know from whence her strength and depth come, her love of freedom and free-roaming nature. It is from deep within her blood that her Ukrainian spirit rises, boils and does not turn away from a fight. My druzhina, my back-up in battle, my foxhole buddy and partner. We stayed because of her and because of the Marine buried deep within me. Our symbol is now the trident, our flag is now the blue sky and golden fields of wheat or sunflowers below.

We have been forged together as Ukrainians, her in spirit and blood, me in spirit. Our souls soar with every victory, and our tears flow with every death, but we continue just like these brave Cossacks, Hutsuls, Crimeans and all the others. One day, maybe they will make us one of them. Will we have earned it? Could we have done more? These are questions that cannot be answered now. In our souls, we will be one with them and of them, even if there is no paper that says it is so. Slava Ukraina! Our beloved new country. On to victory! And then, we will have a party unlike the planet earth has ever seen! We are Ukrainian Patriots forged from American metal by this war.

A Sword of Ukraine
Written for President Volodymyr Zelensky
On His Birthday January 25, 2024

I was a piece of pig iron in the bogs of Jersey
Maybe to be a nail and the hammer that strikes it
Yet I always wanted to be a sword
I laid in the bog and waited
Oh, I tried to be made ready for battle
Was not strong enough or properly aged
And I failed and was thrown onto the scrap heap
A woman found me, decided to test my mettle
She began to forge me, added stronger steel
Between anvil and hammer heated for melding
Strong Scythian warrior head, Amazon arms
Her fire made me, shaped me, gave strength
Ready, she gave me over to her lost homeland
Ukraine took me in and polished me
Refined the strength forged by Her lost daughter
Ukraine held me firmly and then wielded me
Made me into the sword I always wanted to be
The nicks of battle and tests of mettle apparent
And I am Her weapon until this land is free
Or am I utterly destroyed by the enemy.

8

Overcaffeinated in the Ukraine War

Agitation because of potential annihilation by a malevolent nation. Have another cup of coffee! Desecration by defecation on eternal sanctification, oh, they will not find salvation. Pour another cuppa Joe, two, three, four, what the fuck is with this damn war? On they go, old Soviet missiles all shot in a row. Killing kids, old people, morals on the skids. Walking dead, no brains in their heads, their hordes we still dread. Zombies with their Zs, attacking with salvos in threes and mostly hitting trees in yards where pensioners play cards. What, what, smoke another butt, ok, pour me another espresso, pronto! News of earthquakes, missiles make our ground shake, man, we all have a headache! Who are these demon seeds planting themselves among Ukrainian reeds whilst carrying out their evil deeds? Oh woe, that bitch is a ho', don't want to see her no mo'. Rockets fly, more die, and the cappuccino continues to flow.

Anxiety, notoriety, a distinct lack of sobriety. March, march onward cretin soldiers, marching toward the whore with a Z mob sign going on before. Sing a song of six kopecks, hope our pilot had time to eject. Before they shot him down dead over polluted sunflower fields, no flowers to yield. Plow, plow, our brave ones, mow them down, kill every single one! The only good ones are dead ones, much to our dismay these thoughts frequently on display. Don't make us like them, oh please, gods of war, don't let us become like them. Let us love and play, send us a dove of peace for which we pray. Hold on there, sailor, the end is not come.

Disillusioned by victory's illusion, we plod forward in confusion. Hey, barista, another one! Mental health deteriorates with dark stealth. Oh Jesus, when will it end? Are we going crazy? Sleeping late and being lazy in war's hazy daze. What'll we do? Where will we go? Is this a nervous breakdown? No fool, it's cup number eight. Nothing's wrong, you're ok. You drank too much coffee, buffoon. Ah, laughter is the best medicine. What strange existence based on our own insistence that we can't end this pestilence. Funny money there ain't no honey, a salve for the salvos. Tomorrow, just drink water, avoid the caffeine or for no reason, again you will scream.

9

Forgiveness Sunday

Last year, Russia invaded during what we Orthodox call Cheesefare Week but is celebrated in Slavic countries as 'Butter Week' or Maslenitsa. Right now, for the first time in possibly centuries, two majority Orthodox Christian nations are directly at war. Now, to the Average Joe, this matters little or may not even be relevant. Let's start with explaining Great Lent and move from there, sound reasonable?

First, the Eastern Orthodox Church does not tell us that we 'must' observe the fasting rules of Great Lent. The Church does not say we will burn in hell, be denied services or anything else that might sound vaguely torturous. What Great Lent does is give us a chance to 'Rewind, Reset and Begin Again' should we use our free will to choose to observe it. Monastics and clergy do their best to observe the rules, with the monks and nuns being the marathon runners. Observing Great Lent is a very difficult task because it requires self-sacrifice. The self-sacrificial nature of it also builds willpower, discipline and usually a deeper inner journey.

Our Church begins preparing us weeks in advance for the coming of Great Lent. This starts with what we call the Lenten Triodion, which begins on the Sunday of the Publican and the Pharisee. Once we reach this pinnacle of the Orthodox calendar, we know we must begin to prepare ourselves if we are going to observe Great Lent. At this point, our minds and spirits are preparing as no fasting rules have begun. The next week is the Sunday of the Prodigal Son, which is also called Meatfare Week and is totally free from fasting (normally, Wednesday and Friday are fast days for us throughout most of the year). Thus, we stuff ourselves silly with whatever meat we crave or desire during this week because, on the Sunday of the Last Judgement (Meatfare Sunday), we know it is our last day to consume any kind of animal flesh.

Does the Sunday of the Last Judgement sound ominous? It does, right? Well, surprise, it is not a dark fire and brimstone day for us at all. It is a day of hope that we will be saved from unceasing fires. We put our trust in God's mercy on this day and usually eat leftovers because on the next day, Cheesefare (Maslenitsa) begins. Last year, Russia invaded Ukraine during this week. But what is Cheesefare and what do we eat and do? Well, clearly, we eat a lot of dairy unless we are lactose intolerant (both my wife and I fall into this category, unfortunately). However, there is hope for us because, well, we can eat as many fish and egg dishes as we want. So as the missiles and rockets began to fall, as tanks rolled across the border from Belarus and Russian paratroopers started landing in Hostomel, we were celebrating Cheesefare and eating French Toast. Marking the first year of war also falls during this week here in Ukraine.

Yet, it (the Russian Invasion) didn't matter last year, and it doesn't matter this year (the one-year mark). Nope. We went to church on what is called 'Forgiveness Sunday', which is the last Sunday before the official start of Great Lent. We went to church, lit candles, prayed for forgiveness from our enemies and tried to grant forgiveness to them while having Confession and Communion. Traditionally, much like the time from Rosh Hashanah to Yom Kippur, we must close out our books of sin, grudges and other spiritual offenses on Forgiveness Sunday. Sometimes, we have to call someone to ask for forgiveness and in church, we usually look each other in the eye and say, 'Forgive me for all the sins I have committed against you' to our fellow parishioners and to God, the Saints and Angels. Think about this from a purely psychological perspective for a minute and take the spiritual out of it. Do you see the cleansing we are given the opportunity to take part in? Now, on Forgiveness Sunday 2023, will any of us in Ukraine be able to forgive the Russians and anyone who supports them? I am not sure that I will be able to.

Great Lent began just a few days after the Russian Invasion last year, and that was much to our benefit. We were already prepared for fasting, so the lack of groceries on the shelves was, in the end, not really a problem. This year, the shelves are full, but we will still abstain. We fast from meat, dairy, eggs, wine, olive oil and fish with a backbone. Well, that's what we are supposed to do, but most laypeople just do their best. My wife and I fast from most of it, with the exception of the occasional dairy and eggs. Since we are active, protein deficiency becomes a problem after a bit. So, basically, the observation of Great Lent turns you into a vegan for about 50 days if you follow it to the rule. Forty days is the length of Great Lent, but we then also fast during Holy Week, which is the lead up to Pascha (Easter) so officially, Great Lent ends on the Saturday (Lazarus Saturday) before Palm Sunday.

Now, here's the other part of Great Lent. Not only are we supposed to fast from food but also from entertainment, digital media, news, and anything not edifying for the soul. We are told to read more Scripture, Lives of the Saints, or other literature with a religious theme. Additionally, we should attend Church Services more often (many more services are made available for us by the Church during Great Lent), and we should also take part in the Sacraments (Confession, Communion and Holy Unction, which is anointing with Holy Oil). Basically, Great Lent is like being a soldier who goes back to Boot Camp every year. It's a choice, yes. Those of us who do observe it find the journey to really be deep on a spiritual level. My wife and I also hold off on making any major life decisions during Great Lent and have found that when we do, the answer is crystal clear. Spiritual warfare is fought by many throughout this most Holy time of year. We don't always win the battles, but we fight on, in order to win the war.

10

Coming Back Home

John, Philly, and I returned from Chernivtsi safe and sound in March of 2023. Going there felt necessary for two reasons:

> 1. The bombings were getting closer to the building we live in. The route we take to walk Philly daily was compromised by two direct hits and two giant craters staring back at us, the sad reminder of the new reality where the children's playground is the successful target of the Russian military, stated so on multiple Russian media, videos playing over and over to share the results with exhilarated 'special military operation' supporters back in the mighty Moscovia.

The impact of both hits was too sensitive to process quickly. Not the craters, the noise, the shattered windows of the gorgeous architectural monument in the old city center I kept admiring every time I passed it, or the disfigured kiddy playground with one of the oldest poplar trees in the perimeter, smashed to a pulp, or the restaurant across that was left without the glass entrance doors, or the coffee place right behind it, where the barista knows how I take my latte…, but *the cheering* afterwards that we couldn't understand. We saw the comments of the opposing side, heard their 'take this, khokhly', were equally revolted by it, the khokhlukha and the American in me, here on the Ukrainian soil.

> 2. We started losing electricity regularly, abruptly, ominously. I needed to finish what I started; my college reality did not change or have a special 'bombing shell-shock accommodations' available at the time. What was I supposed to do if the internet was no more? Pull the war card? I did not want pity. The college was my ticket to normalcy. It was the one thing that allowed me to feel sane, that had no interest in anything but my brain cells' performance, and I desperately needed to know that my brain was still ok.

The sensation of being at home filled my body and soul when we opened the front door. The smell of our flat, the look of it, the familiarity of everything made me want to twirl on the spot. We are the travelers alright. It was not the first time we had come back home on either continent. Somehow, it felt dearer to me than any other house I ever owned. Maybe because this one was still standing despite it all? It was still our safe haven in a profoundly unsafe environment. It survived WWI and WWII and instilled the hope in us that it will pull through somehow, with or without us in it. The decision was ours. It was not a straightforward discussion between spouses about the current situation and the logical way to proceed in it. It was a mutual feeling that ripened after enough fermenting. We didn't consciously realize it to properly articulate that the only way to proceed was to stay.

See, the 'going back to the States' thing had an expiration date attached to it. The place was found, the universities were chosen, and the plan was theoretically in place for what-are-were-going-to-do-once-on-the-ground. John had applied and was approved for a program that would pay for our relocation to a particular state of choice, if he kept his remote job (not an issue), and I would either enroll in the university, go back to teaching at a local school, or work as an SLP aid to begin my new career. They needed an answer and papers signed. We started by asking for an extension, then for another one… Until we realized we were simply deflecting, unwilling to admit, that neither of us wanted to go back. We had to reason ourselves into it, agreeing both with 'how insane' we sounded for making an argument to stay, where there was NO ARGUMENT to be made. There was a pros and cons list, seriously lopsided towards 'you need to leave'. And yet we stayed.

The fact is, when you go through something so dramatic with a country that begins to defend itself against the enemy with its bare hands, the grit of it rubs off on you. The mixed feelings of all kinds are entangled over time that only a seriously relevant group of professionals would be able to help you untangle. We felt 'wrong' leaving, like the betrayal of a family member who needed you by his side, but you chose what was good for you. Guilt? Shame? Self-masochistic tendency? Low self-esteem? The need to do the right thing? Some principles? Pride? I don't know yet. I can't answer this with undeniable clarity. Maybe it was all of it, or none of it. And here we still were.

We went to Chernivtsi with the intention to cross the border and exhale in peace somewhere in Romania, if the situation became completely unbearable. For the first time in a year of war, we did just that in Chernivtsi. The reality of civilian life on the ground was limited to occasional air raids and planned power outages for a couple of hours in the mornings and a couple of hours at night. THAT was quite manageable. I could work with that. I could study around 'the inconvenience'. I did not need to grab my cell phone in the middle of the night if the siren went off. I could sleep with confidence that a trajectory of Russian rockets to this place was unlikely, if not impossible. It was enough to release my hyper-awareness, body tension, and sleep deprivation into the 'safe bosom' of Chernivtsi.

The Romanian border seemed almost accessible by foot, but it lost its appeal the closer we got to it. It meant leaving Ukraine, possibly for good. If crossing the closest border felt icky somehow, then crossing the ocean was even more surreal. We were not in not the right mindset to proceed. This much was obvious.

11

Displaced Kyivans Return

There is some redundancy in this chapter, and I apologize for that. It is kept 'as-is' in its original form because my chapters were mostly written in the moment. Thus, all the elements of the 'now' that were occurring 'then' are intact to include anger, fear, frustration, sarcasm and cynicism, along with the most important; hope and faith.

14:33, the train from Chernivtsi to Poltava pulled away from the station. This train's final destination was not our own; we were headed to Kyiv. Onboard, two Canadians were on their way to Lviv to bring hand-warmers to Ukrainian troops in Bakhmut. They would stop in Lviv for a meeting before heading east to the lines of death and destruction. Both men were resolute and determined despite the fluidity of the military situation in that 'Unbreakable Fortress' that is another symbol in this tragic and criminal war. We remember Bucha, Hostomel, Irpin, Izium, Mariupol, and so many others that either survived or succumbed to the enemy. Those of us who have stayed on Ukrainian soil throughout the war probably see things differently than those who left and may never return. People on the front most likely view things in another way than those who have spent the war mostly in the rear. When the war started, we were one of the fronts.

Artillery fire and missiles fell quickly when the full-scale Russian invasion began just over year ago. Air raid sirens were frequent. Occasional bursts of small-arms fire were heard close by. Legends have already risen from the Battle of the Kyiv, the city we call home. Kyiv was a front in what seems like a lifetime ago. City streets were empty, churches that are always open were closed, most stores, pharmacies, and coffee shops did not operate. Barely anyone was on the streets except soldiers when we took the dogs out. Curfews lasted anywhere from 14 to 72 hours. No cars passed or drove that were not military. No rideshare services seemed to be around. Kyiv was a ghost town then. This made it feel even more ours since we are both introverts, and the lack of people, noise, traffic and bustle seemed peaceful in between the explosions and air raids.

We, like our elderly neighbors and about a million other people, stayed in Kyiv throughout that battle. Pre-war Kyiv had a population of over three million and we watched as they sat in cars, lined up at train stations and shivered at the bus depot waiting to get out. We didn't celebrate their departure, nor did we celebrate their return in late spring as the fighting nearby subsided. Those of us who stayed could easily pick out those who had fled. Soon enough, we would be standing in their shoes.

Missile attacks in the autumn brought a different reaction and reality to the war. Clearly, they were intensifying, and one struck just blocks from our house along the route we walk our surviving dog. Had we left 15 minutes earlier, we could have been killed. We had accepted God's will on our survival or demise. The truth is that we could not function economically without real-time Internet and electricity. On October 24, 2022, we left Kyiv for Chernivtsi so one of us could continue to earn while the other pursued prerequisite classes for a masters through a US university. Situational awareness, tactical reality, just plain survival. We returned once in December and had intermittent power while taking care of some important paperwork.

Four months in Chernivtsi. Well, a little over that, but who's counting? The train arrived at 03:41, and there was a curfew in Kyiv until 05:00. We were too tired to wait and took a taxi, breaking the rules. Now, back home. We had a hard time unpacking as we forgot where certain things were supposed to go. We forgot where we kept this, where to put that. Oh, we have a dishwasher! Forgot that, too. So, if this happened to us just after four months, what would it be like for those who have no home to return to, those who have been gone longer and whatever other situations may be out there? How will people cope? How will they function? Who will be there to help them? Is it possible for those who have not experienced this war to even really be helpful? There's this bond that forms in war for those who go through it, and everyone who didn't is just, well, not us. Not us as a whole. There's no decent explanation; it just is. Some of us survivors will have to be strong because we may be the only ones that others will be willing to talk to, to deal with.

When the end of the war comes, many will need your patience and understanding. It will be a different kind than it is now when the war is still raging. Yes, we will celebrate in a big way, and then millions of us will have to begin the long process of healing. Have mercy on us as we do, please.

12

Missile Terror Again!

Part I. Written from Kyiv – March 9, 2023
Part II. Written from Kyiv – May 16, 2023

Part I

March 9, 2023, I awoke in the middle of the night to use the bathroom. This is life for we men over fifty. A familiar noise came to bear as I passed the window on the way. I checked my phone, it was 02:33 and then I looked at the Telegram Channel #War_Monitor as it gives updates on all air strike activity in Ukraine. This is how technology and communication keep us alive in the War on Ukraine. First, I did my business, then I let my wife (Natasha) know about the Air Raid Siren. She hustled out of bed and went into the bathroom, which is the safest place in our house, structure-wise. We rarely go down to the bomb shelter unless the first explosion hits close. Since we don't live close to civilian infrastructure and are in the neighborhood where there are many foreign embassies, our area rarely ever gets direct hits. Lackadaisical? Maybe so, maybe so… but this is how we now operate in a war zone.

I went back to bed. Surprised? Yes, after over a year of war, that's pretty much my attitude. If the explosions come and they are not near, I just keep on keeping on. My wife would hear them, but I slept straight through. Natasha said they were not close and that was why she didn't wake me to come shelter in the bathroom. I had to work in the morning, and she decided they were not enough of a threat to call me into our bathroom shelter. Plus, at my age, I can be a bit cranky due to lack of sleep. Natasha is my foxhole buddy, and I trust her completely to make the appropriate tactical decisions when presented. She's a good Marine in my book.

Now, over a year of war gives you certain insights into life, survival, and especially not to waste your time. There is also that acceptance that if death comes, it's just because your time is up. I always think of that scene from Apocalypse Now where Robert Duvall's character (Colonel something or other) is standing straight up talking about loving the smell of napalm in the morning. It's not that now famous line that gets me, but the fact that he is standing, drinking coffee, while hell is breaking loose around him. That is a symbol of someone who accepts death and does not fear it. Are we that brave? Probably not, but we live a pretty good percentage of that attitude.

Death is coming for us all, whether we like it or not. Why fear it? The thing is, once you get past the fear of death, you begin to live even more. Seems oppositional? Maybe it is. The thing is that life just becomes all that more precious when you know it could be over any second. A missile could hit us, and boom, we're gone. Just like that. Hopefully, our souls are clean enough if and when it does. Faith also keeps us alive.

War is not exhilarating for us despite what you just read. However, once you pray, crawl, bite, scratch, shoot, drink, screw, smoke cigars, or whatever it takes to survive, you realize that all those little things make life worth living. Dreams? 'Dreams I'm never gonna see', as Molly Hatchet put it. Who needs dreams when everyday life is so rich with living? Goals are ok, but most of us have put our dreams aside in Ukraine. That's tough for the young, but those of us getting up there in years are just grateful to be alive, to walk the streets of Kyiv and to go on. Die another day, Mr Bond.

Part II

May 16, 2023. Before I speak about the missiles, let me tell you the significance of this day in Ukraine. Let's start with the good news first, shall we? Today is Vyshyvanka Day in Ukraine pronounced 'vishievanka'. What is it you say? It is a celebration of that style of Ukrainian embroidery that I am sure you have seen now that Ukraine and its culture are all over the news due to the war. A vyshyvanka is worn as a shirt, skirt or dress by women and as a shirt by men. Ukraine had to be invaded and attacked in order for its rich culture and history to be exposed to the world. That's a real big backfire for Moscow, but it's not like we are celebrating it as the attacks keep coming on the front and in the rear. It's just one of those realities that are an unexpected result of the Muscovites' fumbled plans, which more and more resemble the antics of Larry, Moe and Curly (Google 'The Three Stooges' if you haven't heard of 'em).

Ok, back to Vyshyvanka Day. Here in Kyiv, as you walk the streets, it's like an art gallery is passing you by everywhere. Almost every shirt, skirt or dress is individual and unique in its designs, colors and background. Yes, some are similar, but none ever seem to be the same. These are very vibrant pieces of clothing that express life, happiness, nature and beauty. Many contain flowers, birds, butterflies and intricate Ukrainian-style designs. Natasha owns two. Today, she wore the shirt version as we ventured out to a small French-style café near the Golden Gate for breakfast. She looked fabulous in her ensemble, and we took a bunch of pictures. She looks like a Ukrainian hippie to me, and that suits us both. We sat in the sidewalk café as busy commuters walked to their jobs, most dressed in their best vyshyvankas. Today was significant because we had survived another almost sleepless night of missile attacks from multiple directions.

Missile attacks have been ever more frequent this whole last week, with every night but one forcing us from our beds to seek cover. Kyiv seems to be the primary target. So, everyone is nervous at night but goes about their business during the day. Yes, the streets were packed this morning with colorful Ukrainians everywhere. People survived the night and went to work in the morning, showing off their culture. No matter what happens, Muscovy will never take this from them again.

This past week has been rough. Rumors circulated for two days that the Muscovites had taken out the Patriot system that protects Kyiv. This is one of two systems in the whole vast country, or so they say. We have no idea where the other one is stationed and that's ok. This system is not mobile and has a strong radar built in, which means it is easier for enemy forces to locate and possibly destroy. So, the rumors had us all running a little nervous. Last night, which means from about midnight to 05:00, they kept firing from land, air, and sea-based platforms with hypersonic and other missiles. In total, some 30 ballistic missiles were launched, and some 29 of them were shot down by Ukraine's Air Defense Forces. What an awesome job! Broken and destroyed Patriot System, my ass. Yeah, we knew that it was slightly damaged the other night by falling missile debris. And, yeah, we also knew that one missile can't take out the whole thing at once since it is dispersed. Nothing confirms that like 29 out of 30 destroyed missiles along with Unmanned Aerial Vehicles (UAVs or drones).

Are we scared? Yes. Everyone is to some extent. Nobody seems to be running and leaving. In fact, it seems like Kyiv gets busier by the day. More and more voices are heard in languages other than Ukrainian and Russian as well. This past week, they have fired in the range of or over a hundred of these super-fast missiles. Somewhere around ninety-eight percent have been shot down. The other night, when it was really bad, there were multiple explosions, pink light from tracer rounds of air the defenses were lighting up the night, a bunch of vloggers posted videos and images of air defenses shooting them down. This, after the government of Ukraine specifically banned this activity. Within minutes, this data was all over social and defense networks in Russia. Now, twenty-three of these 'vloggers' are in custody and facing eight years in prison. Any soldier will tell you, it's the morons that get you killed. The enemy will do the shooting, but the idiots will expose you, give away positions and, in this day and age, post it on Instagram, Facebook, TikTok and whatever other platform exists. Selfies will kill you! Or get you an eight-year prison term.

13

Kyiv Shopping Malls and Air Raids

March 13, 2023, started like any normal day prior to the Muscovite invasion of Ukraine. That is, it probably wasn't all that different from your Sunday morning. Yes, I know that it was actually Monday, but my weekend starts on Sunday, which makes Monday my Sunday and Sunday my Saturday. That's life for someone who works in the hospitality industry (and many others). Here in Ukraine, our soldiers, medics, surgeons and many volunteers don't get days off. I woke up a little later than usual although Natasha was up by 07:00 as she likes the quiet mornings to begin her studies for prerequisite classes in Speech Language Pathology (SLP). She chose to become an SLP during the war. One of the reasons we came to Ukraine is because she burned out as public school teacher in Florida after only six years. Natasha likes to help people and figured it's a good choice because there is plenty of room for growth in the profession for the next 10 years at least even with the AI revolution. Maybe she'll tell you all about it in one of her chapters.

Philly slept in with me and, after his morning grub, was eyeing me for a walk. I drank down a glass of kefir and another of water as Natasha sipped her coffee. Philly and I took our time, walking down one of Kyiv's main boulevards and then cutting over to Taras Shevchenko Park. This the park where we narrowly avoided being hit by a missile only five months ago. You remember? Maybe not, but we remember them all. The missile in question successfully hit the extremely important tactical target called 'Children's Playground.' In the Muscovite social and news media sphere they cheered the destruction of this highly valuable target. Luckily, no children were playing there that day. Our mayor, Vitali Klitschko, quickly sent crews to repair the playground, and today, as we passed by, it was as if the missile had never hit.

The air was brisk, and Philly sniffed his regular sniffs as we circled toward the other side of the park. People were out and about on their way to work, stopping for their morning coffee or, like us, having a walk. Traffic was heavy as usual on a Monday morning rush hour in a war zone. Philly and I headed through the Botanical Garden in the center of the city as the sun warmed us gradually. We passed St. Volodymyr's Cathedral on our way back to our flat. All was well and normal.

Natasha was waiting and ready to go when we returned. First, a little background. Natasha and I left the US in November 2020 to move to Ukraine in the midst of the heavy masking rules and without being vaccinated yet. No, no, not because we were anti-vaccine or anything right-wing crazy like that. In fact, we were leaving that state of right-wing craziness, Florida. We took a trip to the St. Augustine Outlets, or maybe it was Daytona, before packing our meager two pallets of belongings to ship off. Natasha and I were well aware that clothing costs are higher in Ukraine than in the US, so we stocked up on a lot of warm-weather clothing of good quality because, well, after seven years in Florida, we really didn't have any. Now, after three years in Ukraine, much of it is wearing out and needs replacing.

This day was the one we chose to head to the Ocean Plaza Mall to replace some items. You get it, right? Just a day off excursion to the mall, like the ones you take. We decided to walk to the subway station with a direct link to Ocean Plaza instead of going to one close to the house where we would have to transfer. Those of you who live in cities get it. We live in the dead center of Kyiv, and it makes no sense to own a car here, just like in Manhattan, Philly or any other number of cities. Kyiv is Europe's seventh largest city, with a pre-war population of over three million. It's still somewhere in that range, and public transportation is easy and readily available. Natasha and I passed through Taras Shevchenko Park on our way and passed a yurt donated by the People of Kazakhstan. This yurt serves as a place to keep warm, charge phones, drink tea and provide other comforts during power outages. In Ukraine, they are named 'Points of Invincibility'. Carved wooden doors in the Kazakh style make this a pretty interesting point in the middle of our city park. Natasha and I glanced and continued on toward our Kyiv Blue Line Metro stop.

Just as we were about to exit the park, the ominous droning of the Air Raid Alert started. We decided to keep going as the subway is a shelter anyway. I love this particular subway stop because there is an underground flower market there. Natasha and I had once owned a flower shop in Watertown, Massachusetts and my father, Bill, had owned a very successful and thriving flower shop in my hometown of Woodbury, New Jersey. That's where I learned the business, a strong work ethic, and the logistical skills that I use in my current profession. Our flower shops (mine and Pop's) met the same fate and went belly-up within a few years of each other. However, the memories are always there, as are the appreciation of flowers. As you enter this subway stop, in the bleak Soviet-style underground, you are met with bursts of colors and the smells, ah, the smells of hundreds of varieties of fresh flowers. How can that not make you smile?

The Air Raid was in full swing as I made my klutzy way through the turnstiles with Natasha by my side. Some Kyivans had already arrived to use the subway as a shelter, while others like us headed to the platform to wait for the train. Natasha and I got off at the station where the mall is located, and there, people were sitting on mats and chairs, checking their phones. We continued on, knowing that Ocean Plaza shuts during air raids, as do most other businesses. Other potential shoppers were milling around outside, also waiting for the air raid to end, hoping that it would. Telegram channels updated us about Kaliber missile carriers in the Black Sea and Sea of Azov as well as the take-off and directions of enemy aviation. Just a typical trip to the mall, right?

Several targets of the enemy were struck in the east and the south of Ukraine which meant more could come. We gave it forty minutes before heading back to the subway to trek back home. As we emerged onto the street from the flower market, the Air Raid ended. We decided to try to make the most of it and check some stores on Kreshchatyk Street, although they tend to be a bit more expensive. We passed through a smaller underground mall and Natasha tried on walking boots that were too tight. I was hungry by now, and Natasha was getting there. We headed to TSUM, which is a high-end department store with cafés and dining on the top two floors. We figured we'd check prices after we ate and see if we could find at least one or two of the items we had originally set out for. We chatted, I drank buckwheat tea and Natasha had a latte as we waited for our food. Our order came out relatively quickly.

Sometimes, it takes forever compared to the US, and as Natasha and I are not patient people, we were pleased. Natasha always references an appearance by Governor Chris Christie on Saturday Night Live's Weekend Update after Hurricane Sandy. Governor Christie makes a joke about how 'patient' we people from Jersey are, along with our sarcastic traits. Strangely, we were living at the Jersey Shore when Sandy hit but just so happened to be on a family vacation with Natasha's parents, brother, and his wife in Moscow. We had to delay our return because our town, Ventnor, was closed and not allowing people back in since it is one of many barrier islands that make up the landscape of the Jersey Shore. We finished our meal, paid our check, and Air Raid Number Two came.

Shopping was just not meant to be that day. Home was a fifteen-minute walk, and we decided to brave it. People calmly left TSUM and headed to the parking garage and nearest subway stop. Shops were being closed and locked. Metal windows and doors came down and Kyiv had to stop normal living once again. Natasha and I easily would have spent at least a few hundred dollars on what we needed that day adding to the Ukraine War Economy. This is just one of the crimes that the Muscovites are perpetrating on Ukraine, its people, and its economy. The next time someone cuts in line at checkout, steals your parking space or some other minor slight, remember that you are living in safe zone, and our lives are constantly disrupted, put on hold or turned into debris, blood and body parts. Now, where and when can we go to get a new pair of jeans?

14

2nd Easter at War

The wind was cold on (Holy) Saturday morning in the center of Kyiv as Philly the dog and I exited our old Tsar-era building. Across the street, the coffee shop was just opening. A flowering tree in full bloom was gently swaying in the breeze outside the Stalinka (Stalin era building). Bright red tulips, just opened, on the green grass outside this Soviet era piece of architecture. Barely a soul was on the street. Saturday and Sunday mornings early are the best in Kyiv's center. There is a quiet stillness to the city at that time. Living here, you begin to understand why Manhattanites always rail against the 'bridge and tunnel' people who invade their neighborhoods. Unwelcome visitors are necessary for the economy to roll, but that doesn't mean you have to like them. Living in a busy, trendy neighborhood has its advantages, but also, well, all those people who are trying to be cool are just, well, annoying. You develop a slight arrogance as a resident when you see them acting like fools in the place you call home.

Philly and I travel up the street and cross while the light is green, as there is little traffic. We pass a couple European embassies where National Police huddle, drink coffee and try to keep warm while guarding the offices and abodes of foreign diplomats. Sovietsky Father B. is just exiting his old BMW as we pass the cathedral. We don't say hello. He doesn't like dogs and Philly senses that kind and expresses his mutual dislike rather easily. I don't dislike Father B., we all have our idiosyncrasies, and who is to judge others in a war zone?

Traffic hummed along but not at the usual weekday rush hour pace as we crossed the boulevard to the Fomin Botanical Garden. Bare traces of blooms getting ready on trees welcomed us with their mauve smiles, promising bursting colors in days to come. Bright yellow forsythia danced for our eyes as an older woman took a selfie with them in the background. The soft pulse of electronic music from the Grky Coffee Shop made me wonder who listens to that first thing in the morning? Grky means bitter in Ukrainian for their signature espresso. But I am no longer a coffee person, so we didn't stop.

The path goes down into what is almost a ravine, and we pass no one on the descent. Local Territorial Defense guys were drinking coffee and smoking as we passed at the bottom and began our ascent on the other side of the park. I like the ascent because it is very steep and gets my heart rate going; who needs coffee? Philly is always on the lookout in this area for other dogs to attack. Don't worry. He doesn't go out without a muzzle but wants to fight either way. True to his name, a Broad Street Bully. We pass one other dog that Philly determines is not a threat to our very existence and we keep moving. He's a good dog to have in a war zone. I know he would die to protect me and my wife if that duty called. That kind of loyalty is hard to find in a human being. Natasha lives up to it, but surely, I would die for her first. I am grateful to have her. She always has my back and vice versa.

Whilst out walking, Natasha is at home preparing for the Feast of Feasts. The spiritual significance is important, and I'll maybe discuss that later. Here's the real skinny: we haven't eaten meat since Meatfare Sunday (February 19th). Today is April 15th, so that's two months almost. We are not vegans or vegetarians and we both like to eat. Also, protein is essential since both of us are active. You can't live in Kyiv and not be active. The city is full of hills and unless you sit and have everything delivered, you will walk uphill to get somewhere at some point. American couch-potatoism is not a thing here. People walk to get groceries mostly. I assume the same as other big cities. Anyway, Great Lent calls for us to not eat meat, dairy, eggs, fish (with a backbone), olive oil and, well, no wine. Natasha and I simply can't comply with all that although we do limit dairy, eggs and olive oil, as well as only eating actual fish on days it is allowed (Feast of the Annunciation and Palm Sunday). This year, we ate scallops once, but the price was very high, and no shrimp looked good enough to buy. So, that pork roast that we will have to smell all day but not be able to eat will be sweet torture. Maybe that's how marathon runners feel as they hit the home stretch.

We made our way to Shevchenko Park, only passing the occasional pedestrian. Usually, we take the back-oval route, but today we went the front way. Tulips with tight buds were dancing in the cold breeze. I looked up, and there was the statue of Shevchenko, well, he was covered with sandbags and a façade to protect him from missile attacks. Good thing, too, as one landed just thirty meters away in a playground last October. I noticed that the statue had a sign saying it was erected in 1939 and thought of my father. That's the year he was born. He had a stroke about a year ago and is now in long-term care. If this damn war wasn't raging, I would have already gone to see him (my Mom is also not in the best of health). I can't leave Philly or my foxhole buddy behind in an active war zone. So, that's just my little sacrifice for them and Ukraine. We're used to making sacrifices here. I can't tell how much money I have given away to individuals, the military and other causes. Those funds normally would have gone to savings but now are being used to help Ukraine win.

Exiting the park, we enter onto Volodymyrska Street. This street, according to local historians, is the oldest in the city at 1,000 years. There is this feeling when you know that that really can't be adequately described. Once, traders, peasants, hucksters, diplomats, military attaches and millions of others trekked up this piece of ground to enter Old Kyiv. Up, as in uphill. Philly and I now do our trek but not to meet with President Zelensky or anyone else. Just Kyivans out for a walk. Philly loves the soft green grass in front of the National Opera of Ukraine. He rolls and sniffs as I stare at the façade of this grand building. Natasha and I had attended a performance here just two days before the full-scale invasion. Some of the faces seemingly staring in permanent terror from the façade remind me of how many in Ukraine feel every day as their cities and villages get attacked relentlessly. Although, we got used to it when it was happening, just as most of them probably are now. Strange is life in war. Humanity gets used to its circumstances, adjusts and keeps on living. We headed uphill, and the cherry trees teased up with their pink buds not quite open yet.

Now, the icing on the cake of our morning walk. Zoloti Varota (Golden Gate) stands on the hill as we approach. This is the original entrance to the Kyivan Rus, starting in the 11th century. Here, in my neighborhood, stands this amazing reconstruction of a former dynasty and age. Inside, remnants of the original still stand and are visible. Now, albeit, the truth is that our flat lays at the bottom of a ravine (Yar in Ukrainian) where they probably dumped offal and other waste a thousand years ago. I can tell we live just outside the original city walls based ancient maps of Kyiv that also show topography. Doesn't really matter if we were a dump then. It's not a dump now as I stop and look up at the new balcony we installed. The one Natasha designed as she painstakingly brought an old flat in the center back to life, gave it new energy, and retained the original pieces throughout. She greets me as I walk through the door, and the smell of pork roast teases the senses and makes my stomach growl. But we won't touch it until about 05:30 or so on Easter Sunday after the midnight service. The curfew this year runs from midnight until 05:00, so we won't be there as long as last year. Kyiv City and Ukraine National authorities have given permission to attend services in small numbers this year as long as the curfew is observed. No air raids accompanied the bells of St. Michael's this year, and the night and day passed in peace. The service ended around 03:00, so we all hung out, drank coffee and ate sausages, eggs, sweets and other treats. All the parishioners brought something to share. We left at 05:00 to head home, walk Philly, sleep and then woke up to feast. We are grateful to God and Ukraine.

15

Pulse of War

'Check my pulse, it don't change. Stay seventy-two come shine or rain. Wave the flag, pop the bag, rock the boat, skin the goat.' – Lyrics from US Blues by The Grateful Dead.

A war is almost its own organism, a living thing with a pulse. Like most living organisms, you have to be able to put your finger on it in order to really feel it, to feel the heartbeat of it. Yes, you can read the tea leaves or check the heart monitor from some remote location. You can watch battles and reports, listen to testimony and also get first-person accounts from various social media and messaging apps. But can you feel the actual heartbeat? Does the pulse extend beyond the borders of Ukraine at this point? No, the pulse itself is confined much like it is to an organism that is wrapped in a body. Now, this is not to disillusion those who support Ukraine and are trying with all their might to feel that pulse. This goes into a deeper sense of the war.

We know that in Uzhorod on the far western border of Ukraine, they can barely feel the pulse. In fact, there, it is easy not to feel it because the beat is so faint that it is easy to ignore. Yet, even there, the presence of internally displaced persons (IDPs), international aid organizations, and possibly supplies for the frontlines pass through or exist on the streets. Maybe soldiers are recovering from wounds or other trauma, but the pulse is still faint. No curfews, no major attacks suffered by the population.

In other parts of western Ukraine, like Lutsk and Lviv, which have been hit, there is a stronger pulse. These parts are home to the strongest and fiercest pro-Western politics of Ukraine because of their history and location. They have been targeted, lost electricity, had to hide in shelters and worse, suffered the deaths of innocents. International aid and other shipments move through here a lot. Soldiers on leave and civilians from the East often go there for quiet, away from the intense fighting on the frontlines. These frontliners bring the pulse with them when they come, upping one's sensitivity to war's heartbeat.

Travel southeast to a place like Chernivtsi, which has never been hit by an attack, and you expect the pulse to grow fainter. No, just because a place has not suffered under the attacks does not necessarily mean the pulse is less intense. Territorial Border Guards and soldiers are everywhere. Romania has a consulate in this city. Aid from that country in all forms comes through here much of the time. Heavily laden semis roll through and stop at the truck stop on the edge of the city, where the drivers grab coffee or something to eat at the local choke and puke. Trains roll with passengers on their way from or going to the hot zone. Convalescing soldiers wander the parks and streets on crutches, limping or slightly dazed from their battles on the frontline. Thump, thump, thump, the heartbeat of war in its further extremities.

Take the road now to Ternopil, to Ivano Frankivsk through the Carpathians. Even small villages that pass by have Territorial Defense on duty. Collaborators are caught throughout Ukraine, and the Security Service of Ukraine (SBU) is often nabbing guilty parties in what seem like obscure places. These cities have also been hit with missiles, lost power and muddled through with IDPs and aid shipments. The pulse grows louder here. Sometimes you have to put your finger on it to feel it. While it is sometimes just a faint beat, you can hear it at other times.

Once you begin to approach the Dnipro from north to south, the pounding of war's pulse grows louder. Odesa feels it every day. Cherkasy knows it is right on the river and holds strategic value. Reaching Kyiv, it's like you're standing next to an athlete who just ran a race; the sweat is pouring off, and their heartbeat is loud. You can count the beats here in the heart of Ukraine without ever feeling for the pulse. Sure, you can go into an underground bar and escape it as well. But sooner or later, you have to emerge and hear it. Every subway station shows signs of the war, as does every street. Whether it's anti-tank structures (hedgehogs) or certain buildings with sandbags protecting entrances. Don't ask what they do there; it's not your business. Strictly need-to-know. Know this, the war is being run for the most part from these streets and buildings. Pound-pound-pound goes the beat of war's heart.

Cross the Dnipro in any direction, and the pulse of war grows louder with each kilometer. Dnipro, Kherson, Donetsk, Kharkiv, Mykolaiv and many other cities, towns and villages where the pulse of war is the constant thump of artillery. Doesn't matter if it's outgoing from Ukrainian forces or the incoming from the enemy's guns. It's a pulse, a heartbeat that is always there. One that could drive certain people mad, but soldiers and civilians live through and put up with it 24/7 for well over 400 days now. Maybe you can't call it a pulse anymore. It is the center of the war's life along a front that is very long. Many human heartbeats will stop permanently here today, tomorrow, next week, next month and for who knows how long. But the war will live, and its heavy pounding will continue. Even when the fighting is done, the pulse of the war will beat on until Ukraine is restored. Maybe that pulse will never die in anyone who is living now's lifetime. The scars of it are too deep. Wounds will lie open for many years to come. Not just the wounds of humans but the wounds of cities, fields, villages and the land.

Thump-thump-thump goes the war. Can you feel it? That's the thing, if you can feel it, life is very different. War brings all your faculties to the forefront. It creates a sort of sixth sense, which we'll call 'War Sense.' That's right. Any soldier who has fought in a war will tell you that it's something that comes with the fight. Civilians will tell you it comes with the fight for survival. Either way, we who feel the pulse or hear the constant pounding of war's heart are different than you on the outside. We are the same species, but now we are a war animal. Yes, because our animal instincts or our lizard brains kick in so we can survive as soldiers and civilians. We don't know where the heart of the war actually is, nor do we really care. We want to live, and we want to win. That's our only real objective in life. Nothing else really matters very much. We'll deal with the vagaries of life after the fighting stops. Now, we'll do what we have to, pay attention to what we have to, and live as normally as we can, depending on our situation.

The thing is, we can feel the life of this war. In general, our war sense gives us an idea of what to expect and when. Most of us don't listen to speculation and predictions from those outside the war. That's all based on logic, reason and a lot of wishful thinking. We do listen to what weapons they will send and their official policy regarding Ukraine. We can feel and sense a lot based on the pulse of this war. Not everything but most. We're still existing, working, eating, drinking coffee, watching Netflix, having sex, getting drunk, smelling flowers and all the other little things that seem normal. But how we live is not normal because war is not. We're still on social media and other communication platforms. If you are sitting somewhere comfortable making comments and we blow you off, ignore you completely or hit you with sarcastic dark or gallows humor, don't get your panties in a bunch. We need air defense, attack helicopters, and multi-platform fighter jets, not pity, empathy, speculation, predictions or any of that other touchy-feely malarkey. All you former soldiers out there, ask yourselves this: would you be willing to go on a major ground offensive without proper air defense and support? We need all those things like yesterday. Are you feeling it?

16

Hurry Up and Wait!

Military veterans and those on active duty are well aware of the 'Hurry up and Wait' (HUAW) conundrum. This begins on Day One in most basic training across all the services. Rush, rush, rush and then stand in line at attention, parade rest or at ease for hours to sign some obscure form or get issued some equipment. This is psychological training at its best. I can't speak to whether foreign militaries employ this in their training. Why is it psychological? It teaches one patience under duress. You get this habit drilled into you throughout basic training and again on regular duty, training exercises and any way they can indoctrinate you into HUAW. Why?

Well, for many males of my generation, it began with our introduction into quasi-military structures. What's that? The Boy Scouts of America (I can't speak to the Girl Scouts for obvious gender reasons). What's the motto of the BSA? 'Be prepared.' Looking back, it almost seems that many of us young men were being prepped for a life in the military. That's ok. The US defined itself as a global leader through military intervention in both world wars. We have become absolute experts at logistics, which means planning, staging and launching. This process often takes time, and personnel must 'be prepared' to get their staff and equipment ready, moved into place and then sit around waiting for the launch order. This, HUAW, is an essential skill for soldiers. You must remain alert, sober and ready for hours, days, weeks and maybe even months on end.

Civilians don't get it. Most of the world doesn't get it, especially in this age of instant gratification, responses and results. Ukraine is dealing with this right now. Civil society wants the counteroffensive to happen now! Western observers want it to happen now! In the case of the counteroffensive, patience is a virtue and might also save lives. General Zaluzhny, President Zelensky, General Budanov and all the other Ukrainian leaders know what they are doing and will know when it is best to do it.

Yet, people seem to want the big boom-boom now. What happens if it is not a big boom-boom? Most are also expecting a monstrous thunder run against the Russians, which may very well work and be the case. First, you have to HUAW for the proper reconnaissance, weather, disruption of supply lines and other pieces of the puzzle that must be assembled prior to anything substantial. Additionally, most people seem to forget that Ukraine's Armed Forces are going into this with almost non-existent air support. The Ukrainian Armed Forces (UAF) are well aware of this shortfall and obviously have contingency plans for it.

The explosion at the fuel depot in Sevastopol this morning looked apocalyptic, that's for sure. Really, that's just one event in what will be a series of events that lead to the counteroffensive. Psychologically, that raging fire with smoke forming a massive black cloud that could probably be seen from space has a lot of enemy soldiers and civilians shaking with fear. Yes, it puts a huge dent in fuel supplies, but it also creates the 'It's Coming' effect for all the UAF soldiers who have hurried and waited. In fact, now that this event has taken place, a few more high-profile strikes on strategic locations behind Russian lines on enhances the effect. Why? Well, the Russians don't have the luxury of hurry up and wait.

The enemy is now sitting and waiting. You see, there's the difference. There's the mentality of the offensive military that is moving equipment around, gathering strength, information and plans with a clear set goal. For them, within the HUAW is a clear, defined purpose. Sitting in your trench and waiting for the onslaught that you know is coming and is most likely going to be devastating and will possibly be your personal end is not the same as motivated troops on an offensive. The psychological factor for those just waiting only gets worse as they sit and wait, and wait, and wait some more. Meanwhile, the UAF is eating well, hydrating, and raising morale and confidence. On the other side, Russian troops are poorly fed and just waiting to be killed. This battle looks very different for both sides, and that's what works to Ukraine's advantage.

So, if you are impatient while waiting in the rear or somewhere abroad, go grab a coffee, have a drink, you'll know when it comes. If you're on the front line? At ease, smoke'em if you got'em.

POSTSCRIPT: I edited this chapter on February 23, 2024 after the counteroffensive went nowhere and a complete change of command of the UAF took place. Now, we just hope to hold the defense.

17

Night of Pink Tracer Trails

Kaa-blamm! 03:16 on a worknight. Whizz!!! A missile flies over. Dull-thud-thud-thud of antiaircraft cannons. Scrambling. Grabbing the phone and a t-shirt. Outside the windows, the pink light of antiaircraft tracer rounds lighting up the sky. They look like fireworks from the Fourth of July with their smoky trails. Pow-pow-pow! They hit their target. Suddenly, reverberations from the falling of a downed ballistic missile. The bathroom floor is warm to my bare feet as I set the kitchen chair down that I grabbed passing the windows and was temporarily mesmerized by the pink trails in the sky. We might be here for a while, and it's more comfortable than sitting on the toilet. Natasha is already seated on the heated floor, wrapped in a blanket. Philly is agitated and nervous, his tail wagging a-mile-a-minute as I enter. Ka-bang! Another loud explosion, the flat shakes a little as the debris falls. That's what we wait for now. A slight sigh of relief when it doesn't. We pray that it hasn't fallen on anyone else either. Tonight's debris fell and broke limbs in the Kyiv Zoo. No animals were injured… this time.

I can't recall what night this was now. Since May 1st (2023), this has been happening more nights than it has not. Now, as I write this on May 20th, there is the fuzziness left over from last night's Shaheed drone attacks. Twenty of them were shot down. The Kyiv Zoo night they shot 30 missiles plus drones. That's the night (I think) the Muscovites claimed they had destroyed the Patriot system. Maybe it was the pink trails I saw in the sky. Panic ensued for about a day as the rumors circulated that the Patriot protecting Kyiv had been destroyed. That is until they shot down all the missiles the next night. Air defense or no air defense, the psychological effect is the same. Explosions still mean something is probably going to fall and hit something or, worse, someone. Yes, the fear factor subsides somewhat because the devastating payload of the missile is eradicated. But that shit's gotta fall somewhere. It's not like, oh, explosions again!… Hmmph! Air defense has got it, and I'll just roll over and go back to sleep.

Zombification sets in after multiple nights of disrupted sleep. You see rings under people's eyes as you pass them on the street. Yeah, during the day, we are out on the streets, in the cafes, and walking in the parks. We are alive. We are living our war lives, and unless you were dead drunk, we're all short on sleep. Despite this, we look at each other with will and resilience. Even when someone does or says something stupid, we don't judge or get angry. Maybe they're just tired and not thinking straight. War camaraderie exists in the trenches and in the rear.

Now, don't get me wrong. We tolerate a certain level of moronic behavior. The Night of the Pink Trails is another story. I remember this night clearly because, to my memory, it was the first night we witnessed firsthand the Patriot system in action. Well, turns out, so did a few million people in Russia and around the globe. Yep. Pretty much instantaneously, too. A whole slew of morons was posting the air defense in action as it happened over Kyiv that night. Some of the photos and video were really good. Hey, Putin, lookie here. Wanna know where the Patriot is stationed? Want to see where the antiaircraft cannons are stationed? Let me go ahead and post it all over Telegram, Facebook, Instagram, TikTok and YouTube. How's that, Vova? This is the kind of behavior we can't tolerate.

Ukraine made that pretty clear the next day when they went out and arrested around twenty-three of the increasing number of morons of war who posted that info. The UAF, SBU and a bunch of other official Ukrainian government and defense ministries had clearly stated in the past, 'Don't post images, videos of air defense or any troop movements.' Um, that's pretty clear, right? Apparently not! Turns out that all those who were caught are now facing up to eight years in prison. It's a shame they have to resort to that sort of penalty, but this is fucking national security. So, yea, they only way some people learn is a very direct punch in the nose, lightening of their pocketbook or, well, some serious time behind bars. We see this on the streets of Kyiv in regard to parking where owning a vehicle is allegedly a sign of status…not! Thus, since they have 'status' well, they can park wherever they please. Make sure to bow and kowtow as they exit the vehicle.

Tow truck drivers learn quick. Mayor Klitschko and his retinue are starting to crack down, and that means revenue for someone and loss for another. Illegal parking is being addressed. Now, if only they would outlaw them parking on the sidewalks as well. They never tow the people parked there! It's frustrating as hell to try and walk your dog or just go for a stroll with a bunch of cars parked in what really looks like a pedestrian zone to me. Sorry, I'm ranting, but that's what you do when you don't get a normal night's sleep but once in maybe the last twenty days.

Ok. Ok. Drank some caffeine. Thinking a little more rationally and logically now. Wait. I'll be back in a minute. A dose of chocolate ought to give my brain a good dose of glucose to finish out this chapter. Ok, back to the subject at hand. You should know that the air raid sirens are not loud enough to hear when I am in a deep sleep. Natasha often checks the Telegram channels before going to bed, but if nothing looks imminent, she drifts off to sleep. Ka-boom is often the sound that sends us to our bathroom shelter. I can see the trauma that she suffers, and it pains me greatly. She is younger and has more life in front of her. We again discussed getting away from Kyiv but instead chose to stay. She says she might begin to go to the bomb shelter instead of the bathroom, and I will stay in the flat with Philly. We will have to see how that works out.

POSTSCRIPT: December 30, 2024. Natasha never once went to the shelter and decided it was better to stay at home with us instead of underground with a bunch of strangers.

18

Life's War Chapter

Kyiv May 24, 2023

This war is not our life. Our life is not this war. The war is just a chapter in all our lives in Ukraine and beyond, I suppose. Many have lived their last chapter in this war beginning in 2014. May God have mercy on their souls. Some have been born into war, and it is their first chapter of life. Among them, some had their first and last chapter in this war. Dead children who knew nothing but war from the day they were born until a Muscovite projectile took their little life. How can we feel mercy toward those who would do this to a child? What power has been unleashed upon us? What has that power achieved at the cost of all these lives? Nothing. A blank chapter for one hundred and ninety million Russians or so. We will write that chapter for them when the war ends. Their own people are writing it in Belgorod right now as Russian volunteers fighting for Ukraine infiltrate their own homeland.

Each book of life is different from every other. Those whose books are written with chapters of war may seem completely removed from those outside the war. However, the human condition is also the same now for many, no matter what external circumstances exist. Suffering in war, though, would seem to be its own particular type. It may be the same on a physical level. Lack of food, an empty belly, a cold basement, ringing in the ears from explosions, and burning skin are all experienced on that human level. The feelings of fear, anger, rage, sadness, grief and everything else might be similar. A monk (Archimandrite Zacharias of the Monastery of St. John the Baptist in Essex, UK) once stated that the new human condition of modern life is collective pain and suffering.

There is no breath of life in watching others suffer, even though we in Ukraine may think otherwise of our enemies across the border. Pain and suffering are only making us stronger here. These chapters of suffering in war will soon enough be written and read while the Muscovites are only beginning. Theirs is a chapter they have chosen to write and brought upon themselves. Ours is one we have not chosen but strive to live through no matter what they inflict upon us.

A fool is the only one who may think they are the author of their own book of life. Yes, we all get to write some of the chapters of our book. But it is the Chief Author and Editor who writes the rest. Whether one calls it fate, destiny or God, does not matter.

War makes you realize that the preceding chapters might be relevant or interesting, but it is the now that matters. The past is written and read. A time for edits is over no matter how hard you might try to cover it up. It is the story of life that you will know no matter what you do to bury it. We can bury the dead, but we cannot bury the truth. Many may disagree. We can, however, rise from that past and go from antihero to hero. Well, some of us can. Others may be too tainted or drowning in greed, addiction and other sundry vices.

We cannot write our future chapters. No one can. Plenty out there actually believe they will write them themselves. The one thing we can be sure of is that those chapters will tap into all the genres. Tragedy, comedy, horror, mystery and everything else. Some ending chapters will be absolutely boring, while others will contain a complete transformation. Most of those that are written will just be some variation of millions that have already been written and read. Others will be completely unique, new masterpieces. Masterpieces of human living, of surviving, of giving. Books that only the one who lives them will know. Their stories will die with them, except what is left behind on Instagram, Facebook, TikTok and all the other distractions which steal our lives from us. Most will be judging those books by their covers.

What will your book of life look like? Will you tell your story? The other day, I read a post about the importance of stories to humans. About how most of the sages and other wise ones told stories as a form of teaching. I never looked at it that way. Furthermore, I don't know if our story is interesting to you, only that it seems so to us. We hope we have not bored you so far. We hope what we have told you of our story inspires or makes you think. Right now, I am reading stories written by Ukrainian writers relating to their stories in the war. These stories matter because we can feel them in our own lives because we are here with them. Our cross is upon our backs, and we are carrying it up Volodomorska Hill. We chose to carry it, just like He did. We asked our Father to take the burden from us, but He didn't. So, with as much grace as we can muster, we trudge forward to our own Golgotha just like millions of others in Ukraine. We don't ask for pity, and we spit out the sponge filled with bile when the Muscovites splash it on our mouths. Maybe we will survive. Maybe a missile will kill us.

There is no fiction in war. Everything is real. Maybe some can turn to it for escape, but I have not been able to. Reading fiction during the war is like swallowing a big chunk of dry bread with no water. You chew, and you chew while your mouth grows drier with each bite. Truth is stranger than fiction? I don't know. Life is just more interesting than fantasy. Living has taken on new meaning. Don't get me wrong. I still watch movies and TV shows on Netflix during the war. That's just a mind-numbing escape. Personally, I don't think I could write fiction during the war either. There's just too much truth that still has to be told.

We will keep writing in our book of life until our end comes. We don't know how the story will end. We know we have some small parts to write ourselves, but most will be written for us. Therein, our books, like yours, are a mystery. Embrace your own mystery. Be comfortable with not knowing how it ends or what the next chapter may contain. What I can tell you is this: the war here is just a chapter in the lives of millions. Like all chapters, it will also end. Some will still be born into their first chapter, while others' last chapter will be written before the war ends. Readers, write your own books. Writers, read the stories of others. Stories are what makes us human, whether we are the ones being slaughtered or the ones who slaughter. Yes, their horror stories must also be told, if not by them, then by us.

The sun rises over the Dnipro just like it has every day. We go on, walking the streets and paths of Kyiv. The river flows, the wind blows, the ravens crow, our spirits grow even when our bodies are weary. Ukraine is alive, and she will continue to live. She will lick her wounds, repair her bridges, houses and dams. New buildings will appear alongside parks, museums and businesses. All of them will be part of their Greatest Generation. All of us who will survive this war no matter what our age or nationality. A catalyst for growth, new definitions of freedom, justice and expression. We will die but our art will live, a rekindled civilization and culture. These will no longer be chapters in our war book. They will be a new book that we all write together. And I turn on the soundtrack of that life as I think about it. The music rises, the raspy voice of Bob Seger begins with the chorus 'Here I am on a road again… There I go, turn the page.'

POSTCSRIPT: I began reading fiction again a few months after this post. Most notable I started with *Septology* by Jon Fosse. That book has changed my outlook on some things and reaffirmed my belief in others. I also took a crack at writing some fiction which I hope to revisit at some point to complete.

Photo from Kyiv Art Gallery of Art Depicting Bombed Building.

An old Babycia (grandmother) in our neighborhood who comes out every day on two canes to exercise throughout the war.

An art display of a ballerina made from bullet casings outside Kyiv National Opera.

Sniper Shells from Bakhmut, sent to us by a friend.

Christmas Photo from the ReadEat Bookstore in Kyiv.

Natasha's Chocolate Chip Cookie Day for St. Nicholas Day/Christmas.

Display outside the Frankly Coffee Café, which opened during the war.

Father Bohdan with John as Altar Server at St. Yuri's Church.

A 'Hero' vehicle on display outside the Kyiv City Administration Building.

Above: Home Depot boxes containing aid being unloaded at St. Michael's Monastery.

Left: An art sculpture from Kyiv Gallery depicting the Kremlin on fire with 'cotton'.

Statues of the Founders of Kyiv in St. Michael's Square.

A display of Moscow Patriarch Kirrill outside Kyiv Pechersk Lavra (Monastery).

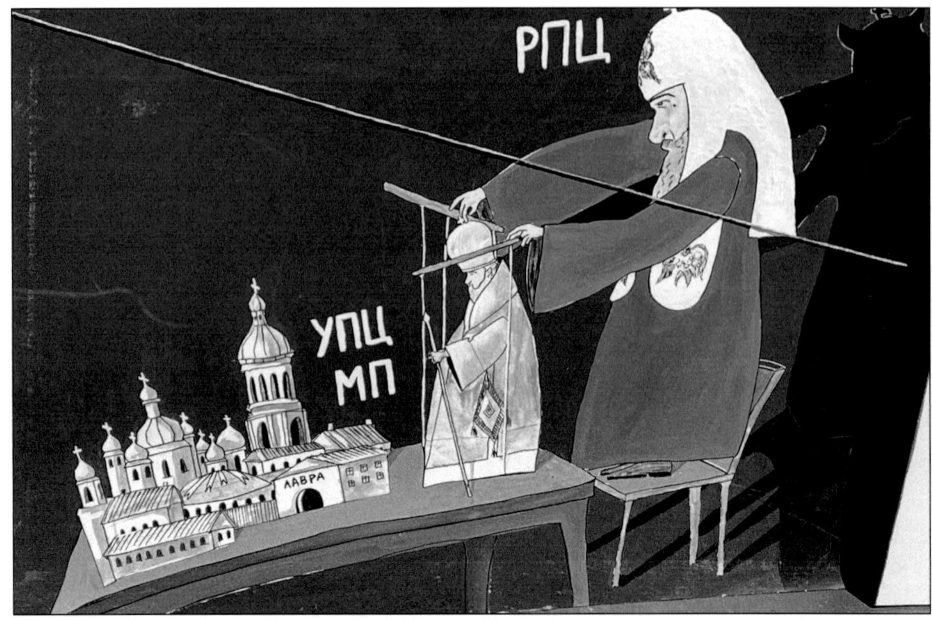

A display showing Russia controlling the Metropolitain Onioufry of Ukrainian Orthodox Church-Moscow Patriarchate.

Our neighbor Lena greeting Philly.

Lilacs in bloom at Kyiv Pechersk Lavra.

A mural on the wall in Lviv, from our trip.

Out for ribs in Lviv.

Natasha's all-time favorite, Lviv ribs.

View from the window of the train in Chernivusti returning to Kyiv.

An empty street with an early morning snow reminder of the Battle of Kyiv.

Flags for the Fallen on Maidian Square, Spring 2023.

Above: Mud season slows down everything at the front. The photo shows how saturated the ground is.

Left: Another example of mud season.

Above: Natasha's first day at work at Pechersk School International.

Right: Natasha's model of the inner ear she made for her Speech Language Pathology class.

Natasha at Golden Gate on Vyshyvanka Day.

Natasha in Warsaw's Old City.

Natasha and a photo in Kyiv while General Zaluzhny was still C-n-C with Putin in handcuffs.

A sign that appeared on our streets during a recruiting and fundraising drive for the AFU.

Philly eyeballing a visitor at our first AirBnB in Chernivtsi.

Philly guarding the spring blooms at Fomin Botanical Garden.

Ominous faceless sculptures at St. Sophia's Kyiv.

Bust of Petro Prokopovych, the first commercial Ukrainian beekeeper, at Ukraine National Beekeeping Museum (Kyiv).

Flowers in bloom at the memorial to Belarusian journalist Pavla Sheremets, who was killed on our street.

Pascha (Easter) at St. Volodymyr's Cathedral. The faithful have come to have their Easter baskets blessed.

Top and British Cossack with John on their Christmas Aid run. Both are veterans of the Queen's Regiment.

Destroyed Russian military equipment on display at St. Michael's.

19

Ukraine War Therapy

May 30, 2023 – Kyiv

There are no longer words waiting to be written or so it seems. The mundane minutiae of everyday life in a war simply takes over. Who cares what I have to say when I don't really care what they say? Tit-for-tat, this for that. Online life seems a waste of time when it takes away from those you can break bread with. It's nice that people care out there, but I can't see your face, give you a hug or drink wine and laugh with you at the table. No more energy for this glowing machine with its promises of connections. Words simply do not wish to come, nor do I wish to share them. There is only life now. Real life. War life.

Yes, the writing for the first 15 months was helpful and most importantly, therapeutic. Engagement with people around the world also brought comfort, but now we are facing the long haul. The truth is that the reality of this war could be our way of life for years to come. We know they will not stop, their desire to destroy is relentless, their resources barely even tapped. No utter destruction of their military-industrial complex will happen. Even if power in the Kremlin changes hands, the hate that exists for Ukraine will not just miraculously go away. Their hate is a cancer that is growing among them. They hate Ukraine now because it has stood up to them, has not fallen and is steadfast in its resolve never to surrender. Some of their own lands and people no longer being safe only makes them angrier and more hateful.

Hate at this level exudes its own energy. You can feel it, smell it, see it. You can only hope that it doesn't infect your own body and soul, but it does. No matter how full of love you may be, rage and anger rise when you see dead children, elderly people and other innocents. You can't just turn away from that and forgive. You have to learn to exist without hate. That means (for me) that I must turn away from this digital non-existence and turn back to those I can touch, feel and see. The people we draw strength from and those we must give strength to. No one else really exists for us in war.

Maybe those who grew up with the digital life cope better than those of us who knew life before all this fake mode. In fact, I admire those who can do it. Their coping mechanisms may be stronger than those of us raised on true human connections. So, I cannot judge the online people because it is their time now. That doesn't mean I have to participate in it just because the world tells me to. What does the world know anyway? We are just a show for them to watch, an episode to read, video images of death, suffering and destruction. Our real life plays out as a fictional existence for most of them. We feel the empathy, the support and the positive vibes, but that doesn't really help many of us coming through in bytes. We need the warmth of a smile, the glance directly in our eyes, a hand on a shoulder.

My story is not yet over, I know that. Yet, I am so very tired of telling it. Now, I go to those who are living similar stories. I sit with them, talk to them or just wave as I pass them on Kyiv's war streets. Sure, I connect online with some, but mostly with others in Ukraine who are fighting, helping or struggling. Life outside Ukraine all seems like Disneyland now. None of it seems real at all even though I know it is. It's just a different reality to that which I now live in. Yes, it was my (our) choice to stay but my (our) principles would not let us just turn our backs and leave. We now face 15 months of this and know that in the future, we may have to leave. This will be as much for physical survival as for psychological.

Gratitude comes to us every day we are alive in the war zone. I am grateful especially to all of those who supported and communicated from outside Ukraine. Truth is, I would not have made it through without that. War is fluid, just like life. Forward movement is what wins wars and leads to success in life. Hardened after this time in war, we must prioritize that which brings security, comfort, and confidence. Someday, it will end. We have to prepare ourselves for that day. We have to be ready to process, grieve and start anew. Life that seems normal will be its own transition. This applies to everyone from soldiers to civilians. We in the rear will need to help those who survived at the front and won the war for us. We will also have to help those who lost everything from loved ones to businesses to property and everything they owned. There will be different echelons from the front to the rear to the diaspora to the world community.

In the beginning, getting the truth out was my highest priority. Letting people outside Ukraine know the history, motivations, atrocities and all other things from just an Average Joe. One who was experiencing the war firsthand told from an American perspective. A lot of people listened and reacted, and I thank you all for that. Maybe I got too personal and now that I have pulled back, you resent it. This is war and I can't expect you to understand the necessity of survival, nor can I really explain it properly. Here's the point of this paragraph. The truth is out there. It has been told, shown, documented, videotaped, telegrammed and everything else. If you don't see it by now, then you are either blind or choose to be blind. I have done my job up to this point.

Now, it is time for the next stage. In this stage, I stay focused on those who I help and those in my immediate live circle. These are the people who stood in church with me (us) as missiles rained down and the service continued. These are the people I have connected with online who go to the front to take supplies or give art therapy to children in Kharkiv, Odesa, Izium, Kherson and other previously occupied territories. Our neighbors who stayed and the people in the neighborhood. Businesses in Kyiv who stayed open or opened early in the war. We must now maintain as we wait for the counteroffensive. None of us have blinders on about this. We know it will most likely not be the decisive victory we all would like to see. Our hopes are not up for that but deep down we all wonder if maybe… just maybe… it will end the war. Yet, we really can't think too much and are sick, tired and fed up with all these experts who tell us how things are going to go. We know they don't know because things change quickly on the battlefield.

Writing therapy is what got me through up until now, but it has lost its usefulness and taste. I have to now prepare to function and recover should the victory come. Additionally, I must at the same time prepare to depart Ukraine if the war drags on. Maybe not permanently, but for at least three to six months. Why? Just to go somewhere and remember what normal life is like. Frankly, I fear normal life now. I fear that I prefer war life. Normal life seems so mundane and meaningless even though I know it isn't. Functioning outside the war zone or after the war is not going to be easy for any of us. We in the rear have no true idea what those in the front are experiencing directly. We are closer to them than most, but our existence is not theirs. They will need our help just as we will need yours. We are depending on our fellow humans to be patient with us as we emerge. We will not be like you anymore. We may never be like you ever again. Some of us will assimilate better than others. Others may never assimilate.

Healing will be essential. Those of us who are strong are already treating ourselves so we can help those who are weaker or have simply suffered far more than we have. Writing was good therapy for nearly fifteen months. The words just no longer come, nor am I interested in writing them. Please don't take it personally, as it is a transitional stage. My new therapy is the pencil, ink and paint. I have moved from writing therapy to art therapy because I have grown tired of thinking. Art allows me to swim in the colors that I use. Vibrant blues of seas that I cannot dip my feet in. Browns and greens of mountains that I cannot climb right now. Painting forces you to be in the picture and in the moment. Outside distractions fade as you craft something with your fingers and hands. I can't say that anything I am working on is good, and well, it doesn't matter, does it? It's therapy, self-prescribed and self-treated. And it's working. The cost of it is abandoning some who were supportive. Survival is selfish. Survival is necessary. Survival is written in our history and DNA, so no excuses are needed.

So, I part for now. Maybe sometimes, a poem will appear if the mood strikes. Maybe even some prose, even though I have no desire for it. There are no new words for now. However, old words, already written are being poured over, adjusted, edited. Some old words are being put in illustrative form. The words are still there in various forms, but I do not wish to tell them. If you run across Ukrainian refugees or displaced persons, please try to be kind and patient with them. Ukrainians are a strong and proud people, but they are imperfect, just like the rest of us. What they are suffering and living through can't really be described by anybody but them. I see it, feel it and live it here with them. But they are going to have to be the ones to tell it from their own unique perspectives.

20

Attention, Teachers and Students!

If I was making a dumb move at the crossroads, it would not be obvious till later. In the meantime, I needed a job in Ukraine. I simply could not sit on my hands, as nice as being a housewife might seem in peacetime: running the house, making new recipes to impress the palate, walking the dog in the city I love… Blah, blah, blah. It sucks you into a trap of comfort and delusion from reality. My mind got tired of the stimulation of reading smart books for pleasure and personal development. It no longer appealed to my senses or reason. Plus, since the war broke out, the majority of my time was wasted on media channels selling hope to civilians. Maybe we are finally going to break through on the eastern front? Did you follow the speech of the so-and-so? Did you know what we hit last night? When will the numbers be confirmed? Does it mean we are making gains? It was a never-ending circle of an 'almost but not quite' vacuum that kept sucking all the life out of you. I felt on edge continually, watching the interviews, following 'experts', making my own predictions, having discussions with John and the neighbors… Nothing changed. Nothing broke through. Nothing big happened. My mind was exhausted from staring at the phone screen searching for the 'truth', or something I possibly missed that would keep me from making informed speculation about the Ukrainian soon-to-be victory. The conclusion was writing itself: too much time on my hands.

So, Ukraine, here I come, looking for a job on the market at war, with an American expectation of a salary to be made on Ukrainian soil for it to be worth my time. I knew one thing for sure: if I couldn't get worthy employment, I would not be able to continue to stay in Ukraine, no matter how much at home I felt in it. It was a long-term impossibility if she couldn't provide for me. The reality was the plan to stay with an expiration date looming around, so I went out to search for my stay ticket.

As it turned out, Benjamin Franklin was right; God helps those who help themselves. The ad for an international school 'hiring now' was around the corner, on Yaroslaviv Val Street, as I was walking Philly one morning. I clung to it with hope and humility, updated my resume, and made a call. Two schools were looking for teachers. Native speakers. Can I call myself that? Almost, but not quite. However, I do prefer English to my native languages for its comfort, structure, the habit of using it daily, and the jokes that somehow sound better in English. My whole adult life happened in this language, so, you be the judge, if it is native or not. To me, it is. My sentence structure starts with an active subject predicate system; it just makes more sense... First of all, my thinking happens in English. I am a different Natasha when I speak it: a self-made person who matured into adulthood in English. It was my passion since fourth grade. I loved everything about it: the logical approach, the movies and cartoons, the ability of it to connect me to the rest of the civilized world. I wanted things in English, I thought about myself in English, my favorite person in the whole world is communicating with me in English, my life as I know it exists in English, and is to be continued, God willing, in English.

That was one advantage I had over everyone else, I kept telling myself. My 20 years of life in the States included multiple jobs, sights, and experiences... It is mine to share or not.

My future employer offered something I was not looking for: a homeroom teacher position, grade 1. Everything I knew about homeroom teaching from the States came flooding into my body, and it reacted adversely. For those of you who have never taught in the public schools of Florida – move on to the next chapter because I am about to ramble for a bit. It helps me process and explains my pitiful 'housewife' situation to those interested. And, if someone out there is reading this and thinks 'I know what it's like, I've been a teacher somewhere', you might want to stick around, and read what I am about to say because otherwise you will be comparing apples and oranges for the rest of your life, and we don't want that. The only way you might know what it's like is if you actually taught in the public schools of Florida. I specify the state because I have not the slightest clue what it is like in any other state as far as the public school system is concerned. The private sector is an entirely different beast altogether. So, let's get to it, and over with it, shall we?

21

Teaching Career Begins

For starters, I was avoiding getting into that profession for as long as I could. Was it true that I got a teaching degree? Check! Was it true that my parents had been telling me I was meant to be a teacher, not a flight attendant (the job of my dreams at 14)? Check! Was it true that my family had already showed a tendency toward teaching degrees and proudly reminded me about the fact? Check! So, excuse me for getting a bit impatient when everyone around assumed in advance that was going to be my path.

Active resistance on my part took me around different career choices that proved to be great life experiences and jobs but have never amounted to careers. I will not get into those just yet. The only thing I will mention at present is that at one point when I was working at a casino in Atlantic City, NJ, I realized I had outgrown that job. It was an easy kind, 6-hour shifts, half an hour break in between, protected by the Union, full health insurance for myself and my spouse, and loads of 'free money' to be collected, if you get 'lucky'. The requirements of my 'intelligence' included smiling, looking pretty in the uniform provided, stepping on the casino floor, offering free drinks to the gambling customers, and collecting 'as much cash as I could carry'. Even this kind of employment eventually exhausts its pros into cons. For me, it was the dread of getting old in that uniform, trying the hardest to compete with 18-year-olds popping out everywhere with perkier limbs in place. I could successfully continue doing so for a long while, but the fact was that I did not want to. I remember looking at 55-year-old waitresses, still in good shape, not hard on the eyes, trimmed in the right places, enhancements done as they should be, because who wanted to look at saggy numbers serving you liquor? Maybe at a diner. A casino floor? Nah. It was not going to be me! I wanted to get older with dignity, on my terms. But the fast-forward scenario of my future in the casino, if I stayed there, would not leave me alone. I had to start a different path, say no to all the cash flowing into my hands and go for a career where I could talk to people about things other than facials, manis and pedis. I might even need to work hard, possibly 40 hours a week?! Wasn't it what normal people did? I also knew I would find every possible excuse in the book to return to the casino or procrastinate to a point of no return to the actual workforce. How long should I wait then, with thoughts like 'why fix what's not broken' coming at me logically, forcefully, persistently?

Moving states, on the other hand, would cut the cord! So, we did. After all, we always wanted to live some place warm with reasonable taxes (sorry, NJ, but you've always been too steep, and I too lazy to earn so much just for your taxes). Palm trees have been seducing suckers like us for a long while. The grass seemed greener over there, temperatures milder, flip-flops year-round... Ha! In our defense, we learned from experience – the best teacher in the world that charges a high price but explains the best.

It took me about a year to get my ducks in a row for American schools. I needed to see if my degree was worth anything there. I was expecting to get an answer stating I needed more college credits, or that my diploma was somehow incompatible, outdated, irrelevant... But come what may, I needed to start somewhere and getting my transcripts in order was it. Much to my surprise, I came out with a master's degree, as I should have, and my GPA in the right digits.

The next step was the exams. All to prove I knew the subjects I was going to teach, but be it in K-6 or K-12 was up to me. I figured I would start small. That decision kept me on the elementary school spectrum for years to come. Much prepping and studying was done prior, except for English. I didn't need prepping. English was my jam! I had a degree in it and was not going to waste any more precious time (which equals money in America) studying it. After my English exam was over, I marched up confidently to the front desk receptionist to get my results. She handed me the paper. I looked at it. It stated: *Not Pass*, so I turned around to get MY paper, not someone else's she obviously handed me by mistake:

> Me: My name is Natasha Sennett (handing over the paper).
> The lady looked at it and replied: Yes. NOT PASS.
> Me: Who got NOT PASS??
> The lady: Natasha Sennett.
> Me: Huh?

Ouch. So, after living in the States for about six years (and with my English degree at that!) I still did not know everything I needed to about the language I spoke and studied extensively in college. My time to claim I was almost a 'native speaker' was not yet. What an arrogant rookie mistake.

The papers were in order eventually. The next step followed: getting the job. I was looking along with hundreds of native speakers right out of college, or tens of hundreds of potential employees with experience, just moving states. Who do you think was a priority in the eyes of the district? No brainer. The job fairs were a waste. I pivoted: I took a substitute teacher position for a year at *literally* every school in the perimeter, hoping they would hire me at some point on a permanent basis as a homeroom teacher. Meanwhile, I needed my experience.

A year passed in ten different schools, with all kinds of classes, teachers, students. The hiring time came about. No one hired me. You might think I was not doing a good job, but that was not the case. My phone number was on a speed dial with teachers who requested me specifically to substitute in their classroom for weeks in advance. Then what? It turned out one more requirement was not met. Yet another exam. The most extensive one. The one I was told could be done after I got a job. However, when it came down to it, I could not get a valid teaching certificate without it. Therefore, I needed to retrace my steps. I did. A few months were devoted to learning various teaching strategies I needed to know to get my PASS result after a two-and-a-half-hour exam. But before another school year started, I needed something solid. Searches followed, extending to schools no longer in my living perimeter. I wanted my own classroom. I was ready. There was not a chance for me to pass the exam and secure a job at the same time. It was either or at the time. So, I kept studying and looking for a job that would take me on a leap of faith that I would pass the exam later, a contingency of sorts.

June was under way. The worst possible timing to secure a job. It smells of the last-minute hires and desperation for both sides. My hopes were low to either get a decent school or a homeroom teacher position. I couldn't sleep one night, stressing out over my situation of going back to being a substitute for another year. I got up and sent an email around 5 am to some schools still looking to hire. At eight am sharp, I was on the phone with the receptionist of a school an hour and a half away from my home. By 10 am I had an interview with a principal, an assistant principal, and a leader of the second-grade team, all seated across from me in one tiny office. I came out with a contract, starting July, and hurried over to John to share the joy.

22

Teaching Career Ends for Good?

My first official public school position was in a Title 1 elementary school in Auburndale, Fl. If you have ever experienced working in a Title 1 school, then you know everything it entails: classrooms full of diverse students, low school budgets, overworked teachers, and, most likely, an overall school grade that urgently needs to go up from either F or D to the next best option.

That typically means the district will be at the school and in your classroom regularly, adding pressure to an already stressful environment. That scenario would often include a more affluent school being built in the neighborhood that immediately begins a very strict student selection process (no student with a grade lower than B would ever see the inside of that establishment, and, in most cases – only an occasional B will seep through the cracks). That means all the 'better academically endowed' kiddos have already left or are on the way out. Can you blame the parents for wanting a better environment for their child?

The Title 1 school, on the other hand, is left to educate children of migrant workers coming to the state to pick oranges or other fruit, which in itself is not an issue other than their children's brief involvement will contribute to an overall grade of the school where they settle for a few months. Typically, after the picking season is over, those families are never to be seen or heard of again. But the overall grade of the school reflects the 'contribution' of the children who passed through it.

There is another piece of the puzzle: the students of families where education was never a priority for anyone, but a free breakfast and lunch was, might find themselves in a Title 1 school. And, finally, the small percentage of good ole hardworking, blue-collar families who are trying to educate and raise their children right, sending their kids to a public school, making sure they listen to the teacher, do their best, and try to make something of themselves when they grow up. See, all of it comes into play for the overall school 'performance'. Everyone 'contributes', and the grade shows what it shows. The district tends to overlook all the factors in favor of one: the teachers and the administrators of such schools do not do their jobs; therefore, we need to show them what teaching is all about. So, they come, all in suits, looking strict and professional, judging everyone's performance, coming up to the students at random, asking them 'what are you learning about'… The teachers praying they wouldn't ask that one 'particular student' because they would not respond immediately or intelligibly (why would they? They came to school yesterday straight from Puerto Rico and they don't speak a word of English). And so it goes, day after day, year after year… Students learning to the test, teachers teaching to the test, everyone shaking over the numbers the students will show towards that grade. See, unnecessary stress for everyone. Then, we add the paperwork for each individual child in the classroom for differentiated instruction, Tier 2 and 3 students that are no longer at the top of the pyramid – but are the pyramid, and here you have it – a perfect recipe to become a burned-out teacher.

I burned out, just a tad. I loved the kids and the magic times we managed to have despite the insanity of the educational system, but loads of paperwork, data collection, Professional Learning Communities (PLCS), professional development courses, mandatory trainings, summers full of everything at once, plus the classroom-take-apart at the end of the year/setup for the upcoming school year was getting heavier by the minute, with no time in the 24 hour stretch to do it all.

After about six years of my husband doing almost all the housework, renovations, cooking, and shopping while having a full-time job, he informed me that I needed to quit. Just like that. As much as I was fighting the concept of being a quitter, I was also conscious of the fact that I looked seven years older than my age, pushing into a 'hag' category by the minute (because I just couldn't remember if I took my shower earlier that morning or was it last night before going to bed??). I was well on the way to a 'cancer candidate highway' due to the stress of it… So, I agreed. It was settled: I was not going to be a teacher ever again!

When my future principal of Pechersk International informed me that they were looking for a homeroom teacher, I wasn't thrilled. I was going for an ESL support position I wanted (no stress of building anything from scratch, no teaching seven (7) subjects, procedures, thinking skills… the list goes on when you are a homeroom teacher). It pays less but comes with a glorious peace of mind, and you get to leave your work at work. No more planning till 11 pm! I wanted to know what that felt like. Plus, first grade strongly implied you were going to deal with a 5-min-ago-diaper-factory, a bit harsh, I know, but that's how I imagined it to be: too needy. I replied, 'thanks but no thanks', and continued my search. I landed a few interviews in the process, but somehow, that first-grade position kept coming at me from all angles. Eventually, I thought it was the Universe trying to tell me something, and I needed to respond with a 'yes', regardless of my position on the six-year-olds. After much deliberation, I ended up taking the job at PSI as a homeroom teacher, grade 1.

We were staying put. Ukraine had spoken.

23

A Fresh Start and a Bump

The excitement I felt to begin teaching again was two-fold. First of all, if you ever (better never) find yourself in a war that is not obviously coming to an end but takes on the shape of a marathon, it's better to find a long-term job/volunteering/occupation that takes you out of your misery and occupies the mind with productive versus destructive thoughts and helps someone along the way. I knew this job was going to be a saving grace for me. I desperately needed schedules, routines, lessons to teach and knowledge to share with those who wanted it. Plus, working with children is so much more rewarding than working with adults. They are so much better than us, not yet tainted by the world, authentic in every expression of their little personalities that you can't help but feel blessed and privileged to be a part of their journey, even on the rough teaching days.

Another thought pattern has gradually settled with clarity as an inspiration of sorts, and I wanted to share it here. Having a school reopen in the midst of a war was a huge risk. No one can predict the future, but one can consider the odds. I am glad those odds were not the driving force behind that decision! The step was bold and heart-warming. It united teachers, students, parents, maintenance and management as an island of hope. It has captured a long-gone sense of normalcy and brought it back to all of us.

With that amazing feeling, my school year had begun, and with it, a very familiar sense of chaos that comes with setting up classrooms, getting the list of students, getting to know your co-workers, general surroundings, procedures, protocols… It was a breath of fresh air: a welcomed chaos completely unrelated to the war. My head space was occupied with more pressing matters: do I want my tables round or rectangular, my bookshelves to the left or right, my bulletin boards blue or yellow, my projector lamps, cords, and beanbags brought in gradually or at once? Somehow, it felt like I had never left my teaching job. I was simply taking a long nap.

The difference between my previous experience and the current one was not one but many. I didn't realize it at the time, but I landed a teacher's dream job (it only works if you have *enjoyed* teaching before). The number of students in the classroom was only a third of what I was used to. I also had a co-teacher (basically my right hand in all things organizational), working with me daily side-by-side, which meant I was given permission to breathe, prepare for my lessons, differentiate many tasks, and go to the bathroom when I needed to! On the other hand, I have never taught in Ukraine or in a war zone.

At the start of the year, I was informed that, at some point, I had to travel abroad. My visa status needed an upgrade and the only possible way to accomplish that was during my October break. Unfortunately, it meant the hassle of traveling during the war (John flat out refused to be OK with having me go out of the country on my own and separate for that long). If you are the person who lives to travel, explore, and soak up the new exciting views forever to be treasured, and filling up your bucket list to the brim with all possible travel entries in your passport is like your life's mission… Even then, traveling abroad during the war would be a hassle for you.

The nearest country with a Ukrainian Embassy was Poland. John and I are the type of folk who actively seek something positive in any given situation as a self-preservation mechanism. We were coming up on four years straight with no real vacation behind or ahead. It was time. During the war? Maybe, if traveling is sort of imposed on you, so be it!

John had taken time off from work specifically for this occasion. We even started to look forward to it a little bit. A week of that was going to be in Warsaw running errands in between, but, hey, we no longer remembered what it was like to sleep through the night with both eyes shut in peace. Philly, the dog, was coming with us, his papers ready, and an AirBnB was rented in walking distance of the old town. We booked a car service, dog-friendly, comfy and fast. You see, the last time we went to Chernivtsi by train, Philly ripped his nail straight off on the twisty iron step in the middle of the night, trying to jump down to tinkle during the stop. No one saw what happened until we got back on the train, and I felt something sticky dripping down my hand. A flashlight revealed a blood bath inside the train cart. The conductor was super sweet and helpful about the mess, but blood was everywhere! And my poor dog had a raw-looking paw for a month to come.

So, this time, we changed things up a bit.

Philly loves traveling. He pokes his wet nose all over the glass, changes his spot for a better view in the back seat every ten minutes, completely disregards anyone's personal space, and prefers to have a window cracked open just enough to stick his head out, eyes filled with bliss, tongue hanging out in the wind. Oh, the joy (maybe not to the driver of the vehicle)!

The ride started out smooth and promised adventure. We settled peacefully, enjoying the view, the junk food (hello Nathan's hotdogs, what's up), and the whole enchilada of a long car ride. Eight hours or so, give or take, based on the traffic and some checkpoints along the way. We switched the drivers and a vehicle in Lviv, as we were approaching the border and needed a person with a permit to leave the country. The first question he asked was if Philly's papers were in order. I reassured him. Somehow, he kept pressing the issue, sharing unpleasant stories and 'harshing my mellow'. I double-checked the papers, just in case, and he seemed satisfied.

The Ukrainian-Polish border was backed up for miles. It took us almost four hours to finally get to the checkpoint. My lawyer called twice to straighten out a few 'questionable details' the guards had regarding my papers. Everything was checked, double-checked, and questioned just to the breaking point of your will to move on to another border and do it all over again. Slow, tedious, nerve-racking.

Yet, we finally crossed to the Polish side. The waiting continued for a few hours. Our turn came up for a car search and other pleasantries, around midnight. Philly was tired but actively protecting my 'bubble' from an invasive gentleman by staring him in the eye but not yet growling. The guard requested my dog's passport and other traveling documents. Yes, sir! He examined everything for what seemed like an hour. Unsatisfied, he requested one more 'document'. I replied that was everything I had. He proceeded to tell me there had to be a form signed by the state-owned vet clinic in Ukraine, stating my dog was fit to travel. I asked if Philly's passport did not have everything listed (all the recent vaccinations and stamps)? *It did.* However, the proper way of crossing the border was to have Philly's international passport *plus* the paper from the state clinic stating all the above on a different template as additional insurance.

I felt a knot in my stomach that somehow paused my breathing. I swallowed, anticipating a disaster I had no control over. It was done: without that wretched piece of paper, he was not letting us into the country. As the driver took a hard turn around to head back to the Ukrainian side, my heart was pounding in my temples. I was wide awake at that point, and a few hours of waiting in a gigantic car line to get back to Ukraine did not help me settle.

Ukrainian guards: Didn't you just...What happened? The process of admittance started all over.

When we were done at the border, the driver needed to know where we were going. John and I needed to think. I wanted to go back to Kyiv and call it off. So, what if I won't be able to work? I will decide when I am not furious with all of Poland! John was echoing my stress in his baffled response. The driver, God bless his heart, heard both sides of the story and offered a suggestion: what if you just slept on it in Lviv, and tried to locate the state clinic in the morning (Sunday)? Now, that was a plan! I booked a dog-friendly hotel ten minutes later, and we crashed in the room next door to a party of sorts, loud, young, and obnoxious. Last thing I remember was drifting off to some bad pop tune circa 1995.

The following morning was wet, brutally cold, and windy. We set off on a wild goose chase to some clinics that could issue the special paper. We got soaked through, trying. Only private vet clinics were open on Sunday. Nice, warm, polite, ready to sign whatever, but it was of no use to the border guards that specifically required a state clinic form. My last resort was a state clinic located at the back of the train station. We ran as fast as we could. Philly must have thought it was a racing game, dragging me full force, leash tight and snappy, until I sprinted in the freezing rain.

The vet clinic was closed. At that point I sank on the little step right by the entrance, and tears of frustration and fury poured out as if someone flipped the switch. By the time John caught up with us, I couldn't explain intelligibly what I was feeling at the moment, other than telling him it was over. See, my appointment at the consulate was on Monday afternoon, in 24 hours. John offered a solution: I could still make it to Poland with the driver, if I left alone. Meanwhile, they would stay in the hotel and wait for me in Lviv. I didn't see a better option, all things considered. My ability to stay in Ukraine depended on a multiple-entry visa, which would be issued in Poland. My current temporary residence permit was expiring in a few days.

The trip back to the border felt like some dark cloud gripped my entire body. During the war, under regular bombings and chaos, the sense of being together through it all gives you strength. If we were to die, I did not intend to leave my husband by himself, not after we made it through an entire year of war, going on two. I also know that Philly likes it when we are all together, otherwise he gets stressed out. God had pity on me. The road was smooth and fast, the sun was shining out of season, the lines to the checkpoints were nowhere near to be found, as if everyone has already left yesterday. I couldn't enjoy any of it. I don't think the whole crossing the border to the other side procedure took us longer than 40 minutes. By that point, the guards warmed up to me and even managed a compassionate smile of sorts.

The Polish side was just as quick. Same checkpoint as the other night, different guard. A much more pleasant individual, who took his time asking about the refusal stamp in my passport from the other night and what the problem was. I explained everything. He said, 'You should have asked him to get the vet on call to come and quickly examine the dog'. Was that an option? I did not know! But *the guard knew*. He could have accommodated as they often did in such situations on the border, but he didn't. Now, instead of thinking about the horrendous bureaucratic procedure we all had to follow, I had simply encountered a very small petty man on a power trip. I thought about his choice that night and decided to bless, not to curse. But you know, karma does what it does to all of us.

I was exhausted by the time my driver pulled up to the flat in Warsaw. The host was checking in frantically (whatever the reason, I ask you??, just tell me where the keys are!) because she wanted to meet in person and show me where everything was. Huh? You must think I was a prize idiot to be unable to figure out my way around a two-room flat. Be that as it may, she waited up until 2 am by the entrance. Forgive me, but at that point I was not in a very social mood to be thinking and remembering where the light switches were and how to turn on the stove. For crying out loud! It was ten years behind in terms of appliance progress in the big wide world. The observation I made was that the lady must have never set foot in Ukraine before. I kept my cool but withheld a review afterwards and left the flat a few days early. Sorry, but in Ukraine, we keep the washer and dryer in the flat where we live, not in the attic, sharing it with the entire building after you sign in your name. And on the way out, don't forget to record the amount of water you used for a load of washing: that means you need to remember what the meter was saying on the washing machine before you placed your load there! I decided to bring my dirty laundry back to Ukraine and wash it at home in peace. I was not amused! John had a chuckle when I told him about the 'protocol' of doing laundry in a certain apartment building in Warsaw.

My visa was upgraded at the consulate, and absolutely nothing was going to prolong my stay in Warsaw. I gave myself an extra day to wrap up a module of my IB PYP training I was simultaneously taking online during my autumn break and hopped on a Flixbus as soon as I could.

One little glitch on the way back kept me nervous: my suitcase lock got jammed. It locked all right but wouldn't open, no matter how hard I tried to play with it or change the lock combo, it just wouldn't budge! My concern was the borders again. What if they asked to open it, and I would be left behind to fetch for myself in the middle of nowhere? I saw what happened to 'suspicious' individuals at the border: the driver is not obligated to wait for anyone, a 'not my circus, not my monkeys' kinda situation. The worst-case scenario remained in my head until we hit the border and waited patiently to be allowed to leave Poland and enter Ukraine. But all is well that ends well!

The bus pulled up to the same station in Lviv that housed the state-owned vet clinic (the one that closes on Sundays and has obnoxiously long lunch breaks). But my attitude was different now, I was coming home, with an upgraded visa in my pocket, a secured stay for a couple of years in Ukraine, and a few days left to enjoy Lviv with my family. So, we did! The best ribs I have ever tasted (and I know my way around meat) were in Lviv! I still remember the look, the aroma, the savory melty goodness of that unpretentious joint that I would travel to again in a heartbeat just to have those ribs again! People who know us call us foodies. I am not sure about all that, but I do enjoy good food. As a matter of fact, John and I bonded over food when we were just friends, twenty-three years ago. Lviv had satisfied our palate, reunited us safely, allowed for some shopping and fun along the way, and sent us back to Kyiv.

Lesson learned: not everything that starts out bumpy, ends that way. The lemonade out of Polish lemons turned out to be palatable. It might have lacked refreshment and zest, but it certainly made for a good story.

24

July 4th From the New War for Independence

This weekend in the country of my birth and citizenship, people will be celebrating at barbecues, picnics, beaches and their own backyards. They will be commemorating the signing of the Declaration of Independence on July 4, 1776, by the Continental Congress at Independence Hall in Philadelphia, a place just twenty-five minutes by car from the house where I grew up. We visited it regularly on class trips and as individuals because it is one of the pillars of the American Republic. Fireworks will take place in the evening, but I cannot imagine anyone here in Ukraine wanting to hear them right now as they are, in fact, banned during the war. The rockets' red glare and the bombs bursting in the air here are the real ones.

Let's take a minute and remember our own Declaration of Independence, which, when accusing King George states:

'He has plundered our seas, ravaged our Coasts, burnt our towns, and destroyed the lives of our peoples.

He is at this time transporting large Armies of foreign Mercenaries to complete the works of death, desolation and tyranny, already begun with circumstances of cruelty and perfidy scarcely paralleled in the most barbarous ages, and totally unworthy the Head of a civilized nation.

He has constrained our fellow Citizens taken captive on the high seas to bear Arms against their Country, to become the executioners of their friends and Brethren, or to fall themselves by their Hands.'

Ukraine is now suffering almost word-for-word what is stated above by the tyrant in Moscow and his countrymen and women. The Black Sea is under a naval blockade where cities and villages have been burned to the ground, killing women, children, the elderly and others. Mercenaries from Chechnya, Syria and other places have been employed by this despot for the murder and rape of Ukrainians. Residents of Donetsk and Luhansk have been conscripted to kill their own people. This is just the tip of the iceberg of comparisons that we Americans, who fought so bravely in battle those two hundred and thirty-six years ago, could make. Battles that were fought just a bike ride from my home at Red Bank Battlefield (Fort Mercer), where my distant relative, Jonas

Cattell, ran 10 miles from his home to warn the troops there that Hessians (foreign mercenaries) were coming to attack them in October 1777.

Ukraine's Lexington and Concord have names like Irpin, Bucha, Hostomel, Chernihiv and that of other small villages along Russia's path of destruction when their troops first entered this country. The Minutemen of Ukraine are not only men but also women who go by the name of Territorial Defense Forces. They gathered and took up arms immediately after Russia crossed into Ukraine. I went to sign up on the third day of the war and was turned away because they had more volunteers than they had weapons.

This is not Russia's war. This is Ukraine's War for Independence. Ukraine may not have a Jefferson and an official Declaration of Independence. Maybe they don't need one because the despot in Moscow wouldn't even read it, and they declared their independence on February 24, 2022, when they resisted the invasion. Russia has, for over 500 years, treated Ukraine as a vassal state. Citing another great American document, Ukraine issued its own Emancipation Proclamation from being a slave to Russia back in 2014 at the beginning of the war that is currently raging.

Lincoln said:

> 'And by virtue of the power and for the purpose aforesaid, I do order and declare that all persons held as slaves within said designated States and parts of States are, and henceforward shall be, free...'

Ukraine said this collectively to their assumed masters in Moscow when they refused to accept the slavery of those who would rule over and subjugate them. They took up arms and stood their ground in the Donbas and are now doing it all over Ukraine. You can almost hear those Ukrainian voices quoting our great and famous Declaration of Independence, which states:

'But when a long train abuses and usurpations, pursuing invariably the same object evinces a design to reduce them under absolute Despotism, it is their right, it is their duty, to throw off such Government, and to provide new Guards for their future security.'

Moscow has assumed its rule over Ukraine since at least the 1600s. Ukraine has attempted independence before. Ukraine stated it was independent in 1991, but now in 2022, it is showing the world that it will fight and die to the last person standing for that independence. My fellow, Americans, their story is not all that different from ours. I am here with them. I see it every hour, every day. They are strong-willed and brave and are only seeking that which our forefathers sought all those years ago on the battlefields of our original Thirteen Colonies. Ukrainians, like us, are seeking the right to Life, Liberty and the Pursuit of Happiness.

We, the people of the United States, should be doing all we can to help the Ukrainians achieve complete independence. Would our forefathers have settled for partial independence? Would you settle for it, given the option? This is what we must understand about our brothers and sisters in the fight for a new democratic republic. Their fight is our fight, and it is based on the same principles that we hold so highly, no matter what our own political leanings may be.

America and the United Kingdom were foes in our War for Independence. Now, we, along with the Brits, must play the role that France did in our Revolutionary War. Yes, we are doing it to some extent, but we have not sent them a Lafayette. We have not sent ships to undo the naval blockade. We need not do it alone nor under the auspices of NATO. We can use our power and influence to get the job done.

Ukraine's War for Independence is also ours whether we like it or not. I see the bravery and resolve of these Ukrainians every day. Their desires are the same as ours. Their will to fight and die for freedom is the same as ours has been through so many wars. Since day one of this war, I have been here on the ground in Ukraine with them all doing what I can when I can. I love the stars and stripes, but now I also love the blue and gold. Yes, I am a Patriot of Ukraine, and all I ask is that in whatever way you can, you join me and so many others in standing with Ukraine in its War for Independence. May God have mercy on all of us. God Bless America... and Ukraine. Happy 4th of July... have a hot dog and a hamburger in my name, please.

25

Morning Missiles from Muscovy

September 21, 2023

05:37. This is my missive on the morning missiles from the Muscovites. Vreem! Vroom! Sounds singing over our heads in our slumber. We slept through the Air Raid Alarms as many here do. That's how the malicious, malcontent marauders murder more and more. Killing us not so softly with their song. This morning, our war intuition woke us up and we could hear the KH 101 missiles flying their patterns overhead. No time to go to the shelter, so we used our only chance, standing under two retaining walls. That's our go-to most of the time. You go outside to run to the Air Raid Shelter and run the risk of missile debris falling, injuring or killing you. Usually, I think of a few lines from Bob Seger's song *Night Moves* when the explosions wake us up. They came into my head as we sat and listened to the Kyiv Air Defense shooting the missiles down. The lines are this 'I woke last night to the sound of thunder. How far off I sat and wondered? Started hummin' a song from 1962. Ain't it funny how the night moves?' Now, I haven't changed the words to reflect the woe of war life. There are just certain tunes that trim the terror a tad in war.

We got the All-Clear and Natasha started getting ready for work. I made coffee and sat with the dog, getting ready for our morning constitutional. Funny that I wanted to get up earlier today as I had some errands I wanted to run before starting my remote duties in the US at 11:00. No, not nutty enough to need missiles for a wake-up call. Natasha made her way out the door to her job in another district and I decided to finish my coffee before taking Philly out for a walk. Telegram Channels already showed some of the damage from the missile salvo. Parts of the district north of us lost power. Somewhere, missile debris fell on a gas line. Here we go again! The Muscovites are studying the energy grid again and looking for vulnerabilities. They will probably find some, and we will have another long, cold and possibly dark winter.

07:23 (or thereabouts). Eerie screech of that blasted Second Air Raid Alarm! I worried as Natasha was still probably in her rideshare when the alarm went off. This is not our first time apart when the attacks come. We have to earn a living, and her job requires offline presence. WhatsApp is our go to, and sometimes Telegram. She quickly answered that she was already safely in the Air Raid Shelter at work. Offline employers have to have close access to shelters. Natasha works at a school, and they are required to have their own air raid facilities for students and staff. She asked me if I heard any additional explosions and I replied in the negative.

08:13 (or thereabouts). The Air Raid All-Clear message came in across my phone. I gotta get movin, gotta get goin, grab the dog and get out the door. Usually, the streets of Kyiv are bustling this time of morning. People are in line at the coffee kiosks. Others are walking briskly to work. Not today. It wasn't empty like it was during the Battle of Kyiv. There are now more people in Kyiv than before the full-scale invasion, or so we are told. It makes sense. Millions have been displaced from where the fighting is concentrated. International visitors, volunteers and whatever else people who come to a war zone do are milling about constantly. Once you have endured war this long, you get a sense for who is who. I am guessing that the street activity this morning was at about 35% of what it is normally. There were not many other dog walkers out, so we made our way through the Fomin Botanical Garden without any major encounters. Philly is not a fan of other dogs, so this was a welcome peace for me.

09:11. Weird time now that I look at it. That's when Philly and I got home. He needed feeding, and his paws cleaned from the grit of the Kyiv streets. Within seven minutes, he was curled up and ready for a nap. I grabbed my backpack and set off for my errands. The first stop would be St. Volodymyr's Cathedral and as I exited my building, a car was blasting Depeche Mode's 'Personal Jesus'. First, this made me smile and remember my younger days when I was a metalhead, and Depeche Mode's music was for *derogatory word*. However, after the pride and stupidity of youth passed away, I found out that I actually liked the music. Lyrics lifted from the car stereo speakers 'Reach out and touch faith.' Hah! Strange coincidence. You see, I was on my way to visit the relics of St. Barbara. She is our protector from sudden death and missile attacks. So far, she has done that for us, our clergy and our friends. Knowing she is there just a five-minute walk away brings comfort. Of course, I visited the icons of other Saints, but she is there, spiritually and physically. You can put your hand directly on the coffin where she rests. Today is also the celebration of the Nativity of the Theotokos (Mary) but I did not have time to stay for the service due to errands and work.

10:02. My next stop was the pet store. Philly needed food and some of his preventative medicine for heartworm and the like. Tired eyes were all around. You could sense that tiredness throughout, and some had that foreboding sadness

> of a rough winter to come. Cafes that usually are full and bustling at this time of day sat empty. Kyiv is a tightly packed city, and we live in the center. Thus, anything we don't order online, we have to physically walk and pick up. Owning a car in the center is pretty much like living in Times Square and owning one. It's ludicrous. Loaded up with Philly's food, I humped uphill to make another stop. Today, I would be buying 'sausage rolls', which are basically full-size pigs-in-a-blanket. Titka Klara (translates as Aunt Clara) is my go-to for these junk-food goodies.

That also got me thinking. It would be so easy in war to eat like a maniac and become obese or sink into alcoholism or drug addiction. I can see the reasons as in, well, probably gonna die anyway, so what's the point in trying? Screw the Muscovites. We're living life to the fullest. Ok, you want to make us sleep-deprived? Go ahead. Most of us will live no matter what you shoot at us. So, we are going to eat healthy and live life. BTW, Kyiv is very hilly, and run a few errands in a day with a heavy backpack and, well, there's your cardio.

So, as I am about to enter Titka Klara, I can hear the orchestra of the Kyiv National Opera rehearsing. Those sounds! Kyiv is alive with the sound of music! Yea, maybe they started late but they were at it. I enter Titka Klara and place my order. Again, music. This time it is Fleetwood Mac's *The Chain*; a song I have long loved and also a reminder that Ukraine will not be stopped. We will live, we will sing, and we will eat junk-food! Well, on occasion, we'll eat junk-food.

The last stop with a heavy backpack, which reminded me of forced marches with a rucksack, would be the local convenience store Kolo. Elena, who has been here since the beginning of the full-scale invasion, was behind the counter. She is one of the 'ones'. As in, the strong ones who stayed. We all know who we are, and there is that unspoken acknowledgement as our eyes meet. I grabbed five liters of water and two liters of sparkling mineral water and headed home. The heavy load weighed on me as I climbed the four stories of my walk-up. Well, a little strength training combined with cardio means I already burned some sausage rolls, eh?

That was my day, up until I unpacked everything and started work. Now, I don't know where you are or what you do for a living. But here's what I will leave you with. If we can live through this shit, how bad can it be elsewhere? Next time you feel self-pity, remember the strength of the human spirit and all of us in Ukraine.

26

Christmas Story Ukraine

December 16, 2023

Christmas Spirit. Is it something we learn, or does it naturally exist inside us? In the US and UK, it is ingrained within us, and I am not talking about the consumerism side. There's that energy that fills our souls and spills over into those around us as we spread it around. Ukraine has not quite grasped it to the full extent yet. They are still trying to shake off prioritizing the Soviet worship of New Year. New Year's is celebrated in almost a cultish fashion throughout Ukraine, Belarus and Russia. Christmas takes a back seat to it, but Ukraine is now in the process of changing that. Some are beginning to catch that fever of giving, joy, celebration and the Christmas Miracle. These past few days I have been part of an event that so fulfilled within me that Christmas Spirit that it is important to tell all of you about it. First, it requires an introduction to the characters and a bit of a backstory, so grab some hot chocolate, throw on your warm pajamas, let the Christmas lights glow in the background and give yourself just enough light on your screen to read. Ready?

Let's start with the characters and I can't give actual names other than myself and my wife Natasha. Now, I must say also that this is just one event in Ukraine's Christmas season in Kyiv for Natasha and me. We have had others and will have more, I am sure, as we are still nine days from the holiday. So, here is the cast of characters:

Grizzly – Now, he is not called Grizzly because he is angry like a bear but because he is a Ukrainian biker who helps the military. So, the name is apt. I met Grizzly on Medium, and we have now been working together for over a year, helping a military unit at the front. He is a private person, as am I, so I'm only giving as much info as needed for this story. Grizzly and I have never met in person, but we hold a bond of brotherhood that is as strong as any in person.

UTCBN – The Unit That Cannot Be Named is who Grizzly and I support.

BC – British Cossack is the name of a twenty-seven-year veteran of the British Military that I met through a Facebook Group (EEMC) over a year ago as well. This story revolves around BC's eleventh trip to Ukraine with military and humanitarian aid. BC and I have worked together at a distance but met in person for the first time on his tenth trip a few months ago. BC was kind enough to bring this Yank a nice supply of Marmite. BC and I have also formed that bond of brotherhood, and we have broken bread twice to seal it so far.

Top – Top is the name for a British veteran and former Sergeant Major who served for twenty years with BC. I also met Top through the EEMC Group thus discovering the link to BC. Top has revealed that he has long-term PTSD from serving in conflicts in the Middle East. He decided to come despite that to meet Grizzly and support BC. This is his first visit to Ukraine.

PT – PT is another guy I met in the EEMC Group who is from my side of the river in South Jersey. PT plays a support role for another organization that serves one of the only other US citizens that has been in Ukraine the whole time and is based in Lviv. PT and I have worked on fundraising, information dissemination and other projects related to the war. He is a Physical Therapist, hence the PT, and former US Army medic. PT has a young family, so can't really come to Ukraine without getting in big trouble with his wife.

Nicky – Nicky is the money man from what Top has told me. So, we are calling him Nicky in deference to St. Nicholas. Nicky has spent a very large sum helping Ukraine on various fronts since the invasion began to include housing upwards of forty families and supporting up to four hundred displaced persons since February 2022. Nicky has been doing most of his support up until now from a top-down perspective but is now more interested in assisting those who are directly involved. Top brought Nicky into the loop due to their friendship and association in their respective professions in the UK, where they have worked together for some years. This is Nicky's first trip to Ukraine since the invasion.

Philly FF – Philly French Fry is somehow associated with Nicky from what I can gather. One learns not to get too personal or ask too many questions. Philly FF is now a French citizen, although originally from Philadelphia. Top, Nicky and BC all say he looks like General Custer, but I say he is 'The Dude' from *The Big Lebowski*. Philly FF has also sponsored and housed Ukrainian Displaced Persons. His part in the story is minimal, but there is an important element that must be told. I never met him (until now) or knew about him other than he is also on his first trip to Kyiv since the invasion.

UA Ants – This is an NGO that stayed behind the scenes but helped with paperwork on this shipment and all the ones that came after. They are Grizzly's partners and now ours through him.

The EEMC Facebook Group – Eastern Europe's Modern Conflict = EEMC. This is a closed Group on Facebook that requires an invite or vetting through answering various questions related to supporting Ukraine. Members are from all over the world, from former soldiers (including Generals down to NCOs), academics, intelligence analysts, volunteers, active-duty Ukrainian military and many more. The Group was started by RC, who served in the UK Military with both Top and BC.

Now, these are the major characters, but there are some minor characters who I will give attention to within the story who also embodied that Christmas Spirit and all of them are Ukrainians. Also, Grizzly, BC, Top and I are not part of any charity organizations. We are all former soldiers or closely affiliated with the military who each do our part on an individual basis. None of us like the media or want attention; we just want to get the job done and do what it takes to complete the mission. Top and BC are still on their mission and departed Kyiv this morning as I sit here writing this. Nicky and Philly FF departed Kyiv for Lviv two nights ago and will head toward their final destination in Western Europe the following morning.

The Backstory

A few months ago, Top contacted me and a few others in the EEMC Group that he knew were either boots on the ground or had worked with smaller military and humanitarian aid individuals or military units. He told us that Nicky (who was anonymous at that point) wanted to get more involved on a personal level. Top did not say anything about Nicky other than he was fairly well off and had been helping for a long time.

Top and BC obviously already had a long-term military relationship. Now, I had done a shotgun approach in the first 14-16 months after the full-scale invasion. Pretty much helping anyone I could trust, from monetary aid to writing/editing/proofreading for the likes of UNITED24 and the Ukrainian PR Army. However, I am not much into public relations and am quite a bit older than most involved. My outlook on social media and life in general contrasts with theirs and eventually they found more volunteers within their generation who could be more involved on the various apps and platforms. I quietly made my exit and started developing a direct relationship with Grizzly as well as Margosha who does art therapy for children near the front, along with assisting military units, the elderly and pretty much anyone who comes her way. Natasha and I are only involved with Margosha on a financial level, meaning we give every month from our income. Here's an important point, though: we broke bread with Margosha when she was doing training in Kyiv on how to deal with children's trauma and art therapy. Old schoolers breaking bread sealed the deal.

Yes, I digressed. We help some others financially on a minimal level, that's TMI. I gave Top the rundown on Grizzly and the UTCBN. This included how long we worked together and very, and I mean, very basic information about the UTCBN. Now, at this time, nothing was promised or guaranteed to us or BC. I reached out to BC, and we, of course, did not allow ourselves to get excited because we know better than to build hope around what people say in a war zone. There are big talkers everywhere when it comes to this war, and not a lot of doers. You learn quickly to not waste time on the talkers. Top seemed serious and committed though. He was frank with us both that the decision all relied on Nicky. BC was planning his eleventh trip regardless, and I was doing my best to assist him because, inevitably, I knew he would find a way to get something to Grizzly and the UTCBN, even if it was just some symbolic supplies. He is my brother, and I know he would do that for me more than for them. That's how this bond works.

I let Grizzly know what Top was up to, and his response was the same as BC's. We'll see if and when it happens. We trade only in reality and don't count on anything until it's in one of our 'hot little hands'. That's how we survive. We also know that once that personal bond is made, it either becomes thick or washes down the drain. War intuition reveals the truth rather quickly. We can't waste our time on hopes, dreams or promises.

Top got back to us and let us know that Nicky would be supporting BC, Grizzly and the UTCBN. I don't need support but provide counsel and connections when needed or asked. Nicky wanted a shopping list for what was needed. Grizzly sent me a doozy of a list with a total cost of probably north of $100k just for the UTCBN. PT's guys, who are Border Guards, didn't need anything at the moment. I am not sure what was on BC's list, as it's really not my business. Everything within this small group is based on the standard operating procedure (SOP) of 'need to know'. Frankly, it becomes TMI if you know more than you need to anyway, and I can say, for one, that my cognitive abilities within the war zone have been negatively affected so I can only process and deal with so much. It's not PTSD because there's no 'Post' about it; rather it is more like Current TSD. However, I am very much functional and focused as long as I don't take on too much.

We deal with our respective units and share if there is extra. I edited Grizzly's communication and removed some of the higher cost items so as not to scare away Nicky. Top, I am guessing, nearly shit himself when he saw our list (and it was pared down). He took it back to Nicky anyway, with the caveat that he couldn't promise anything.

Messages flew back and forth. Nicky wanted to provide cold weather gear, medical supplies and basic stuff that soldiers need to survive; I could tell Grizzly was disappointed that the high-tech stuff we needed for UTCBN to go on assaults was probably not going to come.

Me: 'It's ok, brother. We should take what we can get. Right now, it's better to build a relationship for future assistance. You know as well as I do that we are a long way from the end of this thing. We need to build a relationship with Top and Nicky.'

Grizzly: 'I know, bro. Maybe just tell them the only thing we really, really need is Night Vision Goggles (NVG) for the boys. It gets dark by like 15:45 now and they can't go on assault at night without them otherwise they'll take casualties or worse, lose some of our boys.'

Me: 'Yea, I know. Let me get with Top and see what I can do.'

Grizzly was persistent with his messaging on NVG. I sort as served as the communications middleman between him and Top. Basically, I was filtering the message so as not to turn Top and Nicky away. NVG is hard to come by since the Israel-Hamas War broke out, and the prices have gone up considerably. The top-level technology which the UTCBN needs to be effective runs about $4000 for one set with the mount. Sometimes, we have to source them from the black market. UTCBN does not get much from the Ukraine Ministry of Defense because they are a small volunteer unit, so they are dependent on people like Grizzly and me to help. This is the fate of many Ukrainian units. Much of the supplies for the military are crowdfunded. The problem with that is the huge number of hucksters taking advantage of people. That's why most of us narrowed our focus to people we have already vetted. Top was utilizing BC, PT and my networks to protect Nicky and make sure his donations go where they are effective and truly needed.

Nicky was set on what he wanted to supply by now. Top and I decided the least we could do was work together and fund one NVG. BC was not involved other than as a consultant for potential sources of supply. PT got fully on board with helping us fundraise for one set. Top's friend gave some money. Some of my oldest and dearest friends pitched in, as well as some digital friends that I have never met. Natasha and I matched the donations from our friends. Top made up the shortfall with his own funds and some help from Nicky.

Grizzly sourced the NVG from his clandestine contacts. Two days before Top, BC, Nicky and Philly FF departed the UK, we received a thank you video forwarded by Grizzly from the UTCBN from a guy our age on the front in winter military camouflage fatigues wearing the NVG. That's more than enough of a thank you for us.

Sorry, you thought the back story was finished? Not quite. While all of the above was going on, a whole other shitstorm brewed and abated. A new set of rules for bringing aid into Ukraine was due to take effect on December 1st which was after our boys were set to depart. Polish truckers were majorly fucking things up at all the Poland-Ukraine border crossings. All but BC were Ukraine War Virgins (UWV) regarding their coming to a live war zone. On December 1st, just a week before departure, a social media Russian disinformation campaign caught us off guard. BC and Top were very worried. The story was that vehicles and cargo were being seized at the border and held.

I fell for it as well in the first few hours and contacted Grizzly, who was his normal calm self. He started checking into it, and I used my sources to do the same. Nope, nothing, nada. It was all a fake. Of course, that took some time for UWV to accept and understand. BC was already a bit nervous because they were all depending on him for the itinerary and a smooth trip. Grizzly and I warned them that the likelihood of smoothness was rough. Somebody within the group had a contact in Lviv that assured them they would be ok getting through the border. There was more frantic last-minute communication regarding the proper paperwork needed for Customs at the border. Grizzly came through with ours a day before departure.

Day I

There was not much communication on this day. I went to St. Volodymyr's Cathedral lit candles, and said prayers for their safe journey. I checked in with Top in the afternoon, who told me they had made the ferry and were now passing through Antwerp.

Day II

Just one message between me and Top. I checked in. They had just crossed into Poland. That's nearly a full day's ride, so we went dark.

Day III

Top told Grizzly and I they would be at the Poland-Ukraine Border at around 05:00 so I figured that might be an all-day affair. Natasha and I went to Divine Liturgy as I serve as an altar server in my church, and that, like the military, is also a duty only to a Higher Power and my Priest, Father Bohdan. After the service, I checked my phone and saw that Top had stated they crossed over, and BC sent me a message that he now had a Ukrainian SIM and was in country. Believe what you want, but as hard as I prayed on that first day and while behind the altar at church, you will never convince me that God did not hear and answer my prayers on that morning. Nicky and Philly FF were in one van with two Ukrainian Nationals (women), while Top and BC were in a second van. Both groups had stops in Lviv, where they planned to layover briefly and continue on to Grizzly's place a couple of hours east of there. They were pooped at this point, and understandably so, as it's a long drive with a lot of stress. Collectively, they decided to stay the night in Lviv and stop to see Grizzly the next day. Top informed us that most of the military kit that Philly FF was bringing for a military unit would now go to Grizzly and UTCBN. Turns out that Philly FF's guys couldn't supply the paperwork and seemed to be running a scam. All communication between Philly FF and them just dropped off the map when he started asking for details. That's why caution and trust are essential. Now, I don't really know Philly FF or what he has been doing but I can only imagine how he felt at that moment and wondered if they had taken cash donations from him in the past.

Day IV

The Group decided the night before that they would travel to Grizzly's, drop the supplies for UTCBN and continue on to one of BC's drops a few hours away. Now, other stops and contacts were made based on conversations I heard, but I stayed out of seeking information because we all operate on the assumption that the less known, the better. Grizzly sent me a photo of them having coffee at his house. Everyone looks happy but tired. He tells me that they plan to head to Queen Bee's, which is someone that BC has been supporting on nearly every trip he has made. They will spend the night at Queen Bee's. Top contacts me and ask if I will be available to meet up for dinner the next night. I ask if Natasha can join us, and he agrees.

Day V

One brief message from BC in the early AM stating they expect to arrive in Kyiv around 18:00. Everything goes dark. Kyivstar, the major cellular provider, gets hacked, and most communications with the Group are cut off. No communication all day. I send a general text to both BC and Top around 16:30, letting them know that I don't expect to see them for dinner.

13:38. Me to BC: 'Kyivstar network is down country-wide. Not sure if that is the SIM you are using. At this point. I am assuming we will see each other tomorrow and not tonight.'

16:04. Me to BC and Top: 'Sending this message to both of you since I assume at least one of you has been affected by the Kyivstar hack. Assuming dinner is off at this point which is ok. We can figure things out once you are safely in Kyiv and back in communication. I am going to start prepping dinner at home about 16:30 just so I have backup when Natasha gets home from work.'

Natasha is due home soon and will be hungry, so I heat up the borscht I made so she has a hot meal when she gets home. I had told my client in the US that I wouldn't be available for a few hours when we went to dinner, so I text him and let him know I am staying home and am around if he needs me.

18:14. Top to Me: 'We are still an hour away from Kyiv. May we meet for breakfast at 09:00 for breakfast at the Golden Gate?' (My response in the affirmative)

19:43. Top to Me: 'Can you come to breakfast at 08:00 at the hotel as Nicky has to leave early.' (Again, I respond in the affirmative).

Below is me and BC

20:01. BC: 'Hi brother, now in Kyiv and yes I'm on Kyivstar (two angry emojis) I think all is arranged for hotel breakfast tomorrow.'

Me: 'Glad you guys made it. See you in the morning.'

BC: 'OK brother. Been a very emotional day for both teams. We need to go shopping tomorrow for x50 soldiers in the hospital. Please advise where to buy underwear, toiletries, tracksuits.'

Me: I send him some links.

BC: 'I have about 1000 pounds to spend but also need baby stuff.'

Me: '1000 should go pretty far.'
BC: 'Happy Day!! Looks like loads of shopping bags then.'
Me: 'Tis the season to be jolly.'
BC: 'I love the gift of giving. (prayer hands emoji x 2).'
Me: 'Do you need to come help with shopping?'
BC: 'if you don't mind brother.'

Natasha and I talked it out and decided it was a good idea. I called my client in the US, explained the situation and asked if it was ok to take a few hours off in the morning to help out. He asked me if I just wanted to take the whole day off. There, I had to think about it. That's a whole days' worth of income out the door just before Christmas, on top of the fact that since I am self-employed, the vacation time I start on December 17th through the 25th is uncompensated. So, I again turned to Natasha, who, along with being my wife, is my counsel, my best friend and my foxhole buddy. She, of course, agreed as it is in the Christmas Spirit to do such a thing. I confirmed with BC and decided I was in a festive mood, so drank some Ukrainian cognac and smoked a cigar. The day finished, Natasha and I were warm, tucked in our beds with Philly the dog in the middle, snoring as usual. Almost a Norman Rockwell painting.

Now, it must be noted that I feed PT tidbits of information throughout the mission and even throw some to the Admins of the EEMC Group so that they are all aware that everyone is safe, and the mission is continuing.

Day VI

03:03. Kaboom! Blam! Windows rattle. More explosions. Natasha, Philly and I run for the strong walls. I forget my phone. Natasha has hers and checks the Telegram Channel Monitor. No Air Raid alarms went off. No warning. Hah, stinking Russians. The Patriots quickly and ably did their jobs. Debris fell, and civilians were injured (of course, that's the primary target of this insidious enemy), but no direct hits.

03:37. War intuition kicks in. Natasha and I say fuck it and go back to bed. Philly follows.

05:20. Natasha's alarm goes off. She gets up to do her yoga and grabs a shower. This is a seriously disciplined woman that any soldier would be honored to be married to. Yes, I got very lucky, and I never forget it.

06:45. My alarm goes off. Natasha is still in the shower. I make coffee and give Philly some small treats to keep him happy. At about 06:45 after the caffeine has taken effect, I leave to take Philly for a walk. Natasha has left for work by the time I get home.

07:34. I realize that I am running late for the 08:00 breakfast at the hotel and order an Uber Black since it is the fastest option. First time I ever used an Uber Black, and, well, it is a Mercedes, so who's complaining, although I do feel a bit ostentatious and out of place. No familiar faces in the lobby, so I take a seat.

A few minutes later, I recognize Nicky from a photo and walk up to introduce myself. We chit-chat and soon enough, Top shows up. We figure out where the breakfast buffet is and go on our way. BC shows up a few minutes later and we decide we should eat. We eat, and chat about their experience so far. They begin to review their itinerary for the day. Philly FF shows up and introductions are made. More chit-chat. They all talk about seeing the missiles shot down from their rooms on the 18th floor. Now that's brave, I think to myself. I, as someone who has been here throughout the invasion, would never take a room above the 3rd floor. What becomes clear listening to the conversation is that all the UWV's cherries have officially been broken. Now, they know what our lives here are like. Like most, they are even more resolved to come back and continue helping.

BC already began talking about his next trip in about two months, which will be his twelfth. Top and Nicky stated they couldn't make that one but would try to make the following one. Philly FF was clearly affected by the incident that happened to him. He was slightly guarded, and rightfully so. We adjourned as Nicky was due to meet some contacts of his in the lobby, all of them Ukrainians. I managed to speak with them as they planned to take Nicky and Philly FF on a few hour's walking tour of Kyiv. Barrel is the name I will give the one guy who spoke English, French, Ukrainian and Russian. He literally looked like a big barrel of a dude. We sat after breakfast and had coffee in the lobby, where Barrel consulted me on where they should take Nicky and Philly FF. This, of course, after finding out I live downtown and have a rudimentary working knowledge of Ukrainian. Imagine that, Ukrainians consulting me about what route to take. I gave my suggestion, and Barrel thought it was better than the one they originally planned. Although this is not the first time, I felt like a true Kyivan. We all need someone else at times to assure us of our place in this war, and Barrel gave me mine that morning.

Nicky and Philly FF let BC and Top know they planned to depart Kyiv for Lviv at 13:00. We transferred some cargo from Nicky's van in case we were not back in time for their departure. BC, Top and I decided we would drive in BC's old beat-up lorry to a mega store on the outskirts of the city to buy the supplies we needed for the wounded soldiers, mothers and children, all aged one to three. All parties went their separate ways.

I don't have Kyivstar but am forever grateful to Google for my GoogleFi service, which seems to find whatever network it needs to operate. The three of us had a pleasant drive through downtown Kyiv, and I pointed out landmarks and also where missiles had hit a while back. We arrived at the megastore with enthusiasm. Soon enough, we had long faces. They didn't seem to have what we needed, especially for the soldiers. The place is massive, so we searched every part of it. BC said he knew of a warehouse for one of the military units he supports nearby and maybe they had stuff we could buy. No one was there when we arrived.

Our soldier heads kicked in. There was another megastore across the street, which is a French chain called Auchan. The other store was more like a Home Depot, whereas Auchan seemed more like a Walmart if you need a frame of reference. Inside, we came across the toiletry and baby aisles. We each grabbed carts. We decided we would at least get the basics. We just started piling stuff into carts with wanton abandon. Top grabbed the wrong nappies for the kids, but we quickly adjusted as the shop assistant pointed us to the most economical choices. Locals in the aisles had bewildered looks on their faces. Soon enough, some employees showed up, and between my broken Ukrainian and Google Translate our message was conveyed. We need lots of stuff for injured soldiers and children, and we need the best prices. The employees were all women, and they quickly sprang into action. A couple directed us to the lower-priced products that were still of good quality. Others disappeared and then came back with dozens of empty boxes for packing. It was like some scene out of one of those crazy Christmas movies with a mad rush of retail.

I told BC that I had eyed some clothing and would do a quick recon to see if they had the clothing we needed for the injured soldiers. Wow! They did, and at very much affordable prices. I went back to BC and told him I'd organize the baby food and toiletries. Top was a little overwhelmed, so I directed him where and what to start loading. Now, I needed shower shoes. Ah, my sturdy elf appeared, and she directed me to the location. She helped me load them, but we needed fifty pairs and there was not that many on the shelves. In a flurry, she let me know she would go to the back of the store and bring more! Whoosh! She was off like another one of those magical Christmas characters from those children's shows.

As I stood there with loads of shower shoes, an old couple was looking for the same. The old man went to take some from my cart and I politely in basic Ukrainian said they were for injured soldiers. His wife gave him a look that wives so famously do to us husbands and he backed off. They kept searching for them close by and I figured they only needed one pair, so it wasn't a big deal. In my broken Ukrainian I asked if they just needed the one pair and that it was ok. They both smiled and said, 'No, no, for the soldiers. They come first.' Christmas Spirit! Angels we have heard on high!

BC soon showed up with carts full of warm socks, comfortable sweatpants, t-shirts, hoodies, and fleece pullovers. Our injured soldiers would be warm and cozy! Oh, how lucky BC and Top would be to see the faces of the soldiers when they show up. But my part was not with them. That's the essence of a true mission. Do your part and get out if you are not needed.

An Assistant Manager was now involved in this scurrying about, and she gave us a designated aisle, organized some of her employees to help us and the checkout process began. Top unloaded everything. I, along with one of the Auchan elves, packed and labeled the boxes. BC stood back, took pics and served as commander. Top informed us that Nicky had given him a wad of cash, so going over budget wasn't an issue.

Ching! We reached the limit of what the cash register was allowed to process at one time. I took a break from packing and organized additional boxes. My elf went to fetch another pallet as the first one was already almost full. Then it started again. This time, it was all clothing. The children's goods were now packed on Pallet One. Ching! Soon enough, we reached the cash register's allotted amount, and there went all the cash we had on hand. Top quickly stepped up and said put the rest on the card. All said and done, we spent £3000, going £2000 over budget. Nobody blinked an eye or complained.

So, the General Manager came and thanked us. He gave us his business card for any future runs and said to contact him in advance so they could be ready to help us better.

You see, that's the thing. The trip to the hospital and supplies for the injured soldiers was never on the agenda or part of the planned itinerary. BC and Top just happened to visit the hospital when making another stop, and after seeing what the soldiers needed, they simply couldn't say no or not do anything. That's often the way it works when you are not an official charity. You have more leeway and are able to adjust to the conditions, much like properly trained soldiers in battle.

The lorry was loaded, and they dropped me near home so I could get to Philly who was overdue for his walk. BC and Top returned to their hotel and then set off to do some Christmas shopping for wives and families on Kreshchatyk (Kyiv's main downtown shopping area). Later I joined them for dinner and dropped them at their hotel using my Uber account. We all assumed Nicky and Philly FF got off ok on their own. Our parting was a quick handshake as they had an early morning ahead, and I had to work.

The next evening, I heard from Top that they were in a church community hall preparing the baby items to distribute tomorrow. They will be like Father Christmas, handing out goodies, smiling and enjoying the Christmas Spirit. They still have to drop more supplies for military units and take the items we bought to the injured soldiers in the hospital. None of us are young. Our stamina, thankfully, still remains. BC is 54. Top is 61. All the others, including Grizzly, are over 50. The thing we Yanks and Brits laughed about at dinner was that we all are married to younger women. Almost all of us could pass for Santa Claus with a little padding, and some of us without.

This is a true story. This is a Christmas story, one about sacrifice, generosity, bravery, and the coming together of cultures. We Yanks owe a lot to our former imperial masters, the Brits, for that very unique take on the Christmas Spirit all wrapped up in Dickens and traditions. That relationship between our peoples is probably the strongest one we have as Americans. I don't know if anything like this will ever exist between Russia and Ukraine. Frankly it is doubtful. We may have attacked the British in Trenton on Christmas Eve all those years ago but there was no hate for them as a people like the Russians have for Ukraine. It was militarily expedient in our case, and now, we, once mortal enemies, stand together against tyranny and imperialism. We don our Christmas hats, smile wide, hug the children and salute the soldiers. Merry Christmas Ukraine!

27

The Holiday Queen

January 13, 2024 (Kyiv)

December 17, 2023 (Sunday) was the day we started celebrating Christmas. The Brits from the previous chapter were back in Kyiv and had meetings with AZOV soldiers to supply them some kit. BC was also due to visit one of his AZOV liaisons, who had recently been injured in a firefight and was now recovering at a military hospital in Kyiv. We had hoped to meet up for coffee before they started their journey back home to their families in England. I got a text message from Top that they were just going to wrap up and start driving. So, I told Natasha I was free for the day.

Natasha's Christmas Break vacation from teaching 1st grade at Pechersk School International had officially started the day before. She had decided to have a 'cookie project' for her students just before the break, and they had all made chocolate chip cookies in the school kitchen, which her class shared with students, teachers and staff. Natasha absolutely adores the American/British style Christmas celebration that she had grown used to and fond of after living in the US for some twenty-one years. Chocolate chip cookies are a big holiday event in my family. When I was young, my mother, grandmothers, aunts and cousins all made huge batches of these cookies. Some had M&Ms, others had peanut butter chips, but needless to say, we had cookies that lasted about a month or more.

So, Natasha was like, 'Since you're free today, should we just make it a cookie day?' And I was like, 'Yeah!' Now a cookie day for me is relaxing while Natasha does her cookie magic. She rules the kitchen, especially for the holidays. I am there if she needs a hand, but Natasha really never asks. Frankly, I don't remember if there were any air raids that day. I do remember that after Natasha finished her first batch of cookies, we went to the flower shop to get Christmas greens for the holidays.

Natasha really liked this one arrangement that was pink, including a soft pink Nutcracker. Of course, I was extraordinarily surprised that she would pick one with a Nutcracker, given the association with Russia. However, it's what she wanted at the moment and what we bought. I do remember as the season drew on, she regretted buying it and swore she would never have another Nutcracker in the house after some particularly tense days of missile attacks. Later that night, we feasted on cookies, and I started reading aloud the section called 'Marley's Ghost' of *A Christmas Carol*.

December 18 (Monday) came, and we decided we wanted to go and see an exhibit at a certain museum near Taras Shevchenko Park in Kyiv. Natasha took Philly for a walk that morning and stopped by to check their hours, and the sign read 'Closed on Mondays'. Oh well, time to figure out a Plan B. I had told Natasha about a new bookstore called 'ReadEat' here in Kyiv and so that quickly became our destination. We are both bookstore bugs. We took the nice walk and grabbed some coffee before heading to the second floor to browse the section with books in English. Natasha was giddy, and I managed to purchase Jon Fosse's *Septology* because I had heard it takes place around Christmas. Additionally, I had heard it was his magnum opus, and I had to check it out, being that he had just been awarded the Nobel Prize for Literature.

Natasha was giddy with excitement at finding some books she could bring to her classroom for her students. There was a beautiful Christmas tree with two comfortable chairs and so we recruited an employee of the bookstore to take what turned out to be a very nice holiday picture in the midst of a war. It was a good day, and later we went to meet with our friend, Oleksandr who had been mobilized into Ukraine's Armed Forces. He had been granted leave to go visit his wife and her daughters in Germany. We drank a little, ate a little and had a good time while wishing him a safe journey. We got home and received a phone call from Father Bohdan who asked if I could come the next day for a 9:00 a.m. service at our little church (St. Yuri's). I said yes, of course.

December 19 (Tuesday) The alarm went off, and I rolled out of bed, leaving Natasha to rest and walk Philly at her leisure. Just before I left, Natasha decided to take Philly and go to Confession at St. Volodymyr's Cathedral since it was closer, and the service started later. The wind was cold as I walked to St. Yuri's with no idea what the service was for. You see, our church stayed on the Old Calendar this year regarding Christmas, which means it's two weeks behind most other churches. We struggled with this decision by Patriarch Filaret because the Russians follow the same tradition. Natasha and I are very American and pretty much always celebrate Christmas on December 25th. I could go into detail about our personal beliefs and philosophy on this, but it would take away too much from this chapter's theme.

When I arrived at St. Yuri's, I noticed that the icon of St. Nicholas was displayed first, and then it dawned on me that this was his day on the Old Calendar. At that very moment, I felt blessed because St. Nicholas has always been our protector and saint as a couple, going way back to when I bought his icon in Belarus to bring home to the US in January 2001. That icon is now with us in Kyiv. Father Bohdan gives a good service. I did my part as an altar server and the few of us who attended parted ways.

Walking home, I decided that why not take advantage of this day even if the calendars are different? It's about the joy and celebration of Christ's birth, not a particular dogma. So, well, it called for a stop at the cigar store and then to pop in at my favorite liquor store (OK Wine) which is basically right below. Normally, I would buy some scotch or cognac, but I had a suspicion that Natasha would be getting me something for Christmas. Thus, I just grabbed a bottle of Saperavi, a dry red Georgian wine that we both love. That wonderful Christmas spirit was surging through my soul as I walked the few blocks home.

Natasha was home when I arrived and told me she had Confession but didn't take Communion as she had come early, thinking the Akathist to St. Barbara was being held that day. We laughed at the fact that we didn't realize it was St. Nick's Day and then felt bad that we were not properly prepared to celebrate. Natasha suggested we exchange gifts since that is a tradition on St. Nicholas Day. I agreed. My gift to Natasha was well received and she presented me with The Dalmore Cigar Malt Reserve Single Malt Whiskey which showed me how much she loves me and just how well she knows me. Good thing I bought that cigar, eh? We soon discovered that we missed each other by only about ten minutes at OK Wine and, of course, got a good chuckle out of that one. But, oh my, what to do about dinner? We hadn't prepared or bought anything befitting a holiday meal. Food is one of those things that bonds our marriage, and we had to seriously consider our options.

Easy enough, right? Go out to dinner. Natasha had really been wanting to try a traditional Ukrainian restaurant called Korchma Tara Bulba which translates as 'The Inn Tara Bulba'. So off we went to drink traditional uzvar (a Ukrainian fruit drink), a salo platter, roasted meats and other fare. Absolutely delicious, good call babe!

We made our way home after dinner and Natasha had some wine while I retired to the balcony with my cigar and Dalmore. Wow! I was sold. Truly the best scotch I had tasted since Natasha had bought me the Knockando Single Malt all those years ago at Green's Liquors in Wildwood, NJ when we were newly married. Yes, I can say that I am not a sophisticated connoisseur, but I have an awesome wife who has gifted me the two single malts that I love the most.

The journal entry format is now over as I don't want to bore you with that style. Natasha cooked different holiday treats for the rest of the week. We went to the Kyiv National Art Gallery to see 'Shevchenkiana' which is a series of paintings by the Ukrainian artist Ivan Marchuk based on the poems of Taras Shevchenko. Dark, haunting, gloomy with undertones of horror but poignant and apt in an active war. Ukrainians are willing to suffer in order to be free, whereas Russians wear suffering like a badge that makes them somehow special. We sort of glided through the week and only stopped on Friday to go shopping for our Christmas Feast.

Throughout the week, we took turns reading Dickens aloud to each other. Natasha made more cookies to give to our fellow parishioners at St. Yuri's. We had purchased a crackling candle scented with cinnamon, which we burned almost every day. Sunday would be Christmas Eve on the new calendar, so we made our way there for liturgy. We arrived to find out that Father Bohdan had a fever and would not make it to the service. I decided to stay and serve the Akathist while Natasha dashed off to St. Volodymyr's for Confession and Communion. We try to do both as often as possible, and I had taken mine on St. Nicholas Day.

I returned home and arrived as Natasha was preparing the roast. An air raid siren rang out just as she put it in the oven. We checked our phones and decided it was not that big of a threat. I popped the wine, and as we raised our glasses, I told Natasha she was the Holiday Queen. She blushed and told me it was the best compliment… ever. She is really, I meant it. In all the years of our marriage, she has always made Christmas special. Out there, wherever you are, I hope you have a Holiday Queen or King who brings the Christmas Spirit into your home. I pray that you never have to celebrate in a war, but if you do, don't let it stop you.

28

Ukraine OPSEC NATION

January 16, 2024

The definition of OPSEC is most likely not in most people's everyday vocabulary, so let's provide a definition from the US Department of Defense (DOD) in document DoDD 5205.02E:

> *A process of identifying critical information and analyzing friendly actions attendant to military operations and other activities to: identify those actions that can be observed by adversary intelligence systems; determine indicators and vulnerabilities that adversary intelligence systems might obtain that could be interpreted or pieced together to derive critical information in time to be useful to adversaries, and determine which of these represent an unacceptable risk; then select and execute countermeasures that eliminate the risk to friendly actions and operations or reduce it to an acceptable level.*

Basically, keep your mouth, your phone, your computer, and your camera shut!

You who are observing the War on Ukraine may notice that you receive only a limited amount of information. We are coming up on the second year of the full-scale invasion, and it may seem to you outside Ukraine that you are getting even fewer details. Pretty much everything leaked in the beginning which was both good and bad. Good in that the world got to see firsthand the atrocities being committed by the enemy. Bad because the enemy could also see it and use it. Ukraine was hands down winning the Information War along with the conventional one throughout all of 2022 and a portion of 2023. Those tides have now changed.

Changing tides are not the subject of this article. Those of us fighting at whatever level know that the enemy has gained the advantage in the information space. That's why the borders have been blocked for goods and also why the US Congress and White House can't seem to act regarding additional military aid to a nation that is struggling for its freedom. Yes, every day, we are struggling to set Ukraine free.

Now, why is less information coming out of Ukraine? Why are there very few images of the piles and stacks of war dead, both ours and the enemy's? Why aren't there images of enemy missiles being shot down by air defense? Because we got on war footing as a society. Unfortunately, the morons of war in the beginning were publishing everything on TikTok, YouTube, Facebook and just about everywhere else. That was like handing the enemy a bullet and a gun and pointing it at your head for them.

Civilians in war can't be expected to just know the importance of OPSEC. The digital media is part of our lives, and everyone is fighting for likes, influence and popularity. Of course, the government of Ukraine warned everyone about how dangerous it was to their own security. They only started listening when bloggers and others started being arrested and charged.

Here we are in January 2023 and it finally seems like the vast majority of people now understand that publishing this kind of content gives free ammunition to the enemy. This precedent of almost an entire society now voluntarily practicing OPSEC is most likely the first of its kind. Yes, some material gets out, but nowhere near what many of us know about but do not reveal. Most of the important information about the movement and use of military equipment is rarely seen unless Ukraine wants you to see it.

Ukraine now must also be careful to allow enough information out so that the free world stays on our side. We here know that 2024 brings many new challenges on all battlefields. A new strategy is essential in the information and narrative that is coming out of Ukraine. Sometimes, it takes that outside eye to accomplish that which is not necessarily seen from the inside. We must not look away from the suffering, death and destruction, and here in the war zone, we see and hear about it just about every hour and most assuredly every day. But we need the American people to see it on their level, not that of the talking heads. We need them to see the victories that occur in Ukraine daily.

Personally, if I were in charge, I would teach English to those who have triumphed in Ukraine: soldiers with prosthetics; children from destroyed cities who go to school underground; mothers who cook for frontline soldiers; workers who sweep the streets and pick up the garbage as air raids are blaring; to all the other amazing Ukrainians who have accomplished their own small victories. Then I would send them out into the cities, towns and rural hamlets of the English-speaking world as Average Joe Ambassadors. That's where we get our support because eventually, they might write letters to their representatives on why it is important to continue supporting Ukraine. All without violating the crucial Ukraine OPSEC Nation.

29

Missiles and Rockets and Drones! Oh my!

February 11, 2024

There is no Yellow Brick Road. There is no Wizard. The Haunted Forest is our life, every day, day in, day out: air raids; news of civilians killed by rockets and artillery; soldiers dead on the front; ammo shortages; dwindling support; abducted children taken to Russia to be brainwashed against their home and families; and all other sorts of horror. Those of us who stayed were very much the Scarecrow, Tin Man and the Cowardly Lion, but there was no Dorothy among us because we were already home. Sure, we wished we could click our heels, if only for a day or a moment and be someplace peaceful, but something held us here. Something stronger than anything else we have ever experienced in our lives.

Like the Scarecrow, we didn't have 'war brains'. Like the Tin Man, we didn't have 'war hearts', but unlike the Cowardly Lion, it seems that we did have courage. Courage which we wondered was instead plain stupidity at first. My war brain kicked in pretty quickly and Natasha's quickly followed suit. Our hearts beat together and rose in the face of death. I really cannot describe the how or why of any of it. Somehow things happened the way they did, and we stayed. We are still here as I write this sentence and just thirteen days from the second-year mark of the full-scale invasion.

On December 29, 2023, the missiles, rockets and drones came at Kyiv again. Plop dab in the midst of our continuing holiday celebration. Yes, we celebrate the holidays from mid-December until almost the end of January here, so I guess we were bound to get hit somewhere in there. We know when the attacks are coming well in advance most of the time, but not always. Sometimes, they are strictly drone attacks, which are the least worrisome. We don't sit on the balcony waiting for the fireworks show or anything like that. People have been killed by falling debris doing that. The warheads on the drones can only do so much damage, so we feel pretty safe hiding out away from windows because the walls in our building are about a meter thick. Our building was built while Tzar Nicholas II was still in power and has withstood both World Wars.

Often, the drones come first, followed by missiles. This tactic is well known among Ukraine's Air Defense Forces and us civilians as well. The drones sort of test for weaknesses in the air defense and then the missiles come where those weaknesses are perceived. These attacks usually last a while, with the occasional lull between launches. Most of the time, the attacks come in the middle of the night or in the very early hours of the morning before the sun comes up. Lately, the combined drone-missile attacks have petered out a bit. Sounds mundane when I write this, does it seem that way when you read it? Well, the truth is, for us, it has become sort of routine. We take precautions, of course. Most of the time these drones and missiles are shot down before they get close to our area of Kyiv. We can hear the dull thuds of explosions in the distance sometimes, and at other times, we just sleep through them. It's always strange to wake up on a night that attacks came and find out you had no clue about them.

I am saving the worst for last. These are the full-on missile attacks. The ones that our war senses often detect before we even begin checking the Telegram channels. Most of the time, it is a certain type of insomnia, let's call it ominous insomnious. Yes, it's different than your run-of-the-mill insomnia, as there is a deep sense of foreboding. Sometimes, I feel it, other times, it is Natasha, and we check Telegram right away. Usually. They are large-scale attacks. Bombers from deep inside Russia take off from one to three different locations to launch areas near the Caspian Sea. These bombers usually take a couple of hours to reach their launch zones, so we sometimes set the alarm and go back to sleep. Once the missiles are launched, they take another good hour to cross into Ukraine's airspace most of the time. That means we sometimes go back to bed for 2–3 hours. This type of attack almost always kicks off around 3 a.m., with missiles reaching us between 6–7 a.m., as the sun is rising. We are sheltering when they come.

Dull thuds come first most of the time. Sometimes, the Russians simultaneously launch missiles from ships and submarines in the Black Sea. Often, all the missiles go around circles or head one direction only to turn around and come straight back at us. We actively watch the Telegram channel called 'War Monitor' and have a pretty good idea when they are headed directly at us. These cruise missiles are not the superfast ones, but that doesn't mean they all get shot down. Even if one does get shot down, the debris has to fall somewhere. We can sometimes hear them flying overhead as it is a very recognizable noise for us by now. The distance of explosions becomes easy to read rather quickly, and sometimes, it's just one after another.

Now, the worst part is that often, during these missile attacks, another bomber or series of bombers takes off. These planes carry and launch what are known as hypersonic missiles. We have maybe a five-minute lead time from when they are launched to when they arrive, and often these are the scariest of them all. Many have been shot down not far from where we live. The blast is powerful and sometimes shakes the whole building, with the concussive blast setting off car alarms outside the windows. Sometimes, the slower-moving missiles continue to follow these, and at other times, they are the last of a given missile attack. Words really don't describe the impact it has on a personal level, and I certainly wouldn't wish you to experience it firsthand.

Just the other day, and I am sorry, but I do not keep a running journal of when the attacks occur, so I can't give an exact date. Who wants to remember that shit? A wave of slow missiles came through, and it seemed like it was all clear. Natasha checked her chat with the other Pechersk School International (PSI) employees to see if they were heading to work. Everyone was either on their way or getting ready to leave. That's what we do. We go on as soon as the attacks are over. Natasha called her rideshare (she uses Bolt most of the time) and headed out despite my having a feeling it was not over. We have learned to trust each other's instincts and not to argue about this type of thing. Twenty minutes after she left, the Russians launched a modified anti-ship hypersonic missile, and it hit close. Well, it felt close for me as it impacted a high-rise just one district over and much closer for Natasha.

She had just taken off her backpack in her classroom when it hit in the same district where she works. In a New York minute, she was in the school shelter. Fifteen minutes later, she was texting me a photo of getting coffee in the school cafeteria. That day was particularly bad for both of us because we would rather die together than apart. We couldn't shake that feeling. A guy I know here posted on his social media how he had watched the cruise missile come in horizontally with a direct hit on the high-rise. You have probably seen pictures of this online if you follow the news in Ukraine. I won't go into body counts, but they were there just like the one on December 29th, which was the highest number of civilian casualties from one strike on Kyiv. That's our life. What can we say?

I can say that if you can't sleep at night after nearly two years of full-scale war. It's missiles and rockets and drones! Oh my!

30

A Night in Podil

February 23, 2024

I kissed Natasha goodbye on the night of Wednesday, February 22, 2024, as I left the flat. She was not happy to see me go that night, but she is a good wife who respects that my weekly saunter into the nightlife of Kyiv is important for me and even more so for our friend, Oleksandr. His wife, Lesya, had just returned to Germany, where she had gone as a displaced Ukrainian. Lesya has her daughters and grandchildren, but all Oleksandr has are a few friends and his fellow soldiers that he spends his days with. The week prior, we had all had dinner at Korchma Taras Bulba in the city center. It translates into the 'Inn of Taras Bulba', whose atmosphere is more like an old Ukrainian grandma's home. Antique Ukrainian farm implements and old-style art decorate the thick-walled interior. Staff wear traditional Ukrainian garb and are always very friendly and the food is the best traditional Ukrainian fare we have tasted. Those times passed, and now Oleksandr and I are back to our regular weekly routine.

Oleksandr has other business, so we planned on meeting later than our normal time. Earlier in the day, I had coffee with an American musician from Ohio, Benya Stewart, who has been exploring the folk traditions of Ukrainian music and helping to document, celebrate, promote, and preserve Ukraine's cultural heritage. He told me that there was a gathering in the Old Podil neighborhood of Kyiv that night. We had broken from our traditional time, so I decided to see if Oleksandr was up for something completely different than our routine meeting place in the shadows of hulking Stalinist buildings on Kreschatyk, the main thoroughfare of this teeming war-time city. He was enthusiastic, so we set the meeting place.

Earlier, I had looked at the Kyiv metro map to determine my route. Home alone while Natasha was at work, I had time on my hands and had been watching the Ukrainian film 'Dovbush' on Netflix. So, I checked the walking distance on the map out of boredom, loneliness and curiosity. Life without Natasha at home is sometimes challenging, but at least I have Philly to keep me company. Our first three years in Ukraine, we were always together. Natasha has just this year taken a job as a 1st Grade Teacher at PSI. She never flourished at her Title 1 public school teaching job in Florida like she has at PSI. I am glad she has found a niche for herself, but I do miss her dearly. She is a gift, and some gifts are meant to be shared, so I watch her as she goes sleepily into the early morning. This means that I have to find activities to keep my mind occupied and my time filled. I searched Google Maps, which showed that it was only a thirty-nine-minute journey on foot. It felt good that Natasha wanted me to stay but also that it might be a welcome change of pace.

War makes you want to live even more, so I embraced a stroll instead of the metro. The route is through some of my favorite areas of Kyiv, and I, being ever the logistician, decided I knew a better and shorter route than Google Maps. This also drove home the knowledge that Kyiv is my city, my home. First, the stairs that lead up the steep hill on Ivana Franka greeted me soon after leaving behind the woman I love with every fiber of my being, body and soul. I realized then that I could count the trip as a bit of my daily workout. My heart rate climbed with every step. Yaroslav Val was teeming with life like it almost always is as I reached the top and crossed.

The police guard was on duty as I passed the Embassy of Norway. Finland's is also just down the street, almost next to Korea. Crossing Reitarska Street, I recalled a Ukrainian movie we recently watched called 'The Best Weekend' about the Atlas Weekend Music Festival in the summer of 2021. Funny, how culture sort of melds together as I also recalled we skipped Liturgy at the Cathedral of the Transfiguration the week of Atlas Weekend because the metro stops were the same. I smiled as I stepped foot on the far corner because, in the movie, a scene was shot showing young revelers in a blow-up pool right there. Walking on, the rear walls of St. Sophia's stood tall and strong in their white-washed simplicity. How long had those walls stood there? St. Sophia's is over a thousand years old, but who knows when the walls were added. I brushed my hand against them as I passed, feeling the age, pulse and soul of Kyiv.

People were all over the streets. Soon I used a cut-through and joined the ranks of my fellow Kyivans out for their evening strolls on Landscape Alley. Lights illuminated the long set of stairs that ran alongside the path. This was a project put together by Mayor Vitali Klitschko and the Kyiv City Administration. Many people are very critical of him and those he is affiliated with, but I only see the good he has done for this city. Much of it has been accomplished since we moved here three years ago, and some of it has been done during the full-scale war. Opinions are like... well, you know the rest.

Checking the time, I saw that I was very early and decided to walk behind the Ukraine Museum of History (which is on my list to visit) so I could look out at the Dnipro River and the Podil District glittering below. A young couple played and joked as I passed. Older folks walked slowly with their hands behind their backs. A drunk sat teetering as if ready to collapse. All seemed well with the world even though I knew it was not. That's the kind of moment you grasp and hold onto for as long as it lasts because any day, missiles may come your way once again. But not tonight, so far, at least.

Slowly, I made my way down the lighted stairs onto the lower part of the path. A woman sat reflecting and eating a sandwich. Others strolled hand-in-hand. I walked through the *Alice in Wonderland* themed tunnel and stepped onto Andriivts'kyi Descent as a young man strummed a guitar and sang a soft, mellow tune beneath the shadow of the masterpiece of Baroque St. Andrew's Church. This area is one of those 'must-see' locations in Kyiv, and well, it's just a short walk from where Natasha and I have planted our flag. How amazing is that? You know you are in the right place when you feel that way about where you live.

The descent is rather steep, and I definitely wouldn't try it if it were icy out. Gritty sand from previous snows lay all over the street. A tractor on one side seemed to be trying to clean some of the leftover mess from winter that comes every year and seems to miraculously disappear by the time the flowers of spring are in full bloom. I saw some tulip shoots just beginning to make their appearance as I walked Philly earlier in the day. Again, say what you want about the mayor and administration, but many aspects of this city run like a well-oiled machine. Once you hit the bottom of the descent, you are smack dab in the start of Podil. There, a bar was overflowing with Kyiv's young professionals at a 'Meet-Market' bar, music was playing, their chatter lively. I passed by on my way and turned the corner.

There in front of me was the Ferris wheel on Kontraktvoa Ploshcha (Square of Contracts), which is where in the times of Old Kyiv, merchants and others came to complete and sign, well… contracts naturally. The Ferris wheel is lit like a colorful Christmas tree as it goes round and round… what goes up must come down. Funny enough, the movie I mentioned earlier has quite an impactful scene shot in, around and on that Ferris wheel. I took my time crossing the vast square where there are multiple historic buildings, including the Kyiv-Mohyla Academy (National University), originally founded in 1615 as the Kyiv Brotherhood School. Its motto, '*Tempus fugit, Academia sempiternal*', which translates as 'Time passes, but the Academy is eternal', seems fitting when I think of how Ukraine is fighting for its life, future, culture and values on all fronts.

Oleksandr texted me that he was five minutes from our meetup location, so I quickened my step. Meandering about, the vibe very felt like the Greenwich Village of my youth. Rounding the corner, I could hear choral voices singing an ancient Ukrainian folk song. Yes, I was certainly in the right place. Oleksandr greeted me outside, and I heard at least one more American voice outside as we entered. Normally, I don't react or speak in English much because I don't always want to draw attention to myself. We entered quietly into the loudness of the interior of the bar. Benya was standing on the stage playing something between a violin and a cello, surrounded by four or five fiddle players with one lone drummer. The place was packed with all variations of Ukrainian twenty- or thirty-somethings. We looked at each other and realized we were out of our element. Screw it, we said, let's get a drink. Beer and wine only? No way. Tonight was cognac night. The bartender directed us across the street, where the bar was under the same ownership. We did our thing, returned and could only find seating outside, where we barely heard any of the music.

We chatted, and Oleksandr seemed pleased as the tunes are part of his history. Once we caught up, we headed across the street for another round and then back into the sweaty, grungy masses on the dance floor. We stood against the bar and took it all in. Benya had moved to a fiddle and joined the small circle of fiddlers. Two new drums and drummers banged out a beat. Traditional folk dancing, or at least what seemed like that, was ongoing. A transvestite in a bodice danced with a girl in a traditional Ukrainian shirt and skirt; couples attempted Cossack moves unsuccessfully; everyone was smiling, energetic and having fun. Young Ukrainians openly expressing their freedom despite the horrors of the war. The song ended and Benya stopped by for a chat. Energy, sweat, grunge, music, dancing swirled around us as we sipped our Zakarpatian cognac.

Oleksandr needed a smoke, so we stepped out into the cool air, which felt unseasonably warm for February. Beautiful voices greeted us on the street, singing songs well over a hundred years old. Oleksandr came to find out that one of the singers was studying to be an opera singer at a less-than-well-known Ukrainian university. The bar door swung wide, and out came the Soundgarden twins like they stepped out of some strange time machine from Seattle. They introduced themselves as the two Andrukhas, and both engaged us in English. Apparently, they were in competing grunge bands. Music swirled, my head grew foggier from the cognac, and I just sat back and soaked it all in.

Eventually, the night ended, and we gave one of the Andrukhas a ride close to his home. He corrected my terrible pronunciation of Ukrainian words on several occasions, proudly announced that he was a native Kyivan, and was pleasantly surprised how much I knew of my neighborhood's history. It was time to go. Oleksandr had hired a driver so as not to drive drunk, and we went our separate ways.

Needless to say, I had drunk about one hundred more grams of cognac than usual, and boy could I tell. Natasha was already asleep when I got home, so I downed some cold water to try to hamper the effects of a potential hangover in the morning. I reflected on the whirlwind of a night, from the imagery to the atmosphere to the music, as I sat on the couch with Philly. An escape from your comfort zone always seems to help. The two-year mark of the beginning of the full-scale invasion is just two days away. Today is two years since Natasha and I went to see the Gogol ballet at the Kyiv Opera House. February seems to be the month where so much of our history happens.

Benya told me they do the folk activity every two weeks. Natasha has spring break right when the next one is scheduled. She is Ukrainian, and I kinda hope I can talk her into attending the next one. There are parts she will hate and others she will love, but that's the essence of life, isn't it? Is it something you want to make a habit out of? No. But it is something worth experiencing once… or twice in my case, hopefully. Most importantly, it is those young people who now bear that weight on their shoulders, to survive war and keep the culture alive.

31

Accidental Ukrainians

February 24–26, 2024

February 24, 2024, was the two-year mark for Ukraine's 'Day that will live in infamy.' Waking in the morning, all those memories came flooding back. You can't not remember those experiences once you have lived through them. You can file them in the back, but certain dates and events just reach down and pull them back to the forefront. I still can't tell you why exactly we stayed. Natasha and I were determined not to be consumed by the fires of our memories of that day, so we planned to hit a café near St. Michael's Square after she walked Philly. The date fell on a Saturday, which meant we both were off, and she was on Philly Walk Duty in the morning since I usually take him Sunday through Friday. I call this my lazy morning as I don't have to rush to do anything. My phone is turned to silent, and I try not to look at the news and even ignore some messages and pretty much all phone calls. Working four 12-hour shifts means that I am on high alert on the days I do work, and it can be maddening.

Now, I think back to February 27, 2022, which is the day I decided to sign up for Kyiv Territorial Defense while Natasha was out walking Philly. That morning, I wanted most of all to protect Kyiv, my city. The decision came like lightning, and I knew if I gave Natasha time to 'discuss' she would probably freak out. Not like a screaming, emotional 'freak out' but a subdued plead for me not to leave her and the dogs. A latent warrior flame was lit, and I felt the need. Fate or God had other plans. I didn't give her time but waited by the door for her to get home, hugged her, kissed her and told her I was off. Her immediate reaction was support as she has warrior energy herself. But the Kyiv Military Administration was already out of weapons and the recruiting office was not where it was supposed to be. In that moment, I felt it was best to just go home and be with my family. Maybe to protect them as a first line of defense should the enemy make it into our neighborhood.

Back to the morning of the two-year mark. Natasha was off with Philly on her long Saturday morning walk. My phone needed to be charged and, as I grabbed it, I saw a message on the secure messaging app from Benya Stewart. You'll remember Benya from the chapter 'A Night in Podil' as the American musician from Ohio who is exploring, promoting and playing Ukrainian folk music. He released a song on the two-year mark called *Mighty Big War* which is an adaptation of *So Long, It's Been Good to Know You* by Woody Guthrie. The song was released with a video on YouTube, and man, it's good; hell, it's the best message tailored to the American audience that I have seen throughout this war. That was a great way to start this day. Natasha had tears in her eyes when she watched and listened to it.

Philly came in with his usual dog enthusiasm while we got ready to check out the café. We left Philly and strolled past Ukraine's SBU building, across St. Sophia's Square, which had Ukrainian families holding signs to bring their mobilized family members home. Press was milling about on St. Michael's Square, with military and police forming a perimeter. The café was off-limits as President Zelensky, along with other foreign leaders, were expected to come lay wreaths for the fallen whose photos line the walls of the monastery. Natasha pushed to head over to Andriivts'kyi Descent to find a coffee shop there since the other one was within the security zone.

We strolled in that direction, passing the artists selling their work, the tourist hawkers selling all things Ukrainian and down toward St. Andrew's Church. Streets are not very full in the hours before noon as Ukrainians like to take their time on the weekends. Many of our fellow Kyivans know this and take advantage of the quiet before the 'bridge and tunnel' people start to arrive. This day was not to be marked by anything but an attempt at normalcy. We can only ever attempt normal in a war zone because it's just never normal to accept that missiles can come at any moment, or is it? It is for us, I guess.

Drinking our coffee, we chatted, looked at old photos from before the invasion, remembered our old dog, Sammi, and reminisced about all the crap we went through before February 24, 2022, in Ukraine. We talked about the stories I wrote about my summers in Cape May Point as those memories came to the surface when death was staring us dead in the face. I thought about Pamela Hines in Morgantown, West Virginia. She was someone I connected with and have had to reduce contact with since I am focused now on military aid, and she works in the humanitarian sphere. She has done great work with her charity Gold and Blue United. Funny, we were almost neighbors, but it just didn't work out for us to return to the United States. War causes us all to focus on our priorities, and inevitably, we must reduce contact with some and increase it with others. You can't not be sad on this day because our lives changed so dramatically, and we had no say in it whatsoever. As we sat, we decided that today we would celebrate living through those first days, weeks, months and the Battle of Kyiv. Natasha planned on that day to make what she calls 'Soviet burgers' or kotlety. A trip to the underground grocery store, NOVUS, was in order. Soon enough, we were fully laden with our provisions and Philly was greeting us as dogs always do.

Natasha unpacked the groceries and so I checked my messages and found one from Andrii about a writing source. He was still working on the Foreword for this book, and so he sent me a writing resource that he found at the University of Wisconsin's Writing Center. We bantered a bit, and he ended with this message:

> 'After the war, we will take pens, paper, whisky and cigars… and go to the mountains like two Hemingways?'

This made me smile, of course, even though I am more of a Steinbeck guy. I decided that maybe I should check in with Tristan in Odesa. We exchanged messages about the Epilogue he was writing for the book, how they were spending the day and, most importantly, that all was quiet. His parting message was:

> 'We're about to walk down to the sea I heard it's crazy. It's pretty windy here.'

The two people I communicated with most were ok, so I turned off the ringer and sat back. There was nothing hanging over our heads that day, including missiles and rockets.

Natasha decided it was time to cook and decided to set the mood. She opened Pandora and put the Bob Seger Station on. Bob started belting out *Still the Same* as I poured us some Odesa Black wine. Fleetwood Mac's *Dreams* came on soon after, followed by Dire Straits with *The Sultans of Swing*. Natasha is a huge fan of Dire Straits. I like them, but she absolutely loves them. Sitting there, I realized how American we both really are on many fronts, from culture, business and communication to our tastes in food. Van Morrison began to sing how his mama told him there'd be days like this… and I thought, yea, that's what today feels like. Queen came on with *Another One Bites the Dust,* and Natasha said she hoped that's what was happening to Russian troops and equipment on the front right now as the song played. War, it's a fucking mess. I sipped my wine and Bob Seger's raspy rendition of *Turn the Page* came on, and realized that's what we did when we moved to Ukraine…

Ukraine was not our intended destination, nor did we come here thinking we would 'Go Ukrainian'. Like most others in the US, we were woefully ignorant of the actual situation. We knew about Maidan and also were well aware that there was a 'frozen' conflict struck by the Minsk Accords. In Tampa, we had attended an Orthodox Church directly under the Moscow-Patriarch and donated money to the children of Donetsk there. Never in our lives did we think the conflict would unfreeze. We went about our business, decided we loved Kyiv and bought property. Everything seemed hunky-dory until it wasn't. We, as stated before, did not believe that Russia would attack directly and that all the troops on the border were just saber rattling.

Ancient Kyiv had become our home, and we had just begun to find our place in it as the enemy crossed the border. I don't know if either one of us can tell you the exact moment we became 'Accidental Ukrainians'. Maybe it was the first day of the invasion when we decided to stay put. Could be for me that it was the day I went to sign up for Kyiv Territorial Defense, knowing full well we were outgunned, outnumbered and that I might never see Natasha again after being shot dead by a Russian weapon? Somewhere at some time, the spark was lit, and it has only grown as the war has dragged on.

Now, frankly, I personally don't want to be anywhere else but Ukraine. Of course, I want to travel, especially to Italy, Switzerland, Norway, Portugal, England and Scotland. Not until the war is resolved, though. Joe Lindsley of Ukraine Freedom News once stated that Ukraine is the location of 'Wild Freedom'. He is one of the few, the proud, who has also been here throughout the invasion, and he pretty much nails the definition of Ukraine as a people and country. Wildness is messy, though. Bless this mess!

We don't think or talk much about the future anymore. Living through the day is what we primarily think about. We don't make plans beyond a week or so. Increasingly, we turn off the news and don't listen to speculation or alleged 'western' expertise. We also are wary of the emotional nature of some of the internal channels as well. All we do is try to live and survive. I guess maybe it's more than that. We do our best to help Ukraine in any way we can. Our arrival here might have been accidental, but our staying is not. We have firmly planted our flag in Ukrainian soil. One day, I hope to be buried here, but not too soon, mind you. The future is hopeful despite the war. Natasha and I both see something in this country; in these people, there is a kindred nature that only grows stronger. Yes, Natasha has Ukrainian blood coursing through her veins, and she has tapped it well. I have absorbed Ukraine into my soul. They are in us, and we are in them. In fact, there no longer is an us and them; there is now just a 'We'. We were Accidental Ukrainians; maybe we are now becoming 'Intentional Ukrainians'.

Tristan will tell you his standpoint in the Epilogue. We are of the same mind on many things Ukrainian. This place, this culture, this people, this faith, courage, humor and this messy, wild freedom grows on us daily. Maybe it's not for everyone. Our lives have been spent wandering because we never quite fit, but here we do to an extent that we never have before. And it was all accidental.

When I am dead, bury me
In my beloved Ukraine,
My tomb upon a grave mound high
Amid the spreading plain,
So that the fields, the boundless steppes,
The Dnieper's plunging shore
My eyes could see, my ears could hear
The mighty river roar.

When from Ukraine the Dnieper bears
Into the deep blue sea
The blood of foes … then will I leave
These hills and fertile fields –
I'll leave them all and fly away
To the abode of God,
And then I'll pray … But till that day
I nothing know of God.

Oh bury me, then rise ye up
And break your heavy chains
And water with the tyrants' blood
The freedom you have gained.
And in the great new family,
The family of the free,
With softly spoken, kindly word
Remember also me.

My Testament by Taras Shevchenko
Translation by John Weir

Epilogue

By Tristan Ruark

I can't be happy here.

Living in Romania as displaced persons, we had a good life. A nice apartment, lots of friends, and many things to do. We made the most of our new life. Although we had days filled with happiness and joy, it was only a thin coat of primer over depression and homesickness. My wife would get lost in the news of the war in her homeland. One night, she came across the photos of children with their names and contact numbers written on their skin in permanent marker. Written by mothers trying to get their children safely out of the country.

The paint cracked and peeled away.

Discussions of moving back would quickly devolve into arguments. Her cornerstone was that plenty of people lived in war-torn countries and carried on with their lives. Many people she knew still lived in Odesa –her family and her friends – and they adjusted to the new way of life.

I had lived in a war zone for a while – occupied would be a more appropriate word. Willfully moving my family back into a war zone seemed to me to be a bad idea. Crazy and stupid are just a few things I was thinking about. A man takes care of his family. Here we were, living this nice life, but my wife was depressed. No family, no business.

Our first trip back to Odesa after she had left was for Christmas. We passed several checkpoints, and then, as the route grew familiar to her, I could feel my wife's happiness ebb out of the fourteen hours of fatigue in the car.

My first Ukrainian air raid siren bleated out while playing basketball with my stepson. I hadn't downloaded Telegram yet and had no idea what the threat was, just the siren beating the hell out of the sky. I looked around. I had no idea what the hell to do. The biggest thing I had ever had dropped on me in Iraq was an improvised lob bomb. Maybe just shy of a 120mm artillery round. The Russians were sending in Kinjals, Daggars, and Shahed drones. I decided to just keep playing. Knowing that if we did run, we would most likely just die tired. I'd rather go out shit talking to a thirteen-year-old about his lay-ups.

The happiness that filled my wife's being was the answer I needed to make a bad decision. I told her she should stay, and the boy and I would go back to Romania so he could finish out the school year, and we would join her in the summer. She wasn't ready to leave us for that long, so she came back with us.

Three months later, I sent my pregnant wife back to Ukraine, where she lived alone on powerless and heatless nights, bundled up in blankets and sometimes sleeping in the corridor while missiles and drones blew up in the city. She only told me about the power and the heat. The bombs, she would tell me about much later. She didn't want to worry me.

Meanwhile, the boy and I lived carefree in Romania. We lived in two completely different worlds: one where half the family was in danger, and the other half went to the movies, birthday parties, and basketball games.

The months went by with the quickness of a slug crawling across a glue trap. Our final day in Romania was bittersweet, but I was excited to be back with my wife. As a going-away present, a friend of mine paid for my stepson to take a joy ride up in a private plane. It was the last time he would be taken to the sky and the last time we would see a plane that wasn't a fighter jet in the sky.

Life happened in a blur back in Ukraine. We were officially married. We had a baby whose first hours were spent in a bunker without her parents. We celebrated a christening and another New Year in the corridor as 30 Shahed drones were engaged by air defense. We toasted as explosions shook the windows and set off car alarms in the street.

Two years of war. So much senseless death and destruction, millions of people fleeing their homes. My wife drove around Europe trying to find a landing pad. I worked on the borders of Romania with a friend who I served with in Iraq, delivering clothes and food to border crossings and displaced persons. I flew to Spain and drove my wife across Europe to Romania. Romania welcomed us with open arms. We came back to Ukraine and had a baby. We learned to live with alarms. We've been terrified in the parking garage with our neighbors when hypersonic missiles blew the doors open and rattled windows when they detonated three kilometers away. I've huddled over the baby's stroller while air defense missiles tore across the sky and Shahed drones buzzed above us.

Two years of war. Life stopped and started. War is part of our daily lives. When the alarm sounds, we run or check Telegram to see where the threat is. We get the all-clear and go to the market to get tomatoes.

I love Ukraine. After two years of war and one year of living back in Odesa, people asked me why we stayed. I don't have an answer that would make sense to someone living in the U.S. or some other place tucked away under a long-term security blanket. The answer doesn't make sense to me. It makes sense to my wife. It makes sense to John, Natasha, and Philly. It makes sense to the people who stay. Ukrainians will ask me, why I stay and if I'm afraid of the war. I ask them the same question. They tell me because it's their home. Those that don't fight support the country with their work. Paying taxes, volunteering, and existing in the face of terrorism.

I stay because it's my home, and we won't give up on her.

Part 3

Introduction

by Barbara Nickless

As I write this introduction in the fall of 2025, Ukraine has become a litmus test for who we are as Americans and Europeans. Supporting Ukraine's fight for freedom means accepting risks few democracies have faced since the devastation of the Second World War: economic instability, political division, and even the shadow of nuclear escalation. Yet the benefits of standing firm are even more profound – defending sovereignty, deterring tyranny, and proving that alliances and ideals still have weight in a volatile, fragmented world.

The stakes are global, but for some, they are also profoundly personal. For Americans John and Natasha, a husband and wife who chose to stay in Kyiv during and after the Russian invasion in 2022, the cost is not abstract. They have endured missiles and blackouts, dark-of-night terror and the haunting, persistent presence of Churchill's black dog. Through their choice to keep faith with a nation fighting for its right to exist, they remind those of us far removed from the conflict that the value of freedom should not be measured in defense budgets or approval ratings.

John and Natasha's first book, *Accidental Ukrainians: Part One,* documented the shock and moral clarity of 2022: the year they chose to remain in solidarity. *Part Two* traced the long months of 2023, as chaos hardened into a grim routine and survival required both defiance and adaptation. *Accidental Ukrainians, Part Three* captures 2024, a year when war has become the background noise of ordinary life – and yet still demands extraordinary resolve.

John and Natasha write not as war correspondents or soldiers, but as witnesses who refuse to look away. 'You on the outside call it resilience,' John writes. 'We on the inside call it resistance and defiance.' That distinction defines this memoir. For those still living in Ukraine, endurance is not passive; it is an act of moral will. As Natasha, John, and their friends work their day jobs, volunteer, help deliver aid to soldiers at the front or bring bodies back, they prove how ordinary citizens fight against tyranny.

What shines through most powerfully in this memoir is John's love for Natasha and hers for him. Theirs is a marriage rooted in shared purpose: two people holding fast to each other and to a country they have accepted as their own. In a world numbed by statistics – how many missiles, how many drones, how many dead and wounded – their story rehumanizes the war by showing how devotion and decency survive amid devastation.

Alongside this struggle with daily life runs a fierce moral questioning. John's friend, a former Green Beret, asks his audience: 'Are you worth dying for?' The question rings through the book like a bell – calling all of us to self-examination. What do we owe those who fight in our name? What kind of life, what kind of society, is worthy of their sacrifice? It is the same question Michael Connelly's detective Harry Bosch poses in his own moral universe: 'Everybody counts, or nobody counts.' That line could serve as the credo of *Accidental Ukrainians.*

Part Three also confronts the fractures within a nation at war. Natasha observes the growing divide between those who serve and those who evade service – the 'elephant in the room,' as she calls it. She anticipates the reckoning to come when veterans return home carrying both moral injury and the burden of seeing who chose to remain safe. The book does not preach, but it refuses sentimentality. War, the authors remind us, exposes not only heroism but cowardice, not only resilience but vanity and denial.

Yet through it all runs the thread of faith – sometimes shaken, sometimes renewed. Natasha's reflections on God's silence recall the spiritual questioning of all who have lived through catastrophe: Why does evil thrive? Where is justice? Her honesty and John's place this memoir in the lineage of war literature that seeks not answers but understanding – from the mud-and-blood-soaked realism of *All Quiet on the Western Front* to the moral anguish of *The Things They Carried.*

What makes *Accidental Ukrainians* distinctive, however, is its texture of daily life amid an apocalypse. Air raids interrupt morning beauty routines. Schoolchildren learn to treat the bomb shelter as their 'other' classroom. There are chocolate-chip cookies baked under bombardment, cigars enjoyed as rare luxuries, and Christmas celebrated with gratitude for simply being alive. These moments of grace remind us that love and humor are also acts of resistance.

John writes: 'First comes the inner searching. Am I doing enough? What constitutes enough?' To read this book is to share the authors' ultimate conviction that 'everybody counts' – that each act of care, each recorded memory, pushes back against erasure. *Accidental Ukrainians, Part Three* is more than a chronicle of survival; it is an argument for moral presence in an age of distraction. In staying, writing, and loving where they might have fled, John and Natasha have answered the soldier's question with their lives.

Are they worth saving? Of course – and so is every life, every act of courage, every stubborn insistence on freedom documented in this book.

Barbara Nickless
Colorado Springs, Colorado
October 2025

1

Dark Winter of the Soul

Winter 2023 to 2024 was probably the roughest one for me on a personal level. This is the reason that *Part Three* is not quite as much in chronological order as *Parts One* and *Two*. Darkness started to spread in November. Luckily, the Orthodox Nativity Fast drew me out of it toward the end of the month and all through December. Faith played a constant role in my psychological well-being. There is a distinct picture of humanity that I still have in my head at that time.

Early Christmas Eve morning, I was out with Philly for our morning walk. I approached the intersection and stopped to wait for the light. There were not many other people around at that time of day. As I glanced up, I saw a young girl, maybe six- or seven-years old, standing across the street waiting for the light with her grandfather holding his hand. They were laughing at something. A moment came, and the grandfather looked down at her, directly into her eyes, and you could see the human light of love as he did so. A huge smile broke across the girl's face, and her eyes lit up with love right back at him. That brief moment brought me joy for a good week, maybe longer.

Soon enough, Christmas would come. Natasha and I would go to church and have our feast afterwards, exchange presents, and then watch as people put more effort into New Year's than Christmas. The holidays were in the past, and the dark pall of a very difficult winter lay ahead. January was bleak and soon rolled into the second anniversary of full-scale war. My only respite was on 23 February 2024, when I went to Podil with my friend, Oleksandr. I wrote about that outing 'Night in Podil' in *Part Two*. That rolled past, and it only seemed to get darker. I guess I should tell you why.

First, it was the holdup of military aid that was stuck in a major rut of partisan politics in the US Congress. There didn't seem to be any way forward with it. Nothing looked like it was working. The only way I got through it was to accept that it just wasn't going to come. We knew that Europe would do its best, but that would probably only hold off the enemy to a certain extent. More death, destruction and missile strikes were bound to come our way. There simply was no joy in the air for months.

Second, my friend Grizzly, whom you know by now from reading the Foreword, was in a deep dive of darkness. Normally, if he was down, I lifted him up and the other way around. Grizzly is my spiritual brother, along with my main contact with soldiers on the front. These are men and women that we support regularly. His reports from them were increasingly bleak. We don't sugarcoat things and just tell the truth. War makes you a realist, no matter how hard you might fight it. We both still tried to cite Scripture or other Christian messages when the other was worse off. They helped some, but we had sunk up to our necks into a rotting hole of mud and sewage that seemed to be drowning everyone we knew who was directly involved in the war effort. Those who are not involved seemed to be doing just fine. You can tell who is involved and who is not easily. This applies to people on the street as well as those who post on social media. You get angry, and then you begin to wonder if they are smarter by not being engaged but going on with their lives as if no war is happening in the country. Some of us just can't exist in Disneyland, I guess. I'm not going to pass judgement. Just know that only about forty percent or so of the population seems to be directly contributing or involved in the war effort. That's based on surveys taken by organizations within Ukraine. This is also why there have been major problems with mobilization.

We sometimes wondered among ourselves if the other sixty percent would have been just as happy rolling over for the Russians. I can't say for sure, but it makes you think, right? One day, I ran into a guy from Mariupol. He told me his friends had stayed and were doing just fine. They had new houses, and their utility bills were much cheaper. I could only wonder if they were willing to sell their souls for lower electricity bills. That revelation got to me. He seemed unmoved by it but told me that he would not go back as long as the city was occupied. This conversation only drew me deeper into the darkness.

Third, the reports we were getting from the soldiers were bad, no, just plain awful. They didn't have enough artillery rounds. They hadn't seen a Javelin or Stinger for months. They could barely muster any counterfire. Vehicles were destroyed, and new ones were hard to come by. Our guys had modified a BMW sedan and were launching GRAD rockets off the back of it. Now, despite all this, the soldiers still felt ok. They still felt they could hold off the enemy. That provided some comfort, but we knew we would lose more of them than needed because of the shortages.

This bleakness didn't lift for a long time. The reality of it made me realize that my psychological and spiritual state was in deep decline. If I didn't make some sort of change, I would be of no use when things did get better. Reality kicked in, and I eventually began to climb out of the black hole. Grizzly had to have an intervention for him to climb out. When I felt myself begin to get a grip, I could sense he was still losing his. His story is his to tell, but he did eventually climb out of the hole. Tristan dealt with it by just ignoring all outside news and not paying attention to his phone. That's my understanding of how he made it through, but he has been in the suck before, so he is better equipped.

2

When Time Was Not on Our Side

Time is very often a cruel enemy in war, as, unlike the Stones, it is not always on your side. The Brits had left, and we were exhilarated for that very short time frame until the sweeping cold of mid-January rolled in. We let them alone for a bit so they could decompress from their time here and enjoy the holidays with their families. Soon enough, the messages started to roll in. Nicky had business and other obligations. His wife's activities for Ukraine were going to take precedence for a while. We didn't show it, but Andrii Getun (Grizzly) and I were completely dejected. We were still in the space where the US Congress was not acting. Essential American weapons and ammunition were almost out of stock among our units and others. Bitter snow fell, and the soldiers kept fighting with what they had. Grizzly and I felt useless to them beyond the occasional supplies we could either give or raise money for in Ukraine.

These are things you don't speak about with those who support you. We maintain the axis of strength while feeling utterly alone. Luckily, Grizzly and I have each other. We openly share the bad news and do our best to support each other. The Brits finally informed us that they would not be able to return for another run for our unit until August. They did add that they could supply some funds for items we could source in Ukraine before that. This helped some. Damon Warren (British Cossack) would be in and out a few times before Nicky, Jon Allison (Top) and Paul Tregouet (Philly FF) would return in August. BC told us he would make small drops to Grizzly as he could. That also helped to some extent.

Truth is, if you allow yourself, you will spin far into the abyss and not be able to climb out. Psychological and spiritual resiliency requires a certain aloofness to suffering. If you or people you know are not directly affected, you can empathize but must not allow yourself to go too far in that direction. Additionally, if you want people to keep helping, well, you can't turn into a little whiny bitch (not gender related). Strength is what gets things done. The projection of strength makes people want to help. We never felt weak in those times; it was just that the Black Dog was nearly always with us in those days, in bed, in the shower, on the toilet, at meals, at rest, just bloody fucking everywhere. The Black Dog is not a puppy, but sure felt like it in those days. He followed us no matter how hard we tried to get away from him. Me, personally, the best places I kept him away were in church and certain intimate moments with Natasha.

Focus being the name of the game to keep the Black Dog in his kennel. If you can take time to completely focus on another person (intimacy and conversation), then the Black Dog retreats. If you are a person of faith and can totally focus on God, the Liturgy or some other service, then the Black Dog takes a nap. Now, I know that I have written a whole chapter on the Black Dog, but that never contained strategies for overcoming those deep-seated feelings of dread. Maybe I should write a self-help book? Nah, I have a bit of a tainted view of psychology after watching 'The Sopranos'. Here's the kicker, I probably could have watched the series in that time to lift me up.

Now, you are probably wondering if I am some sort of sick, deranged person for taking comfort in 'The Sopranos.' So, I guess I should explain. Natasha and I both feel this way about the show, so we are on the same page. We have watched the series several times when feeling homesick. This doesn't mean we have ties to il Cosa Nostra or a penchant for watching violence. We watch it because of how 'dey tawk to each otha'. People from New Jersey are often considered rude because of our ethnic, cultural style of communication. We just happen to be blunt, quick to the point with a heavy pinch of sarcasm. You can stand in line at any store and make wisecracks to complete strangers or normally join in or affirm without anyone getting offended or blinking an eye. If they do, you mostly identify them as an outsider. Philly and New Yorkers fit right in as they are of the same communication breed. Anyway, I did digress, didn't I? Wadyyagunnadoaboutit? Yes, you're stuck as a reader. No offense to you that are sensitive.

In essence, we were dealing with walking the Black Dog deeper into an abyss. The British weren't coming any time soon. I had my job to look after, along with Natasha and Philly, as well as occasional duties as an Altar Server at church. Grizzly's whole life is helping the military, so he took it much harder. His oldest daughter had already established herself in the US, and his younger one was soon to depart. This was clearly taking a toll on him and his wife. Luckily, his wife (Anna) recognized how deep he had crawled and brought in help in the form of a spiritual intervention. I won't share too much beyond that, as it is his business. Thank God we both have very good and dedicated wives. I also have PT (Matt Boben) in Philadelphia. He is another person I met through the Eastern Europe's Modern Conflict (EEMC) group on Facebook. Roy Cauldery (British veteran) started the group way back when and served with both Damon and Jon in the Queen's Regiment, if I understand it correctly. Matt is a retired US Army Captain who now serves as a Physical Therapist in the US Veterans Administration. I can turn to him in times of trouble, frustration, or to vent. Matt very much wants to help out physically on the ground in Ukraine, but his wife (Sara) is not in the best of health, and he has young children. So, I help deal with that, and he helps me deal with my shit. Plus, we are both Philadelphia Eagles fans who love cheesesteaks and the Jersey Shore. Our circles are small but extremely effective and supportive. We are still here, and we made it through, but it was a very dark and long walk with the Black Dog.

Proverbs 31:10-12 'Who can find a virtuous wife? For her worth is far above rubies. The heart of her husband safely trusts her; So he will have no lack of gain. She does him good and not evil All the days of her life.'

3

Guerrilla Volunteering

Blaming others for your shortcomings or mistakes is weak. Facing them is Step One. Admitting them is Step Two. Dealing with them is Step Three. Correcting them is Step Four. My spirit kept slipping into darkness, and I thought that my way to climb out was to volunteer more. I had been practicing Guerilla Volunteering since the beginning of the full-scale invasion. Basically, I jumped in and volunteered where needed, when needed. Sometimes this was signing up as an official volunteer with an organization. Other times, this was simply stepping in for a task or two whenever anyone asked. I had left a couple of well-known NGO's in the first year of war for reasons I don't want to disclose. This jumping around had helped. The only place where I stayed consistent was with Grizzly and our soldiers. I stayed on because I had a deeper personal relationship with him and a direct connection to men and women who were fighting, risking and losing their lives every day.

Black days and nights just followed one after another, yet I continued volunteering. Most of this was done in providing writing and editorial duties for various organizations. Deadlines always seemed to loom over me. A weight lay upon me and was crushing, driving me further into a grave. Grizzly and I still spoke regularly. I don't know when the light in my head went off or what set it off. The realization came that the weight I had was put there by me. Volunteering more only added to the stress of war.

Difficult days lay ahead as now I was faced with having to let people know I just couldn't help any more. This process was much like triage by combat medics. First, I knew they all could survive without me, but who to cut first? Instead of naming the actual organizations, I will just explain how I came to the decision. First, I cut out any organizations or people who were not actually in Ukraine. This was not easy, as I really liked one organization and enjoyed the work. However, there were deadlines involved all the time, which just added to the already existing war stress. Sliced it off much to their chagrin. I think they thought they really had a hook in me, but they really had no idea of the reality we face in a war zone, no matter how much they want to understand. They stopped communicating altogether, even when I tried to check in later. Thus, I didn't really feel bad about it after a few months had passed.

Next, I had to go through a deeper assessment of those still in Ukraine. I took a deep look at all individuals and organizations. My criteria came down to only helping those who are actively working towards military victory, not information victory, not diplomatic victory. Now, I had signed an agreement with at least one of these organizations, but looking through it, I found it really wasn't legally binding. They took a while to get the message, but it finally seemed to sink in. I only wanted to help the soldiers and veterans. Not with words but with material. A woman I knew and helped had left the country after nearly two years volunteering on the front, so that one went easy.

Angst had not left yet, but the weight was lifting, and a ray of sunshine found its way through. A sense of guilt lasted for quite some time, so that needed to dissipate before I could get back to 'normal'. We make fun of that word a lot in Ukraine. There is no normal during war, although at times I guess we feel 'war normal', whatever the hell that is. Time heals all wounds? I guess these wounds were not very deep. Natasha was having her own issues, so we worked on her and me together. She went to Warsaw for free trauma training sponsored by Rotary International through a grant for teachers at Pechersk School International. Natasha brought back valuable lessons which she taught me. That's the plus of having someone you love and trust in the foxhole with you. Cobwebs of dread began to clear, and some of the real work would begin later.

Being outside of it all now, this is what I discovered as a non-combatant who once served in the military. There is a code that exists within each of us. No code is still a code. My code is to do everything I can within my means to help those who are fighting or helping those who are fighting. The problem we have as non-combatants is that we must exist within the vagaries of life in a war zone. Distractions come quickly and easily. Doing more often ends up making you do less. Doing what matters must become the key. Jumping around does no one any good in life and war. You've got to stick to something in order to gain expertise, discipline and commitment. Guerilla warfare is one thing, guerilla volunteering just causes one to become ineffective. Although some personality types might just thrive in it. I can't say anything other than from my own experience. What I can say is that it was the first step in overcoming what seemed to be a major pending case of PTSD, which would have rendered me completely useless. But that was only lifting the weight; more work was still ahead.

4

Teaching Under Fire

In our school, every teacher has two classrooms: the regular one and the bomb shelter one. We set them up in a way that invites students to learn, explore and feel welcomed before the kiddos start their school year. It is a natural part of their learning experience since the war broke out. The bomb shelter locations affect every field trip and possible outing for students and teachers alike. Where is the nearest shelter? Question number 1 with an answer on every permission slip we hand out to parents and each other in cases of 'emergency'.

This might not seem 'normal' to any outsider, but to those of us who have been dealing with the realities of war for quite some time, it is basically routine. As the children are welcomed on the first day of school, their number one priority on the agenda is not to get to know their classmates and play teambuilding games. Within the first half hour, the students are introduced to the routine of travelling to the bomb shelter and seeing their other classroom in case of air raids. The process of getting to the bomb shelter should take less than five minutes, be quiet and calm (to the best of everyone's ability), and be ready to learn in the next location in under 10. Believe it or not, it is quite possible with just enough practice for the 6-year-olds to simply roll their eyes at the next air raid wailing about in the perimeter instead of crying uncontrollably, grab their water bottles/jackets and line up quietly (with some groaning) to proceed to the bomb shelter. I have seen it happen. I have made it happen. The routine. No questions. No arguments. No bewildered looks anymore. Occasional cursing from the middle schooler having a rough morning causes more reactions than the air raid routine.

The children respond to your calm. If you, the teacher, are unphased, they simply follow the lead. After plenty of practice, it becomes second nature to all involved. Sorry to disappoint a possible Russian reader looking for teary dramatic outbursts for all the efforts put into this, but the staple reaction from the kiddos is the deep eye roll and a groan. It, in itself, cancels out the terror (chaotic and life-threatening as it may be) and leaves a number of teachers dealing with 'unacceptable' situations of reprimanding the students for buying chocolate croissants during the air raid!

First, the students are familiarized with the protocol and the steps we follow to be safe. Next, the students practice following the steps. Then, the steps lose their eerie feel and become the routine that no longer carries the unbearable weight. Just something we do every day, like reciting the digraphs.

The students feel comforted by the calendar hanging in the bomb shelter. It has the photos of our local soldiers with their call signs. Many times, I saw the students looking at them, making confident remarks:

– They took down that rocket. They know what they doin'. I can't argue with that.

As a teacher, there are a few things to keep in mind. First, when you prep for your lessons, always have activities in mind that are appropriate for the bomb shelter. Ultimately, there should be a number of them prepped and ready to go when the need arises: social-emotional learning, fun math, guided reading, or read-alouds are popular choices. There are numerous sorting, categorizing, and hands-on authentic learning options that can be utilized, depending on the emotional state of your students. If the routine is followed to a T, there is almost no time wasted between transitions, and the kiddos are learning in either classroom. My computer goes with me everywhere, and by the time they take their seats, my projector is up and running. It is always good to have a Plan B. Sometimes, Plan B is your most important one. If I can anticipate it, I can avoid turning my bomb shelter learning into complete chaos. It helps to have a teaching partner who anticipates with you and helps move things along smoothly.

Looking back at my year of teaching, remembering those days in the shelter, I am happy to announce that, all in all, there are no horror stories to hold your attention. It is rather what I called it earlier – a pretty boring routine, with tons of eye rolling on the part of my students, quick remarks 'argh, again' or something similar, quick hands and feet travelling to the shelter under five minutes, settling in and learning, learning, learning! Nothing to see here, folks, nothing much to tell beyond what it is. Once in the shelter, the rest is the job of our skilled soldiers to get us through the day. So far, my respect and gratitude to all of them. God bless you guys for making it possible for us to move on with our jobs and our lives.

Kids always seem fine. They do not show any obvious signs of fear. There is no drama. Almost 'disappointing' for a teacher like me, who spent an entire week participating in trauma-related workshops in Poland, a training organized by the Rotary Club International in May of 2024.

Before I decided to travel all the way to Poland and back, I had weighed my pros and cons. We know that traveling is a major hassle during the war. Waiting on the borders to check in and check out, waiting again… Plus, leaving your family behind to 'enjoy' their stay in Kyiv through bombings is no fun either. Your mind is not at rest until everyone is in the same place. At least for us it is. We have been together through thick and thin; we are foxhole buddies. Plus, my dog gets nervous when one of us is gone for a while. First, he gets a major attitude, then he gets mad, and finally, very unsettled in his perimeter.

On the other hand, I have never taken an official trauma-informed training. I was bothered by my observations of students and their response to trauma; so far, nothing, zinch, nada. All is well, business as usual for them, just another Tuesday. I was missing something. Some clues that were not obvious, the behavior indications I was so diligently looking for, missed my vigilance entirely. I needed to talk to the pros. Here, on the ground, we mostly had professionals dealing with post-traumatic events in children and adults. But what happens in the case of ongoing trauma? How do we all deal with that? Making it up as we go, that's how. PTSD cannot happen if you are still in the middle of traumatic events. There is no 'Post' just yet.

I signed up for the training that was taking place during my spring break, when I was supposed to veg out on the couch, binge-watching *The House of Cards* or whatever with a glass of wine and a pack of truffles accompanying my 'rest'. I packed my bags, still frustrated with myself for missing the most important Christian holiday – Pascha, which was falling right on the week I was away participating in the workshops! How could I be so forgetful towards something that I patiently wait and prepare for? The most culminating event of the Christian world in the Universe. I have committed to the training, and there was no backing out of it because people flying to Poland have also committed their time.

With my husband's blessings, I set off on the train to Warsaw.

5

Rest and Peace

Train rides can be very soothing to a restless and tired spirit. Their night rocking, and occasional light in the fields touching the passing cart ever so lightly, connects to here and now every passing second. The only available reality is that of a tiny moving compartment that welcomed you for just a few hours. It's a great setup for those of us who can never seem to find a moment of peace outside of it, in a real world, where we are spread too thin between its obligations. They say it's important to have time for yourself. I agree. I even try. Somehow, I tend to prefer my couch after a long day of obligations. I am pretty sure it does not fit into a self-care category, where yoga, fruits and vegetables eaten with mindfulness, no coffee after 2:00 p.m., and lots of walking take a rightful crown of the Gold Standard. In a train car, the internet goes in and out, so there goes the phone. People around you might be sleeping, so there goes the opportunity to catch up on some reading. The view outside is readily available for a moment if you pass some lonely streetlight. Otherwise, get ready to rest between the border stops and checkpoints, with guards suspiciously eyeing everyone's face and proof of residence/belonging. Once that part is behind, on to a new 'adventure' of getting to yet another location with 'god-knows-what' awaiting you there.

Most of our destinations never match the picture in our heads. They are either better or worse, but never quite what we imagined them to be. In my case, I had no expectations, other than sharing a room in a hotel with one of my colleagues. Not a perfect scenario if one of you were trying to hibernate peacefully for a week or so. The last-minute cancellations played in my favor, and the first pleasant surprise consisted of my staying in a quaint whitewashed room all by myself.

There comes a time in everyone's existence when cancelled plans or the unexpected change of circumstances do what needs doing. In my case-forcing their unpredictable variables into my already chaotic state-of-affairs and producing the least awaited but much needed result – a complete island of rest. Until I closed that small hotel room door, I had no idea how exhausted my body and mind were. I realized the advantages of being transported to another country with no air raids or loud explosions for the next few days were going to be magical. The purpose of my training was to gain knowledge about ongoing trauma in children and apply it to the best of my ability back home.

What I did not expect was a gift of peace for myself. I am forever grateful to the Rotary Club for that.

Dwor Konstancin was situated outside of Warsaw, in the woods, inviting all the guests to explore the *Konstancin-Jeziorna* National Park right in front of the main entrance and listen to the birds singing all day long. The blanket of soft pine needles under the soles of my Converse sneakers that were beating the asphalt just a few days ago prompted my feet to slow down and reset immediately, like a spa hostess with a hushed voice greeting you in the quiet rest zone. The aroma of blooming field flowers and a spread of lovely hydrangea bushes all around the entrance perimeter promised that I was going to love the place.

Refreshed and excited despite myself, I went out to explore the small perimeter without venturing into the woods. After all, it was a Friday night, and the sleeping exercise was not going to work just yet: the hotel was booked solid for an upcoming wedding party over the weekend, and the guests were enjoying themselves in every possible square meter of space filled with music, chatter, and laughter. It felt so normal. Like, life is going on outside the war zone in its usual tempo, with karaoke singing, dancing, and large groups of people gathering in one place that might not be safe, militarily speaking. Things like that cross your mind quickly, in orderly fashion: a) the nearest bomb shelter, don't see the sign, b) the crowd is too big, how are they planning to abort, c) the only possible safe exit into the woods, spreading in pairs for safety, d) the loud music attracts attention unnecessarily, e) the electricity is everywhere… The switch in your brain doesn't turn off automatically, just because you find yourself in a fancier place. You have to consciously make an effort – do a 5, 4, 3, 2, 1 – quietly to snap out of survival mode. It takes time, an attitude adjustment of sorts, like stepping into a new reality, with water, electricity, no blackouts, and planes flying in the sky are simply a signal of travelling by air, not a possible threat. And in the quiet slumber of the morning hours, when one of the guests decides to take his motorcycle out for a spin around 5:00 a.m., there is no need to jump up in a hurry, grab your cell phone and a T-shirt off the nightstand, run to the hallway for 'safety', and check the local channels for ballistic threats. You are ok for now.

Having a mental conversation with myself during the first couple of hours of the stay was a necessary transition into a life with no air raids or hiding in the hallway, just like it used to be a while back. Tactical breathing worked its magic. As I was quietly exploring the safety of my immediate perimeter, I walked into a lovely outside seating area with a few guests enjoying their food from the restaurant. I thought of grabbing a table, even though eating alone in a restaurant was never my thing (it just looks weird). However, my mission was slowly shaping up to revisit life as I know it currently. My husband kept nudging with 'enjoy for the both of us, will you, please', and I gave it a go.

I met Lisa and John, who just settled at their table, waiting for food. I overheard them speak English in a way American people do, making you feel instantly at home anywhere in the world. I introduced myself and said hello. It turned out they were the trauma workshop organizers! It felt warm and personable to share our meal together, be American together before the official meet and greet of the following days, and I was instantly wrapped up in a sensation of being in the right place at the right time.

My days in Dwor Konstancin were a mixture of timely psychology, human connection, truth revealing and raw, strengthening in the end, generously mixed with American-style luncheons (sorry to disappoint some European readers, but Americans are way past their obsession with burgers as a staple of their diet and are not at all embarrassed to ask for healthier options). In between the sessions, I was hiking every imaginable and visible trail of flat luscious woods, sharing my bliss with horse riding enthusiasts, galloping here and there for the fun of it, spraying perfectly peaceful sand around the tracks and leaving a savory smell of the horse sweat behind. I managed to do the same on the very last day of my stay. The last time I rode a horse was in the village, when I was nine or 10, on a sunny day just like that. Except the safety measures were quite different: no saddle, no training prior, just a crazy uncle giving in to our request to try it out. I remember feeling the horse's back swaying naturally between the steps it peacefully took, and me trying so hard not to slide down with it immediately to my left or right. I would never hear the end of it from my cousins about the 'city girl' riding a horse. I pretended to have fun and keep my poker face, sweating a little on my forehead from the effort of it all…

The owner of the horse-riding farm was a young kid, speaking very little English. We got to talking the small talk. Turned out his grandfather was an immigrant from Ukraine, who settled in Poland after WWII. The farm was everything I wanted to see and smell: horses, sheep, chickens, cats and dogs running about protecting the place, squeaky gates. The experience of horse riding started with me getting to know the horse and brushing its mane, rubbing the beast with a soft sponge all around, speaking to it and letting him know I meant no harm. The time we spent together lasted for an hour, but I was filled with all the right emotions for days to come. There was another version of me hiding behind all the tough layers, just a kid who loves nature and bugs, the animals running about, minding their own business, and I am in the midst. Somehow, that felt rewarding, made me human again, connected me back to my sense of wildness. Like I am barefoot and pregnant somewhere in the village, baking bread, wearing sheepskin to keep warm from the chilly wind, making borscht and baking bread in the fire pit or the brick oven. Maybe one day?

After the training, I was inspired to implement as many exercises as I could in the classroom. One of them was a tree craft. The roots the kiddos painted represented their memories, the trunk represented their strength, the branches were the people they held dear, and the leaves were the events they remembered. I thought I was taking a risk with it. Would the first graders even understand the metaphorical sense of it? Is it even age-appropriate at this point in their development? I was completely floored by the result. First, they got so into it, that the timer going off was completely ignored and the extension of 10 more minutes was awaiting the same fate. After all was painted, they took their time sharing with each other the great and the saddest parts of their lives. It was almost the end of the school year at that point. As a teacher, I thought I had learned everything there was to learn about each and single one of them as a person, their background, their hopes and dreams, concerns, preferences, etc. I do remember feeling somewhat shocked when one of my outspoken students shared one event, which he was still feeling sad about. He held his head low, was serenely calm, obviously sad, and hadn't formed a complete thought at first. 'This is my horse', he said. 'I loved it'. I knew I was going to regret asking what happened to it, but it seemed a natural progression at that point. I probed gently: 'Do you want to share some things about it? You do not have to, if you do not want to, but we are here for you.'

'When the war started, my ranch got bombed. The shrapnel killed the horse I loved. I miss him.'

6

Tristan and Yevgheny

24 February 2024 came and went with only a very long walk with the Black Dog, even though I was blind to its existence. Who wants to celebrate or commemorate yet another year of war? I did have something to look forward to as Tristan and I were scheduled to meet in person for the first time. We were due to present at a conference on developing a veteran's program for Ukraine. Natasha was skeptical as the conference was scheduled for 29 February. She was adamant that events scheduled for this leap year day would never result in anything. I am unsure if anything came as a result of the conference or not, as I was still in my 'Guerilla Volunteering' mode. Conferences, forums, blah, blah, blah and yada, yada, yada have become all the rage in Ukraine, as well as outside it. The best results we have seen so far are that they have injected money into certain people's pockets, elevated the alleged 'concern' and 'expertise' of others and given a boon to hotels, caterers and special events organizers. Action is what we want, not talk. Yes, I am cynical, but talk is just a waste of time unless it yields real results. Of course, neither Tristan nor I had that attitude on the eve of the conference. We were excited at the prospect of making a difference in this sphere.

Tristan and Yevgheny took the overnight train from Odesa and were due in fairly early. Luckily, their arrival coincided with my day off and Philly's walk. Tristan is hard-core, so they planned to hump from Kyiv's main rail station. Their route would bring them along one of the areas where Philly and I go in the morning. Philly did his business as we passed Leontovicha Street on the side of St Volodymyr's Cathedral. We crossed Taras Shevchenko Boulevard and headed into the middle of it, which contains a park setting reminiscent of Park Avenue in Manhattan. I scanned both sides of the street as we slowly meandered away from the city center. Tristan's long red beard and gait came into view on the far side of the street. It was way too early for them to check in to their AirBnB located overlooking Maidan, so we slowly walked back toward my flat, where they could relax and sit for a few. It wasn't particularly cold that day, and they soon passed Philly's muster. After catching up and showing them our place, and giving Tristan a copy of John Steinbeck's .A Russian Journal., we headed out so they could check in.

Yevgheny was impressed by Kyiv, as was Tristan on our short walk. The place wasn't ready yet, so we headed down to Kreshchatyk to Pashtet for breakfast. Pashtet is a Kyiv or maybe even Ukraine-wide restaurant chain. It's significant to me because it was one of Roman Cybriwsky's favorite haunts. Roman loved Kyiv and Ukraine, so I think he would have approved of my taking these Kyiv virgins (as in first-time visit virgins) to his favorite place. There's a whole chapter dedicated to Roman coming up later. We took a seat overlooking the busy street as the life of Kyiv scuttled about. Breakfast was good as usual, and we chatted about our lives in war, family, literature, but never touched on US politics. There are reasons people like Tristan and I are living and staying in Ukraine, and US politics is one of them. We dudes cannot abide by them any longer.

Soon enough, their rental was ready, so we headed over so they could check it out and check in. What an awesome view they had with two balconies overlooking Maidan. I can only imagine what the place might have looked like in 2014. This would just have been a week after, and the cleanup would have still been going on if we went nine years back in time. We chilled. They checked out their accommodations. Jenya handled the Host since he is a native and fluent in both Ukrainian and Russian. Yes, many people in Kyiv still speak Russian as they do in Odesa, where Tristan and Jenya live. This is not Lviv. There are very few Language Checkers here. Everyone goes about their business in whichever language is most comfortable. We who speak neither language get confused because most people speak a version of both languages (Surzhyk). I myself often speak a different one, which is a mixture of English, Ukrainian and Russian. They haven't named this dialect yet, but they should because many of us native English speakers with history in Ukraine speak it. Surzhyk allegedly refers to any mixture of two languages, but doesn't seem to take into account a third language. The symbol of Ukraine is the trident (tryzub), so let's call it Tryzhyk for now.

Tristan and Jenya were excited to see the city, so we soon made our way back onto the streets and headed for what used to be the Friendship Monument. Well, we have all had friends who have come after us, but maybe not try to execute us. That symbol of the 'relations' between Ukraine and Russia has long since died. However, the views over the Dnipro River from that point are widespread, and you can see far into the horizon to the east, where all the fighting is concentrated. Parts of the outskirts of Kyiv were occupied within that distance. There is a pedestrian bridge where a missile strike hit early in the war, which brings you up to the now sand-bagged statue of St Volodymyr the Great, one of the fathers of the Golden Age of Kyivan Rus. The path meanders along and is called Volodymyr's Hill. High hills overlook the river below, with the teeming city life there, but sometimes hidden from the ears and eyes. Eventually, the path leads to St Andrew's Church and the beginning of Artists' Alley.

Legend has it that St Andrew the First-Called planted a cross at the top of the hill and stated that this place would become a holy place. We don't know if he meant that particular spot or the entire settlement of what would have been the pagan land of Kyi or some other warrior tribe of nature worshippers. It's nice to feel like the place you live is holy, whether you are a believer or not. Toward the end, we ran into some of the artists, or maybe they're just art dealers who sell their wares. Weekdays only find a few, but on the weekends, they are bountiful. Tristan is a great lover of art in all its forms, so he enjoyed it. The path empties onto Andrew's Descent (Andriivskyi's Descent), which is a very steep hill coming up from another ancient part of the city (Podil). It's full of art galleries, cafes and souvenir hawkers. Basically, a tourist trap.

We cruised up and around the church, stopped at the spot where the first church built by St Volodymyr once stood. This was called the Church of the Tithes, built between 989 and 996. Batu Khan destroyed it around 1240 during the Mongol Invasion. It was rebuilt again, some six hundred years later, only to be destroyed again by the Soviets. Tragedy, horror, hate, death, destruction, along with joy, creativity, ostentatiousness and spirit all live together as neighbors here in Kyiv. The Ukrainian branch of the Russian Orthodox Church had built a small chapel next to the original foundation of the Church of the Tithes in trying to stake their claim to the church and the grounds so that Russia could continue to propagate its great myth of history. Now, as I type this, the chapel has been torn down, and Ukraine is claiming its religious rights to this blood-soaked holy site. Spilling blood seems to be the path to salvation. Someone has to bleed so others can be saved and that's what Kyiv and the whole nation are doing. Tristan and I know and understand that. We also know that we must stand with them and also bleed if we must. You can't escape the grip this country has on you once it grabs you. That's the horror and beauty of it.

We spent the whole day on our feet. I was beat up after taking them around the old city. They were, too, and we had the conference scheduled for later in the day so people in the US could take part. We went our separate ways and met later at the venue. The conference gave about 40 people a three-to-five-minute window to speak. It was exhausting. Tristan spoke on one panel, and mine was the last panel. Luckily, coffee and sweets were supplied in ample quantities. We met interesting people and listened to some very good ideas. But we were both glad when it was over.

The next day was Friday, and I was due to work, so the boys would be on their own. They took a trip to Bucha, which I thought was way overpriced. War Tourism is a thing, and it's good to put money in the pockets of those who are suffering, so Tristan didn't think twice about it. Tristan said their visit to Kyiv was transformational for Jenya, especially their tour of Irpin and Bucha, where they experienced the war on a far more personal level. Odesa has been targeted frequently, but there were no tanks and artillery outside the city. No one in Odesa's suburbs had been raped, tortured, and killed by the enemy. I never really looked at it that way since we had lived through it all and tried to move on from the horrors. Jenya seemed to be enjoying himself as a teenager amongst the old dudes, so that was a plus. My day passed rather easily. The next day, Natasha would be off, so we would all get together. Natasha needs her coffee and her sleep on the weekends, so I took Philly duty in the morning. We set a meeting time with the boys late that morning and headed out.

Jenya, being a growing teen, was already hungry by the time we met up. We stopped at a St Sophia's Cafe where Natasha and I had eaten during warmer weather, which opens up onto the grounds of St Sophia's Cathedral. This is the oldest standing church and was built by Yaroslave the Wise, the estranged son of Volodymyr the Great. We planned to take the boys inside after breakfast. Funny enough, indoor breakfast was a bit too pretentious and fancy for our taste, but we decided to muddle through, much to the chagrin of a few ostentatious diners. Yes, Kyiv has many of them. Somehow, here, people think that their level of income makes them better than everybody else whereas back in Jersey, we have no problem putting millionaires in their place. Clearly, none of the diners were anywhere near that level, but they certainly wanted you to think that. These types have a very difficult time with us foreigners, who just aren't impressed and will be vocal about it if given the opportunity. Nobody said or did anything, and we went on to have a pleasant and fun breakfast with occasional glances at us Americans in jeans and t-shirts eating off fine china and sipping coffee from fancypants cups and saucers. Looking back, it would have been a funny Ukrainian or American sitcom moment.

We entered the cathedral grounds with full stomachs and light spirits. Natasha connected very well with both guys. She educated. I educated. We gave a grand tour of this, our home city, which we both love and hate, but that's material for another time. Tristan and Jenya loved the icon painting, but my impression is that they were most impressed with the diorama of Ancient Kyiv inside the cathedral. This is a very clear illustration of the topography and buildings of Kyivan Rus. Imagination allows you to transport back in time to those days when this nation was established. You can smell the horses, hear the calls of peasant and noble alike and feel the energy of this metropolis that has existed for over a thousand years. There was a new art display in the Bakery section of the grounds, and we purchased tickets for entry.

Ukrainian art has something indescribable about it, or at least much of it does. You can almost feel the soul of the artists in their work. I sometimes wonder if the myth of the great 'Russian Soul' is what they have been searching for and trying to steal from Ukrainians. That somehow, this place, Kyivan Rus, is where the soul began, and somehow, they want it and can't have it, so they would rather kill and destroy those who do have it. Maybe that's too philosophical a thought for this particular book. The Bakery has five different galleries, and they all featured the work of varied artists that day. Tristan was giving Jenya official Art Appreciation lessons. Natasha was mesmerized, as she always is by art. I felt the soul of the paintings. Tristan seemed most impressed with the art by a soldier in the trenches who had used mud, dust, ash and carbon from expended weapons. Here was a guy who sat there while being attacked by artillery and created art. That's the indomitable Ukrainian spirit which gives all of us confidence. It was one combat veteran calling out to another in the midst of death, destruction, stench, rats, cold, fatigue, discomfort, hunger and camaraderie. We spent quite a bit of time amongst those creations that day before heading toward home to take Philly for a walk, which meant all of us.

Hours had passed, and soon enough, we were all hungry again, with Jenya in the lead, of course. Tonight, it would be Georgian cuisine at Mama Manana. Natasha and I love this place and always stuff ourselves silly whether we eat there or order takeout. The food is that good. We were a party of four, and they asked if we had a reservation. I could feel Natasha holding back her sarcasm. We rarely go out on Saturdays because of the moron crowds that come to our part of the city to be seen and act cool. Basically, the Kyiv version of the 'Bridge and Tunnel' crowd. Yes, yes, it doesn't reflect well on either of us, I know. But do you want the truth or a comfortable and convenient lie? Neither of us are really city people nor do we like crowds due to our more introverted nature. But we are not the mousy types that most people classify as introverts. Instead, we are more like the Tony Sopranos of introverts, capiche? Anyway, they miraculously found us a table.

Tristan was certainly in heaven. I think Jenya might have preferred burgers and fries. They had done that quest on the day they went to Bucha, so Jenya was stuck with us adults and our love for Georgian food. These people have made their mark in Ukraine, and boy, are we happy about it. Frankly, I can't remember what we ordered, as I leave that part to Natasha since she is an expert. I do know that we got stares from other diners when they saw the amount of food delivered to our table. Well, we love to eat, and none of us is shy about it. Somewhere in Tristan's deep memories, I feel like he has this vivid recollection of that dining experience. We ate. We laughed. We talked. We ate some more. It was a jovial and interesting evening, but soon enough it came to an end.

Outside on the street, the early March air was crisp but not exceedingly cold. We stood in front of Mama Manana and said our good-byes as the boys would depart on an early train to Odesa, and I had duty as an Altar Server at our church the next morning. It wasn't a long goodbye. Natasha and I both hate goodbyes, so we're not very good at it. Tristan and Jenya were truly thankful for our hosting them in Kyiv and showing them the sights. Tristan remarked that he could tell we love the city and its history. He is right. We love it far more than we hate it. He insisted that we come to Odesa so they could return the favor, and we agreed. Natasha has been to Odesa many times, but I have never been and still have not made it. I think now of the popular response for the Jewish Seder, 'Next year in Jerusalem' but in my case it's 'Next time in Odesa.' If we live, we will go.

7

Don't Think, Act

Fiction. Literature. These were once very important to me but had seemed to have lost their luster once the invasion broke out. I couldn't escape into them, couldn't learn from them for the longest time after 24 February 2022. A few novellas were all I had managed to muddle through at a very slow pace as the war raged outside. This gave me a new appreciation for the novella over the novel. Short, sweet, to the point and didn't take as much time to read. Reading long novels that were deeply woven used to be my go-to. Mainly, I read classics of literary fiction. Science fiction, horror and fantasy fell by the wayside of youthful tastes as I grew older. Who wants to read horror when you are living in it? Christmas 2023 was when I first bought a long novel.

There's a story behind the selection. Somewhere, while the battles were far away, I had come across the Nobel Prize Winner for Literature for 2023, Jon Fosse. Now, I have never been one to follow these sorts of literary prizes nor buy the winners' book or books. Information came across that Fosse's book 'Septology' was his magnum opus. Since I am up in years, these swan songs often catch my attention. Once I did deeper research, I heard that he had used a completely new style for the novel. One of a rambling chain of thought with no punctuation. Those who do not follow conventions also appeal to me. A rebel at an advanced age is not what we often picture. There must be something deep in your soul to rebel as you grow older.

Natasha had wanted to check out a new bookstore in Kyiv called ReadEat, and one day during Christmas Break, we decided to give it a shot. We both are kind of crazy for bookstores. I was curious if they would have a decent selection of works in English, as most places here only carry standard, mundane fare with an occasional gem. Discipline would be required so I had to set one. The decision was made that the only book I would buy would be 'Septology', should they have it in stock. This was self-discipline; I didn't share it with Natasha.

The bookstore was set up nicely with a café on the first floor serving coffee and sweets. This brought back memories of my early days in DC when I worked as a busboy at what was then called Kramerbooks and Afterwords Café in Dupont Circle. I Googled it, and they are still in business but now simply called Kramer's. That place always had the feel of one that would stay. Celebrities were often patrons. I cleared dishes for Lily Tomlin. While I was working there, the Red-Hot Chili Peppers visited twice when they were on tour. Years later, I would drive them as a chauffeur for the HFS Festival. These forays into our past are the habit of older people, I guess. Our stories are our lives. We never tell anyone the full story, as it's something that is uniquely ours.

We grabbed some lattes, and I picked up a brownie to satisfy my sweet tooth. Most of the books are on the second floor, so we made our way up. ReadEat is laid out on the second floor in an industrial loft style, much like many places in Brooklyn. A very well-decorated Christmas tree with plush chairs was displayed in the middle of the floor. I took my seat in another section on a fine velvet couch to enjoy my coffee and treat. Natasha started browsing the English section of children's books for her 1st grade students at Pechersk School International. Once finished, I wandered over to the English literature section. Same old, same old, or so it seemed. A whole section of blue books caught my eye. These were nondescript with very simple fonts on the spines. The print is relatively small, so I had to get close with my old eyes. There it was, 'Septology' by Jon Fosse.

The book was very thick for a paperback, a whopping 825 pages. Examining the book, I opened a random page. Whoa, brother! This seems like just a jumble of words with no end. There's simply no way I am going to be able to read this format for that many pages straight. Those were my first impressions. I put the book back on the shelf and wandered on. Nothing grabbed my eye or appealed to me, so I eventually returned. Maybe if there wasn't a war on, I would not have given it a go. There is something strangely metaphysical about living through war, or at least in Ukraine, there is. I haven't experienced war anywhere else, so I can't really say, can I? The thought came that I should stick to my discipline and the word I had given myself. So, Natasha had her pile, and I had my one as we made our way to the checkout.

'Septology' to me is an old man's book. Maybe it appeals to older women, also. That's the first thing I will say about the work. The story takes place at Christmas, so it was certainly an appropriate buy for the season. I started it as the holiday season began, but did not finish it until after the second anniversary of the full-scale war. That's why this chapter is included in *Part Three*. Work was busy. Life was busy. War was busy. Busy, busy, busy. Well, that does help us maintain our sanity, but it also means I could only read in small snatches when I could focus and have my wits about me. The setting was a nice escape as I could picture myself looking out the same window at a beautiful Norwegian fjord, watching the wind blow the trees or the rain fall on the water. 'Septology' is like a deep cavern which you must mine. Once you get past the repetitive structure, you start to find gems. The main character, Asle, talks about facing death daily on a few occasions. This was something I had forgotten about as related to Orthodox Christianity. It's a core tenet of the faith's teaching. Kyiv doesn't always physically face death daily like they do in other parts of the country, but that doesn't mean you don't have to be ready for it. We never know when the next attack will come, so it's always there, lurking about. Fosse's Catholic faith is a central influence on the book. I began to sleep better after coming back to the active participation of facing death daily.

There are so many more gems than that within it that helped me on a therapeutic level. Fosse also describes being trapped by our thoughts, and his line reads 'the key to freedom is not to think too much but to act instead.' This completely grounded me and brought me back to getting mission-focused. The Brits' mission had kept me focused for months, and once they left, I felt without purpose again. Grizzly was riding the same wave. We were afloat in the fjord of discontent with no oars. I began to get to shore, only to step on land and start walking the Black Dog.

8

Walking the Black Dog

'Black Dog' was my favorite Led Zeppelin song for most of my teenage years in the late seventies and early eighties. Of course, I never knew why the song was given that name since it has absolutely nothing to do with a dog of any kind. Somewhere in my history, I also remember that t-shirts from The Black Dog Tavern on Martha's Vineyard were the rage, but I'm a Jersey Shore guy, so that pretty much meant nothing. Apparently, I was also ignorant of another Black Dog, even though people told me it was following me around. This particular Black Dog exists everywhere for a huge portion of the population, and from what I have been told, was made famous by Winston Churchill. There are many disputes about the term's origin from the Roman poet, Horace (65 B.C.E.), through to English folklore about hell hounds and so on. Thus, the origin is of little consequence, but the expression is what makes an impact. The Black Dog can be melancholia, depression, dark moods, and well, a bent for the demonic. Grizzly was the first one to bring the term to my attention when he said that he had a bout with the beast. Jon (Top) also confirmed his regular run-ins with this canine during his struggles with long-term PTSD.

Well, I have always liked black dogs, so defining the image of a domesticated canine with a particular darkness didn't take hold so easily. My description for those moods within myself, others and people with particularly dark personalities or dispositions was always 'a black cloud hanging over their heads' which often followed them everywhere they went and engulfed those they encountered. However, I decided to embrace the terminology and not hold it against any individual black dogs I might encounter. Admitting you have a Black Dog is the first step toward recovery, like anything else. Maybe this one doesn't need 12 steps to resolve. My black dog probably started out as a Chihuahua, but by the time I turned around to find that I was holding the leash, it was an English Mastiff that constantly needed to go pottie.

All of us in Ukraine who were involved in the war seemed to have had black dogs that winter. Tristan Ruark, along with his stepson Yevgeny, had visited in the late days of February, which made me forget mine for a few days. My Black Dog was in the kennel as I showed them the city and introduced them to Natasha. Tristan and I spoke at a conference about developing a policy for veterans' recovery, employment and treatment. They soon parted, and the Black Dog started howling. At that time, I didn't even know or acknowledge that I had a Black Dog. Grizzly was in a downward spiral; I was sniffing the grey mists and darkness of existence. The abyss was swirling and pulling us down. A leash was attached to us. Grizzly's text about his 'Churchill Black Dog' came on 1 April 2024.

Personally, I knew I was in a bad place. Depression is not something we males like to admit or try to cope with. Brush it aside and it will go away is our usual tactic. Plus, it is not always depression, per se. Sometimes it boils up as aggression, impatience or just very dark thoughts about Russians. Some days, you just want to commandeer a heavy machine gun at the front and start mowing down the enemy regardless of your personal safety. You develop a picture in your head of firing the weapon as it rips apart the bodies of the enemy, their heads explode, and you wish for the screams of pain and agony. But let's face it, this is not a realistic outlet for frustration or depression. Who knows what one would become if they did? My usual self-treatment was whiskey and a cigar. Yes, I know that can be dangerous, but as a former addict, I know how to self-regulate. However, the cigars and whiskey did nothing, were bland, tasteless and did not bring the subtle buzz of calm like they used to. I had to admit that I had a Black Dog.

Males, I guess, process things differently than females. We tend to be more visual, from what I have read of psychology. Thus, visualizing all those dark feelings and moods into a big Back Dog actually helped to understand the problem. Now, the Black Dog was there and acknowledged, and I, being a responsible dog owner, would have to take it for a walk, but I, as a husband and friend, also had the responsibility not to feed that dog. Feeding the dog means giving in to the thoughts and actions that bring it out of its kennel. Walking it is different.

Walking the Black Dog is the realization that it's there and must be taken out. Further, you also must understand that it's not just going to go away because you are walking it. Walking the Black Dog is developing coping mechanisms when it shows up and wants to go out. My first method was always prayer, which helped a majority of the time. Sometimes it was communicating with Grizzly on both important and mundane things. When Natasha was home, it was by being totally focused and in her presence. She will tell you that I am often distant, which is true because sometimes I am simply distracted, and other times, I am walking the Black Dog in my head. 'Septology' was also a help because there is a darkness of the human condition in that book. Knowing that others go through their struggles helps you feel like you are not alone. This does not mean to revel in their suffering or celebrate, but instead that you nod in acknowledgement. Of course, it's best to walk the Black Dog as soon as he wants to go out. The longer you make him wait, the more difficult it is when you do take him for a walk.

9

Walking the Real Dog

Philly Cheesesteak is now 10 or 11 years old, but still thinks he is a puppy. He has very high energy. Philly needs to be walked three times a day, once in the morning, afternoon and evening. The first two are almost always my responsibility since Natasha works away from the house and usually departs around 07:00. Sometimes I will take the third one for her if she has a lot on her plate or is simply exhausted from dealing with rowdy 1st graders. Other times, I just feel like taking Philly the third time, and that's sort of a good way to start.

Walking the Black Dog is often an arduous task that doesn't require movement. Other times it absolutely requires doing push-ups, walking around the house, taking a shower and best of all, walking the real dog. There are few physical acts that chase away the Black Dog better than taking Philly out. If you are a dog owner, you will understand. If not, well… Philly is not a fan of other animals, children, drunks or skateboarders. He will sometimes even jump at an apparent stranger for no reason. Philly does not leave the flat and enter the streets or anyplace else without a muzzle. He isn't an overtly aggressive dog unless he truly doesn't like something or somebody. Watch out if that happens. Beast mode comes instantaneously with full-bore attack mode. This means that when walking Philly, your full attention is required to him and his possible triggers.

Full alert means that the Black Dog can run off without a leash. I don't know if Philly realizes that he is an actual mental health treatment, but he sure likes to get out and be a dog on the street. He's quite docile at home unless you mess with his food or his space. Territorial in everything and very upset when his full pack is not at home. Natasha and I have grown used to his idiosyncrasies. He is very different to the prim and proper Samantha, who we lost on 25 March 2022 to cancer. Maybe Philly is a bit of a reflection of Natasha and me. We both have our moments as well, as we tend not to be big socializers who prefer familiar territory and our own space. Both of us also have a temper.

Philly is also very loving and affectionate; I don't want to give the wrong impression. But he is also one not to be tangled with. Those months when the Black Dog was really with me, Philly saved my ass from going deeper into the abyss. I will always be grateful to him for that, although he might never know it. He has been my rock since Natasha started working outside the house and Sammi passed. I know there is all kinds of research about the value of having a pet, and I know that Natasha and I are living proof in a war zone. Ukrainians love their pets, so we fit right in.

One day, the Black Dog was scratching at me, so I took Philly out. It was a crisp morning where the ice still hung around with small piles of snow. Work was crazy with emails, but had seemed to slow down. We made our way through Shevchenko Park, and at the very same moment, about 15 email requests came through as the air raid blared. I looked at Philly, he looked at me. We seemed to connect and just say to hell with it. Screw the emails. Screw the air raid. And screw the Big Black Dog. I let that Black Dog off the leash that day and let him run in the yard. Once in a while, I still feed him, and he comes around still on occasion. Mainly, I have learned to deal with it and accept that he is there lingering most of the time, but that doesn't mean he needs to be petted, fed or walked.

10

Can We Handle the Truth?

My big plan of travelling around Europe and experiencing all things refined on this continent came to a full stop. First of all, as the days of war turned into months (still counting), the appeal of it lost the luster and mystic of the unknown. I became somewhat revolted by any kind of surprises in my life and preferred a boring known, tried and true. It offered stability. The unknown territory meant scoping the perimeter even though subconsciously, looking at *potentially Russian* tourists *if they kept their mouth closed* or actually coming into contact, *Hello Russian Bolt driver, please learn some English, you seem overly confident around here, cocky and loud, you know what they say about the loudest in the room? Of course you don't, that would require reading...* Essentially, my feelings would be exposed via my facial expression and a strong angst towards anything russki. That's the truth. It is not pretty, but it does not need to be. I couldn't possibly be civil. It takes the strength I do not yet possess to pretend nothing happened and chit-chat about the weather, ignoring the giant elephant right between us. Could you?

For me things are clear. I know who the enemy is, I know who the allies are. I know who is pro-war and who is not. See, people are not that complicated. You do not need to ask questions or talk about politics to get the idea where everyone is and, therefore, how to proceed. In a war, it is self-preservation and survival.

What the war has done to me is rudely knock off my pink-colored glasses through which I saw people. I think I'd have preferred to wear them. Those lenses had a protective shield. Ignorance is bliss for a reason! I did not choose to categorize people I came into contact with after the war had started. I enjoyed my little belief that the world was a decent place, people meant well, and the curve of the universe inclined towards justice of its own accord. Therefore, if we chose to work hard, tried to be honest, and did the best we could, things would fall into the right places, eventually. I miss that kind of thinking. In its place, a hard-core reality took hold of my philosophical musings. It stripped away the safety cushion from under me, baring its ugly teeth and laughing in my face. Things are a bit different now. I grew out of my comfort zone, became familiar with some raw truths that might have always been there, but didn't get a chance to climb out until the circumstances were 'just right'. I might have a change of heart when the traumatic events stop happening and healing gets underway, but for now, it's like this.

I steer clear of anyone who calls Ukrainians 'ukropy'. This is a highly derogatory term that typically follows or precedes the wish for murder (somewhere in their social media account it is either buried deep or is in the *get to know me section,* but scroll around for a minute and eventually it reveals itself). Those are the kind that will cheer on and pass the news of a successful hit on a hospital, playground, or local college with civilians in it. They are BFF with the ones who appropriated the WWII victory to their grandfathers and claim to defend what they started, adorned with USSR memorabilia and slogans calling for slaughter in the name of Christ.

I stay away from people who never once supported Ukraine after the war broke out. They talk about everything but… It would seem they did not exactly choose a side, or they assumed a politically neutral angle. But look closer, they have chosen. They keep quiet on the topic, so as to not draw negative attention to themselves from the rest, who knew right away where they stood with it. If you really want to make sure, ask whose Crimea is. It is not a trick question. Hear them fumble, something like, *well… blah blah, all are welcome, does it really matter, Ukrainians, Russians… Is it really black and white? We will pray for all.* Very considerate and clean. Sorry folks, but Jesus' disciples had a stash for those in need, not just prayers. Heard of a good Samaritan and those other ones? Heard of 'not hot, not cold, but lukewarm'? That noise ain't gonna cut it when you are in the war and need a support team.

Some folk realized a year or two into it, that, after all, russki could not possibly bring peace as they had hoped they would and wasted much time listening to the russki channels for a few years that eliminated the majority of their working brain cells. Believe me, russka propaganda has been working its foul magic for years, building an intricate web of lies and 'news' to listen to. How do you think traitors got to be traitors? Well, besides the obvious payout, they have been listening to russkis masquerading as Ukrainians, even speaking half-decent Ukrainian in some cases. What good are you to those who need to be able to trust you? You sway like a summer breeze in your jumbled opinions about everything.

There is another category: the sheltered kind. I can sympathize with them. I was in that category once, sheltered by a beautiful bubble of Starbucks and mortgages of gated communities' residences, and the community church and the golf course… Pitying the wronged, vaguely aware of the issues outside the bubble, but identifying with them? Nah. *It is so sad about Ukraine, what's happening out there, isn't it, what a shame, we are not going to stop going to our church, though, just because it is under Moscow??! What can we do?*

That said, I do not judge anymore. Each made their choice, just like Ukrainians made theirs. I know where I stand with a few of my former 'friends', even if some of them are still listed as such on my FB account. The reason I did not delete your sorry ass is yet TBD. You are someone from my past, and this is where you will stay, like a muted ghost.

It was painful in the beginning. First to realize, then to process, actively trying to *explain* the reality we found ourselves in, and how different it was from what they must have heard. Surely, they would get it after I spoke to them about it! Surely, they care! They are simply misinformed! But after much explanation, then waiting, agonizing about the thickness of their skulls, there comes a time of letting go. It is very unsettling at first. Some of those people you have known since childhood, others have been a part of your life for so long, you no longer imagine them as a separate entity outside of your core. They broke your heart and took a piece with it. With time, it gets better. Life brings new people and asks that you welcome them *for now*. You do, because the common cause dictates it. After a while, the 'for now' part falls off, and you realize it has been a fair trade: five assholes for one standup individual is not such a bad deal. And so, it goes.

Our reality will forever be defined by the war and how we handled ourselves in it. WHO we were with before, during, and after. It will never be just a small chapter that we get to rewrite or give a second chance to those who excluded themselves from it. There is no going back and fixing anything. We survived without your support so far; you will never know about that brutal night or that shattering day. You simply excused yourself from all of it. But we stand a bit taller because it was this much harder. You are simply one of the two: a good neighbor or a schmuck. We can handle either. Life goes on. Here is to good neighbors, Cheers!

11

And I Say to Myself, What a Wonderful World

If you ever been in a war, you will quickly realize how fast the world around you becomes smaller and smaller, until you feel safe in your own perimeter, where every nook and cranny is familiar. I am not talking about people who happened to be here in passing, went home to safety somewhere in Bali, and try to tell people around how they made it out of a war zone. Their world is still nice and wide after the fact. Or the ones who came here for a few nights and caught a glimpse of the russki hatred toward anything Ukrainian, barraging bombs into residential districts for the heck of it. They are, hopefully, somewhere safe and sound right now, telling people around them about the traumatic event they lived through in another country.

It is an entirely different experience, however unfortunate, from the one where you've met the war in your own home when it started and stayed there without knowing what tomorrow would bring, but had a strong feeling that it was the end of life as you knew it. And, for some unknown reason, stayed in that home as if some invisible force pinned you down there, even though the narrow paths of escape had beckoned plenty of times with their manageability. You dug out a 'safety' perimeter for yourself in the midst of madness and that became your new world.

The vacation in Europe we had been dreaming of in Solomenskiy District in 2020 got postponed till our apartment renovations were completed. We moved in, enjoyed the awesome feeling of accomplishment for a couple of months, unpacking the boxes, moving around the brand-new furniture to just the right spot, when the war knocked on our then sparkling entrance door. A meme comes to mind from the first week of the war: the photo of Putin adorned in red catholic garments, knocking on the locked door. Speech bubble above: Let me in, so I can save you. Behind the closed door, a speech bubble says, Save me from what? Answer: From what I am going to do to you, if you don't let me in!!!

Many days have passed since that meme. I remember a huge sense of relief washing over me when I saw that joke. It confirmed that life has not ended, just yet. People still had a sense of humor in the darkest of times to allow some release. Things just got hard. I can adjust to the hard, like so many locals who stayed for their own reasons. The war has united the strangers, the neighbors, random drifters, seemingly good for nothing, in the peaceful circumstances of the day-to-day rat race. In the war, everyone discovered a new sense of self, lurking somewhere below the surface of the mask we put on to deal with the world as we know it. Suddenly, the banal and mundane star dust was no longer in demand, but the true and authentic self was, whatever that might be. We carefully looked at one another on the block to make sure we were on the same side, eyeballing every move. It was not hard to do in the perimeter where 20-some people still remained alive and were staying put. We went through a lot together.

I remember taking the dogs out for a walk around the neighborhood in the first few weeks. The food stores were closed except for the bodega on the corner, a Silpo (fancy supermarket some ways out), and VK (Velyka Kyshenia), kind of a super 7-eleven. I was walking briskly, almost trotting, because we needed to stock up on some groceries, and the rumor had it Silpo was still open for business if you could handle the lines. It was early morning, and I figured I would let my dogs enjoy some grass patches scattered around the building. As I looked up, I saw a man walking his Dachshund back to the flat in the Stalinka across from my own building. We must have seen each other hundreds of times before the war. We only knew the dogs, not the owners. He stopped before the buzzer, and unlocked his front door:

To Silpo?

Yeah, I figured I would get in early.

My thinking exactly! If you get there before I do, let them know I am in line right behind you, will you?

You got it. But if you are there before me, please do the same.

We suddenly started to look out for one another. We didn't bother exchanging names. It was not essential anymore. Survival was, and we couldn't do it alone; we needed the good neighbors.

At Silpo I was swiping down everything canned and whatever was left of 'fresh' produce. If the mold was only starting to show, it got folded into my cart. At some point, I simply looked around, paralyzed by the scene: people moving about, trying to decide if things were edible enough, foreign reporters flooding the supermarket, coming up to the random 'customers of war'.

I remember thinking: do we really need the goddamn fiber right now?!! The mic suddenly appearing in my face snapped me out of my contemplations about the nutritional value of the produce in my cart. The light of the camera seemed invasive. The voice in the microphone offered a pitiful comment of sorts that I could not digest. It seemed like the journalists wanted to capture the pain and despair of the people around them. Were we trying to fatten up for the upcoming slaughter? I registered the hunt for sensationalism. I remember answering questions briefly about my concerns in regard to surviving. I pointed to the lobster tails (the only expensive item left fully in bulk, unwanted by most folk for the steep price) as my exquisite plan to beat depression and potential hunger. That's right! Bet you didn't expect sarcasm, did you? Bet you wanted tears and screaming? Nah. I was going to go out eating fucking lobster tails, how you like that??

Silpo was allowing 10–15 people at a time in a first-come, first-served fashion. I remembered suddenly that I left cash back home, hence mild panic seeped its way through my nostrils, prompting me to please answer a question: how are you planning on paying for those lobster tails after all??? Breathe in, we are going to die, aren't we? Breathe out: talk to the lady in uniform, kindly ask if there is a chance of opening those doors for me to get my husband in with cash to pay for my cart. I kept my cart close; I could not let go of the stupid lettuce in it, because it could literally be my last chance to eat a half-fresh vegetable! As I opened my mouth, I realized the lady did not need to be persuaded. She grabbed the key and motioned me to follow her. She opened the door and told the mob right outside their turn was coming in a few minutes, but for now, she just needed John! John!! Who is John over here? Step to the front, your wife needs you here!

I came to my senses. Babe, I forgot cash at home. You there? I saw the crowd shuffling around, allowing someone through. Like a 3D wave, it lifted my husband up the stairs to the entrance door. I saw his strained face, I saw a bit of bewilderment there, as he was saying my name, trying to get to the top of the stairs. I kept thinking, oh honey, the concept is so new to you… But I have been here before. Those lines are about the same size as back in my USSR days. A fucking deja vu with Russia poking her stinky nose in. Now you know what that was like firsthand, not just from the stories of my soviet past. We made it out of the store alive and well, sporting some expensive items to tie us through a week or two, if rationed wisely.

Anywho. This is the second time I attempted to write about Yaremche, but my brain took me on a detour to way back when. The point of this story is that I was not going to Europe anytime soon. Not because I could not. I did not want to leave Ukraine behind. Naïve? Check. Stupid? Maybe. But I wanted to be with the people I felt safe with, not somewhere in Europe, God knows where, hearing pity in someone's voice over how sad a life must have been for me. I don't think so. Plus, we were in it together. I wanted to see how everything would play out. Maybe a few months of this hell and things would 'normalize' for all of us? Wishful thinking is a strong force when hope is nowhere to be found.

Time kept turning season after season, and the madness was only getting worse. I managed to find a job in it so as not to get carried away with it. In year two of the full-blown invasion, PSI reopened its doors for students and staff. I stepped in as a grade 1 homeroom teacher for the 2023–2024 school year.

12

War Work Lent Life Balance

Joseph Lindsley of Ukraine Freedom News often states that Ukraine is the ultimate self-help guide. I can't say I disagree with him at this point in the war. How we self-regulate and manage our time is an exercise in efficiency and survival. Imagine for a minute that you have a deadline looming. The electricity shuts down, an air raid goes off, and explosions rock your perimeter. You sit in a shelter with your laptop because it has WiFi and continue working while all THAT is happening. Could you handle that? You are on your way to work on your morning commute as a missile strikes a building in front of you. Do you freeze or just take an alternate route to work? You wake up early to go for a run or take your dog for a walk, and the air raid goes off, Shahed drones enter your city as the air defense shoots them down. That's what many of us have been dealing with for nearly three years. Yet, deadlines still get met, dogs still get walked, and people go to work every day. Do you imagine that you could balance something like all of those while maintaining your sanity?

There is no magic formula for doing it. In fact, I don't think there is even a real, actual formula. Life must go on. There are no gurus or books that explain how to live through war. Even if there were, would that fit your needs on an individual basis? No. We are all different in how we deal with a crisis. Our personalities don't align. There is no common thing we really hold that would work for everyone, given the circumstances of our lives in war. The one thing we do hold onto is that we can look each other in the eye and acknowledge that so far, we are making it. Truthfully, I think some people don't know how they are doing it; they're just like Bo from Nike and 'Just Doing It'. However, doing it does take certain coping mechanisms, and those are probably also completely different for each one of us depending on our age, gender, level of education, maturity and psychological development, life experience, military background or lack thereof, spiritual belief system or lack thereof, personality type and a whole range of other factors.

What works for me might not necessarily work for you. There is no Manual of Standard Operating Procedures (SOP) for non-combatants in a war zone. You couldn't write one unless it factored in such specific demographics as listed above. You'd literally have to take an extensive test just to see which particular SOP might work for you, and even then, it might not be effective. Could you imagine all of us in Ukraine taking the time to do such an undertaking with a tailor-made manual delivered at the end? Ludicrous, right? So, Joe is right, and I am sure some will capitalize on the opportunity at some point. Yes, some lessons will be applicable and useful. I won't knock that.

Author Kostiatyn Koshelenko has written 'Management in Times of War', which I assume is sort of a self-help guide for businesses in dealing with crisis management and pivoting quickly. This is where practical applications from the war can be applied to real-life situations outside the war. To date, I have not read the book as it seems to be directed toward business and government. That's my time management at work in an active war zone. We only pay attention to that which we need to survive and what we can do to help Ukraine achieve victory. After that, only our families and immediate circles matter. That's the selfishness we must adopt to survive. But is it? Maybe that's universal inside and outside of war. We are not programmed to have 1,000 friends to keep up with. Humans as social animals really only need a limited number of real-life friends and even fewer online ones, don't they?

Natasha and I have both learned to adjust. We have mechanisms we share and those we employ individually. These become more symbiotic the longer the war drags on. Natasha's, in a nutshell, are her work as a teacher, the students themselves, yoga, reading and the occasional glasses of Prosecco. Mine are my work, volunteering to help the military, writing, walks, sweets and the once or twice a week Scotch/Cognac and a cigar. Our joint coping mechanisms are going to our favorite coffee places to relax, watching television for escapist reasons, cooking for each other, church and that other thing that most couples do.

By the time that we started to recognize the need for War Work-Life Balance, Great Lent was about to begin. The burden grew even more difficult as I looked at fasting and going to church while just beginning to deal with my own snowballing psychological decline. Faith and the church have been one of our main coping mechanisms, so I couldn't just ignore Great Lent. Natasha and I have always benefited from the observation of the fast rules. We grew from these experiences.

This year, I decided not to try too hard with fasting but instead to focus on prayer and communication with God on a personal level. Natasha pretty much followed suit but she was more disciplined in the fasting department. This would be our first Pascha apart since I became Orthodox, and we started celebrating. I had encouraged her to attend a training organized by PSI and funded by a grant from Rotary International in Warsaw. We didn't realize until after she signed up that she would not be in Kyiv for this most Holy of Orthodox Holidays. She struggled, and I served behind the altar for Pascha. We got through it, but we are certainly no self-help gurus. There's no guidance or advice either of us could give you that would fit you personally. But Nike can: 'Just Do it'. Don't think too much and act more.

13

Wozza Kicks the Black Dog

A day in war can seem like a month. Waiting is the name of the game more often than not. Sometimes you have to find a way to fill the time between awaiting messages or the next shipment. Nicky and Jon, along with others, had donated a good sum of money for a 4x4 for our soldiers. Natasha and I kicked in what we could afford. Grizzly was busy working out where to source the vehicle and just letting the money sit in the account. He had to go to the front on a few occasions, and it would sometimes be days before I would hear from him. Funny, I never once worried about his safety there. There's an energy about him that says he has God's protection. Maybe it's just wishful thinking, but it certainly provides a certain sense of reassurance when the Black Dog is constantly nipping at your heels.

Wozza (Damon) informed us that he would be coming for a trip in March and was bringing gear for our guys along with his. Matt had run a fundraiser through the EEMC Facebook Group and had some funds left over. These funds would be used to purchase field dressings made up of Chest Seals, BCB Pressure Dressings and stretchers. These items are essential on the front for saving wounded soldiers from bleeding out or losing air due to a punctured lung. Stretchers are also always in short supply. Wozza runs a military surplus store in the UK, so he always throws in the necessary military kit or clothing.

We had MAVIC drones stuck in Poland over some customs glitch. The money was sitting in Grizzly's account (about $6,000). Good news came in that our unit would receive some donated vehicles from donors in Lithuania. Some things still get lost in translation, and cognitive function and memory retention can be severely affected at times. Jon knew Wozza was coming. He needed information quickly about immediate needs, as he and Nicky wanted to take advantage of Wozza's trip into Ukraine. Grizzly checked with the soldiers and was told that Starlinks were the highest priority at the moment. We checked with Wozza to see if he had room. A flurry of messages went back and forth, individually and collectively. Frankly, I have to run through my Signal messages to even keep track of things that happened. Due to the disjointed communications, I can't keep track of every event and every piece of equipment that comes in. Grizzly might have a better handle on that. My job is primarily to intercede where needed and to stay on top of movement, along with morale.

Grizzly fell out of communication for a while, so I texted him.

Me: 'You ok out there?'

Grizzly: 'Slight depression. My Black Dog as Churchill said.'

In the midst of this, we were pushing Jon on what Starlinks to buy. He was pushing back for specifics. We were pushing Wozza to see if he would bring them with him. Back and forth, intercede, more back and forth. Plastic storage boxes were also requested for storing drones in dirty, wet weather. Ones with wheels that could be moved around as needed. Had to get back to Wozza on that to see if he had room. Jon needed specifics on how big the boxes needed to be and what kind. I had to Google search for sources in the UK to provide to Jon. Wozza got back to us. Yes, he could fit the cargo. The deadline was approaching fast. No Starlinks and nearly no time to ship. I messaged Grizzly.

Me: 'How are you feeling? Natasha says you sent something?'

Grizzly: 'Hi bro. A little better but still sick. I was on the road for two days, arrived and was back in bed. I sent you some cigars.'

Me: Thank you, bro., Did you go to the front or waiting until Wozza comes. Soup always makes me feel better. Hot tea with honey and lemon also is good.'

Grizzly: Yes, this is my main drink now.'

A few days passed.

Me: Cigars arrived. Thank you.'

Some other messages went back and forth between Jon, Grizzly and me due to other confusion about Starlinks and miscommunication. Wozza clarified a few things with me in the meantime. Texted Grizzly.

Me: 'I gave Wozza the heads up about the plastic boxes.'

Grizzly: 'And how is he? Did you two agree?'

Me: 'Yes. He is ok and adjustable. Excited to come back to Ukraine.'

Grizzly: 'Super bro! Thank you for your support and communication. My Black Dog ran away.'

Wozza came, and the Black Dog couldn't even be heard barking in the distance. The Starlinks never came in due to glitches. Instead, they were purchased in Germany, where Grizzly arranged their transfer to Ukraine. Azov Special Operations received all eight of them. That high lasted only a short time for me and Grizzly personally. My Black Dog was still running around in the backyard, unfortunately.

14

Hey, You Guys!

Rita Moreno yelling 'Hey, you guys!' from the PBS show 'The Electric Company' has nothing to do at all with the Russo-Ukrainian War, but somehow the reference sticks. Why? Our electricity grid was heavily targeted and attacked by the Russians in the late winter/early spring of 2024… again. This was what had led us to leave in October 2022 for Chernivtsi. We were having none of it this time. Being displaced comes with its own logistical, psychological and spiritual challenges, and we just weren't in the mood… at all. As soon as it began, Natasha and I worked out what the minimum power would be to function. We concluded that if we could run the Router, keep the computer going and charge our cellphones, we could make it. Earning while without electricity was priority one. Plus, the weather was warming, and we knew we could get by without heat even on chilly nights once the communal heat was turned off. A small Bluetti was the answer. So, we would not be out on the streets of Kyiv yelling 'Hey, you guys!'

Days came and went. Power was intermittent. The allegedly published official 'Electric Shutdown Schedule' seemed to be rarely accurate. We ran into problems with Internet service, mainly because of my lack of technical know-how. Google to the rescue again. Well, Google Fi, to be exact. I just turned my phone into a hotspot and voila! I was in business, and Natasha could still do her lesson plans for school. Time crawled on, and the shutdowns became more predictable. Funny, how your biorhythm adapts with the light.

Natasha and I sat in our flat one evening as the shadows of night made their way through the big windows. Both of us were relaxing as the natural light became dimmer. We are often on the same spiritual and psychological page. Maybe that's what a good marriage eventually settles into. Simultaneously, we looked at each other and said, 'It's kinda nice, isn't it?' We laughed together as we said we should be quiet in case the FSB was listening, but wait, their listening devices wouldn't have power, would they? More laughter.

'Can you imagine how pissed those crazy Russians would be if they knew we were actually enjoying this?'

'God forbid anyone experiences joy, right?'

Yes, war is hell, but once you have been in it for a while, you quickly learn to adapt to whatever conditions present themselves. We have it relatively easy in Kyiv, but we hear tales of cities and villages near the front that also find those same moments. Those moments that people share that make them more human, more connected, more appreciative of what they do have than over obsessing about what they don't. Many nights would pass like this. No loud music. No television. An annoying gaggle of gas-powered generators, which soon enough just turned into a background hum. Natasha and I would just sit there in the growing dark and watch how the light slowly danced and faded in the home we loved. How beautiful the different parts of the room looked as the light changed. We would sit and do this for hours unless an email came in for work or I had to pay attention to other duties. Philly would lounge on the couch, which he had officially marked as his, and we would just be our little family.

Of course, we wondered if our neighbors and others in the darkened areas of Kyiv were doing the same. Nobody seemed stressed on the streets. If you wanted coffee or a cocktail, everything was open. You could still buy groceries and pay for them with Google Pay or Apple Pay on your phone. All the payment terminals were working. Not feeling well? The pharmacies were open and fully lit by generators. Could Americans and other Westerners live this way if they had to? Only those who have been through hurricanes and major storms seem to understand the experience, and only a little. If you see the sensationalist news after these events, you'd think it's the end of the world. Now, I can understand that it's life-threatening for many if you get hit with a hurricane in Florida when the heat is full blast. That's the main thing I hated about that state; it's just unbearable for a few months out of the year. But could any of them bear lack of sleep, constant air raids, missile and drone attacks, on top of no power?

One of the reasons why populations outside Ukraine cannot understand how we do it is that it's not even imaginable for them. Europe has some historic memory, but other places have never experienced a full-scale war on their territory. There simply is no frame of reference. No grandparents telling stories of some long-ago war. No old news footage of villages, cities and towns reduced to rubble and now rebuilt where they now live. No photos of bodies lying in the streets where memorials now stand. This may be one of the reasons that Ukraine doesn't get the overwhelming support it should get. Simply because people cannot know and understand what is going on here on a personal level. It's just soundbites or propaganda, sometimes a mixture of both. That's entertainment for those on the outside, or so it seems from the inside.

Thoughts race when there is no electricity, just like the two paragraphs above. The key is not to control them, channel them or even better, just be. Most of the time, that's what we did. I like simply being in Natasha's presence. No need for conversation, just knowing that she's there is enough. Our lives filled themselves with meaning on those dark evenings. Life also required a serious adjustment to the regular ins and outs of existence. This became easier once the shutdowns took place at the same intervals every day.

Electric back on? Laundry, cook the roast, charge the Bluetti and a bunch of other seemingly mundane tasks. They are not boring at all, but instead give a sense of purpose. Shazam! Maximum efficiency for work. Pump out schedules, Excel sheets, settle accounts, update the client, call the client. Funny, how our productivity became hyper-focused. I was never more productive than in those days. Too bad nobody did a productivity study, huh? This was true for everyone across Ukraine. You, on the outside, call it resilience. We, on the inside, call it resistance and defiance. Damn near the whole country is an ever-evolving Resistance Movement. Hey, you guys!

15

Are You Worth Dying For?

June swept in with a baking heat wave, and we were still a month away from our first Official War Vacation as the 80th Anniversary of D-Day landed. A guy I occasionally interact with on LinkedIn was there for the commemoration. Ryan Hendrickson is a former Green Beret who was wounded in Afghanistan and slated for a Medical Discharge due to an injury to his foot. He was not willing to accept that. Ryan soldiered on, healed and returned to theater, where he received the Silver Cross for his actions after his injury. That's grit and perseverance, the soldier's way. He wrote a book about his experience called 'Tip of the Spear'. What has that got to do with Ukraine? Well, Ryan now runs Tip of the Spear Demining and has made multiple trips to Ukraine to train Ukrainians and perform other related activities.

On the beaches of Normandy, Ryan posted a video that really had an impact on me. He was calling out Americans more than Ukrainians. Ryan spoke of the sacrifices made on that day and what goes into being a soldier. Then, he looked straight at the camera and said 'So, ask yourself, are you worth dying for?' That's heavy, huh? Have you ever sat back and thought about what you do in life, and if you're worth dying for? You know, by a soldier who has dedicated their life to fighting an enemy. I think he was dropping subtle hints to Ukrainian civilians since he has quite a following here. This question has come up on more than one occasion from Ukrainian sources since then.

Some things make you just stop in your tracks. You take it into account and hope you can confidently say 'Yes' to such a question. First comes the inner searching. Am I doing enough? What constitutes enough? In my case, I am lucky as I have a personal connection to one person fighting. I work with Grizzly on supplying another unit, and we have brought in quite a bit of aid for them. So, I know some soldiers who would most likely answer in the affirmative, but is it enough? I can't really tell if it is or it isn't. Every day, I do something, even if it's just sending a message to a couple of people, facilitating connections for military aid, promoting businesses that are supporting the war effort or just posting something that keeps Ukraine in someone's feed. Maybe it's enough, but I certainly wish it were more. Here in Year Three, none of us is having an easy go at it. Once the inner reflection ends, we tend to turn our eyes to the world around us. This is where the trouble begins.

The streets of Kyiv serve as my point of reference, although friends in other locales have reported the same viewpoints there. Military age men wearing the latest fashion and stepping out of brand-new foreign cars is a common sight. Young women hiring professional photographers to take pictures of them on the street for what we suppose is their Instagram. More of these young (Ukrainian) women are posting pics of themselves in beautiful and exotic places, wearing designer clothes throughout the world. They argue that they are patriots, but seem mostly to be promoting themselves and capitalizing on the blood being shed in their country. Fit men in gyms, bars and nightclubs allegedly brag about how much they paid in bribes to avoid mobilization. Of course, we can't know everyone's personal story. Maybe they have suffered or lost many loved ones. But the impressions they are creating do none of us any good, nor does it do any good for Ukraine's image and the belief that corruption is waning here. No, it does the exact opposite. Vanity, greed, and foolishness are thrown in the faces of we who are fully invested in the war every day.

Demoralizing is putting it softly. This is our country now as immigrants, and when we see the indigenous population acting like this, we conclude that only a small part of society is fully invested in the war. Of course, we deal with those Ukrainians who are fully invested like us. They are even more frustrated because it is their own people. Are they worth dying for? The ones we see every day? Somehow, we hope they are, but that will be a question for the soldiers to ask. And ask, they will. That's what we hear from the soldiers we support. They are aware of the goings on in the rear. Soldiers tell us they will mete out justice when the war is over in the form of physical violence and/or death. We don't wish this on these alleged miscreants, but we also can't really blame the soldiers, can we? They will spare those even who are just partially invested, which seems to be the overarching majority of civilian society. Our estimates from our Ukrainian partners are that maybe 35 to 40 percent of Ukrainians are fully invested.

Internally, the following message comes from the Tatarigami Telegram channel, which is written by a Ukrainian veteran:

'Anti-corruption measures during recruitment

The West will not extend its support unless Ukraine can deal with rampant corruption in its military recruitment centers, where those with money and connections can avoid conscription. This has resulted in the army being disproportionately made up of poorer citizens. Ukrainians are increasingly unwilling to serve as cannon fodder in senseless operations often led by Soviet-minded commanders who prioritize saving face over the lives of soldiers. Ukraine cannot afford to treat its troops the way Russia does. Ukraine should also focus on re-equipment of existing brigades, rather than equipping with numerous new units, creating an artificial shortage of manpower on the front lines.'

This statement leads me to recall some of the lyrics to Black Sabbath's 'War Pigs'.

Tatarigami also speaks to poor training. So, there is a reason that many try to avoid mobilization due to the lack of a NATO-standard comprehensive training program. Volunteers to the UAF receive a higher level of training than those being mobilized, but volunteering requires personal motivation, which is waning with every meter the enemy takes in the East. Thus, all of us must be attuned to the factors that influence the decisions of others. Ukraine is in a pickle.

Pointing fingers. Assigning blame. These are all the actions of the weak. We all must take on the burden of responsibility for what is happening here. Collective responsibility leads to collective victory. Why should we turn on those we see as 'not doing enough' or 'doing nothing'? We only see their surface lives as we cannot swim in their depths. What if they had a mental breakdown or became an addict if they were more actively involved? This is where those of us who are strong must take our place and allow the weak to go on with whatever they are doing or not doing. We don't want only the strong to survive, do we? We want everyone to survive. But the questions keep coming, no matter how deep we bury them.

How the hell do you win a war against a giant monster bear of a country when a majority of the citizenry is not fully invested? You don't. That's becoming increasingly apparent with every passing day as the Russians take more ground little by little. Assault by assault. Yet, we stay. We stay because we know that the enemy will never take all of Ukraine because of that percentage. Would the rest just roll over and accept it? We are hearing that many have in the occupied territories. Still, we hold out and don't run. Ukraine has become home with all its weaknesses and failings. Those we work with are some of the best people we have ever known in our entire lives. These are the people we choose to stand with and fight alongside. They are all worth dying for, and we will die with them if that is what it takes. Each individual member of Ukrainian society must face the question on their own personal level. Are you worth dying for?

16

Commander Sto Smert

Our vacation seemed like a lifetime away still. The level of anticipation and impatience only growing with every slow, long, drawn-out day. You might remember this feeling. It's most akin to waiting for Christmas, and when Christmas Eve arrives, the day drags on and on. Where the hell is Santa Claus, and why can't I sleep? Nearly three years of war had taken its toll on us both. We were aching for some quiet respite. So, it became better to fill the days with activities in the hope that time would pass more quickly. Luckily, when you work with a variety of people who are actively involved in the war effort, somebody always seems to need something or to meet someone or to coordinate something. Ryan Grant Little was my savior on this one when we were still two weeks out from the launch of our R-n-R.

Ryan was introduced to me by Andrii Busarov, a friend of mine here in Ukraine who is aiming to be a career diplomat or politician, so he meets a lot of interesting people. Andrii also has a unique and realistic insight into the war since he is originally from Donetsk and lost everything in 2014 during the first incursion. Ryan has been working relentlessly since the beginning of the full-scale invasion, from transporting displaced people to providing multiple 4x4 vehicles for the UAF. He has a vast network of trusted sources in Ukraine. This is essential for effectiveness, as there are plenty out there just trying to line their pockets. War creates destruction, but it also emboldens hustlers on the heart strings. Unfortunately, just about everyone who operates here has fallen victim to that in one form or another before learning the hard lessons. Honey pots are the most often utilized tactic of not only the enemy but also the war hustlers. I vetted Ryan. He vetted me. So, I was glad to be invited to a meeting with his team and their trusted Ukrainian contacts.

Musafir on Bohdana Khmelnytskoho Street was the designated meeting place (that's a mouthful, huh?). This location for this Crimean Tatar chain seems to be the most popular in Kyiv, and according to insiders, the chef is their best one. Natasha and I order takeout from there regularly, so we know it from those experiences. I had never been there physically, and it's big, as in two to three levels of dining. I made my way in and found Andrii already seated at the table, which was set for about 20 people. No one else had arrived yet, so we caught up a little bit. Ryan and his retinue followed soon after. I remember meeting his older brother, Scott, along with some others, but I am lousy with names and excellent with faces. Ryan has been living in Austria for quite some time, so he brought along his friend from there.

Florian Marlovits regularly works with Ryan, but he also volunteers as a tactical combat medic on the front. He is a gentle giant of a man and a faithful Catholic, so we bonded immediately. We now stay in touch regularly and get together for breakfast when time allows. Florian has helped the British/French team with various insights regarding bringing aid in. I was grateful that he was added to the small circle of trust. We all operate on the micro level because we are primarily independent operators. Maximum effectiveness is achieved within these networks. We know we can't save everyone, so focus on those that we can help directly. We do require making some of our activities visible because public reporting helps us to keep and recruit various donors.

A half dozen or so soldiers soon entered as most of the other diners went quiet. Three of these men are part of an organization called the Kyiv Military Chaplains. These are Ryan's primary guys for donating vehicles as they transport them directly to the military units on the front lines themselves. Funny enough, Ryan is an avowed atheist, so I was a bit surprised at the connection. Even stranger is the fact that Ryan is an official Military Chaplain, complete with an official uniform and military ID. We don't judge people by their faith or lack thereof. We look at their actions. Most of them are Orthodox Christian Priests with large social media presences, so I call them the PR Priests. One of them, Father Serhiy Budoviy, stood out with his general demeanor.

Father Serhiy is a barrel of a man, like a wrestler. He was a soldier before he was a priest, so he has seen the worst of this war firsthand. The Light of God shines from his spirit. We sat and broke bread. He ate like a wrestler, and we joked about it being an Orthodox Fast day (Friday), but there were mainly meat dishes on the table despite the fact that Ryan is a vegetarian. Father Serhiy clearly stated that the fasting rules are relaxed because of the war. I wasn't about to make waves. We found out that he serves with a Priest and Metropolitan that I know from when we attended the Cathedral of the Transfiguration near the Hippodrome in Kyiv. Natasha and I went there regularly when we lived in another district. Ryan had pushed a little to make me an official Military Chaplain, but when they found out that I serve under Patriarch Filaret, things sort of fell through. Orthodox church politics are very complicated here, so I didn't make an issue of it. Frankly, I don't feel worthy of the chaplain label anyway, although it would open some doors for me on a personal level. Soon enough, a mountain of a man in full UAF uniform joined us. This is the one I call Commander Sto Smert. He has the presence and charisma of a true soldier's soldier.

Many others sensed this and seemed to avoid looking at him or engaging him in conversation. The battle-hardened are often avoided either out of fear or shame. Father Serhiy obviously knew him. I spoke broken Ukrainian and looked him directly in the eyes as I did. We bonded immediately. He started showing me a modified weapon they had built during the Battle of Bakhmut, which he manned himself. Next came the pictures of the Russian dead. These were not close-up, gory photos, but instead blurred a bit with dozens of them lying in fields. Commander Sto Smert then showed me the medal he received for 100 confirmed kills and said it was probably more than that now.

He didn't speak or act in a boastful way, but rather matter-of-factly by a soldier who is clearly proud to defend his country.

We rolled directly from the photos to sharing pictures of our wives and families. Commander Sto Smert has a beautiful wife and several attractive children. This was where his pride was. That's also where my pride was. We feel blessed to have such strong, independent and gorgeous wives. Father Serhiy got in on the action, and well, his wife is very attractive as well. We all laughed since all our spouses are younger than us, but there were no crude comments. The twinkle in each of our eyes reflected that part of our manhood that understood our deepest desires. Soon enough, the food came, and we had our chow. The Commander had war business to attend to. Father Serhiy and the other PR Priests had to go take the vehicles that Ryan and his team had brought as donations. On his way out, Father Serhiy gave me a big bear hug and quickly ascended the stairs toward the exit.

Andrii and I took this as our cue to depart. We thanked Ryan and his team and left. Outside, we stood on the street as a security detail with armed guards and armored Mercedes eye-balled us. Perceiving us not to be a threat, they let us be. Soon enough, German businesspeople or diplomats came out of Musafir and were whisked away. Andrii said this location is highly popular amongst the 'in' crowd. I took note of that as Natasha, and I tend to avoid these types of places for security and personal reasons. Ryan and his crew soon came out and invited us to the bar. Andrii doesn't drink, so he declined, and I did too because I just wanted to get home to Natasha and Philly, my war family.

17

Hey, Poncho!

June rolled in on a hot note in Kyiv. August seemed like a decade away. Ryan Grant Little and Florian Marlovits were introduced to the group since they are both experts who travel in and out of Ukraine all the time with military and humanitarian aid. Some side conversations took place between them and Jon, along with insights. Matt was constantly in touch. Paul was finally added to the Group chat. Everything seemed to be progressing according to plan. Wozza had come and gone at least twice, but we never met up. Nicky's budget was getting tighter by the day. He was still looking for very practical yet affordable ways to help the soldiers directly. Jon inquired of Grizzly what the troops were asking for. Grizzly sent a list with many items on the expensive side. Mixed in there somewhere were military ponchos. These, I knew, were affordable.

First, I spoke to Jon about them before getting back to Grizzly. Jon and I had both served in wet conditions and knew the value of a good poncho. Grizzly informed us that the ones they were getting were of poor quality, and the guys preferred the British ones. Jon checked with Wozza only to discover that the ones he could get were the same garbage the Ukrainians were already getting. Ponchos didn't seem to be standard military issue in the British Army anymore, which is strange given that famous English weather. Google is my friend, so I researched in great detail about British procurement and issues, but came up empty. Frankly, I got a wild hair up my ass about it. Messages flew back and forth from Ukraine to France to Ukraine to Philadelphia.

Finally, I made an executive decision and started researching standard US military issue. This didn't come easy. Matt checked a US Government procurement system for the military but came up mostly empty. Finally, after several unsuccessful Boolean searches, I found the company that has had the contract in the US for military issue ponchos, which I won't name for reasons that will be revealed later. We all consulted in our Signal chat and decided that Matt would take the lead on procurement since he is based in the States and was a US Army officer at one point in his career. We would have to get the price and shipping information before settling on a quantity.

These events were transpiring in late June while Natasha was decompressing from the school year. We planned a month-long trip to the Carpathians beginning on 6 July. This was our first R-n-R since the full-scale invasion, and I wanted to be fully focused on her and Philly, along with the break from the bustle and heat of Kyiv. War stops for no one.

Alongside this project, Grizzly had found a small group called 'Little Spiders' that was weaving camouflage netting for the front. Their system was slow and inefficient as they were having trouble sourcing the right material. Grizzly had found used fish netting from Norway that was being either donated or sold to them cheaply. The problem was the material for weaving,g which had to be dyed and was inconsistent. Grizzly managed to find a specially made product that would greatly increase production, but the costs were higher than the Little Spiders could afford. This also needed a monthly budget and commitment.

We all put our heads together and decided to recruit donors, including amongst ourselves. Ryan and Florian brought in a couple. Jon grabbed a few from EEMC, and the rest of our crew filled in the rest between Nicky, Paul, Jon, Matt, Natasha and me. Now, we send our donation on the 15th of the month, with Jon and Grizzly staying on top of donors, and me giving a little push when needed. This deal was concluded in our second week in the Carpathians. Meanwhile, Stateside, Matt was having his own issues with the poncho supplier.

A US military poncho is a thing of beauty to any soldier trying to stay dry. It's used as a tent, a stretcher and various other survival uses. These things are incredibly strong and durable. They fit over a rucksack. Apparently, the manufacturer is a bit sensitive about where they are sent. Matt encountered problems when he asked for them to be shipped to Ukraine. He encountered further problems when the manufacturer found out they would go directly to soldiers. I know, I know, it seems moronic, doesn't it? Why should it matter where they would be sent? This is not the first time we have run up against problems sourcing military type aid for Ukraine in the US and elsewhere. I thought it's just business, man, do you want to make a sale or not? Matt finally had to reassure them that the ponchos would come into a humanitarian aid NGO that we work with in Ukraine via Grizzly. Paperwork and bureaucracy are the slow killers of soldiers.

Shipping then became a problem. The manufacturer would not ship to Ukraine. Time was slipping by. The crew's departure date was set. The ponchos would first be sent to Matt in Philadelphia, then he would have to ship them to a staging point in France. There, they would first have to get there and after that, they would have to clear French Customs. Matt took the chance and paid for them all, and the shipping, with me telling him I would back him up if payment went south. He had been burned before, and I don't think Sara would have been too happy footing the bill.

The French end included Matt being paid by a charity based there. They didn't use PayPal, so a bank transfer was the only way to go. The ponchos were en route by the time Matt got the money, after his bank threatened him with being reported to the US State Department for receiving funds from a French charity focused on humanitarian aid for Ukraine. This is the typical shit we have to go through on numerous occasions. We suck it up and plug ahead. Matt got the ponchos packed and shipped. They hung in international postal limbo for about two weeks. The clock was ticking.

Just a few days before departure, the ponchos cleared French Customs and ended up in the hands of Paul. I think they came by way of our new French team members, Frankie and Valery. Frank and Valery had also procured some French military surplus ponchos, which are also of good quality. That was an added bonus. Soon enough, the ponchos were in Grizzly's hands, and just yesterday, we got a report from the front that they were there and about to be delivered directly to the soldiers. This is the kind of report we live for as volunteers.

UPDATE 17 OCTOBER 2024:

This note came through from Grizzly on Signal and says it all.

'Hello to my brothers.

I came back from the front last night. All your latest cargo is already in the hands of our soldiers. It was raining constantly the whole time I was there, so American and French rain ponchos were the most popular cargo. The soldiers send their deepest gratitude to all of you. I asked the guys to make a few videos of thanks mentioning you and the French Foundation. The situation at the front is very difficult now, many wounded and dead. The doctors couldn't hold back their tears when they saw so many tourniquets. This will save many lives. Thank you for everything. From the bottom of my heart.'

18

July 2024, Yaremche

The expats working at PSI in Kyiv typically leave the country every chance they get. Those from Europe go home for a break, those who aren't, leave Kyiv 95% of the time either way. One of the perks of working at an IB school is travelling. But let's face it: if we lived in France or Italy, or any other place that does not require us to hide in the bomb shelters on any given day of the year, we would have been exploring the country we teach in. Someone like me does not quite fit into the title expat easily. I was not born in the States, nor Ukraine. I would be considered who exactly? I am not displaced. I chose a place to live in and stay in it, that's all. There is plenty to explore on the ground. Ukraine is huge. Every location is unique due to its multifaceted history. So, I heard, so I read. But I have not personally seen it or experienced anything outside of Kyiv. The summer of 2024 was when we visited the Carpathian Mountains in person for the very first time.

It was everything I thought it was going to be, just like the internet promised. We hired a driver with a vehicle to take us to a pet-friendly lodging and pick us up in a month and a half. Our first vacation together as a family in Ukraine. Philly was thrilled to travel. He loves road trips! John and I stocked up on everything we might possibly need for the time being and were looking forward to peace and quiet. Everyone talks about Bukovel, a manicured, modernized, commercially attractive, clean, overpriced touristy destination. We did not go out of principle: stay away from the tourists! We accidentally lived in many places that people came to vacation in. Therefore, we avoid the concept of Disney pricing, no matter how great it is for their business. I simply refuse to pay a quadruple rate for whatever. I prefer the reasonable market value. If I feel like sleeping in a 5-star hotel, I expect a price for it. But I do not choose to live in a mediocre lodging infested with everyone and their mother for that same price because it is located in Bukovel. It's a status place for your Instagram photos. Hard pass.

Yaremche is more of a blue-collar place, less pretentious, reasonably priced, and quite friendly. They also make their living on the tourist economy, sell and upsell all day long, but they do not rip you blind midday for a cup of coffee. The views are breathtaking in both areas. The horizon is animated with slopes, hills of lush grassy carpet, peaks of forested mountains touching the sky itself, and then stretching unapologetically beyond the clouds. It gives the impression that this is where the sky and earth meet up for a chat.

I remember the driver looking concerned at the sight of the steep climb toward the resort of our choice, right on the mountain, so we could come out of the front door and hike, hike, hike for hours at a time. Hey, dude, you knew where we were going; we were concerned with your sedan from the beginning of this ride!

The first thing I did after unpacking was grab a blanket, Liane Moriarty's *Apples Never Fall*, and a glass of red. I settled on the porch recliner with all of the above and quickly placed the book on a wobbly table nearby (sorry Liane but the views are mesmerizing, I can't focus with a background like that, it deserves a proper stare). What I did was just sit there and look straight ahead of me, like a rare painting it was, making its appearance at a museum for a limited time to be appreciated temporarily. The longer I looked, the more I wanted to look. It was a feast of nature spread right in front of me, with its aroma of moss, campfire, and evergreens. Even the sounds seemed subdued, like they bounced off the soft blanket of pungent pine needles and reached your mind just for a brief moment to register and move on with the chilly breeze.

The night sky featured the brightest stars I have ever seen. They hung so low, as if eavesdropping on our conversation, twinkling in agreement and making a strong point of their own, shooting across that black canvas of eternity. Magical. I remember thinking I could take the Alps off my bucket list once and for all. I bet it's pretty and worth seeing and all that. But will it make me feel the exact same way? I lost the desire to find out. I was already in love.

I think the intensity I felt toward the Carpathians was not just for their regal beauty scattered everywhere within your touch, but the feeling of peace I felt for the very first time since 24 February 2022. It was the place that fed the starved soul with the quiet days of pure bliss and renewal. There are many places like that around our planet, but to experience them at just the right time is a privilege not many of us get. It woke up my feeling of gratitude toward God for simply being alive and breathing.

The hiking route started right outside our cottage. And hike we did! At the top of the mountain (if you were inclined to get there, of course), there is a polonyna, a small community, open for tourists and locals alike to experience homemade cheeses, wine, sausages, and bograch (western type of borscht, much more savory and a bit spicy), stock up on pickles or ready-made varenyki. You can drag it all back or enjoy the view in their outside kitchen, resting, eating, enjoying the view, checking out goidalka (a giant swing that floats right at the top of the world around you), and just be. I did not mind being a tourist for experiences like that. There is no show, just people going about their business, looking after their sheep and livestock, cooking for themselves, and generously offering their goods to the rest of us. What a great business! What a life. They live in their own cosmos. There is no war here. This place is pristine, untouched by human progress and need for convenience. It's old school. It's raw and real.

In our excitement, we decided to make it our daily escapade. Why bother eating in a restaurant when you have all this? Until the next morning, when our stiff, angry legs protested that decision adamantly. We only made it to the top three times overall. Fast quadricycles are for young folks with healthy lower backs, not for a middle-aged couple with herniated discs. We rely on legwork when we hike.

We discovered that the old soviet style 'jeep' branded UAZ is not as cool if you sit there and ride in it. I swear I felt every single bone in my body violated by a rough ride we booked to visit another polonyna (we really loved the concept and wanted to go to every single one in the area). Besides it being one of the hottest days to venture out in a UAZ with no AC (naturally), it is the least comfortable vehicle I have EVER ridden in. If the road has any tiny bump or a stone, you curse the time you fell for this 'authentic and cool' ride booked for a reasonable price to get to the top of yet another mountain. Philly's expression was priceless when we set out, WTF? Please hold me, I will never bark again at anyone, I promise, if only I make it out of here! Is this your idea of adventure, mom? Ok, ok, I'll just get to that corner in the back, oh shit that's the worst corner! I cringe just thinking about that ride and the sheer discomfort of it for straight 40 minutes. I imagine dirt bikes in terrains make your body go through a similar dilemma: why? It's funny now, but the next day we both were out with a severe case of back pain.

John was pounding at his keyboard in just a short few days and did not mind working in such a gorgeous setup (or so he says). I was looking to explore the area beyond, and the flyers at the reception offered tours of all kinds, including to the salt-fed lakes and pools by the Romanian border in Solotvynovo. The ad promised a full day of relaxation that included a three-hour ride to the salt springs in a comfortable air-conditioned bus with a knowledgeable and fun tour guide. I love an easily achievable sense of adventure that day trips offer right at your fingertips (especially if you are a passenger, not the driver). I was going!

The morning of the trip, I descended towards the bus stop where I was supposed to be picked up. I was excited about the scenery I was about to see for the whole three hours ahead. I stepped into the bus, quickly made a cash transaction and was delighted to see it was almost full but still had great seats to choose from on either side. I tried both before I settled on my left window seat a bit past the middle. I filled out my brief passenger info and relaxed.

I do not remember a single fact shared by the guide, but rather the anecdotal records of local history, tall tales, and legends, which was fun. As we were passing one of the tallest mountains in the area that had a rough terrain to overcome all the way to the top, she informed us that the locals called it a 'bless or curse my man-to-be' place. It has successfully done the job for years and therefore earned its reputation among the ladies, who wanted to know what kind of husband he was going to be. So, the lady in question was supposed to take her man for a hike on the mountain. Since the paths are rough and the climbing is quite lengthy and exhausting, the mountain would create just the right circumstances. There are spots along the way that the ladies without the proper training are simply unable to handle, requiring assistance. According to the guide, the ladies from all over Ukraine would come here with their beloved for a truth-revealing adventure. The passengers in the bus perked up and sat a bit straighter to listen closely:

So, ladies, ready? If the man by your side carries you, stretches his hand for you, lifts you up where climbing is tough, gets the first aid kit out (most people have minor cuts, scrapes, or bruises when they are there) – he will treat you like a queen in the years to come. But if, God forbid, something happens to him there, like a twisted ankle, broken arm or whatever, and you must take care of him – please know, you will be carrying him on your back for the rest of your life. This is a no bullshit mountain; it doesn't play around, it just creates a certain truth-revealing ambience. The rest is up to you! What's that you say? He is way too handsome to ditch? No one said you were gonna like 'the truth', honey.

I was mulling the information over in my head, wondering how John would size up against all that, when the bus suddenly pulled over after one cool story and a 15-minute total trip time. The guide has informed the rest of the passengers that we were going to wait for a young couple to join us, who were riding the cab right behind to catch up and would be there in a few short minutes. After a little while, we were suddenly aware of the full 60 seconds making up a minute. 'Anytime' has lasted 40 excruciating minutes in the heat of the side of the road without the shade and a switched-off AC in the bus due to the idling nature of the event.

The rhythm of the trip was grossly disrupted, the passengers got sweaty and irritable (me included), and the young couple was nowhere to be seen. I thought about the mountain we passed. Does 'its truth-revealing power' apply to men specifically or to any traveling group? Should we brace ourselves for this day of fun?

Eventually, the couple showed up, paid cash, climbed on board, and proceeded to blame the guide for some type of mess-up she was responsible for. The energy of the trip has certainly changed with them being a part of the team. It was replaced by the brooding passengers who probably wondered about the same thing I did. The guide attempted to cheer everyone up with more stories about this on the left and the local brewery on the right, but most passengers had placed their headphones in by then, like resentful grown-ups might do in a situation that can't be sweet-talked after the fact. The young couple seemed full of angst, not gratitude to all of us for not making a fuss and patiently waiting on them to show up.

The bus continued down the slopes, up the slopes, gently curving away with the shape of the road ahead of us, until we came to the checkpoint between Carpathian and Beyond Carpathian (Zakarpatye) border at a picturesque village called Yablunytsia. God it's so pretty! The bus had stopped. It was full of female passengers with a few exceptions: our driver, a man in his sixties, the other half of the young couple we waited for almost an hour, and, what I assumed to be a soldier on leave, travelling with his son. The checkpoint guards scanned the bus with their eyes from where they stood. The driver opened the front door. The guide chitchattingly handed one of the Border Guards the papers, explaining where we were going. The soldier looked at the papers, accepting her general demeanor in a gracious manner. He even cracked a joke or made a small talk comment that put everyone at ease. Meanwhile, a 20-something kid in a uniform with the gun behind his shoulder stepped into the bus. His eyes met the 'soldier on leave' who grabbed an ID card out of his pocket and showed it to the kid, who nodded knowingly and stepped off. I remember thinking to myself: Jeez, you are just a kiddo, I would not give you pass 21, try as you might, looking all serious. I would give you a hug, though, in my head, and say a little prayer for you. You had to volunteer for this. Everyone else right now is waiting till they turn 25. Respect.

It seemed like we were about to hit the road. Then the 'merry-go-round' soldier stepped into the bus. His eyes ignored everyone but one dude. He asked for his papers. The dude in question got out of his seat, made a bit of a fuss looking for them in his bag, meanwhile trying to make a small talk following our tour guide lead. He got zero response. Finally, the papers made it out of the bag and were handed to the soldier waiting.

You from Kharkiv?

Yes.

Wait here a sec, the soldier turned around to run the papers, the dude got nervous.

Well, I'm from the nearabout, technically.

So, which is it, Kharkiv or the nearabout?

I was supposed to get them renewed, I'm all good, I lost track of time travelling.

Where about?

All over.

The soldier stepped off the bus, papers in hand. The guide turned in her seat and was facing the dude, all good, right?

There was no straight answer from either of them. Frankly, it was beginning to look suspicious (like who are you two?). The bus was waiting for the papers to reappear for another 30 minutes. It did not look good. We were travelling toward the Romanian border. Did you really think no one checks the buses? Come to think of it, why would you have a giant bag packed for a day trip?

We left the dude behind. He kept saying something about miscommunication, to come and get him on the way back. Yeah. Some people have a misplaced self-importance syndrome. His girlfriend did not seem that upset and proceeded to the resort with us. The guide probed her with gentle questioning, adding that they were notified yesterday over the phone about the papers being ready. The girlfriend avoided direct answers, going around the bush with her responses, like someone hiding something. Be it as it may, there was no one waiting for us at the checkpoint on the way back from Solotvynovo.

I suddenly made a connection to the 'bless or curse' mountain legend about the man you are with. They did not have to climb it, just stepped into the waiting bus, parked a couple of miles out.

With time, people relaxed and appreciated the views spreading like a gorgeous plush carpet on either side of the bus, a true feast for the eyes. When the sun turned unmerciful in its brightness and heat, we stopped by the side of the road in a tiny village of 10 houses right alongside it, right across one particular house, as ancient as its resident. The lovely babysia residing in it stepped out to welcome us to an underground spring that runs through her property. People are welcome to stop by and fill their takeaway bottles. So, we did. One for me, one for John, one for Philly. I drank some out of my hands and splashed on my back and face. The water was icy cold, naturally carbonated, and delicious. I filled up what I could carry out without paying a dime. The guide told us it was her regular stop every time she was in the area for a quick chit-chat and a cup of water.

At one point, the temperature rose to 98 Fahrenheit. The landscape offered no shade, just the road, the blazing sun, and an AC unit that started resembling a very slow dance song. At that point, I was feeling the back of my knees perspiring. I wanted to be done with the ride before the outside and the inside of the bus fused into a sweat bath for all of us. But the day was young, and the views beyond the bus beckoned to look at despite the rising temperature. I vividly remember the mountains growing larger, swelling up and out, majestically surrounding Rakhiv. They immediately made you feel smaller, somewhat insignificant in their full size. They quietly imposed humility, silencing human progress into an irrelevant nuisance at their feet. The hope of every driver on those roads is a tank full of gas in a very capable, trusted vehicle with a spare that gets them to point B before dark. The views got imprinted into my memory forever as I rode that bus, holding my breath every so often, staring out the window, instantly enriched by the sight of it all, refined by nature's rare masterpiece.

Whatever humans have to offer fades by comparison. I splashed in three kinds of saltwater-fed pools with underwater massages, floated in a gross amount of salt water under the open sun with no shade, and kept my backpack close by as I could not locate any lockers in the area. All of that was accompanied by loud music bursting through the speakers, with no place to hide from it. A spa experience? Not quite what I had in mind. I would also refrain from calling it a resort. An ancient salt mine collapsed and splattered the contents, forming a few lakes around it. The mine remains were peeking out ominously in the area that served as an entrance back in the day. The site was not secured in any way and was a serious eyesore in the middle of the recreational area, which included a few lakes around it, saltwater swimming pools, a kiddie splash area, showers and a restaurant that offered a long waiting line, slow service, and irrelevant food. Healthy business competition would have been nice, but as the only game in town, who cares?

My overall impression was, well, I didn't know what I didn't know. Maybe it was the unbearable heat with a desert-like feel to it, frying your brain cells slowly and unmercifully. Everyone moved in slow motion around the park. Even wasps and flies seemed confused around the littered trash. Maybe it was the salt lakes of room temperature that did not seem all that refreshing or healing at the moment, but promised potential dehydration of the body and skin. Maybe it was that your idea of a good time was quite different from the rest of the sardines in the same tin, but you have already been packed, sorry Charlie.

I got home exhausted, in an urgent need of cold shower and a few stories to share with John, who was better off typing away in the shade of the cottage.

19

Grizzly

I made myself a promise: no telegram channels, no FB, no news, no war-related anything. I only had a bit over a month to decompress and step right back into a school year. It took a conscious effort to remove my fingers from the icons on the phone. It worked. Not that I forgot about the war. I just hit a pause button in processing it and distracted myself with the views all around me, a great book in my lap, and sore legs from invigorating hikes in the woods. Philly followed my lead. He accepted his new perimeter for his guard duty and performed his beloved task with the excellence of a guard dog. No living creature went by unnoticed. It took him a few minutes to readjust, sniff about, pick a spot, head turning rhythmically every few seconds, ears perked up, as if to say, don't worry, I'll kill any bastard trying to make a move!

I loved the staff from the minute I spoke with them on the phone, making reservations. We wanted to book glamping (a luxury tent at the top with direct access to the pool), a cottage, and a suite. All the above would ensure we got a full experience without driving anywhere. The first in the queue was glamping. If you have done it before, you know what I'm talking about. Kinda cool but with quirks. Plus, it was the only option with AC (for some reason, people in the mountains seem to think the weather is cooler than it is, and love the open windows concept a lot more than AC). Access to the pool was available to the entire guest list, though, and the loud splashing with straining music volume got old quickly.

Right next to the tent was the chan, a giant barrel that could easily accommodate four people. At night, when the sun was no longer an obstacle to overcome, and the breeze made up for a hot day left behind, you could book the chan for a few hours. It's a cleansing experience under the open sky with a gorgeous mountain spread all around. I highly recommend this kind of healing for body and soul. A staff member would burn the wood to heat up the water in the chan to the temperature of your liking, add essential oils and some spruce branches for maximum body relaxation, leave the towels and complimentary beverages close by, and voila! After a day of hiking, your sore muscles demanded soaking. We complied. The best part was getting out into the cold night air to grab a drink or jump into a pool, then climb back in, staring into the stars. Star white, star bright, first star I see tonight, wish I may, wish I might, get the wish I wish tonight! It was on a night like that, relaxing in the chan, looking at the sky we spotted the first F-16 flying into the country.

The staff treated us like old friends they've known for a while. The main lobby was the place for all requests, payments, a chat about the weather, booking tours or a BBQ, questions about a restaurant in town, purchasing home-made teas and soaps, dropping a bag of your dirty laundry, and getting a ride to town.

I stepped in to do one of the above on the morning of 10 July 2024. The lobby was empty but for one newcomer, a young mother with two suitcases and a seven- or eight-year-old daughter beside her, browsing through the stash of flyers on the stand. I settled on the comfy couch, covered in sheep rugs, anticipating a slow return of one of our peeps (some were not morning types). It was a bright sunny day, and the sun was beginning to pick its way through the bay windows. I ran my hand through the sheep rug, admiring its feel and texture under my palm, wondering what it would look like in my flat, certain I was going to get myself a couple of those at a local market. A sudden burst of wailing snapped me out of my musings. The woman was on the phone that buzzed in her pocket a few seconds back, her daughter comforting her gently, Mom it's going to be alright, don't worry... Ballistics hit Dnipro a minute ago, and based on her reaction, I assumed it was either a direct hit on the building she resided in or someone she loved got badly injured. I snatched my phone to run through the feed. Kyiv was under attack too. The famous children's hospital, Okhmatdyt, that treated tough oncological cases, was hit directly by a Russian missile. It was a terrible sight. Hard to unsee and stash into a deep little box, following the compartmentalization technique. I still remember where I was, the minute I saw the scene of the disastrous hit with hospice kids on the ground, IVs still in their little bodies, breathing through the oxygen masks by the destroyed wall in place of hospital rooms, their parents crouching beside, trying to protect the little time they had allotted to them together here on Earth. It was in the way the shot was taken, the position of their bodies leaning toward their children, arms hovering about. My own body jerked in an involuntary spasm. I was looking at the girl hugging and comforting her mother in the lobby. It should have been the other way around under the 'normal' circumstances. Adults should be the voice of reason, bringing the child back into the safety net, reassuring little souls of 'things working out'. How much worse it must have felt to a mother who couldn't help but give in to unbearable grief right in front of the scared child. There is going to be an entire generation left to sort out trauma imposed on them by power-seeking monsters under the banner of tragic 'Russian peace'.

We saw the news, the aftermath, the line of people stretching as far as the eye can see, helping to clear out debris in the perimeter of the blast, photos of the child snatched from the operating table in the middle of the surgery, the doctor running with him in his arms, resolved to complete the mission. Bless you all, who lived through this and who didn't, who got terrified or injured, who kept going to save the dying children, risking their own lives for someone else, rescuing, putting out fire, clearing out debris... May the Lord give you strength to heal and save you from wondering, why?

The sunrises and sunsets kept coming and going despite human tragedy. The wheels of life turn, no matter your feelings about it. The world expressed indignation, shook its weak fingers at the countless deaths of children and civilians, sweeping them under the rug of COA by the end of the same day. It's just that it didn't happen in their own backyard, making it into temporarily shocking news on the screen, between switching the channels to something more palatable. It's not personal until you are personally involved. Long-distance relationships do not have the power to last. They are filtered through the same screen, guarding everyone from intimate connections on the other side of it.

On one of those days, we were waiting for a friend we had never met in person but had worked with in hopes of bringing Ukrainian victory closer, one day at a time, one small (and large) project at a time. His job is to bring home our dead soldiers. He goes to the hot zones, and the bodies get loaded into his van 200, stating clearly who is in it.[1] He receives a list with photos and names (if available) and drives dead bodies home to their families. Even though the van is refrigerated, the smell of decomposition claims the interior. Sometimes it takes hours to get to his destination. Grizzly doesn't get paid for it. He is not a contractor. He's a volunteer.

When the war broke out, he sold his most valuable possession – his Harley Davidson motorcycle and donated the money to soldiers. His beloved truck was needed badly at the time, so he gave it away, too. It lasted briefly and got destroyed. I asked him how he was handling death by his side day in and day out, especially since he knew many of those guys, cracked jokes with them, or shook their hands. They were KIA, lying in his van, missing body parts. Doesn't it get to you? How do you stay sane in mortuary affairs? He's been doing it long enough to develop self-preservation mechanisms, which involve not looking at the list of names and photos during loading time. 'I just can't do it no more; the grief is unbearable. So, I get there, load the bodies and take home the bodies, not the names. I stopped looking at the list.'

Grizzly came to see us, driving the only vehicle he had, his beat-up van 200. He pulled up to the side entrance, catching bewildered looks from the residents scattered around the perimeter. The Carpathian Mountains know the war by hearing a random air raid. Individual families know it by waiting for their sons' and daughters' return from the war. There are no explosions, just guards at the checkpoints with guns on their backs, some guards by the railroad bridges. I am not sure if civilians have ever heard approaching drones, let alone missiles. I hope they are spared. Having a van 200 at the resort can sober up any mood and remind everyone of the reality we live in.

There he was, larger than life, a gentle giant stepping out to meet John. I gave them a minute before intruding with Philly, already impatient to run after John and sniff the 'intruder' by his side. I feel blessed to have met truly authentic people in my life. The kind of folk you can skip the small talk with and drop the filter. Grizzly is one of those. Their presence is inspiring because they have faced tough battles already, survived them, and are continuing the journey in a place God has chosen for them. They ask the same questions, their faith gets tested, yet they go on. They are stronger for it, and I can't help but admire that stance. They don't talk much. Their voice is heard through actions instead.

We ordered shashlyk, grabbed bottles of spiced rum and whisky, and settled on the patio overlooking the mountains to break bread and enjoy a couple of cigars. I will keep

1 200 is the Soviet code for the dead.

our talks between the three of us. Grizzly spent the night and rolled out in the morning after breakfast.

I think it's around people like that our broken, heavy hearts begin their healing. Their presence reminds you who you are, and through them, you see your own strength to go on.

20

Judge Not

Our stay continued its blissful path. My lungs greedily inhaled the mountain air, my eyes feasted on the beauty around me, and my brain stopped racing around a never-ending loop of thoughts and to-do lists as it did in the city. The slow pace of life rubs off; you chill with it, catching yourself smiling for no good reason. I found the right market and the right seller of perfect sheep rugs for our flat. The smell of them brought me back to my childhood and both of my babysias in the villages far away. My bare feet would be in heaven every time I stepped on one of those bad boys. It would serve as a point of return into calm and peace every time the city claimed you fully to its grunge. So, I bought three.

We hiked every path possible, ate as much bograch as we could handle, tasted all the local cheeses and wines, stocked up on lavender-ginger teas and hand-made soaps, obtained Hutsul rugs for the entryway, and looked at our bags. Imagine dragging all that to Kyiv. Argh. We called for a car service and the driver.

I do not remember the driver's name. We did enjoy his company. See, an eight-hour drive can feel light and fast or heavy and awkward for the same money if it's not a good match, I thought you were a dog person, please turn up AC already, you are not going to save any money and my dog is panting out of his mind in the back, no we are not big fans of the loud music in a car, and so on. I realized how much I appreciated the drivers who do not probe you with questions unless spoken to and have a small ability to read the room. He did, and Philly settled comfortably in the back seat.

Before we left the mountains, we had a plan: why don't we buy a property here, a second home? In the meantime, in Kyiv, we were going to relax a bit more, take better care of our mental health, and travel every chance we got. I'm beginning to wonder if everyone gets overly excited in places they visit and fall in love with. Like, why can't we live where we vacation?! We scoped the area for potential deals. Dear God, how over-priced everything was! Yea, I get it, it's safe here, but there are literally no jobs other than summer gigs to rob the tourists out of their savings (sorry, but it's the same any place on the planet if you deal with a seasonal economy). Also, safe or not, it's in Ukraine, a country at war, not Miami Beach or the Maldives. I consider the real-estate market grossly inflated in Ukraine. Why are you selling your property for 200K, when your neighbor is selling exactly the same one for 100K? Because 200K is more! That seems to be the logic. We do not overpay for real estate; it's for amateurs.

The plan failed with nothing reasonable or desirable to show for it. Building from scratch on a piece of land wasn't appealing. We looked into buying an investment property in a new resort with residential suites. They advertised mortgages available, so, what the heck, we stopped by their office. The trick everyone on the ground is raving about is getting in early at a low price while the project is still under construction. After the grand opening, the prices triple, they say. We did our research, the company seemed legit, projects all over the world, 'successfully making money for their investors'. So, the lady gave us a tour and displayed the images of the renovated, modern, smashing-looking resort with a rooftop pool, spas, gyms, stores, and restaurants. It was going to be finished by the next summer. It was in the center of town, close to the train station and all possible conveniences. We could choose the dates we wanted to stay in the suite, and the rest of the year it would be rented out and maintained by the staff. This is a very popular investment option for many Ukrainians. As a matter of fact, we came in late, with construction being underway and only six units to choose from. This company is so popular that every time they start a project, or there's a whisper, people rush to invest before the foundation is laid. We wanted to see what the fuss was all about.

Tell us more about the mortgage. I am paraphrasing here, but, basically, this is what followed from the spiel:

The mortgages are available for your convenience. You have a three-month window to pay the full amount, but we can extend it as far as six months, for your convenience, of course.

Of course!! I wasn't sure I heard it correctly, so I repeated it back to her:

You are giving us 'the mortgage' for three months, during which time we need to pay the full cost of the property, but, if needed, we can pay up in six months due to the exceptional customer service you provide, correct?

That's right!

I sat there blinking at her for a second. Then, I went ahead and asked if the concept of mortgage was new to the company because I did not see the point of such an 'investment'. You get all the money from my bank in three to six months, whereas I would be waiting for 11 years or so to make that money back in increments of potential rent? With all the other resorts coming in with bigger spas, bars, pools, and restaurants, at some point into the same perimeter?

That's correct! But you will make a profit after that. After 11 years.

Thank you for your time. We'll see ourselves out.

I do not understand the real estate market over here, but maybe I do not need to.

A bit disappointed, maybe relieved, or a little bit of both, we rode back to Kyiv. Halfway through the ride, we all got chatty. I need to revisit that conversation to make peace with it.

The driver was curious about us, and the questions followed: how long we had been here, did we like it, did we leave and come back, and why were we still here, not at home in America? We've heard them all before, not once, not from one person. We ask ourselves the same exact questions quite often. Depending on the mood we're in or the situation on the ground, we feel different about Ukraine and America. We are exactly what the book says, accidental. It is what it is; we didn't know what we didn't know. Would we choose to get here amid a full-blown invasion? I assure you, NO. So, I feel guarded toward expats, who did. If you look for an angle, in most cases it's for money to be made or the five minutes of fame to be had, which, in the end, is hoping for the money to be made. One man's grief is another man's fortune in the hard world of business. They differ from the volunteers who came and are doing just that with a clear sense of purpose (well, most of them). There's a start and end of their journey of bringing needed supplies, humanitarian aid, going to the front lines, providing medical assistance in the field, demining the Kharkiv and Kyiv area, providing IT assistance, and so much more. I am not talking about them. I'm talking about the kind hanging here with 'good intentions' no one can definitively explain. They fall under the category of white noise, and we've met our fair share.

So, for our new young acquaintance the answers were short and sweet: Ukraine has been home since 2020, we stayed at home when the war started, trying to help out. Your turn, hon! I see you are driving with no issues through the checkpoints.

Yup. I'm 24. They just look at me and send me on my way.

Thank goodness! How about the next year, if you don't mind my asking?

I'm not going. I am not ready to fight. It's not for me. I will never come back the same. They come back, you know, not all there.

Hmm. Fascinating (deep eyeroll). So, walk me through it for a sec, will ya? Crimea, Donetsk, Luhansk, Zaporizhya, Kherson, Kharkiv, all Ukrainian territories, right?

Always were, always will be!

Help me understand. Are you saying eventually your generation will be ready to fight or defend them?

Not me.

Not judging. But if you are not ready to fight, and never will be, are you planning to turn them over to russkis?

I realized an unpleasant truth about men like him. He was separating himself from the soldiers fighting for us, so he could drive around Ukraine and make his living. Was anyone ever ready for this? Some, younger than himself, didn't think twice and went to defend their country, and those who hid behind their backs and are continuing to do so. With time, enough loopholes emerged to avoid the service, get 'disability' papers, bribe your way through, or leave the country. As a society at war, we have come to a division line, subtle at first, barely lurking on the horizon – those who served and those who didn't. It is very pronounced now, like an elephant in the room that everyone tries to avoid looking at, but ignoring it becomes harder the longer you stay in the room with it. I anticipate violent payback as a worst-case scenario, not from the russkis, from our warriors, who will make it home alive. They would have seen and done enough moral injuries by then to worry about inconveniencing the rest of us, who have managed to enjoy life, all limbs intact. Are we ready to answer their inevitable 'where've you been, when we needed cover?'

So, help us God.

21

The British Are Coming!

Natasha and I departed the Carpathians in the first few days of August. We were not looking forward to returning to Kyiv at all. Neither one of us are city people when you get right down to it. Natasha grew up in a small town in Belarus, and I grew up in Woodbury, New Jersey. The last week of the vacation was very restful with no war business at all. Grizzly had come for a visit for our first in-person meeting. There was movement on the F-16s, and we occasionally had fighter jets flying overhead. We couldn't make out the profiles, but the sound was more along the lines of an F-16 versus the very loud Soviet jets that Ukraine had been using. In my mind, they were doing in-country training. Thoughts and experiences of war never take a complete break. Some days you get quiet moments. Others, you can even squeeze out a full day. We drove home by a different route. It did feel good to be back home with our own kitchen and a much more comfortable bed. The power was almost miraculously still on when we walked in the front door. It still felt like home even though we already dreamed of selling and moving to the mountains.

The Brits weren't due until the end of August but within a day or so of returning, the messages started again. Details were still a little fuzzy. Documentation had not yet been worked out. The ponchos were still lost in transit. This is war business. War doesn't take a break, and neither could we. The scalding hot days of mid-August pressed on. Natasha was due back at work at Pechersk School International for a week of training and preparation before the students arrived. August usually sees a cooling at night but not this year. The asphalt baked Philly's feet as we walked the Concrete Jungle of Kyiv. We made it to church a couple times at St Yuri's, and I served behind the altar. The Theotokos Fast started. Natasha's birthday was upon us, and we celebrated to the best of our ability during the busyness. She was due back to work on her actual birthday, so we celebrated the weekend before. Messages were flying back and forth between the French Connection, Grizzly, the Brits and me. Matt and Nicky were sweating heavily over the fact that the ponchos were still lost in transit.

Our first big glitch came when doing the paperwork on the French side. Everything is organized and donated through a French charity there. They submitted the paperwork to whatever King Louis leftover bureaucracy who rejected some Eco-Flow generators for export. Why? Apparently, some genius in the French government determined that these were lethal aid. We joked amongst ourselves that what the Ukrainian soldiers are going to pick up the generators and drop them off bridges as Russian tanks or troops travel below? But it was no joke. Our soldiers really needed those generators to charge drones, drone detection, laptops, phones and other necessary items. Grizzly had a solution. We work with a charity in Ukraine called Ukrainian Ants (UA Ants). We would repurpose the Eco-Flows as humanitarian aid from a French charity to a Ukrainian one. In fact, we would list UA Ants as the receiver of all the donations to reduce paperwork and stress. Ukraine also has very stringent rules for how aid comes in and how it is distributed. There's a lot of graft in a war zone, and there always has been. Vast amounts of wealth are generated in war for those who are honest and especially for those who are not. UA Ants knows the ins and outs of what the important part is: the aid gets delivered to the soldiers and is properly documented.

Paul, Anne, Frankie and Valery had also bought an Eco-Flow generator for a brigade they support. Apparently, this brigade was unwilling to provide documentation as the commander refused to sign for it. This has been a problem since the beginning, with either incompetent commanders and/or ones that are on the take. Grizzly suggested they just add it to the manifest for UA Ants and just work out the details once the Eco-Flow is in-country. As I sit here writing this a week or so later, that generator has still not reached the soldiers who need it. Grizzly and Paul's contact, Bogdana (Dana), seem to have found a solution, but I can't track their conversation in great detail as Google Translate is not always accurate enough for the nuances of the Ukrainian language. I guess it's most important to note that the generator did make it in along with a good score of other high-end equipment and medical supplies provided by Paul and crew, which are also en route to the soldiers.

Wozza was gearing up his crew in the UK for their part of the convoy, which was on a separate mission from Nicky, Jon, Paul, Anne, Frankie, Valery and Dasha, although they would enter the country together with a total of eight vehicles (or so we thought). Nicky has a beautiful summer chateau in Northern France, where all would rally and spend the night before departure. Of course, there was much ado about nothing except sleeping in a really posh place for the night. Just a few days before departure, the ponchos cleared French Customs and made it to the destination. Paul had space and picked them up. He also managed to pick up a box of cigars for Grizzly and me. Cigars and whisky are something Grizzly and I have bonded over via our chats on Signal. These little luxuries are like manna from heaven at times. That, and well, the fact that allegedly the Odesa Mafia has a monopoly on the Ukraine cigar trade. This seems true since there is really only one cigar store chain in the whole country. These are the days when I miss my Thompson's Cigars in the US, where I could order at a loyalty discount and UPS would show up on my doorstep with them, neatly packed and ready. I had pulled off mail order to Ukraine from Cigar World in Dresden a few times, but Customs or the mob got word and that came to an end. Even with shipping, the cigars were still cheaper than on the ground. I know, I digress. However, this was a huge part of the story for me because I didn't tell Grizzly about the cigars coming in. The look on his face was priceless when they handed them over to him on their meetup in Lviv.

Everyone was ready and geared up. Jon texted me the night before while waiting for the ferry to cross the English Channel to the rallying point in France. Natasha had her first week with her new students, so she was busy with that onerous part of the year for teachers. I decided to give Jon a call while he sat there waiting for the ferry (11:19 a.m.). We rarely ever actually talk on the phone. Maybe that's a dude thing, or maybe it's just my thing. I am not a phone conversation kinda guy. However, it was a very pleasant conversation as he sat there with a monstrous seagull on his hood. I could picture it having taken the Cape May–Lewes Ferry on numerous occasions at the Jersey Shore. We managed to pass some time for him and talk about some details of the trip. Jon has combat experience and is familiar with the necessity of proper staging before going on a mission. Nicky was flying in from somewhere and wasn't due in until 22:00, so he would be tired and in a rush. Wozza was at the mercy of other players.

Glitches started immediately for Wozza. Apparently, there were boats with migrants in the English Channel which were disrupting several of the ferry schedules. Glenn Swallow's vehicle drop-off in Poland was moved up a day, and he was behind schedule. I had met Glenn on a prior trip when he came with Wozza, and this was his second. Glenn caught the wrong ferry and was already in Belgium as he had a deadline to meet. Several others also caught different ferries. Vehicles and bodies were not where they were supposed to be. A rallying point was set in France once Wozza got a handle on the situation. That meant that they would have to carry on and not make it to Nicky's posh estate in France. Apparently, Wozza had also managed to promise to bring on what one can only call 'Ukrainian Princesses' who were not only disappointed about not staying at Nicky's but also absolutely insisted that they had to stay in a hotel every night. Wozza, Glenn, Andy and Mickey were all either battle-hardened veterans or simply quite content stopping at rest stops for a sink shower and sleeping on the side of the road. We all had a good laugh at the princesses' expense, but Wozza is an English gentleman, and he accommodated their request much to his chagrin. They were ahead of Nicky's crew and were unsure if they would meet up on the road.

Signal messages went back and forth from both groups on the road. I tried to intermediate from Kyiv when I could. The night passed, and both groups were still far apart, all being somewhere between Germany and Poland. Wozza's princesses were instructed to be ready to roll at 06:00, but they were fashionably late and didn't come out until 06:30. Nicky's crew was able to gain ground in the meantime. The full circle tale is that everyone managed to catch up at a gas station in Poland before crossing the border into Ukraine. Luckily, Grizzly had managed to get the paperwork in good order for the Polish and Ukrainian Customs, so they sailed through without a problem. There was a small glitch with Wozza's crew, but that was sorted out easily. Glenn had dropped his vehicle with his contacts in Poland, and eight lorries full of military and humanitarian aid crossed into the war zone.

Wozza and Jon posted updates on Facebook from Lviv. You could see a sense of relief in the photos. They were enjoying themselves, having a few drinks, sharing fellowship and using toy guns at an indoor range to shoot images of Putin. You can't really get any more Ukrainian than that. The meetup between them and Grizzly was set for 10:00 the next morning. I went to bed with a sense of relief myself. It's hard not to worry about your friends when they come in because missiles and drones rain down everywhere. Just after their departure, a drone struck a building very close to their hotel, killing a mother and her three daughters while leaving the father alive. These images and stories were all over the media space as we watched the face of a man who lost everything. Our hearts and souls dropped, but we also continued on, as any soldier will tell you that you must do. Jon returned to Lviv with Nicky and the crew within days. He is a hardened veteran and stated that it looked like the drone's trajectory was aimed at their hotel and missed. Russia has been targeting aid workers, volunteers and journalists for weeks now. August 2024 was the deadliest month for these people, along with the big strike on Poltava, which killed 58 civilians and other strikes with more deaths and casualties. We were too busy, thank the Lord, to even let the Black Dog in. He was stuck in his kennel.

Grizzly showed up, and the transfer of aid began. His lorry has '200' on it, which is the Soviet code for the dead. This time, he was filling up the vehicle with life. Somehow, they managed to fit all the gear for our guys (12th Special Purpose Unit of the 112th Brigade-Territorial Defense Forces based out of Kyiv). Our soldiers were in the heat of it near Pokvorsk, with some deployed near the Kursk incursion. Nicky, Paul and Jon all stated that Grizzly was an absolute expert at packing his lorry, as they were amazed that he could fit everything in. Paul handed over the cigars, which made his day. Grizzly texted me when he got home, in very high spirits, that he could barely close the doors on his lorry. He was in a state of joy and satisfaction, which was good to know. Wozza and Nicky's crew spent some time and parted ways for their different destinations. Nicky's crew managed to meet up with some Ukrainians in a village that they support and were treated to true Ukrainian village hospitality. Jon kept me updated and told me they would arrive in Kyiv that night. Missiles and drones were still in the sky the night they arrived. Anne got her first taste of going to a bomb shelter, as did Frankie and possibly Valery. We were scheduled for dinner the next night, with Natasha planning to be in attendance.

22

Dinner, Breakfast, Departure and Arrival

Nicky, Jon, Frankie and Valery had an urgent agenda to go check on an orphanage where there were children that they had hosted in France. There was a lot of mistrust about what was occurring there. Nicky and Jon likened the situation to one that seemed to take its cue from the Branch Davidians. A biblical component existed there, which was being used against the children. They gave the impression that things were bad, but there wasn't a whole lot they could do. It's located a couple of hours south of Kyiv, and Valery spent the night close by while Nicky, Jon, and Frankie came back for a meetup at 19:00 for dinner. Natasha and I hopped in an Uber and arrived just before they returned from the orphanage. We gathered in the lobby of their hotel, and Paul soon joined us. Anne was dealing with a crisis back in France as she sits on the St Omer Town Council. A fire of mysterious origin had been set to a church there, and the Internet was already ablaze with conspiracy theories.

Nicky bought a bottle of Prosecco, and we had a toast at the bar while breaking the ice. We soon made our way to the outside terrace to dine. A pleasant breeze was cooling Kyiv that night. More Prosecco made its way around as we waited for the food to come. Ours wasn't very tasty, but the company sure made up for it. Soon enough, we decided to break open a bottle of Dovbush Cognac, which I had brought along with other gifts for the crew. Technically, it's brandy, but they still label it cognac in Ukrainian. The French at the table didn't seem to mind. Paul announced that Bogdana (Dana) would join us at some point. Dana had stayed with them in France back in the early days of the invasion, but missed home as many Ukrainians do. She returned and now helps the 80th Brigade of the UAF with donations and the like. Much of what Paul, Anne, Frankie and Valery brought went to them, with some siphoned off for Grizzly and the 12th.

Natasha fitted in well with the group, and lots of side chats came and went. The cognac was a small bottle and was soon polished off. I like a cigar with my cognac, and so indulged in one of the Vega Fina 1998s that Paul and Nicky had brought as a gift. Smoke swirled, conversations and good times rolled along, and more Prosecco was delivered. Nicky pulled me aside and asked what else they could do to help.

Ryan had asked me a few months back to see what I could do for Kevin Leach of Sabre Training Advisory Group. The past weekend, Kevin had invited me to be an observer for a rifle training course for armed civilians and a few active military. Sabre doesn't charge soldiers and is registered as an NGO in both Ukraine and Canada. I noticed they didn't really have much of a communication strategy, so I decided to help with that, along with trying to find UAF units that they could train. I filled Nicky in on as much as I could. He was very interested in how training was conducted and other details. Some questions I could answer, but there were many I could not. Nicky's profession and his short time in the British military made him a very firm believer in consistent, ongoing training delivered in modules. I promised him I would put him in touch with Kevin on Signal.

Darkness was rising. We were all feeling no pain. Natasha had to work the next day. Kyiv's curfew was approaching. We said our good-byes and well wishes. I assume the rest of them had stayed behind for more good times, as Dana had finally arrived. Paul paid for a room for her for the night so she wouldn't be beholden to the curfew. We called Uber and were on our way. No long good-byes or tears.

06:00 Natasha's alarm went off. Despite the drinks, I was fully awake. Brewed some coffee, which began to take effect as my gears started moving. My thinking cap kicked into high gear, and I decided to take a chance texting Nicky. Kevin was free that week, so I wondered if I could pull off getting him out for a meeting before they all departed. Nicky had informed me that their departure time was scheduled for 10:30, so I figured they would get up for the free hotel buffet breakfast. He already had an 08:30 scheduled with Dana that he informed me about when he texted back. Now, this might all seem mundane but there's a good ending to it. I managed to catch Kevin while he was still groggy and gave him a rundown on who the Brits were and what they were interested in. Nicky, Jon and crew do not tend to move fast, but they usually stay with whoever they decide to assist for the long game. Kevin could make it, so I confirmed with Nicky on an approximate arrival time.

Nicky and Jon asked questions at the breakfast. Kevin provided the answers they needed. We decided to set up a Signal group for future communication. I explained to Kevin that they would need time to decompress after the trip and that Nicky had to fly out the day they returned for a conference related to his work. Everyone seemed satisfied. As I write this, no action has been taken. Kevin received a last-minute order to train troops last Sunday which means he is off comms for the most part and focused on that. The seeds were planted. That's a big part of what I do in Ukraine. Sometimes it's just helping people connect. Other times, it is direct involvement in a project or mission. Frankly, I did this with Kevin for selfish reasons as well. I knew once the Brits left that I would be without purpose and mission again, besides my writing. Taking no action, having no purpose, is asking the Black Dog to come in and firmly sleep on your lap for weeks or months to come. Preventative measures are needed to avoid that, as I have learned now.

Wozza was still out on his mission and checking in occasionally. He operates in a whirlwind at times, so I wrote off catching up with him, Glenn and their other teammates. Nicky and crew made it to Lviv for the night and then on to their final destinations. Jon checked in when he could from the road. Paul also checked in once they were back at Nicky's. The most significant thing that happened when they were at Nicky's was the word from Nicky's wife, whom we will call Mrs Claus. She basically told Nicky she couldn't abide him taking the sled and reindeer into Ukraine again. We all understood her reasoning. Nicky and Mrs Claus operate on a different level than we do. They have obligations, priorities and six children to think about. Mrs Claus had been the driver behind them, starting to help displaced Ukrainians back in 2022. She was a well-known partner of a very well-known firm and knew how to lead without being too authoritative. Nicky was obviously disappointed. I was hopeful because I felt that it might make him even more motivated to help Sabre down the line.

Breaking bread is an important part of developing any relationship. Maybe I am old school that way. If you can share a meal or a drink with someone, it opens up things that get lost in texts, messages, emails and phone calls. Had I not been able to get Nicky and Kevin together that last morning, there would have been far less chance of assistance. None has been committed as of this writing, but I have a feeling that something will happen. I know Nicky and am beginning to understand Kevin and his motivation. These chapters have captured just a part of our third year at war. We have become better at it on many levels. Nobody wants to be better at living through war or spending huge amounts of personal time organizing and communicating so Ukraine can win. We have seen how so many others operate and like our quiet side of the game. It's almost always the 'Quiet Ones' you have to watch out for, isn't it?

Kyiv city worker cleaning snow at Oles Honchar Park (Kyiv).

Stairway leading to an underground hammam and sauna (Kyiv).

St George Icon donated by the Georgian Legion at St Volodymyr's Cathedral (Kyiv).

Natasha in her new vyshyvanka dress (Kyiv).

Birthday cake for Natasha from the Hilton, Kyiv.

Christmas tree at St Sophia's Square (Kyiv).

John and Natasha at Winter Fun Fest-Pechersk School International (Kyiv).

Christmas chocolate chip cookies baked by Natasha.

Ukrainian Christmas tree, Pechersk School International (Kyiv).

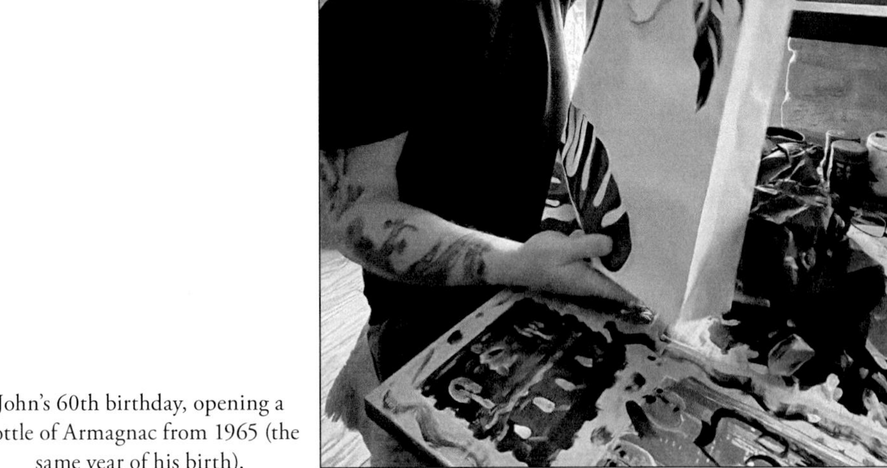

John's 60th birthday, opening a bottle of Armagnac from 1965 (the same year of his birth).

Right: Natasha and Lesya at Korchma Taras Bulba (Kyiv).

Below: John and Aleksandr at Korchma Taras Bulba (Kyiv). Aleksandr was visiting while on leave from the front.

John and Natasha at St Sophia's Museum (Kyiv).

Natasha's students at Pechersk School International (Kyiv).

John as altar server on the Feast of the Holy Spirit (Pentecost) at St Yuri's Church (Kyiv).

Philly relaxing on a Maria Prymachenko blanket (Kyiv).

Left: John and Tristan at breakfast for the first ever in-person meeting (Kyiv).

Below: John and Natasha showing off their Philadelphia Eagles gear after the Eagles won Super Bowl LIX (Kyiv).

Right: John on Maidan with Girl Scout Cookies purchased from the Boben's in New Jersey (Kyiv).

Below: St. Yuri's Church Interior (Kyiv).

Left: Crossing the train tracks with others leaving for Poland from Ukraine (Poland-Ukraine Border).

Below: Natasha with Lisa Groth and John Dewitt (Rotary International). Attending a trauma training seminar for Ukrainian-based educators (Warsaw area).

Right: The forest outside Warsaw.

Below: Natasha attending a hippotherapy session outside Warsaw.

Left: John on an overlook on the Dovbush Trail in the Carpathians (Yaremche).

Below: Philly with his muzzle in the Carpathian Mountains (Yaremche).

John and Philly on a Carpathian mountain trail hike.

The cross at the top of Makovytsia Mountain (Yaremche).

John, Natasha and Philly at the cross on top of Makovytsia Mountain (Yaremche).

John, Natasha and Philly on a Carpathian swing (Yaremche).

Right: Hutsul tour guide on the Dovbush trail (Yaremche).

Below: John and Philly on a very uncomfortable 4x4 tour in the Carpathians (Yaremche).

Left: Grizzly (Andrii Getun) and John with Philly. The first in-person meeting since cooperating online since 2022. (Yaremche).

Below: Hustul sheep herders on Makovytsia mountain (Yaremche).

John overlooking the Prut River (Yaremche).

Natasha on the Prut River in the Carpathians (Yaremche).

Natasha at the
Carpathian Café
(Yaremche).

Natasha on the
Carpathian
mountain trail
(Yaremche).

Right: Natasha and Philly relaxing on the deck during a Carpathian vacation (Yaremche).

Below: Sunset over the Carpathians (Yaremche).

Clay cups and pitchers out to dry in a Hutsul village (Yaremche).

Grizzly, Natasha, John and Philly enjoying some time before an outdoor meal in the Carpathians (Yaremche).

Grizzly and Natasha having a drink on the deck. (Yaremche).

Military patch on display in the Carpathians that says 'Death to Muscovia'.

Old Hutsul house in the mountains (Yaremche).

Thanksgiving Weekend (John and Philly) in Kyiv.

Natasha's students meet a Ukrainian soldier, Pechersk School International (Kyiv).

A Ukrainian soldier teaching Natasha's students, Pechersk School International (Kyiv).

Left: Natasha working from home on the balcony with Philly guarding from intruders on the fourth floor (Kyiv).

Below: Volodymyr Kaplan (former Ukrainian Navy and full-time military volunteer) and John on Maidan (Kyiv).

A tree made from artillery shells. (Kyiv).

Ukrainian soldier giving a presentation to Natasha's students at Pechersk School International (Kyiv).

The old Babycia (grandmom) who walks on two canes around St Volodymyr's Cathedral every day and serves as an inspiration of resilience to John (Kyiv).

Natasha's students at Pechersk School International create notes for the soldiers on the front. (Kyiv).

Right: Tristan Ruark (Odesa Papa), a US combat veteran of Iraq and Afghanistan and now a husband, father and non-combatant living through the war.

Below: Tristan presenting at conference on Veteran Reintegration (Kyiv).

Aleksandr just prior to deploying to the front (Kyiv).

Father Serhit of Kyiv Chaplains with John at a dinner organized by Ryan Grant Little (Kyiv).

Patch (chevron) of the Kyiv Chaplains.

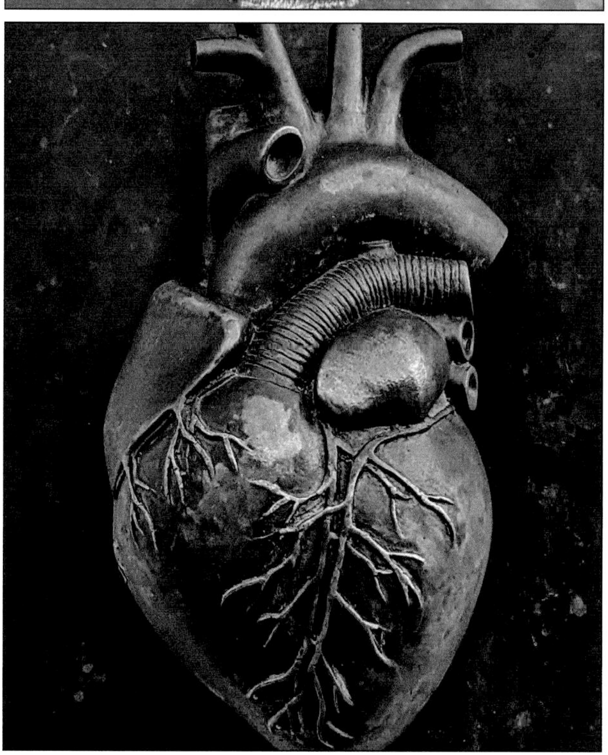

Metal heart sculpture on the street in Kyiv.

Natasha with Deborah Fairlamb of Green Flag Ventures. Two Jersey girls in Kyiv out for pizza.

Grizz, Misha, and Kevin Leach, Director of Sabre Training Advisory Group at some training grounds (Kyiv region).

Kevin Leach giving firearms instructions to civilians.

Starbucks and weapons at the Kyiv region training ground. All weapons are purchased individually by civilians.

Kevin giving instructions on the firing line (Kyiv region).

Firearms training displays by Sabre Training Advisory Group.

23

Ode to Roman

Roman Cybriwsky was my friend for only a brief time, but not because the war took his life. His death was just nature at work. Andrii Getun has stated in the Foreword to *Part One* that God's ways are not our ways. I think Roman was taken before he could see the total devastation happening in Ukraine, and more so the pathetic response of the country he called home. Roman and I both shared that Philadelphia Spirit, that historical place of defiance against tyranny where the US Republic was founded. Living in or near this tough city gives one a true appreciation for the sacrifices that were made by the original colonists. I don't know if it's the same in Des Moines or Boise, but it flows through every part of our being in the Philly area. Maybe there's that part of it that caused Natasha and me to stay in Ukraine. Natasha caught it when she was studying for her exam to become a US citizen. The things she was reading about had taken place only a short drive from where we lived. Natasha also liked Roman for his wit and wisdom. I like to think that God took Roman because the pain his soul would feel would be too much for him to bear. Roman was one of the first public intellectuals to acknowledge and support my writing. This chapter was written during the time that took place in *Part Two*, but it feels more appropriate to insert it here.

The day, 27 March 2023, started slowly, like they always do after the changing of the clocks. Adjusting to the new time seems to take longer as you grow older. There were no Air Raid Sirens this morning, and there haven't been many in the past few weeks here in Kyiv. A crisp spring air was a wake-up call as was the shining sun. It's a Monday here, so the world is back to its regular routine with people going to work, grabbing breakfast on the way to the office and the usual beat of traffic on the city streets.

A bus sat idling in the yard as I walked across the parking lot of St Volodymyr's Cathedral. People stopped before the Cathedral doors, crossed themselves and bowed before entering. I did the same. The old Babucyia behind the counter managed to understand my broken Ukrainian when I purchased candles to light for family, friends, our soldiers and all the innocents killed or suffering because of the war. A Lenten service was being conducted as I made my way around the icons, saying my prayers, remembering those who have departed or as we say, have fallen asleep.

Lenten services are dark and ominous; the curtains are black, as are the vestments of the priests and deacons. Yet, it is still a joyous time because we are preparing ourselves for the coming of Pascha (Easter), which is the greatest of all feasts. The cathedral was slightly abuzz with those lighting candles, saying prayers, as it always is. There are always signs of life in this place, with its ornate icons and artwork filling every nook and cranny of exposed space. Even if you are not Christian, I suspect that the sheer beauty of the place would touch your soul.

I took my place near the front of the church as the deacon and priest sang their parts of the service. The choir sounded particularly harmonious and spiritual this particular morning. We listened to the prayers, bowed and did the prostrations that are common for Great Lent. Bowing and prostrating forces one to be humble, which seems so out of touch with the current state of the world.

Father Bohdan (our priest) came from behind the curtain, saw me and gave his blessing, greeting and touched me with the cross. I was thankful for it since I overslept yesterday and missed Divine Liturgy at his (our) little wooden church tucked away from the big life of the city. St Volodymy's is the headquarters for the Kyiv Patriarchate, and we attend services there at times because it is just a walk down the block, a fixture of our neighborhood. My wife and I are thankful that it is there; we pass it every day when we walk our dog. Completed in 1882, it survived the Bolsheviks, Communism, WWI, and WWII, and so far, it has stood against the Muscovite invasion unleashed on 24 February 2022. A solid structure, a spiritual home to many and today, the location of yet another funeral for yet another fallen soldier of Ukraine.

A red cassock is what Father Bohdan wears when he serves a funeral, and that was what he was wearing when he greeted me at the service. Outside, after the service, Ukrainian soldiers were milling about by the bus. They were doing what soldiers do, smoking, using the bathroom and preparing for the funeral of their fallen comrade. Another life snuffed out for no reason by the pestilence that Moscow has brought to this land.

The sheer scale of death and suffering can't help but affect you in this war. Well, maybe if you are a psychopath, sociopath, or just that egocentric, it doesn't. I stopped to grab coffee and thought of all these soldiers who have left behind families, friends, neighbors and futures. Some will survive, many are long gone, and others may never recover. Sitting down with my coffee, I opened my Ukrainian news channels. President Zelensky had issued a statement saying that many soldiers returning from the front were upset at how lackadaisical people at home seemed to be about the war in the rear. The soldiers would see people acting as if no war existed, as if they were dying for nothing. Sadly, we hear these types in the streets all the time. I think that those who stayed throughout the war, who didn't know if we were going to live when the Battle of Kyiv was raging, look at things realistically and don't take it for granted. Now, in Kyiv, many who are here ran from the fighting and have no real idea what war is really like, besides maybe going to an air raid shelter when the sirens go off. I am not knocking that as stressful because it is, but it's a completely different reality when you can hear active fighting and feel the percussion of the artillery on your windows or the ground shake as you walk. We know many who now speak or wear paraphernalia about 'being brave' but ran like scared rabbits. We don't judge them for running, but we resent them for acting like they didn't.

More bad news greeted me as I decided to check Facebook after a two-day break. There, I read the sad news that another patriot of Ukraine and friend had passed. His name was Roman Cybriwsky. Roman and I had met across the digital sphere when I had emailed him in early 2021 after moving to Kyiv. I had purchased his book 'Kyiv: City of Demons and Domes' when I first moved to Kyiv and decided to look him up. He had retired from Temple University but still had an active email there, so I reached out. Since I grew up in South Jersey, just across the river from Philadelphia, we shared that in common as well.

Roman was very generous and emailed me additional books he had written about Ukraine without asking for a dime. He announced that he would visit Ukraine again in the coming months, so we made plans to meet up when he was in town. At our first meeting, we got to know each other, drank coffee outside on a warm spring day in Kyiv's Solomainskyi District where he had a dentist appointment, and I happened to be living at the time. We met again a few days later in Podil near his beloved Kyiv-Mohyla Academy, where he had met great friends and taught as a Visiting Professor. He gave me a signed copy of his book 'The Sun-Tanned Professor' before leaving. We stayed in touch, sharing stories and insights.

In late October 2021, just a few months before the war, Roman returned. This time, we had moved into our flat in the city center. Roman wanted to meet Natasha, and I wanted to shoot pool on the Left Bank. He picked us up at St Volodymyr's Cathedral in the Megane car he had purchased a few years back. He drove Kyiv like a resident. We shot pool, and he beat me badly, huffing and puffing as he went. Roman was a bit overweight and not in the best of health. He told us he was excited to see his granddaughter and family. Other personal pieces of his life were shared, but those are something only spoken of between friends and not for public consumption. He told me about his new book, 'Incident in Kaliningrad', which was a new writing style for him.

Roman, an accomplished professor and published author, confided in me after reading my novella 'Notes from a Reluctant Alpha Male' that my book had helped him find his 'voice' for his new writing venture. He was also excited to have found a Ukrainian artist in Lviv to do illustrations for the book. He sent me drafts and asked for my critique, which I happily gave and he made changes based on them. This was one of the best compliments I would ever receive as a hobbyist writer.

The muscovite invasion came in February, and Roman stayed in touch through Facebook and regular texts. I updated him about what was happening in Kyiv and on the ground. We hadn't spoken as much lately, but he was always keeping up with my Facebook posts, which served as a kind of war diary. We talked about him visiting when things quieted down and how we would hang out again. Now, that will never happen, and I have lost a new-old friend. Ukraine has also lost Roman. He so loved all of Ukraine and especially Kyiv. In fact, he instilled that love of Kyiv and the Dnipro in me and the desire to see more of Ukraine through his book Ukraine Panorama. Ukraine has lost far too many of its best. We need weapons to finish this war so people can rebuild, heal and go on with their lives. The war didn't kill Roman, but with him, a little part of Ukraine died, just like it does with every death caused by this war.

Later this afternoon, after our neighbor gives us a short lesson in Ukrainian, we will walk to St Volodymyr's Cathedral to light a candle for Roman's soul and life. We will pray that his sins be forgiven and that he sleeps in a place of peace in the light of Christ. Roman was Ukrainian Greek Catholic since his people were from Western Ukraine, but he didn't really practice. That doesn't matter. What matters is that we will remember Roman and be grateful that he came into our lives, that his family bears this grief and does their best to honor yet another Ukrainian Cossack who has crossed the steppes into the afterlife.

Farewell, dear Roman, we will meet again on the shore of the Jordan.

Twenty-Ninth Day of Lent

27 March 2023

396 Days of War

Kyiv, Ukraine

24

Heat and Fog

This chapter covers events from August to October 2024.

Cool nights and mornings in the Carpathians, sounds of birds singing in the trees, a trickle of a small spring-fed stream and clean air were all behind us. We came back to the heat and concrete, heavy smoke of exhaust, stench of garbage and the always bustling urban dwellers of Kyiv. In other words, we were not happy to be home… at all. Neither of us is really an apartment dweller. We prefer a house with a decent-sized yard. Natasha's job demands that she live in the city. This is where the salaries are that make a difference for the standard of living that we have come to enjoy. Sacrifice is part of life. We have given up our love of nature and quiet for this metropolis. It's a love-hate relationship. There's plenty to love about Kyiv, just not in summer.

Heat is something we both abhor after seven years in Florida. How I long for the grey skies of autumn. Natasha has always loved the grey and rainy days. So much so that her boss in New Jersey nicknamed her 'Morticia' (from The Addams Family) when we lived there. I have had skin cancer twice when living in Florida, so I skulk about the city in the summer shadows like a vampire avoiding the sun. We cursed ourselves for not staying longer in Yaremche. All we could speak about was finding a way to move to the mountains for the first two weeks after our return to Kyiv. We concluded that maybe even a country house not far from Kyiv to spend time on the weekends wouldn't be so bad. War made us severe pragmatists, among other things.

Soon enough, Natasha returned to work, and we settled into our school year routine. Since she is a teacher, our life revolves around her schedule. I work remotely and can do it from anywhere. Soon enough, my volunteer activities kicked back in, which means Kyiv is optimal because it seems this is the center of that universe. Lviv has its advantages as well, I presume, but we are Kyivans. It's a different state of mind. The heat lingered and rolled on longer than usual.

Nights began to cool a bit, which often meant the mornings were also pleasant enough. I tried to get everything done in the earlier hours after Philly's walk to avoid the scorching sunlight. Natasha's alarm goes off early so that helped. We had been working with our publisher (Helion) off and on while in the Carpathians and concluded it just as we returned to Kyiv. There was work to do, which I welcomed. Our flat was air-conditioned, and luckily, we had power enough to keep it cool when the electricity was on. The walls are a meter thick and made of brick, so the coolness remains for long durations even when it's hot outside. We quietly celebrated Natasha's birthday when it came, as we always do. Her birthday falls during the Orthodox Theotokos Fast, so I usually make her a tasty vegetarian dish. She is Queen for her birthday month, as we often spread out the celebration. Soon enough, the celebration ended, and we got on with our mundane everyday existence, which includes air raids and attacks. There's nothing mundane about those, but we work around them just like everyone else.

Oleksandyr, the owner of a small business outside our flat and I chat once in a while. He runs what we used to call a 'Head Shop' (Kulture Klub), selling bongs, rolling papers, pipes, etc. We are neighbors. Oleksandyr was smoking on the street one day as I returned from the market. The loud whir of generators could be heard everywhere, which meant the electric was off in our neighborhood. However, no noise was coming from his store, so I asked him why. He had installed an inverter and battery. Natasha and I had researched this and even got a quote from one of our friends from church who had a full solar array. His guy had come in at what seemed like an exorbitant price, so we had resolved to just buy something that would keep us functioning, but without major appliances and possibly the refrigerator. We figured we would store some things on the balcony and just keep a minimal stock of perishable items for the coming winter. Oleksandyr revealed how much he had paid and gave me a referral to his vendor. This came in at about half the price of the other system. So, we had the system installed sometime in late September or early October, which, of course, has only had to kick in half a dozen times so far. Better safe than sorry, I assume, and the full cold of winter still lies ahead.

Qatar is allegedly mediating between Ukraine and Russia for each to stop hitting the other's energy grid. We know how good the Russians are at keeping their promises. We can always add solar down the road and go energy independent. We rolled into October, and the US election nonsense was in full gear, so we avoided anything that had to do with that. Natasha had been off to a rough start with her students but was beginning to find her groove. I had a Defense Tech event coming up. It turned out great for a couple of people and companies that I had helped, but did nothing for me economically. I learned my lesson quickly in that generosity is rewarded until money is involved. Everyone forgets you once that happens. That brought me to return to only the people I trust and have been helping or working with for a long time. Difficult lessons and the ones who turned their backs on me when money stepped up were, of course, Americans. One Ukrainian who was involved took credit and pocketed her share. Another Ukrainian is just simply naïve to the machinations of capitalism. I was dumb enough to think people would do the right thing. Grizzly and I were both hurting financially, and I had hoped to find a way to put some money in his pocket as well. Fog had managed to enter my normally clear thinking. My mistake was not to heed a famous line from a wise man.

'Love flies out the door when money comes innuendo.' – Groucho Marx

25

An Immigrant in Ukraine

2 October 2024

A pale gray and extremely dull October sky hangs above. I exit the flat for a walk with Philly and am immediately greeted with the stench of the streets. It's a cocktail of exhaust fumes, urine, and rotting garbage, garnished with a slight scent of the falling leaves of Autumn. People are rushing to their offices, stopping at the coffee stands, walking their dogs, much to Philly's aggressive reactions and beginning their mornings in this ancient metropolis. I hear Russian, Ukrainian and English with a very strong accent as we make our way toward Shevchenko Boulevard with its park setting, where the mass of commuters sits at lights despite the city having a very efficient public transportation system. A crotchrocket screams past with another moron amidst the vast number of them that occupy the city. It could just as easily be Manhattan, Paris, Warsaw, or any other sprawling urban monstrosity except the sound of the grave-like wailing of an air raid siren.

Traffic keeps moving. People continue walking. No one runs to the shelter. We all stop and check whatever app we use to see if the air raid is an actual threat to our existence. If it's not, we move on with our day. If it is, some of us pick up our pace and head toward a safer place in case of possible incoming missiles or drones. Others of us have grown so used to the thought of death that we just continue on regardless of whether it's a threat or not. Some days, it just feels like a direct hit is a better way. We have grown tired of fear and the disruption of our daily lives. We would rather die than cower like scared rabbits in our holes. Nothing hits, and so Philly and I continue on.

Muscle-bound men step out of brand-new Mercedes, Audis and Bentleys. We look at them with disdain as we know who is fighting on the front and that these men, whose bravado is for appearances, have bribed someone to avoid military service. Stories of them abound about how they work out in the gyms, dine at high-end restaurants and brag about how much they paid to avoid mobilization. How can we not feel utter disgust and disdain for them? Those of us who know and work with soldiers are assured by them that when they return from the front, these types will have hell to pay, and many of them will pay with their lives for their greed and disloyalty. Oddly, this gives us reassurance, and we certainly do not hold it against those who are hiding from drones, dying in trenches and attacking enemy positions so we can be free.

Further along the street, a professional photographer takes photos of painted-up women in the latest fashion for their Instagram and other accounts. Vanity in a war is one of the worst crimes, and it is ominously prevalent here in Kyiv. It breeds disgust but doesn't quite go as deep as hatred. Those of us who are integrated into life in Ukraine are well aware of the country's strengths, while we are also constantly exposed to its weaknesses. We who every day do something for victory, even if it's simply posting something on social media or making a donation, are motivated because we see so many who seemingly do very little or nothing at all. It is up to us to make up for what they lack. Of course, the demon of doubt creeps in when we see all these displays. We begin to wonder if these people would just accept the Russian yoke and live with it. There are those who are already in the occupied territories, as we hear stories of them.

We don't know the exact statistics of those who are fully invested in the war. Amongst our circle, it seems to be somewhere in the 35 to 40 percent range. Sad? Yes, it is. It means that up to 60 percent would accept the yoke or would sit around crying and whining about how 'Ukraine' and 'The World' would let it happen. I don't know if it's the Russian/Soviet influence, but here they spend a lot of time commemorating and celebrating their tragedies. Far too much effort and focus are placed upon suffering. This is alien to us Americans who live on positivity and strength. But we are immigrants and thus, only know part of the story.

Speaking of definitions, we despise the label of expats. We have come here to live out our lives. Of course, this will likely change if Russia prevails, as we would rather die or leave to live under their rule. My wife, Natasha, and I came here to live, not to die, not to exploit the economy, and I will list some of the reasons further on. We do not identify as expats. These people all belong to online forums named for expats, they hang out with other expats, and they all frequent the same cafes, bars and restaurants. Why would you leave the confines of your home country and then hang out with mainly people from that country while living abroad? Neither one of us understands it. There are also those who are short timers who also seem to gravitate toward the same establishments.

The comedian Jim Gaffigan made fun of expats in one of his routines, where he said 'What's up with expats. I stay away from them. They're weird.' Well, the short timers are worse. I guess it might be different in locales outside Ukraine, but this is a war zone. Short timers come, they are loud, often try to be high profile and are ALL experts on Ukraine, Russia, and the war. Let's make it real. Our friend, Tristan Ruark recently texted me about an incident in Odesa. Tristan is a US Combat Veteran (Marine Corps and Army) who served in Iraq and Afghanistan and is trying to quietly live his life with his Ukrainian wife and family. A friend of his, who I assume is also a US Combat Veteran, recently returned from the front where he fought for Ukraine. This friend was getting blackout drunk at a bar in Odesa and had an incident. Natasha and I were sitting at a café on Ukraine Defender's Day (1 October) when Odesa got hit with missiles, and Tristan was letting me know they were ok (we do this often to make sure). Here's our conversation:

Tristan: 'We're good, sounded like it was far from us. Iskander, it was quick.'

Me: 'Dude, I wasn't even paying attention. Chilling with Natasha today. Expert Americans sitting behind us. Can't stand them.'

Tristan: 'Expert Canadians is what started my buddy's trip down the dark road when we met up with Grizz later. Why I try to avoid establishments that have Americans. He told them all to get the fuck out of Ukraine and Walked out. They asked me what his problem was, and I told them he'd been fighting since the full-scale invasion began while they were doing nothing but exploiting the economy.'

Me: 'Pretty much on the same page. Hard to hold my tongue at times.'

Now, you will probably look at us as cynical or maybe even unpatriotic. Tristan was willing to bleed for the US, so you'd be barking up the wrong tree there. I grew up with a great knowledge and pride of the sacrifices the original colonists made. My time in the military was paltry, but at least I gave it a go. We know you will judge us. We also know you will most likely never understand us, and we are very much ok with that. Our tales still need to be told, whether they are pretty or not. Neither of us hates the US; we are just disgusted with what it has become. Neither of us totally loves Ukraine because we know many of its deep, dark secrets. Secrets we keep to ourselves out of loyalty to the land we now call home. We love Ukraine, but we don't view it through rose-colored glasses. Ukraine is a major Charlie Foxtrot, but as I have said before, it is our Charlie Foxtrot, and we choose it. Ukraine did not choose us. We chose Ukraine. We are Immigrant Patriots because here, we see the same values we imagined in those of the Thirteen Colonies, who chose to stand up against an imperial power. Freedom here actually feels like freedom.

Now, I am going to quote a somewhat controversial philosopher who is often sold as Russian. Nikolai Berdyaev was born in the Kyiv Region, was arrested while a student at Taras Shevchenko University in Kyiv and his matrilineal line received lands from the great Ukrainian Hetman, Ivan Mazepa. Berdyaev's biggest fault is that he succumbed to the myth of Russian imperialism and the messianic lie of the Russian Orthodox Church, but in my eyes, that's just a human weakness which still infects plenty of Ukrainians. The quote has significance to my argument for freedom, so here it is.

'*To picture oneself as a free spirit in a consistent and thorough going manner, and to act as a free spirit, means to BE a free spirit.*' Nikolai Berdyaev from his book 'The Beginning and the End'.

This is how we see most Ukrainians, but not Americans. Additionally, this is also why Ukraine is a cluster fuck mess. You simply cannot herd most of these people, and if you try, they will stand up and die in large quantities. Not all of them, but just enough to make it very, very painful for anyone who tries. This is the spirit that runs through the veins of people like Tristan, Natasha and me. Many foreigners here feel the same based on multiple encounters and conversations. Short timers get affected by it but can't quite pinpoint why, because they don't spend enough time here. Expats often identify, and it's why they end up staying, but don't seem to integrate enough into Ukrainian society.

I can't speak for Tristan and his ideas about the US. First, I will say something nice. Natasha and I miss the US, well, specifically, New Jersey. We miss the Shore, humor, food, and the people. We miss Black, Hispanic, and Asian people, their cultures, their food, their modes of speech, and that includes many other minorities of the US landscape, but especially those. We also miss what seems like lightning efficiency of the consumer economy and bureaucracy. Anyone who stands in line at the NJ Division of Motor Vehicles might feel otherwise, but well, they probably haven't lived in a former Soviet state. Those things all look and sound good until you step out and away. Now, it looks more like a Corporate Dictatorship with expertise in making you believe you are free. If slaves believe they are free, they will work harder, keep order and not get too far out of line. I am not saying that all of you in the US are slaves, but I can tell you that you are definitely not free. Freedom is chaos. The US is too orderly, which is enslaving in and of itself. Y'all could use a little chaos in your lives.

Ramble, ramble but not gonna gamble. Tristan, Natasha and I have chosen chaos over order. We choose to live in a nation at war. We have both our collective and individual reasons. Natasha and I are tired of the city. We are both from small towns in our countries. Kyiv is where Natasha has found good employment, so we choose to stay… for now. Sure. We could pick up, sell our flat and buy a cheaper property in a rural area. We're just not ready for that yet. We choose to be here. We choose to be free.

Most of Ukraine chooses to be free. We need more of them to do so. Ukraine has acquaintances, friends, and partners, but it doesn't have allies. Allies would be here on the ground fighting. This is the example from which so many Ukrainians take their lead. So, can we blame them if they are not fully invested? No, we cannot. If just one of Ukraine's partners stepped up and became and actual ally, this whole war would probably change. We don't need the full power of the US for that. We just need one ally with enough conventional weaponry and troops to join the fight. Yes, we also know that it will most likely never happen, and we will have to fight, die, live without power, live without a real future and plug on because we know what it takes to be free. Just one of you, with the backing of your actual allies, could enter this war and end it. Russia is going to retaliate against all of you in one way or another, whether you enter the war or not. You would have to be a fool not to realize that by now. So, take the first step toward freedom and fire a shot.

TRISTAN EMAIL:

I just finished the Black Dog section. I didn't know about the Black Dog from Led Zeppelin.

Once again let me break through to tell you I'm typing this as fast I can to get this out before the baby wakes up.

I have had this black dog following me around on several occasions since being living here. My first experience was talking to a young man on the street who had no desire to be shipped off to die for his country. In one instance I can understand that, and I can't. I wondered then why the fuck do we even attempt to try? We have already lost Ukraine's best and brightest by the thousands.

I experienced it again after talking to some people from Mariupol. They visited they went back. They had to drive through Belarus to get to Odesa from Mariupol. What a crazy fucking drive. They were great people. They had to flee the Donbas in 2014. They had lost everything. They moved to Odesa eventually the husband worked his ass off as a dock worker, seaman, and saved enough money to start up a business which he decided to open in Mariupol. They were not pro russian. They just 'had to be' where they were.

Why the fuck are we doing this?

Why in the fuck are these kids dying?

What the fuck are we doing here if Russia is so great?

It was a spiral. Part of the reason for my commo black out. The other part is American Walmartism ignorant fat fucking consumerism that makes my blood simmer just thinking about it. Or maybe I don't know it's that I can't do more than volunteer some time and money here and there versus going out and slinging lead. It is most likely a combination of all.

I can feel the black dog looking in the window now as I type.

I know that some of the warriors feel this black dog. Guys that believe in Orthodox values then see kids dressed up like furries at the beach on Instagram during a short reprieve from watching their friends being vaporized. I don't know if it is widespread, but I have picked up a big anti homosexuality sentiment. I personally couldn't care less. I was not given the right to judge. I don't know I guess that is a whole other tangent. People that grew up here know better than I what they are fighting for.

The black dog is a great book. It is a great way to describe it. I think it tells the story of the population as a whole. That the black dog is on our heels. As if the average person is being bent to the point of forgetting russian genocidal tendencies towards those who are 'other'. Everyone is tired of being scared. People are sick of the new normal. I don't know. I don't get out enough to talk with people. That and there is a language barrier that is hard for me to breach. I talk mostly to people that can speak English. I don't know what it's like for the people in the Khrushchev housing. Or how ever you spell his name.

I could just be hungry right now.

The point being that the damn black dog is waiting around the corner waiting for the bitch in heat. It can smell it from miles away. I can't say that it's easy to keep the faith. I find myself thinking that maybe the russian flag won't be so bad though I know the facts to the contrary. I studied and continue study Ukrainian history. I know the truth. Do I?

Partly why I can't focus on what I want to write. I flirt with journalism and creative non-fiction to writing children's and YA novels about growing up 90s a Henry Huggins of a different generation if you will. I hate politics. I hate politicians. I feel as if it is a subject that only the people that believe in what you are talking about will read your work. Maybe I just want to write something that makes people feel good. Gives them a sense of nostalgia rather than feed their political porn addiction.

I might rather just want to focus on people. People that don't obsess about politics.

You got me thinking about the black dog. I think that is a very important piece of this war.

Tanya will often get upset about trivial things still. When I get upset about the asshole with no exhaust flying up my street and wanting to follow him to his house and set his car on fire, I have to reset will quick and take into account that I don't live in Kharkiv. Though Odesa is still dangerous it is not bad as most.

I don't know if I envy her ability to get upset about the mundane. AS we live in this weird world where the war has always been. Always will be. Yes, Pizdiets when the dominoes app is down, or when a shirt doesn't fit or when a company sends you the wrong item from an online order.

Is it a good thing or a bad thing? It just is?

We said before moving back to Ukraine that Israel lived in this normal. That they lived with the sirens and took pleasure in the lights of the iron dome. Of course, they weren't being fell upon by hypersonic missiles, but it is no less dangerous to live next to people that don't believe you have the right to exist.

Now with the missile attack from Iran, I find myself laughing a bit. So, you get a few hundred missiles in one day and you had 3 hours to react. We call that lunchtime here.

I love this book, and I feel that it needs to more focused on the black dog. There is so much to this that I, myself am now thinking about that I didn't think about before. I didn't think of it as this damn dog lurking behind me. Though it is and has and I chose not to pay attention to it. I will leave this here. I just saw your other letter come in. I need to wash up the baby and hit the market for some dinner ideas.

I usually stray away from this kind of content in our letters as I like to keep those more optimistic. But the black dog is there. There with dumb fuck Canadians and their dildo conspiracy theories and self-righteousness. It's there with the TCC (True Crime Community) it's there with the American dumpster Walmart politics and the soft ass populace that post memes about not sending another dime to another country while not posting any donations or volunteer time to hurricane relief. Fuck'em.

Ok, time to adult.

Love you guys. I love this new book. It is food for thought for sure. I'll try to read your letter later and respond in kind.

END OF EMAIL. Enough said.

26

Halls of Montezuma

This chapter covers events from 7–11 November 2024.

7 November 2024. The US Presidential Election was decided without any domestic problems. It looked like the Republicans were in line to take both chambers of Congress. Natasha and I expected this outcome and were relieved. The slow walking of the previous administration was causing a lot of unnecessary Ukrainian deaths. Yes, President Trump would be unpredictable, but we also figured he would stir the pot. The status quo was scarier than anything else for us. We needed something different in Ukraine. Europe had to be called to task. Yes, it's all risky, but you don't win battles and wars by being overly careful. Most of the soldiers we know were also of the mindset that things needed to be changed up. We trust their outlook over everyone else's. Of course, many in civil society went apeshit, but the smart ones took the news and started figuring out next steps.

We avoided posting or even talking about the election results with anyone but the level-headed. Emotional reactions were everywhere. Many people in Ukraine, along with those outside of the country who support it, had been vocal about President Trump being a fascist, along with a bunch of other accusations. They were all left eating crow. Many of them changed their tune very quickly, but it was too late; the damage was done. Entering the political fray was never something we ever cared much about, no matter what country we happened to be living in. We have our beliefs and what we support. This is only discussed within the walls of our home. Ukraine lost quite a bit of credibility with the incoming administration because of a bunch of loudmouths.

Life went on as before. We accepted the decision, and I reached out to a couple of Ukraine-friendly Trump supporters to congratulate them. It was time to start building, not knocking more down.

8 November 2024. The lawn mower buzz of a Shahed drone sounded like it was just outside the window. It was somewhere between 06:00 and 07:00 since Natasha was in the bathroom getting ready for work. The bathroom falls under the two-wall protection standard, so I didn't even tell her. I just pulled Philly into the hallway and stood there with him as he sat wagging his tail, thinking we were going for a walk, or he was going to be fed. Ah, the blissful ignorance of a dog's life. This brings comfort that he doesn't

know. I expected an explosion any second, but only heard the steady thunder of air defense. They must have shot down the Shahed without the warhead detonating.

Earlier, around 04:30 or so, there had been explosions relatively close by but not close enough to wake Natasha and Philly. I took the chance and just let them sleep. Yes, it's a tough judgment call. Natasha does the same sometimes when I am sleeping through an attack. You gain a sense for how dangerous the threat really is and go from there. Writing about it doesn't really reflect all the thoughts and sensations that go through our heads when we make those calls. You can't truly understand it unless you have experienced it for as long as we have.

More explosions came as Natasha was wrapping up her morning routine. We have had these Shahed attacks every day for over a month now. No, we are not used to them in a normal way, but we are used to them in a war way. By the time Natasha was ready for work, the threat had minimized, so she headed out. Apparently, she was one of the few who showed up early or on time for work that day. Philly and I hung out a bit longer as I sipped my coffee and prepared to go out in the cold, brisk air. We really don't check the damage reports anymore, but just check on the people in our circle. That's just one of many survival mechanisms.

9 November 2024. Saturday. Natasha and I are both off, but she has a much earlier wake-up up during the week than I do. I decided to let her sleep in and took Philly out for a walk. Our neighborhood is a bustle during the week but is relatively quiet on the weekend mornings. I love this quiet time in the city. Yellow leaves lay strewn about on Shevchenko Blvd and blew with the soft breeze. The air was crisp and fresh, not tainted by exhaust fumes. St Volodymyr's Cathedral stood like a silent guardian, housing the relics of saints and the voices of the choir rising for Divine Liturgy. Philly was his normal self, happy but always on the hunt for something to kill. That's his nature, and we have learned to accept him for what he is after being part of the family for nearly 10 years now. We both know he would die protecting us if he had to, without hesitation. You can't knock that kind of loyalty and aggression when necessary.

Our soldiers have some of those qualities, albeit with logic and reason attached. Not a day goes by that we don't think of them, what they are going through, what they are doing to protect us, how much they miss their families, if they have warm clothes and enough to eat, among many other things. They may never really know our true gratitude. We show it by doing something every day to get them supplies of some sort. Action is what they do, action is what we do. Of course, we back that up with thoughts and prayers. We all fight in the capacity that we are capable of.

Natasha was still sleeping when we got home. That made me feel good. She needs her rest as she is one of the hardest-working people I know. Natasha loves her students and her job. Her level of dedication is admirable. She stumbled out to make coffee, and I cleaned Philly up. The rest of the day we spent just relaxing, sipping coffee, running minor errands and simply all of us being in each other's company. The enemy had probably attacked overnight with more Shahed drones, but our personal memories were filled with warmth and family. This is what life is about, even in war.

10 November 2024. The 249th US Marine Corps Birthday! This is one of our main holiday celebrations every year. Natasha always does it up right. She's one of the few

genuinely good people I have ever known, and I am lucky enough to be married to her. Despite my rather strained relationship with my family, she is a Sennett today because she is making our world-famous Sennett Chicken Dish. This dish has been in my family since I was a child, so somewhere over at least 50 years. That's a tradition. Now, this dish is not something I can describe in its full culinary masterpiece, but I will give you a 'taste'.

First, you cut up the chicken into small bite-sized pieces, then it's marinated overnight in white wine, eggs, garlic, lemon juice and salt. The next day, the chicken is breaded with flour and fried in light oil and layered into a pan with mushrooms and cheese. This is then baked in the oven until the cheese melts and voila! Sennett Family Chicken Dish.

Marines usually drink heavily for their birthday, but in our house, we drink moderately, eat well and top it off with cake. Maybe we are conservative. All I know is that it is a launch into the Nativity Fast and the holiday season, a sort of precursor. We were probably attacked overnight, but that's not the memory either one of us has for the day.

Natasha is a Marine in my book. She has all the qualities that the Corps holds dear and is tough as nails. When we celebrate, I feel like she's a fellow Marine celebrating with me. Yes, she does all the work because she's a good wife and wants to honor me, even though I was not such a great Marine when I was in. To her, I am everything that embodies a Marine, which is what matters most. Basically, becoming that Marine was a delayed reaction for me, although I feel the Corps would approve of the way I have conducted myself since the invasion began. That time on Parris Island paid off for me, and I will always have gratitude to all those who trained me and served with me, as well as all the Marines who went before and will come after. Any day of the week, I can go down to Maidan and honor those US Marines who came to Ukraine, fought and died trying to bring this country the freedom it fights for every day.

Yesterday was Remembrance Sunday for the United Kingdom, which is a far more solemn way to remember the fallen. I made sure I let my British partners know they were not forgotten. Frankly, I lean on the Brits here far more than Americans, who are almost always a disappointment. There are many reasons I feel this way, and it's my own experience. Natasha is on the same page, so it's more our experience. Other Americans and Ukrainians most likely have different experiences. I know there are plenty of good Americans here who are helping and making a difference. It's just that we seem to always run into those who aren't.

11 November 2024. Veterans Day in the US. We woke up to Natasha's work alarm and found that there were bombers in the sky. These we dread because they are far more deadly than Shahed drones and almost always targeted at civilians and infrastructure. All the scuttlebutt is that President Trump spoke to Putin and told him not to escalate, which, well, umm, is continuing to strike civilian targets not escalating? In some people's eyes, probably not. It's more like routine slaughter and not escalation. That's the world we are dealing with now. One in which the routine slaughter of innocents is not escalation. Oh wait, that's pretty much the world since humanity organized around basic society and started coveting what others had.

The missiles struck President Zelensky's hometown of Kryvyi Rih in eastern Ukraine. That's a bit too coincidental in my book, but what the hell do I know? We hear rumors of some kind of deal, but nobody here is willing to believe anything until they see it. Ukraine is like Missouri, we're the 'Show Me' state of Eastern Europe. We just plug ahead and do our thing until there is concrete evidence.

This morning has been challenging, to put it lightly. In the midst of missile attacks, I was on Signal with Nicky, Grizzly and Jon coordinating a military aid package to our Special Forces unit. Nicky sent Jon money, who forwarded it on to Grizzly for FPV drones and Electronic Warfare against drones. Thank you, PayPal! Alongside that, Nicky was also organizing a 20-ton truck with military and humanitarian aid that is due to be delivered in early December. Grizzly and I are coordinating with Nicky to have the truck deliver to our partners in Zakarpattia (beyond the Carpathians), named UA Ants.

UA Ants are quite active and have been since the first days of the full-scale invasion. They are a group of Christians who escaped Donetsk, Dnipro and Kyiv when the invasion started. UA Ants found an unused hotel and set up camp there. They have helped thousands of IDPs (Internally Displaced Persons) and currently house 60 of them in the hotel. They support military units and have six vehicles that regularly run aid to the military and civilians at or near the front. I have hung out with their director, Kalina, in a smoky bar in Kyiv. Lori Jackson, a Floridian missionary who lived in Luhansk since 2004 and has been displaced, is my main contact. People underestimate her because she is a very polite southern girl. Her father is former US Navy, so I wasn't worried and liked her immediately. We have built a strong team and network here. We know who we trust. We know who gets the job done. Today is a good day in the grand scheme of getting things done for the soldiers. That's all we can really ask and be thankful for.

27

1001 and 1002

20 November 2024, day 1,001 of the full-scale invasion. The 1,000th day had passed. It's not a day to celebrate or commemorate. Many in the media, the Ukrainian government and others posted articles, statements, videos and other items to try to grab and keep the world's attention. So many have long ago turned away from our fate here in Ukraine. There's a whole slew of reasons for those who are not going through war to simply drop their support and attention. One can't really stay caught up in this horror day in and day out if it's not required for survival. I know people who care but only give it limited screentime now. It's understandable. Maybe even I would do the same if I were on the outside. We'd been hit by another huge missile and drone barrage throughout the country only days ago. They are more frequent now than at any other time during the war. Sometimes it's only drones, and others it is a combined attack. The whole country is on edge.

President Trump isn't due to take office for another two months, and most of us don't expect him to be some savior who will end the war. We hope he can do something, but we are not sure what, if anything. It seems President Putin and the Russian people have gone completely zombie apocalypse already. We hear the stories from the front of their soldiers running unarmed right into Ukrainian machine guns and being chopped into hamburger. They just keep coming regardless. We aren't necessarily frightened because the front is still very far away from Kyiv. People further away probably feel even more secure from the zombies. But we can't ignore what they are capable of. We also think about the toll it's taking on our soldiers who have to cut them down and let their corpses freeze in the open and cold winter air. Why should our soldiers remove their bodies and put themselves at risk?

Several messages from friends with strong military connections came through today. They warned us not to ignore the air raid alarms because Russia was due to hit us with something new and big. Telegram channels published a text stating the number of missiles and drones that they planned to launch. The numbers were massive, beyond anything we had experienced before in sheer volume. I had plans to attend an event in Podil, and Natasha was scheduled to go to the outskirts of Kyiv to her tutoring client. My plans were easily cancelled, and I asked Natasha to please not go. Her clients understood. For reference, here is the message that came out (translated from Ukrainian):

'TO ALL SUBORDINATED COMPETENT SERVICES!!!

According to the intelligence information received by the MOU GUR from radio intercepts on 20.11.2024 after 2:30 p.m. Kyiv time, a massive combined missile strike will be launched from its existing flotilla, aviation, ballistic launch systems, hails, beechs and others. They also plan to launch more than 317 different types of radio-controlled strike drones with warheads of various capacities at the same time.

The enemy plans to attack energy and gas distribution nodes, as well as strategically important civil infrastructure facilities.

Immediately prove this information, in order to save work documentation, equipment and the lives of employees. Irrespective of the presence of a warning about the air alarm signal, it is necessary to ensure the passage of personnel to the shelters both on the territory of the facility or to leave its borders from 13:00. In connection with the possible loss of coverage of mobile GSM communication, give the employees of the radio station to maintain communication.'

Sounds serious, right? Serious enough for us to change our plans just in case. We were not in fear for our lives. We were in fear that we wouldn't be together if it was time to die. This was scarier to us than actual death. Philly certainly couldn't have been left alone while I was out gallivanting in Podil and Natasha was tutoring a 2nd grader. So, I made the most of it, rustled up some vittles, bought some dessert and grabbed some wine and cognac. Natasha got home from work, and we joked that we were about to have our 1001st Last Supper. Humor gets you through this kind of reality.

Funny enough, not long after Natasha got home from work, we found out the whole thing was a hoax. Well, let's call a spade a spade. It was a massive PSYOPS operation by Russia, and a huge number of us fell for it. Most of the time, we see right through these, but the masses had bought in, and the message certainly looked legitimate. General Budanov of the Ukrainian HUR had nipped it in the bud, but not quite early enough. Here's the thing. It was early enough for me to still attend the event. Instead, I decided I would rather just stay home and enjoy the night. Russia thought they would send everyone into a panic but instead we got a freebie with good food and drinks. It was a Wednesday, which is my evening off and one where Natasha does her tutoring, so I don't see her until 21:30 or so. We spent the night quietly and went to bed at a normal hour.

Day 1,002. Russia fired a 'new' weapon at Dnipro and scared half the world again. This was a nuclear-capable missile with six warheads that were shot empty. Two people in Dnipro died from the kinetic energy. President Putin came out trying to be scary yet again. The warning was true, and the attack was delayed by a day.

28

What Have You Done?

27 November 2024, the eve of Thanksgiving. This morning, I had coffee with my friend, Lamb Wolf (LW). I will explain his deeper story in another chapter, and I am not using his real name, as maybe he doesn't want me to. You will need to have a little background to understand the context of this chapter. LW is in his mid-forties, and prior to the full-scale invasion, he was living his life and running a website. He was there for Maidan in person. LW is a kind and patient person who was mobilized in June 2023. He is not the kind of person that you would expect to be a soldier… at all. Yet, he took his mobilization in stride and was resolved to do his duty for Ukraine. LW didn't go to the front until late summer/early autumn of 2024. He fought in Toretsk and was injured fighting in a close-quarters battle when a round ricocheted and hit his covered position. The round entered his thigh sideways, ripping apart muscle and nerve. This morning, he was still limping with a cane and had his Medical Leave extended for another 30 days.

Our conversation was normal until we left the café. LW insisted on paying for the coffee, and it seemed important to him, so I complied. He had to take a bus back to his duty station to have his paperwork approved, so I decided the least I could do was to walk with him and wait for the bus. We walked slowly toward St Volodymyr's Cathedral, as the bus stop is directly out front. Our conversation continued as we walked about his adjusting to life with an injury. Just as we were passing the Swedish Embassy across the street, he paused and said:

'You know, I think I might have to go see a psychologist.'

I nodded my head but did not reply, deciding to let him speak his mind. Obviously, he felt like opening up, and the key to good listening is to acknowledge and not interrupt.

'It's weird.' He went on. 'I am not upset or bothered by what I witnessed and experienced on the battlefield.'

He stopped and looked me in the eye to make sure he had my full attention. I looked back, letting him know.

'No. My problem is being out here with civilians.'

Ah, I recognized that feeling. There is nothing that matches that strong sense of brotherhood among soldiers who are fighting alongside each other. I made a point to emphasize that. He thought for a moment.

'I wish it were that, and maybe it is to a certain extent. Really, what it is, is that I noticed very strange reactions when I was still wearing my uniform. It was like they were purposely looking away or avoiding me, like I was some kind of pariah.'

As soon as he said this, I told him that I had witnessed the same activity on the streets of Kyiv. It's as if civilians don't know how to approach or speak to soldiers. In the US, we usually say 'Thank you for your service', whenever we find out or see someone in uniform. A recent Facebook post by a combat medic of the Hospitallers (Oleg Magdych), who was touring the US to explain the frontline situation in Ukraine, also spoke to this frustration. These thoughts quickly ran in and out of my head as LW continued.

'I am having real problems with them, especially now that I am in civilian clothes and can hear their conversations and see their actions. It's as if there is no war for many of them. Like we soldiers don't even exist to many of them.'

'Yes. I also see signs within civilian society that trouble me.' I replied, 'As someone who volunteers in some way every day to help soldiers or do something for the country, I also get frustrated. Some people seem to act as if there is no war at all.'

The café we had just left, for instance, was being run by a bunch of young girls in their twenties. They were playing loud nightclub music as we tried to talk over coffee. Coffee? Get it? It was morning. Clearly, the level of noise was bothering us, and I think really getting to LW, but they went about their business as if, well, it was time to start dancing. Soldiers don't like loud noise, and it often really bothers them. What will these types do when the war is over, and they play loud music in the morning, and it triggers a response from a war veteran? LW also has tinnitus from his time in the battle zone, and loud noise exacerbates it. The sheer level of insensitivity to reality is going to cause major problems as more soldiers return injured and damaged. Our conversation continued.

'I don't know how to deal with these emotions toward civilians. I don't want to be violent with them, but just don't feel a part of their society. Nor do I really want to be.'

Briefly, I thought about what he just said. LW is a kind and gentle person. How will soldiers who have experienced total slaughter and destruction react? That rage that exists within them will not take much to bubble to the surface and explode. Are civilians even prepared for this? There are conferences all over the country about mental health, but no national initiative to prepare the civilian population for how to conduct themselves in the presence of veterans of war. You can feel the potential violence that could come. I decided to continue.

'This is understandable, my friend. I often don't want to be a part of it myself.' Reassurance is essential when dealing with someone who is experiencing or has experienced trauma. LW's trauma is focused on how it will be to live amongst people who have not done enough for the war effort. I expressed this myself as he was struggling.

'I have friends who have money and give a little here and there for drones who think it is enough. Yet, they have major skills that could be used to help Ukraine in so many ways, but all they are focused on is earning more. Even if they gave a few hours a week of their time, it would make a difference. But they don't. Increasingly, I feel a distance that grows into a gulf between them, Natasha and I.'

LW looked at me emphatically.

'Yes, there just isn't enough effort. These donations are good, but simply not enough for us to win. It's difficult not to let it affect you, but you have to keep going on.'

We joked a little about Members of Parliament (MPs) and government ministers. How many of the soldiers were already planning to confront them in ways they are not used to? His bus came and he went on his way. A few days later, he texted me to let me know he had been granted Medical Leave and would go to his wife and family in Germany. How difficult it must be for soldiers who fight for their country and then must leave it to see their loved ones. I know many are bothered by those who have left and done well for themselves abroad, who will probably never return. We see many who post all over social media while living abroad, along with those who travel outside to promote themselves while trying to convince us that it's all for Ukraine. You can see right through most of them, and it does not promote anger but depression. You can feel it on the streets and in the fields; there is not even full support for the soldiers among the population. So many are doing only for themselves, and they reek of it.

Increasingly, it becomes more difficult to reach down into that resiliency I know is there. The Black Dog seems to have become a permanent fixture, and he steals all my living energy. If I live through this, I know we will be able to have strong answers if someone asks us what we have done. However, I don't think a large share of society will have an answer when a veteran asks them. Maybe those who didn't step up when the war was raging will help the veterans instead. We could use a second wave because those of us who are fully invested are already fatigued to our limits. Even now, some of us are trying to plan for the veterans and come up with options. Every day is an uphill struggle on all fronts. I almost pity those who won't have good answers when a battle-hardened veteran asks 'What have you done?'

POSTSCRIPT: LW left the country and now lives in Germany with his wife. It just became too difficult for him to return.

29

Dark to Light December

15 December 2024, Sunday. Bleak weather. Apathy. Darkness. Anger. A lack of joy. Death. Destruction. More death. More destruction. Loss of hope. That's where we are now on a societal level, or at least within those we are in touch with. Here stands the difference from those of us who have remained since 24 February 2022, and tried to do something every day to help the military or the needy. Maybe it's just a perception because it's not like I can stop people on the street and ask them. I simply know it's the general consensus among those I do work with. Natasha is sick today. I could not get myself out of bed to go to liturgy, and when I took Philly out, the sidewalks were like a skating rink anyway. At my age, you must consider these things when venturing out. Can you imagine suffering a broken hip whilst in a universal tour of the abyss?

Part of it is our own making. We have stopped going to church. Natasha seems to be sick very often and has not been working out. Sure, we grab small joys where we can, but they dissipate like the smoke from the censer at church. A whiff of the celestial and then the black dog starts barking again. This creature has become more of a pestilence than a pest. We can't ever seem to shake him off completely. Natasha and I are lucky, though; we have each other to discuss our problems with. Frankly, I don't know how we would get through it if we didn't. We've both been skeptical of psychology ever since watching 'The Sopranos' due to its reference by Paulie of being a 'racket'. I am not a talker by nature, so Cognitive Behavioral Therapy wouldn't do me much good. Being a good listener in group sessions would probably only drive me further into the darkness. Alcohol is not an option. Pharmaceuticals? Psychedelics? Pfft! No way, Jose. Did all that recreationally and have no desire to go back to a possible addictive option.

No. This is going to take a fully concentrated effort on both our parts. I bounce my self-treatment ideas off Natasha, and she does the same. Yesterday, it really hit home for me. We were at a holiday party with many children around and chatting to a US combat veteran who has also spent a significant amount of time on the front in Ukraine. A child popped a balloon, and he jumped, clearly shaken. The effects stayed with him for hours. I didn't say anything to him about his apparent case of PTSD. The incident got me thinking of all the veterans and civilians who have it, and we are simply not prepared to treat them all. Of course, I drove myself deeper into the dark tunnel thinking about it.

Coincidentally, I had been putting together ideas for a peer-to-peer type therapy for veterans, families of the fallen, displaced persons, and other affected civilians. The whole thing is coming together nicely on paper. Reflecting on it, I have no background to run such an initiative, and well, I am all screwed up myself. Natasha and I drank our coffee this morning and discussed the steps needed to get out of our funk. Most importantly, I came to realize that for almost three years now, I have been focusing on helping others. I have denied my art, my body and my spirit. Turning 60 is a milestone. Maybe I need to focus on my own healing this coming year. I will still try to get the peer-to-peer project going, but I don't want to be in the driver's seat. Hell, I can't even steer at this point.

17 December 2024. Lately, I have been suffering from insomnia, which was rarely ever a problem. Last night, I prayed for a good sleep so I could get up and go to church this morning. That prayer was answered. Philly was fed and only wanted a short walk since it was wet and rainy. He doesn't care for that kind of weather, so just did his business. Philly is pretty good at communicating. He stops, looks at me with a particular expression, and I ask him 'You wanna go home?' He answers by immediately turning in the direction of home and starts walking. I had time to spare before liturgy because I had planned on a longer walk. Sitting quietly in our flat with the natural light coming in has become a place of peace for me. No, won't call it 'mindfulness', although some might define it that way. I just repeat the Jesus Prayer as I sit there, 'Lord Jesus Christ, Son of God, have mercy on my soul, a sinner.' This is considered an ascetic practice within the Orthodox Church among some. Me, I use it as prayer but also as Orthodox Psychotherapy[1]

As soon as I stepped outside, the air raid alarm went off. I saw people check their phones and then make that familiar expression of, 'Ah, ok, it's not a major attack', and then go about their business. I do this when I am not in the mood to check my own phone, as you can quickly tell by people's reactions what's coming our way. A light drizzle fell, and I could hear the drops dancing on my hood as I walked. The weather had warmed slightly, so it wasn't as bitter. Puddles ran like streams with the falling rain, which was melting the snow that had been falling off and on for a week. In my head, I pictured the running water as a quiet mountain stream. As I came up on the McDonald's, some slight booms seemed to be coming from the Left Bank that sounded like air defense. A Ukrainian guy in his forties looked up and then looked me in the eye. We both looked in the direction of the explosions, looked back at each other, shrugged our shoulders and moved on. The light had changed, and it's a long wait, so I decided to keep heading for church.

The rear gate of the St Volodymyr's Cathedral is closest to our flat, so I entered there across from the Austrian Embassy. My backpack hung loosely off my back, so I removed it so I could take off my hat and gloves before entering the Cathedral. Just then, I heard the lawnmower buzzing sound of a Shahed drone. It's a very distinct sound that all of us have learned to discern from other city noises. People outside the Cathedral started looking up. That's the other thing about the sound, you can pretty much know the

1 Hierotheos Vlachos, *Orthodox Psychotherapy: The Science of the Fathers* (Akrefnio, Greece: Birth of the Theotokos Monastery Press, 2005).

trajectory and distance and whether it's close enough to cause bodily harm. The sky was grey, and the clouds were low, so we couldn't see the drone. Neither apparently could the air defense guys who started firing from the tops of nearby buildings. A lot of rounds were popping off, but nothing sounded like a direct hit. By now, the Shahed was far away as the engine was becoming fainter. I turned to genuflect before entering the church. Boom! Ah, direct hit by air defense as opposed to a direct hit by the drone. You also learn what those sound like. Nobody even flinched or stopped what they were doing. An old babycia (grandmother) with an arm cast asked me to help her up the stairs, so I obliged and held the door for her.

Today is St Barbara's Day on the old calendar (Julian). St Barbara is the protector from sudden death and the saint of artillery soldiers. Odd, I thought as everything sank in.

20 December 2024. 06-something. The air raid sounded, but we were too groggy to check Telegram, so we just rolled over, expecting it was probably Shaheds. Minutes later. Kaboom! A deafening one left the windows shaking. Before we could get out of bed and into the hallway, a second massive explosion, even closer. We knew right away it was the deadly quick Kinzhals. Natasha was getting ready for work in the bathroom, where we were all huddled observing the two-walls-rule. We brought Philly's bed onto the warm flooring we had installed, but he was clearly rattled.

Much to my chagrin, Natasha stated she would go to work. I was worried they would hit us again while she was on the way to work. I gave her a hard time and hurt her feelings, but, in the end, accepted her decision. She looked at me and said in her New Jersey accent:

'Look, I got this! My war intuition is highly developed. I'll be ok. It's a big day for my students and I have to go for them.'

There's no good argument against that reasoning, so I settled down and saw her off. There was very little detail on where the missiles fell, but based on the noise and reverberation, they couldn't be too far away. I worried that Natasha would get held up if they were on the route her Bolt driver would take. Soon enough, she checked in to let me know she was safely at school. Seconds later, another air raid went off, and she let me know she was in the shelter with her co-teacher from last year, Tamara. Natasha and Tamara had become friends, so it reassured me that they were together with the children. Soon enough, the air raid passed.

Damage reports started rolling in. David Nichols from Invest in Bravery was here from Prague. He sent photos of some of the damage, which was near the MacPaw offices where they had held their event just this past October. The missile was shot down but caused significant damage, death and injury. St Nicholas Catholic Church across the street had also suffered damage. This church had caught fire and was in the midst of being repaired, so it was another blow to one of the few Roman Catholic churches in Kyiv. More reports came in. Anger spread all over social media and elsewhere, but as usual, Ukraine's partners were 'indignant' and sending more 'thoughts and prayers.' Oy vey!

21 December 2024. The light began to arrive this morning. Natasha slept in. Philly and I went for a walk after I had some coffee and finished a chapter of Lucy Ash's 'The Baton and the Cross' about the influence and role of the Russian Orthodox Church on

the Kremlin and vice versa. I brewed coffee for her when I returned, and soon enough, she was crawling out of her grogginess. Soon enough, she was on the phone wishing her mother a happy birthday, and I did too in Ukrainian. Fully awake, Natasha started making Christmas Chocolate Chip Cookies. She had started yesterday at school with her students. It's become an annual Christmas event for her. They bake cookies together and then deliver them to school employees and administrators. Christmas Carols played in the background. I taste-tested a cookie from each batch because, well, Natasha insisted.

24 December 2024. We had gone to St Yuri's for Divine Liturgy on Sunday, so I was still riding on that spiritual regeneration. The people there are very nice, but every time we stay for coffee hour, it takes away from the cleanliness we feel after Confession and Communion, so we skipped the social graces this past Sunday. Thus, I attribute my spiritual state partially to that. Philly has been having health problems, so Natasha took him to the veterinarian because he was due for his annual rabies shot. He is a Christmas dog. We adopted him in Polk County, Florida, on 9 December 2015, when he was barely even a year old. The shelter had named him Sinclair, but well, we chose a name that suited him better. I am writing this at 12:32 just to get some words down before focusing on work again. We expect a missile attack in the next few days because the barbarians in Moscow operate that way. Hate runs through their blood and culture so much that we can smell and feel it every second of the day. But it's Christmas, and well, love and joy rule for us no matter what they do. That's how Ukraine and those who support her will beat them and overcome the collective suffering.

Today, though, I must return to my work. Christmas Eve feels like a Bob Cratchit moment for me, although I don't have a complete Scrooge for a boss. It just feels like I must since I'm in a darkened office and bang out the schedule for January, along with all the trips. You see, I have taken some time off for Christmas, but also because Thursday, 26 December, is our 23rd Wedding Anniversary. Philly is a Christmas dog, and we are a Christmas couple. However, I must get back to being Bob and hope to return later and fill you in a bit more.

I hunkered over the keyboard, working all day
What would arise to my dismay?
Missiles and drones in the sky did fly
Orcs won't ruin Christmas although they try
The borscht is simmering on top of the stove
Our spirits dance, St Nick soon to rove
And we'll laugh and we'll cry, have a drink
For one day of the war, we will not think

And so it was that I stopped working and prepared mushrooms for the famous Sennett chicken dish on Christmas. Natasha sat filling in forms, and the night began to creep in. With it, Christ's birthday began to shine, and we went on not knowing what tomorrow would bring.

On a final note, since I was channeling Dickens, it seems the Kyiv weather decided to comply. A deep, heavy fog coated the city as I came out of the door to walk Philly after the little light of day had dissipated. Streetlights were shrouded in the fog's thickness. An ominous baritone bell was slowly making its lonely 'Bong! Bong!' as we approached St Volodymyr's Cathedral. For whom the bell tolls, I do not know, but it certainly isn't a happy tone. Even though it is Christmas Eve, it feels more like an early Scrooge morning. The lightness and joy are not upon people's faces, but it wasn't like that before the invasion either.

They have not quite yet grasped the overwhelming warmth of Christmas here. New Year's still dominates the advertising and theme, a leftover from the Soviet era. What a dark, dank, crushing presence those years still hold. Even the Kyiv Post came out today with an article stating that Ukrainians will spend more on New Year's than on Christmas. This exasperates Natasha, and it gets under my skin as well. I think it's because her time in the US created a true and enduring love for the joy of Christmas, and she misses that most. Maybe we will go to London or thereabouts next year for a proper English Christmas. I think we both could use one. However, we will celebrate here in Kyiv beside hearth and home to make the most of it.

25 December 2024. Darkness seemed to decide to linger this morning as if the night could not quite let go. Maybe it was the heavy grey clouds hanging low. Natasha and Philly still lay tucked away in the bed with visions of feasts and dog biscuits dancing in their heads. I sat in the chair facing the windows, enjoying the quiet, grey dullness of Christmas morning. Natasha and Philly eventually arose from their slumber, and I pulled out the French press to make coffee. I gave her time for the caffeine to kick in.

Just as she was awake enough, I went to fetch her Christmas gifts, and as I did, the blare of the air raid siren sang its sorrowful and ominous tone. No, the Russians were not going to steal this moment. We ignored it instead and just went on with our Christmas morning routine of love, family and Christ. The missiles came and hit energy infrastructure in other parts of Ukraine. We decided it was ok if we depleted our battery to cook something in the oven. The electric went out, and we went on.

Dinner was delicious and the flat was lit up by multiple candles as we sat down. The lack of electric only made it more magical. No, the Grinch of Ivan Grozny would not ruin Christmas in this American-Ukrainian home. We just let it be like millions of others and shared the joy while still others died, fought and froze on the front. We prayed for them and toasted them, knowing we cannot forget but also that we must go on.

31 December 2024. They shot drones, missiles and one hypersonic missile at us in the early morning hours as we expected them to. We slept through the whole thing… again. Some days, it's a herculean chore just to pull ourselves out of bed. It is the holidays, but it probably goes deeper than that. Natasha said she figured they would shoot early so they could start drinking for New Year's. We don't put much on this secular passing of the year, no big plans or resolutions. We call it the Soviet Cult of New Year's, and I guess we don't make much of it. We do the thing we love most, though, cook! Well, Natasha cooks, and I eat.

Right now, it's 14:55 and the pork roast is in the oven. Philly is snoring away in his bed. Natasha is working on her online class for the Florida Teacher Certification in between attending to the food. I am working at my remote job. It's a nuthin' muffin kinda day. I like these quiet days, which still feel filled with warmth and our little family. The little things that make a life a life.

Today, I posted on LinkedIn, which is now my go-to social media network and heard from a couple of people in the US. What's most important is that I wrapped up editing and reviewing *Part Two* of this series, which is due out on 24 February 2025. Maybe I will write another chapter or two for this current book, depending on events and circumstances. My goal really is to write *Part Four* in the here and now, much like the first two, but you know… 'the best laid plans of mice and men.' We don't know what 2025 holds for us, Ukraine, and the world. We don't speculate or hope for peace much. We just march on because it's really all we know how to do. And I think of some of the words from Bob Dylan's song 'Tangled Up in Blue.'

> 'Then he started into dealing with slaves
> And something inside of him died
> She had to sell everything she owned
> And froze up inside
> And when finally the bottom fell out
> I became withdrawn
> The only thing I knew how to do
> Was to keep on keepin' on like a bird that flew
> Tangled up in blue.'

30

20 December 2024

That morning started just like any other teaching day. Early. Groggy. Grey. With tons of little details going through my mind to manifest themselves later in the reality of the last school day before the long-awaited Christmas break for all the teachers and students alike. Teaching 1st grade is full of those tiny details that make up the fabric of the day. Primary school teachers plan a bit differently than the older grades colleagues. The maturity level of their students calls for tasks that are geared towards independent projects. My students require a lot more guidance, interference, and planning for every 15–20-minute time frame, not just one period. It includes time management, engagement activities, a background knowledge assessment (that very often means building the background for them to process what I am about to drop on their little heads), and what the students are actually doing every 15 minutes or so throughout the day. It needs to be clear to them, and for that to happen, it needs to be clear to me. Therefore, my planner looks like a giant draft that has been edited and revised multiple times as the day goes by. Not any different, perhaps, than for many other 1st grade teachers all over the universe.

December 20th was promising to be a crazy, sugar-excitement-filled day, on the scale of 10, a top indicator of crazy. Plus, the school-wide assembly was the wrap-up. It is a special event. The parents and relatives come to see their children on stage, demonstrating the summary of knowledge acquired in the past semester. The whole school gathers in the auditorium, and the performances begin from the youngest to the oldest kids present. It's a climax of the 'story of learning a second language', English for many, French and Spanish for some.

Grade 1 is the cornerstone. This is the glorious passage, when the kiddos step on the big, wide stage with microphones for the very first time. This was their second performance this year. We practiced a lot. The verses were learned, the music was chosen, and the order of lines and mike passing got to an automatic level. It was going to be quick, on point, sharp and entertaining. We made sure of that by smoothing out every possible bump, learning our own lines and those of students already celebrating Christmas break somewhere in Bali, and leaving the rest in God's hands in the event of a much dreaded air raid that could seriously damage the flow of any performance. The kids were ready.

As I was playing out every possible and 'unlikely' scenario in my head and a response to each, and getting ready for school, I heard the air raid wailing its ominous song. I don't automatically reach for my phone anymore. I know I have at least two minutes before the actual update shows up on the screen, dictating my next move. I finished my makeup and beauty routine as quickly as any respectable woman pressed for time would and scrolled down the feed. Ballistics on Kyiv. I ran to the bedroom to warn John and get Philly up and awake enough to entice him to exchange a warm bed for the bathroom floor early in the morning. John is a human with quick reactions and logic; a word or two is enough to get him going. Philly is a beastie with particular habits, who likes his things just so, and he happens to be not a morning dog. He enjoys lounging around in a warm bed next to either one of us, and, if someone bothers his routine, he does not take lightly to it; growling and showing indignation in any way he sees fit for the occasion. I had to grab a quick snack on the way to the bedroom to make the process quick and painless for all. By the time Philly was on his feet, John had already grabbed his dog bed and placed it in the middle of the bathroom floor.

We braced ourselves for the impact. It is a very unsettling feeling, not at all subdued because you experienced that pit in your stomach many times. It is just as overwhelming and unpleasant every time, because you expect the worst, except you are not imagining this in your head. It's in the air, and is about to hit something and kill someone, you just don't know who.

In a matter of minutes, we heard that dull explosion close enough to feel it, but far enough that our building did not shake. Before we had time to process, another missile was headed in our direction. The emotional roller coaster. At this point, the updates were coming up quickly and you have a need to be in the loop of the oncoming disaster, so you follow everything at once, the local channels, the right/left bank channels, the country wide announcements, the official and the 'fun' channels popping up with whatever they think they know, and, by extension, what we feel at the time. Another explosion hit somewhere further up. The whole country was under attack, and another case of missile diarrhea covered the land. Within a few godawful minutes, our perimeter quieted down. Other explosions followed, but not in our district. The channels warned the population of a tough day full of air raids and debris falling around. But for now, it was quiet. I was dressed for work and still had the time to make it by 8:15, the official clock-in time. Many teachers scattered all over Kyiv and beyond were going through the same 'carrying walls/bomb shelter routines' with a definite scenario of running late based on the traffic afterwards. When you live in this reality long enough, your sense of time becomes more acute, you understand clearly where your window is to act, how much time is 'safe enough' to get to the next shelter, and when you can possibly grab Uber or Bolt to make it to work at a reasonable hour.

My thinking placed me in a half-hour 'act on it zone' to call a cab. John was in one of those moods where staying put until the air raid was over was the only option. He had a different feeling about this. My Bolt was three minutes out, and I informed him I was going to work. An argument against my enthusiasm had some valid points. But let me explain. It was not just the last day of school, the day of the long-awaited assembly my kids had been practicing for weeks, it was also the day of the American tradition that

I started last year – making chocolate chip cookies and spreading of the sweet joy, full of carbohydrates, around the school by my first-grade students. The cookie dough had been made and marinated in the refrigerator for 24 hours, for God's sake! How could I leave all of this behind and not show up for the one last final on-stage practice before the culminating event, after which all of us could relax and lie on the couch for about three weeks??! Who is going to watch the kids that did show up, stuck on the road in their parents' cars already on the way to school before the missiles were in the air?

My choice was clear to me. I just wish my husband would see my point. I had enough time in the car to consider my situation from John's perspective: who on Earth would actually show up to school today? It is the last day before the break, and their morning started with loud explosions all over the city. Every child would have heard something somewhere. If I were a parent, I would encourage my own kid to stay home and start the break a day early. Plus, the cookies were a complete surprise this year, sort of an unannounced bonus for all their hard work. Maybe I made a wrong move and should have stayed home?

I clocked in at 8:10. The school premises were quiet and empty. If anyone was here, they were in the bomb shelter. I had a moment to take off my coat, turn on the Christmas lights and the projector with some quiet Christmas music, get a cup of coffee, and proceed to the bomb shelter to assess the situation.

The familiar faces looked up at me as I made my way down the stairs. A few of my kiddos made it to school early. I was relieved to see them, chatting away about something or other, and so were they. They do not express their feelings in the same way a mature adult might, but if you know what to look for, assuming you have truly met all of your students, know their quirks and unique situations, you will also read their faces and body language confidently enough to say to yourself, 'I'm glad I showed up'. Their 'unique situation' manifests itself daily, with air raids disrupting their learning and emotional well-being so many times that their self-talk, so appropriate for their age development, includes phrases like 'Air raid! Proceed to the shelter!' when they are drawing imaginary characters for the story. Some kids may talk to their toys employing the newly learned concepts and rephrasing them to make sense in their minds, including 'don't worry/walk to the shelter/air raid is over'. They need someone who shows up. They might not know this consciously; they simply feel it. And this is what I saw on their faces that day – a relief, that even though the situation represents a type of calamity, there will be some known factors in it, some people who care, who show up for them in the midst of bombings, who practice the protocol procedures with them until the sound of the air raid is no longer expressed with a fear in their eyes, but means a simple routine, that requires for them to not panic and walk quickly to the bomb shelter and stay there until the air raid is over. To feel more 'secure', we have a yearly calendar of our Ukrainian soldiers from Kyiv, looking at us from the pages of the calendar, confidently and furiously. Their call signs are there next to them, making us wonder how they got them. They look at us, we stare back, hoping against all odds that they are going to save us yet another time. 'We know you can!' my students reply to each soldier in the photo, who is 'initiating an imaginary conversation' with the first graders in Pechersk School International bomb shelter.

That day, all my students showed up at school. Let that sink in for a second: every single student showed up that morning, some later than others, but every single one of them came, because they had an assembly, an authentic common project they all worked so hard to perfect, and knew that if one of them was not going to make it, the burden of extra lines and added stress would fall on someone else, and they did not want to be 'that guy'. How is that for maturity? I was proud of the persons they were becoming and felt privileged to be their learning partner in this unpredictable journey.

The chocolate chip cookies bonus did what it intended to do: it put smiles on everyone's exhausted face on the last day of school, which was broken up into the air-raid shelter/clear-classroom periods. The kids loved rolling the balls, smelling the aromas of chocolate and vanilla filling the entire perimeter around the school cafeteria, eating a lot of those later in the classroom, fighting for the ones with more chocolate in them, but, most of all, they enjoyed walking around the school with a large tray and yelling 'Merry Christmas' at everyone they shared the cookies with.

I will cherish that day in my memory for years to come.

31

Christmas

This year, 2024, has been a dark one for me, spiritually speaking. The war has taken its toll. The doubts crept into my soul, suggesting all kinds of outlets for my current state of mind, trying to find logical explanations for the situation Ukraine has found itself in. So much grief, death, losses: young people, old people, children and parents, houses and homes, pets, sanity and clarity of minds, love and health, beliefs, plans for the future…

Tragedy came and settled, singing its devastating song against everyone's will. How come the world is not doing more to stop this madness? How come God allows for such travesty to go unpunished? Why is God not interfering to stop any of it? Why is this taking so long? Are we being punished for the sins of our fathers, or, maybe, our own? Surely God sees everything, when will retribution or justice come? Why is the world turning on its head and evil is getting a sure grip on its throat? Why do people choose this way to be and exercise their free will at someone else's expense? Why is there no strength to resist unchecked power?

With these kinds of thoughts spinning in one's head day in and day out, it's easy to forget your own principles and beliefs, for faith to start shaking and the foundations of everything you held on to crack in many places. A 'new version of you' begins to take shape almost against your will, depending on how much loss you endured, how many people you saw die or suffer in front of your eyes, how many screams you heard… No one will be the same coming out on the other side (if coming out of this is God's will), no matter what positive self-talk you employ or how many times you've practiced mindfulness. To come out untouched by it means you haven't lived through it. You stayed sheltered someplace else. The world you know will shape you up differently, like the product of your environment, with its own issues and problems no less valuable.

My world became entangled with the urgent need to explain why this was happening and who was to blame for it all. Without the possibility of immediate satisfactory answers to those questions, the need persists, but is wrapped in anger, disappointment, rage, and depression. It's like running a marathon without proper training. Inevitably, one is bound to get exhausted and continue slowly, on some autopilot, an unknown force urging to complete 'the race'. When in it, there are stretches of indifference toward everything once enjoyable and precious, including holidays. Celebrations are discolored with a sure anticipation of bombings and lose their full joy because they have a limited window to be experienced and savored.

So, for the very first time in many years, I did not shop for Christmas gifts in 2024. I couldn't find the strength. I did not expect or want to be on the receiving end either. It just did not matter. I also knew that John felt the same way. At this point in our lives, we do not want much. We are blessed with everything we need; we have many things we want and appreciate, and we do not want much else. It makes it very difficult to shop for one another, turning potentially exciting possessions into irrelevant trinkets in the end. I did what the person who likes writing does. I picked a beautiful Christmas card for John and wrote a long message in hopes of brightening his spirit and leaving a keepsake behind in a worst-case scenario.

But John… John did the opposite. I had to sit and unwrap a bunch of stuff. He was so excited to bestow his tokens of love! That in itself became my favorite part of Christmas morning. I will always remember that feeling mingled with a sense of urgency to run between the two carrying walls as the telegram channels announced ballistics shot toward Kyiv. But first things first. I had at least a minute to finish admiring my gifts and read a lovely message. I chose that, knowing in my heart I would rather die happy on Christmas Day, than shake in fear in the hallway. I purposefully sat and savored the moment until I absolutely had to act reasonably. I learned things about my own threshold of resilience. It's not so much that I became brave or less scared of the possibility of dying, but, maybe, more accepting of the fact that we had lived on borrowed time ever since the war had started, and when ballistics are flying toward us, it is a simple reminder to be ready. It took away the comforting knowledge that the life we spent efforts creating can be over in a glimpse, and we have to be ok with it. The sense of security of your own shell was always false; the war has simply reminded us how fragile we really are.

Unconsciously, every holiday ritual becomes more meaningful somehow, like making sure we have plenty of festive candles and lights in the house, a version of a Christmas tree on the balcony and a centerpiece on the table, chocolate chip cookies day set aside for the experience of making, smelling the aromas, baking, and eating. The favorite Christmas movies picked for the day when it finally snows (hadn't had it this year yet, a nice little snowstorm). The chicken marinated in white wine and cooked to perfection according to the years of the Sennett family tradition (and experimenting on our part), spices obtained two weeks prior, the special brandy John loves so much, Prosecco, prosciutto and various sausages waiting on their turn to be gobbled up as the holidays unfold… There is an unspoken determination to celebrate life despite the major disappointments, especially on Christmas, especially for us! Our wedding anniversary is on 26 December. St Nicholas is our family's cherished saint, whose day we celebrate in December also, and there is that long-awaited Christmas break I get to spend with John. Plus, there is that looming feeling that this could be our last Christmas, and it deserves a proper tribute. Old traditions beautifully balanced some new ones we naturally picked up in Ukraine, like getting the next must-have vyshyvanka, intricately designed, handmade and quite gorgeous to simply pass by and leave behind in the store window of one of my favorite places just around the corner.

The feeling of putting on a vyshyvanka deserves a special poem that I am no good at composing, better leave it to the pros who create proper emotions with just the right wording. Somehow, it symbolizes more than just a 'feeling of being Ukrainian and a part of a nation' currently fighting for its existence, but the very roots of these strong, beautiful people, who are carrying on the ancient traditions we got so privileged to experience in the past few years. It's all the babysias and didysias from a long time ago, urging us to run that marathon just like they did, when the soviets imposed a tragedy after tragedy on the people they feared. It is them we honor when we wear our vyshyvankas, all who survived Holodomor, fought WW II and WW I, got tortured in gulags and repressions, all the displaced and wronged, who knowingly and unknowingly contributed to the survival of Ukraine, made it stronger in the spirit of freedom. The vyshyvanka is the symbol of that authentic free spirit, just as intricately woven into the soul of each true patriot of this country. When we put on a vyshyvanka, we reconfirm the strength and beauty within us, still fighting for the cause to be and to make our own destiny.

My Christmas may no longer feel the same way it did in the States, like a wonderful, magical bliss, in the land of no sorrows, but it will feel no less authentic. The unsettled issue of one distinct Ukrainian Orthodox Church has inadvertently created a solid two-week Christmas celebration, not just the anticipation of Christmas. People like us looked deeper into the history of Christmas celebrations and the specific dates of the feast to discover a compromise the Council of Tours came to in 567, introducing Christmas holidays that lasted for 12 days, from 25 December to 6 January. Who are we to argue with that?! So, John and I celebrate the 12 days of Christmas. Along with the gifts and 'koliadky' it will carry a sobering understanding of joy within the limits of borrowed time we live on, and no 'security blanket' to cover it with, tripling the sensation of gratitude for being alive.

32

The New Year's

There is something profoundly sad about this holiday in this part of the world. For me personally, not the rest of the jolly crowd, getting their New Year's trees and running about with gift bags. For them, it is almost divine, the New Year's that is, yet to come. Oh, the parties to be had, the feast to be assembled, the mandarins, the champagne, the olivyie.[1] The joy of sitting somewhere in a restaurant or a corporate event right when the clock strikes midnight, bestowing the 'best of everything on everyone'... Don't get me wrong, I am not a bitter party of one. I do appreciate a good holiday, things to stuff myself with, a nice cold glass of Prosecco that makes everything better, the truffles accumulating around the house, etc. But! I happen to have an issue with the New Year's everything when I am here. A little backstory is a way to go here.

When I was growing up in the USSR, anything religious was banned. There was no Christmas, no Easter, no Ascension, no baptism, and no anything to suggest humility, a trust in a higher power, or simply put, the freedom to worship anything one might choose to. The agenda trickled down ominously from the top of the pyramid to the rest of us mortals, telling everyone what was and what wasn't, and how it was to be forever, in the 'best country, society, and otherwise encompassing best of the best of whatever'. Red kerchiefs tied around necks, buttons with the image of Lenin decorating the outfits, his godawful photo framed in any public office, many homes adorned with communist flair prominently displayed for the guests to see and be assured they were in the 'right kind of home', not some suspicious kind to be reported. Back then, there were no private businesses; everything belonged to the government or 'the people' as they liked to put it. If you wanted to be a 'decent' member of society, a 'good citizen' and so forth, you had to accept that the USSR was the 'best country in the whole wide world' with the 'best services, opportunities, clothes, food, culture, and the mission of communism as the best possible answer to all questions'! Period.

My parents baptized my brother, Alex, and me in secret. Only my godparents were present, and the priest in some abandoned church that remained intact in some village no one had heard of (hence, the church was still standing). Another reason that not every church got destroyed, no matter how hard they tried, was that there were too many to

1 A creamy potato salad that is a staple of holiday meals throughout Ukraine.

'handle the USSR way', and too much work! After enough of them were seized as public properties and offices were erected in place of an altar, the top of the pyramid had its fill and the adequate space to 'educate the society about the evil influence of capitalism and the West on the pure minds of soviet folk'. Lectures were held in the churches, flyers and brochures passed around, crosses of gold and precious metals demolished by the hands of individuals who questionably could recite the alphabet, let alone read a book. But they liked the system, where you could take away someone's property in a snap as proof of their entire existence: 'See?? You don't need to be intelligent or cultured to own things, you just have to be in a place of power to come and take them away'! Those who had nothing will have everything, and those who had everything will be no more. The people will rule. The masses. Uneducated, dumb and proud of it, with no special path in the brain responsible for cause-and-effect connections.

And rule they did! They had to come up with some alternatives for celebrations of joyous seasons (you know, joy to the world, the Lord has come) though, the masses were agitated by all that energy spent on the big job of communism, and, rumors had it, the rest of the world didn't turn out all that evil without it, AND had fun on Christmas!!! Do tell, what it's like out there, in Sweden, is it true??? We know you played hockey there!!!

This is how the cult of New Year came about in the USSR. Instead of Santa Claus, or St Nick, they had Father Frost. Instead of Mrs Claus, they came up with Snegurochka (snow princess, the niece), the Christmas tree was officially renamed the New Year's tree. Everything shut down for two weeks of drinking and making merry in a secular, man-made holiday that had no magical meaning in it other than being forced down people's throats for years to come. People swallowed it, as they did everything else back then. This was it, the Holiday, the New Year's, officially allowed, so everyone could relax, eat, drink, and not worry about 'the good' choices. Everything had been decided for you. Go ahead, celebrate!

Those were the times of no choices and often very little food to go about every few years or so, with the next economic crisis at hand. I personally stood in a six-hour line with my parents, taking turns for bathroom breaks in between (having children meant more quantity received by each family member) for sausages and powdered lemonade from Germany, or some other country, definitely not the USSR. I remember being cold and excited at the same time, for the holidays were coming and we also wanted to feast. But where would it come from if not from the West?! I also remember boxes of soviet chocolates my parents brought from work for us during the holidays. With 'father frost and snegurochka' stamped on the top, naturally.

One time, a friend of mine in 2nd grade, Snezhana, told me face-to-face that Santa Claus was the one who brought the gifts for her and her brother at home. She had the proof! Her parents confirmed! I stated my case: your parents had to be the ones getting it for you, just like for us (because we didn't have Santa Claus here, remember?). She did not flinch: 'He came to my house, I tell you, my parents told me so. He's been doing it for a few years now!' I was devastated for a while, inconsolable. No matter how hard my parents tried to convince me about Father Frost, I thought I wasn't good enough for Santa Claus himself to show up at my doorstep. I was good only for Father Frost. My parents had to come clean about the existence of either one of them. I could swallow the truth about Father Frost. I do remember asking them, 'how could they be so sure about Santa Claus, though, if they never set foot in America?'

When I came to America, I was a bit disappointed with 'a no fuss attitude' about New Year's there. The complete opposite of what I was used to growing up. No one bothered prepping food for two days in advance. No one placed gifts under the tree. No one bothered staying up all night and making holiday wishes that inevitably 'came true' (as long as you wrote everything out on a piece of paper right at midnight and drank a glass of champagne as the clock struck the hour). None of the above. Maybe an occasional bar outing or a symbolic gathering at a friend's house to watch the Times Square Ball Drop and a holiday cookie. That pretty much summed it up. No big deal. I felt like 'my tradition of celebrating New Year's' was going to die in America. In the beginning, I tried to hang on to it, like some ghost from the past to be resurrected or kept alive to pay its dues. I cooked all I could remember from my culture a few days in advance, I bought champagne, I slept late so I could stay up all night, and I bought my favorite New Year's movies to watch (VCR at the time, then DVDs). Oy vei! All to no avail. John supported me as much as he knew how at the time. But the main problem was that his spirit was not in it. He just wanted to make me happy.

It took me about two years to realize something very important that I wanted to share with hope that some former soviet republic residents will read this and realize it too. In civilized countries, where Christmas was never banned, but celebrated and enjoyed for centuries uninterrupted, people did not have the need to create artificial secular holidays to be erected on a pedestal and worshipped. Therefore, a pure, authentic joy and excitement in those Western countries comes around Christmas, not New Year's. The proper order of things as they should be. All the priorities are in the right places, not skewed by some surrogate. In America, the bells of Christmas can be heard right after Thanksgiving. People begin to get their Christmas trees and the ornaments out, decorate their homes, begin Christmas shopping early to make sure they don't forget anyone, stock up on groceries and proper cookie ingredients, and come up with menus and plans to see their families for gift exchanges and a feast. Christmas music can be heard 'everywhere you go', lights adorn every respectable street, and front lawns sport all kinds of seasonal attire to spread the joy of the season. People tend to smile more, proudly show the generosity of spirit everywhere and to everyone they meet… It is truly a magical experience. It envelops you in its glory. Once you have experienced it, you look forward to it every year. Suddenly, you realize, that your priorities shift to their proper places. You honor Christmas because Christ was born, the salvation to mankind has come. You rejoice even if you don't believe, that's how strong is the spirit of Christmas. There is no need to wonder why we celebrate it. If you are a Christian and live in a free country, you are free to celebrate and worship, to get excited and overspend, overeat, overdecorate, and overtravel. You can't help it. It's Christmas! It's the most wonderful time of the year!

I think we have been celebrating the artificial New Year's joy for so long that we never stopped and reflected on why, after the soviets were gone. Why do we still spend so much energy on New Year's? Saving up the energy of celebration for the New Year's and acknowledging Christmas as some afterthought? Why is Christmas taking a back seat in this part of the world? Christian? Check. Free country? Yes, ma'am. Then, I am yet to understand this ongoing obsession. It smells of soviet leftovers on someone's plate. I don't think there is anything wrong with celebrating New Year's. I do think the intensity of celebration is sadly misplaced.

I 'enjoy' the look on anyone's face when they ask me about my plans for New Year's and I provide an honest response, 'we don't really celebrate it, we celebrate Christmas'. At home, no parties, no all-night festivities, no drunken stupor or loud music, and, as of 2020, no fireworks. We do, however, bid farewell to the year gone, in our own way. In 2024, we started a corny but necessary habit of recording something positive that happened to either one of us on any particular day to remind ourselves to be grateful, no matter how things might seem temporarily overall. It is not a diary, more like a jar standing on the shelf, waiting for a deposit here and there. It is a tribute to our life as it is, no frills or 'spectacular' experiences, just a feeling of giving thanks incorporated consciously in a daily hustle, a choice to look for and find the good amidst the crazy. We do not read the notes all year; we write them, place them in a 'jar' and leave them alone until 31 December. On that day, we open the jar and read through the moments that made us happy that day. It is a visual and inspiring reminder of the year that passed, things that happened and were forgotten soon afterwards, and a glorious way to count your blessings. When I open the jar, I flip the notes top-to-bottom, so they go in order. As I write this chapter, I look at one such reminder, dated 2 January 2024, written by John, 'Grateful to be alive. 10 kinzhals, 60 missiles, 35 drones shot down over Kyiv'. I guess I did not quite feel grateful at the time to deposit the note. If it wasn't for him, I would have forgotten what we lived through because, let's face it, it was not the only missile barrage that we dealt with in 2024. I feel grateful now, with a little attitude adjustment, a year later, reading this note. It has done its job, though; it made me feel blessed to be alive, even though it begged the question: how on earth did we make it through this? The only thing I remember was the building reverberating in an unfamiliar way, paintings falling off the shelf on the wall, and a massive steel bookcase on the floor shaking afterwards. It is a pretty good indication of what might happen during the holiday season this year, give or take a few days, and it's better to be prepared for this mentally. It also instilled some hope: if we survived the last New Year's, we just might get through this one.

33

A Joyous January?

1 January 2025, Wednesday. Last night I took Philly out about 23:00, and the streets were empty, much like during the Battle of Kyiv. It was both eerie and joyous as I prefer the quiet time, but those memories of the early days of war never leave. The other part was sadness because New Year's once again shows its prevalence over Christmas. How do you become a free nation if you still partake in the Soviet Cult of New Year's? Natasha will write in detail about this because she is far more of an expert. Of course, New Year's Day was also calm and quiet, more like Christmas Day in the US. I realize the importance of family tradition and celebration, but it just reeks with bad leftovers. But I will not dwell and just enjoy the quietude and Natasha's yummy leftovers. We use New Year's as an excuse for a feast during the 12 days of Christmas. It's not 'if you can't beat'em, join'em'. Instead, it's well, let's take advantage of the time together while the crazy streets of Kyiv are not so crazy.

Part Three is drawing to a close, and so I am experimenting with the format for *Part Four* in trying to return to a running chronicle rather than anything else. I can't guarantee it will work out, but I will attempt to finish out *Part Three* in this manner and see how the style and format fit. Right now, the light is fading and the coolness of night approaches. Philly will need to be walked, and we have homemade mulled wine to make. January is starting on a joyous note, but today as I write this, I have no idea how it will end. We shall see provided we continue to survive.

6–7 January 2025, Monday and Tuesday. Orthodox Christianity in Ukraine is a unique experience for a multitude of reasons. The most important thing to remember is that it has been here in some form for well over a thousand years. The 'official' Orthodox Church of Ukraine (OCU) has switched to the Western calendar for Christmas, which means they celebrate on 25 December. I call it 'official' because it is the one that seems to be most supported and endorsed by the state. Our church, the Ukrainian Orthodox Church-Kyiv Patriarchate (UOC-KP), is accepted but gets sort of brushed aside by many because they decided not to adhere to some of the agreements (Tomos of Autocephaly) that made the OCU legitimate. There is also the Ukrainian Orthodox Church-Moscow Patriarchate (UOC-MP), which allegedly cut ties with Moscow but really can't do this canonically without being released by the Russian Orthodox Church-Moscow Patriarchate.

We, as US citizens, celebrate festively on 25 December with most of the rest of the world. However, our church (UOC-KP), as well as the UOC-MP, uses the old calendar (Julian), which means Christmas is celebrated on 7 January. Yes, it would be very easy to get confused and mixed up, wouldn't it? Natasha struggles a bit more than I do because Russia and Belarus both celebrate on 7 January, so she feels like if she acknowledges it, then she is concelebrating with the enemy. Understandable, right?

Right now, Natasha is sitting in the other room writing about her impressions concerning Christmas. Maybe there will be some redundancies in our telling. However, I think that it will add a certain richness to this book to understand this dilemma. Well, I don't find it to be a dilemma, and that's why I thought you might be interested in my version. This all began last year, 2023–24, but was only made official in 2024. So, we are into our second year, and I have adapted to it by adjusting my whole outlook on celebrating Christmas.

First, I must state that our church (UOC-KP) has taken us in and embraced us as its own. They made us part of their family despite my not speaking Ukrainian or Russian. Father Bohdan has taken me in and allowed me to serve behind the altar, which is the richest spiritual life I have ever led. He even accepts that I do not make it to every service without scalding or judgement. So, I can't just leave them simply because they celebrate Christmas on a different day. What I have done is to improvise, adapt and make the most of the situation, which any good Marine would do.

I think I will spare you the details as you would need a deeper understanding of Orthodox Christianity, its services, dogma and feasts, and this is a chronicle, not a religious text. Today (Tuesday, 7 January) is the official day we conclude our melded Christmas celebration. Last night, I attended Vespers for Christmas Eve. The service is mainly held in the dark with just a few candles burning. Natalia and Daryna (choir) sing their part of the service in the soft lilt of Ukrainian. Father Bohdan chants his parts as he swings the censer, and the smoke lifts into the dim light. He wears white vestments, as do I and the other older altar server, Kostantin. A manger scene lies next to the icons. A star hangs above the large icon above the entrance to the church. Candles flicker, an air raid sounds. There is majestic beauty within all of it for the birth of a King. Municipal workers join us at the invitation of Father Bohdan. I love Ukraine's working class above all else, and it brings joy to my soul as they stand somewhat uncomfortably at the back of the little church. They remind me of the shepherds in the fields on the night Christ was born.

On Tuesday, Natasha went to Divine Liturgy, and I stayed home with Philly. The roles were reversed the evening before. Philly is suffering from arthritis and is very expressive about his pain. We coddle him, but he's all we have got when it comes to family. I stayed home and prepped the food for our last feast. This felt holy. One of the strengths of our marriage is our love for preparing meals for each other. We will spend the day quietly and eat well. It's still festive, but not like the Western Christmas we also celebrate. This second Christmas is more focused on Christ, ritual and ceremony. Tonight, we will have our last feast, and we will remember His words 'Wherever two or three are gathered in My Name, I will be there.'

8–9 January 2025. I had not planned on keeping a nearly daily roundup of events, but so far, it's turning out that way. Natasha returns to work on Monday, so I suspect things will slow a bit as the month develops, but this is war and this is life, so you just never know.

We were invited to St Sophia's Bakery for an art event on 8 January. This was organized by the Museum of Folklore of Ukraine for the unveiling of a project by Volodymyr Koziuk. He is an official People's Artist of Ukraine. Volodymyr began documenting, painting and studying the old-style homes in Ukraine and specifically in Podilya, a region of Ukraine, in the 1990s. Tonight, we attended the launch of his book about the project, which was 28 years in the making. We were the only Americans in attendance.

There were many speakers and some Cossack-style music. The main thing I took from this event was what one of the speakers stated. 'Cultural Diplomacy' for Ukraine is paltry, almost non-existent. The only thing we are known for internationally is 'Shedryk', better known as the 'Carol of the Bells'. I sat there thinking that the world is missing out on some stunning art. That moment also caused me to realize that the main reason the world knows so little about it is because the Russians have been suppressing it for centuries. They claim their Russian luminaries as 'high art' and categorize Ukrainian art as 'peasant art'.

Folk art is more like it, and man, some of it is fascinating. I can't say how they will classify Natasha and me. Non-fiction might not be considered art anyway. Frankly, as working-class Americans, our contribution is more along those lines anyway. We never feel comfortable among elites, even though at times we are invited to events with them. I guess as Jersey people, the spirit of Bruce Springsteen runs through our veins and souls. Bruce is certainly way past the working class, but it seems he never forgets his roots.

On 9 January, I was back to work. One of my friends, a true patriot of Ukraine who I will not name, is working on a study of the Russian Orthodox Church's malign influence in Europe and the US. I had done some research on this early in the war and had a book I thought she could use for her project. We agreed to meet in front of St Volodymyr's Cathedral on her way to another meeting. The night was cool but not cold. People stood waiting for the electric tram to take them home or to some other destination. Cars whizzed by on Shevchenko Boulevard. I am almost always early, so I just stood by the fence and drank in the night.

She soon arrived. We walked toward Maidan Square and chatted. She told me she was on her way to a meeting with one of the Ukrainian Volunteer Battalions, known for their unwavering patriotism and considered controversial by some. I don't question these things, as sometimes I don't understand some internal groups. If they were fighting the Russians and doing it effectively, who was I to question their ideology? She was particularly giddy as we walked and talked. In her hands was a wrapped canister with a Christmas bow.

She stated, 'This is a New Year's gift for the guys.'

I nodded and gave her an inquiring look.

'It's a highly volatile gunpowder-like substance with huge explosive capacity. Only a few grams are enough to detonate a vehicle and destroy it. Don't light a match.' She smiled and chuckled slyly.

So, here we were, two patriots dressed casually and chatting on Leontovycha Street while one of us carried a deadly substance that would cause multiple deaths of the enemy and/or collaborators. The unit that was designated to receive this seemingly nondescript New Year's gift is known for carrying out these types of operations. That's the nature of war. Killing one individual often has strategic importance because of their decision-making responsibilities or past offenses. Vengeance is ugly, but it is understandable given the circumstances. We chatted and then parted ways. Her to her mission and meeting, me on my way home to Natasha and Philly to eat leftover meatloaf. The point I am getting at here is that things are often not what they appear to be in a war zone. More importantly, there is a huge portion of the population who are true patriots that work every day for victory. We all know that the government and military structures cannot handle it all. We also know that sometimes the rules must be bent in war. Grizzly and I have bent the rules on many occasions. Nothing unethical on a grand scale. As they say, 'All's fair in love and war.'

13 January 2025. Natasha had returned to work. I was battling a severe case of COVID. The weather was very dark. President Trump's inauguration is a week away, and already his team has been faltering on negotiations with Russia. US hegemony is dead and gone. The US seems dead or at least brain-dead. Natasha and I had left for many reasons, and that was one of them. Nobody had to pull the wool over our eyes. Nor did we expect Trump and his team to come riding in to save the day. That just wasn't realistic. President Putin was clearly in it for the long game.

Europe would have to enter the war if they really wanted it to end. That seemed to be the only way that Russia could be defeated at this point in time. History may prove me wrong, and maybe I will even be able to write about it. Neither of us would be willing to live under the Kremlin's thumb. Of course, it's doubtful that the Russians could completely erase Ukraine and take over the whole country. We had to face the fact that Kyiv could be defeated if some others did not put troops and equipment on the ground. That, coupled with good air support, could rout the Russians in a short amount of time. On a conventional warfare level, they would not be that difficult to defeat, but there just seemed to be no way for Ukraine to do it on its own. But we don't put our hope in anything this far into the war. Reality is that it was more likely that Ukraine would be sacrificed. It would be a sacrifice for nothing because if Europe allowed Ukraine to fall, the Russians would march on. That much was obvious.

You can call them orcs. You can call them fascists. You can call them anything you want, but what's important to know about them is that they are relentless. They just keep going until somebody kills the source. Ukraine doesn't have that capability, and everyone else lacks the balls. What a waste of so many good Ukrainian lives, cities, villages and businesses. By now, it's apparent that this is full-on World War III, but as long as part of the 'free' world is living relatively comfortably, they'll just go on and ignore it. By the time it reaches them, it will be too late, and the Russians will just keep rolling. Well, that's the way it looks from here, inside the war. I would love to be wrong.

16 January 2025. COVID wreaked havoc on us both for over two weeks. It was the most severe case that either of us has had so far. A major missile attack, or so it was termed, happened yesterday or the day before. The sad truth is that it didn't seem so 'major' to us. Natasha jumped in her Bolt even as missiles were flying toward Western Ukraine. Getting used to war is unsettling. We acknowledge it, we respond to it, we

analyze it, but there's no getting used to the fact that you are used to it. That's more of a dilemma at times than the actual attacks.

I just wanted to write this, as just five minutes ago, air defense seemed to be working right outside the window. It was loud and close. My reaction was calm and not hurried. Philly didn't even move. This is a different kind of hell that most will never understand. Natasha and I are trying. We are writing for the historical record, not fame. We are writing so you can, to some extent, see and feel the reality that we have lived with for almost three full years now. We try to understand those who have lived it for over 10 years and those who are closer to the fighting. Our human experience is all we really have to offer. We hope it helps.

Later in the day, our network received an urgent message from Wozza. He has been supporting an air defense unit. They had just received notice that they were being transferred to infantry units in Kursk. This issue has been all over the news lately, as being considered illegal by many. The criticism being that it is depleting air defense, but also goes against the laws. A lot of problems seem to have arisen with the AFU General Staff, and the voices are rising. Accusations of utilizing Soviet Military Doctrine and cronyism are in the news every day. The British Prime Minister Keir Starmer arrived in Kyiv today with General Valerii Zaluzhny (now Ambassador to the United Kingdom). President Trump takes office in four days. There's a lot of stress and speculation everywhere. President Zelensky is in a tight corner and will have to make some sort of move. Mobilization is not going well. It seems like Trump's Administration may make additional military aid contingent on Ukraine lowering its draft age to 18. President Zelensky and his staff fear this because it will make his already declining approval ratings even worse. Maybe he can blame it on the US as an out.

Fact was, that Wozza needed help, and the politics could take a back seat. His Air Defense guys had been given a few days off to spend time with their families. The rumor was that they were being sent into Kursk to help take a power plant. This, we assumed, was not the nuclear power plant that was out of reach, but a local one. By doing this, the UAF could ensure a constant power supply to the Russian residents under Ukrainian control. Would it win hearts and minds? Well, it wouldn't hurt. But here we were facing a situation where air defense technical and support guys were being thrown into a combat situation that they were ill-prepared for. Wozza was scrambling to get these guys what they needed, including gas masks, Tactical Individual First Aid Kits (IFAK), proper winter uniforms, socks, boots, helmets, body armor, and whatever else was needed to preserve the soldiers' lives. That had to be gathered, packed and ready to go. Gas masks are, for some reason, illegal to transit through the EU, so Wozza had to put on his smuggling hat. I told him to say they were for cannabis consumption, and they'd probably just say ok. Strange how the world works?

What's most important, and I can't stress this enough, our network started gathering and sending funds without hesitation or question. This was Matt Boben, Jon Allison, Paul Tregouet, Lee Tarricone and the world-famous but still anonymous Nicky. It brought joy to my heart and a deep sense of brotherhood. I didn't tell Grizzly as he has much going on. But he was in my heart and on my mind because I knew he would be joyous if he knew how strong our people are. If we live, he'll read this and smile. Within hours, Wozza had enough money to cover gas and lodging, with more promised to come just before his departure. No, we are not in the trenches, but we are fighting for the Ukrainian soldiers we love, respect and support.

Just as I was about to wrap up, our Austrian friend Florian Marlovits connected with Wozza to supply a generator, rangefinders and other equipment. Florian is headed into Kyiv for a few days and then onto Kharkiv before deploying to Pokvorsk for tactical medical transport. Being part of this team is what keeps me revved up and rocking along. What an amazing group of people. I am honored and humbled. We live to fight another day.

18 January 2025. Philly scampers quickly down the stairs of our filthy and decaying walkup. Our flat is beautiful thanks to Natasha, but as soon as you step out into the hall, it's like you live in a drunken leftover of the Soviet Union. This is the great legacy of communal life. No one takes pride in ownership and expects the state to clean up and repair everything. We, as Americans, hate it because it goes against our grain, but we are not wealthy enough to clean and fix it up ourselves, and if we did, none of our neighbors would probably respect and take care of it anyway.

I push the door open and get blasted with the smell of war. That sickening smell was with us for months during the Battle of Kyiv. Strange how this January has been conjuring the Battle of Kyiv abundantly. No, I don't take it as a 'sign' or portend some ominous end for us all. But there is an eerie quality to it all. War has its own smell, and it had come to haunt us again. Early-Dark-Thirty there had been explosions as we slept snugly with Philly curled up between us. Concussive blasts had caused all the car alarms in the yard to scream out. The air alarm went off after the explosions. Iskanders are fast and were shot down before the authorities could even warn us that they were coming. We rolled over and went back to bed.

Before the smell, I checked the channels and found that our district had been hit with falling debris. The part of our district that has suffered the most has suffered again. Some of our fellow Kyivans were killed. The metro stop was damaged, and trains would be functioning, but wouldn't stop there. Firefighters, EMTs and residents were out doing their jobs or surveying the damage. Nobody in the free world would live with this, I thought, but they are quite comfortable with letting Ukraine suffer. Now, I don't have any rose-colored glasses on about Ukraine or Ukrainians. They are far from perfect, but they are not subhuman. We always blame the Russians for wanting to erase their ethnicity, culture and history, but we rarely talk about how many who are supposed to be our allies seem to be ok with our erasure.

I say 'our' because we have become one with them. Natasha and I both know we are flawed, and yet they have embraced us, and we have embraced them back. It's a roguish family of sorts. Some of us are likeable rogues, while many are just rogues. We are in it together, and I guess that is what is comforting. Of course, the problem is that we (Natasha and I) begin to view much of the outside world like them (Ukrainians). This is becoming an ever-increasing issue as we watch the world sit on the sidelines while sending weapons when we now need people and better training. We fear that Ukraine will turn on those who helped but didn't help enough, and we will also be in those ranks. That is, we as residents of Ukraine will resent those who didn't help enough, and we as US citizens might become a target of remorse by some Ukrainians. Talk about existential dilemmas, right?

We just don't want to abandon our Ukraine. Will we ever be completely integrated? Will it matter? Well, it won't matter at all if Ukraine were to lose. The Russians will kill, rape, torture and rob us all.

19 January 2025. I wrote yesterday's piece in the afternoon and went to church around 20:00 for Epiphany (Blessing of the Waters). This feast and service is one of my favorites as it commemorates Jesus' Baptism in the Jordan River. It is a beautiful, joyous and fun service. We do a basic service on the Eve of Epiphany and another one the next morning, which includes Divine Liturgy.

Father Bohdan takes great joy in dousing us with Holy Water on both occasions. Everybody smiles and laughs as they get soaked. The whole church, icons and everyone gets wet. Afterwards, it's customary to drink some of the Holy Water and take some home. This water tastes fresher and cleaner than anything. Maybe it's wishful thinking, but who couldn't use a joyous service and a decent shower?

31 January 2025. Kyiv has been relatively quiet as far as missile attacks are concerned. Drones come through every night, though. More civilians are killed here and throughout Ukraine. You might think the lack of missile attacks is a good thing, but it's not. This means they are building up their arsenal for another massive one. That's the only way they have any success, which is to run a blitz attack. You can almost smell it coming. But it's joyous to an extent because it hasn't happened, and this is the last January.

This last half of the month has been a whirlwind with meetings, shipments, putting out fires and all the other stuff I do to help Ukraine outside the public eye. I had to make some 'Marine' decisions this last half of the month that I think might have hurt some feelings. They are Marine decisions because they are purely tactical, which means no emotion, no sensitivity, just straight get the job done. Sometimes this is allowing people or organizations to fall flat on their face to see how or if they get up and keep going. There's a lot of that going on in Ukraine right now since President Trump suspended all foreign funding. His action revealed just how many have been sucking on the American tit for a long time in Ukraine and worldwide. He has become the 'Great Disruptor'. Many I know and work with on the ground actually embrace this disruption. Why? It forces action and jettisons the unnecessary or the highly costly.

Just last night, I sat at a dinner hosted by Ryan Grant Little. A mutual friend in attendance, Kevin Leach of Sabre Training Advisory Group, was explaining that a certain USAID-backed NGO paid its Director $32k a month in salary. WTF? Seriously, that sounds corrupt to me, except its legalized corruption. Yes, Ukraine is struggling with illegal corruption, but the US (and others, I suspect) have basically found a way to legalize corruption so that taxpayer money pays some douchebag $32K a month. We needed disruption. Maybe I subliminally took my cue from President Trump with my Marine decisions.

Thing is, I don't regret them. I regret that maybe I lost some trust and friends. This is war. Nobody wins by making only easy decisions. Maybe my decisions were wrong, but the Marine Corps always taught us to decide, act and clean up the mess if you fuck it up. Nicky tells me that an alternative has already been found, which is the outcome I was seeking from the Marine decision. Feelings are hurt, but the mission continues. Nope, I don't like the smell of napalm in the morning, but I can live with it.

34

Hounds of Hell

The hounds of hell are all black dogs, and here in late February 2025, they are in a rage, frothing, teeth-bared, ready to strike while all wanting to be taken for a walk. Outside, explosions and air defense rain down every night. Just two nights ago, Natasha was out walking Philly as the projectiles could be seen in the air. Social media is full of rage and, as usual, lies and disinformation. Politicians throw barbs at each other while trying to flex their muscles and make deals. And the hounds of hell rage on with us individually and collectively.

Meanwhile, soldiers on the front line fight and die. They are relegated to the background in the political melee, but woe it would be if they just stopped fighting. Civilians are being maimed and killed every day. They are lost to the fiasco of world politics. Good people are still rising up and sending aid to the military and people in need. We are soldiering on despite the blabbermouths who, in the end, say nothing and do nothing. And the hounds of hell are biting our ankles.

Snow falls almost daily and quickly turns into a dirty brown and grey muck on the streets of Kyiv. People still trudge along their way to work to a bookstore or café. USAID workers have all but disappeared from their offices and haunts. Ukraine marches on. We march on, and the hounds of hell on their chains pull us out to walk in the hellscape of war.

There are hounds for each of us. There are hounds for families, companies, cities, nations and the world. The pack has no leader other than evil. Evil we can see, hear, smell and feel. Hate hangs everywhere in the air. It is the breath of the hounds. Sharp fangs bared; they scare many but embolden others to fight. There's a lot of fight left in many of us, so we strike a deal with the hounds and take them for a walk. Walks in trenches on the front. Walks through ruined cities and towns in Eastern and Southern Ukraine. Walks through hospital wards where the injured lay mangled and maimed. Walks through seemingly quiet cities where projectiles fall at night. And the worst walk, the ones in our minds, spirits and bodies. That's why we all have three hounds.

The hell hound of the body is the one that you feel. Our physical existence is shredded by lack of sleep, exhaustion, excessive drinking, smoking, and the vices we turn to in order to survive war. Some physical bodies turn to cheap sex. Others push themselves at the gym. But the hound of our physical body seems always to be there and is often the easiest one to control. He is a strong dog but one that we can walk for relief. This hound must be walked often for if our bodies deteriorate, we lose the energy and will to fight. And fight we must.

The hell hound of the mind, the psyche, is a much more insidious beast. He comes at us in the full light of day and also in our dreams. This one is hard to fight because his attack patterns can be unpredictable. He might come at us by our own fault because we pay attention to something we shouldn't, like a social media post, a soundbite or a piece of news. This hound also rises up deep within the bile that lives within our minds. It swirls around and then rises deep in our dark recesses, seeking attention, the light of day. He is caged, but sometimes the lock is loose, and he gets out. In our dreams, we have no control over the pull of this beast. We are unprotected there. This hound is probably the one we must walk most often and for the longest period. He is difficult to satisfy, and we must utterly exhaust him and push him from our minds.

Then comes the hound of the spirit. This is the most dangerous of them all. Our spirit cannot be destroyed, but it can be severely injured. Once the spirit dissipates, the will to fight, the will to live and to love fades. Our faith comes into question. Our faith in God, if we are believers, our faith in those around us, our faith in the military, our faith in anything that matters, is what this hound attacks. A weakened spirit causes havoc as we lose that driving power, that deeper source of energy that pushes us on. The hell hound of the spirit bites hard, and if we don't take the time to walk him diligently and focus our spirit on the light, then he awakens the hounds of the psyche and the body.

Walking three hounds at once. This is the worst. Often, we can subdue them singly, but once all three begin to drag us on their chains, it is no longer just a walk they need. No, this becomes a journey through the netherworld of all we are. Three hounds together are not measured in hours, not even days, maybe. These beasts take weeks if we are lucky, months sometimes, maybe years, or they never go away, and our lives change forever. Change in a bad way. The darkness of the three hounds can consume you, suck out life, hope and joy. That's why we fight to subdue one at a time as they come because once three are out, we can focus on nothing else but ridding ourselves of them. And we can never really rid ourselves of themes because they are dogs who need attention. They are dogs who are immortal, so we can't put them down. We have to walk them our whole lives.

Lucky are those who only have to walk their hounds through comfortable lives who only get occasional visits. Here in Ukraine, where evil walks among us, the hounds are stronger, more demanding and infinitely hungrier. We love our dogs; they are part of us. That's what we must embrace. We must accept our hell hounds because once we do, we can domesticate them. Well, we can to a certain extent because they will bite the hand that feeds. In fact, if you feed them, they bite you harder. The better strategy is to put them on a chain in the yard and let them bark and howl. We must do more than just survive. We must fight every day. Fight our demons, fight our hounds and fight a real enemy.

Right now, my dogs are in the yard, but they never stop howling.

Epilogue

by Tristan Ruark

'There's a burlap'—

BOOOOOM!

Cordite burned the nostrils, and moon dust wrapped around the Humvee, blurring out the sun. It was cool for a moment, a nice reprieve from the brutal summer heat, once the overpressure made its way back out of the hatch and let the oxygen, dust, and smoke inside.

The overpressure from the IED blew my brother, Gary Gaudioso from Long Island, onto the floor of truck.

'Gaudi, GAUDI!'

'I'm good.' moaned Gary.

The explosion had rung my bell good. The truck commander was yelling at me.

'Is the truck good?'

I put the pedal to the floor. It sprang to life, and we sped through the ambush. Comms were down, it was chaos of the painfully slow kind, but unwraveling outside at the speed of light and sound.

It was August of 2005, in Samarra, Iraq. We had just been the target of a complex ambush initiated on us while making a right turn at an intersection. The insurgents waited until my truck was separated from our trail truck and detonated IEDs on us and our trail. We were lucky. The IED on us was deeply buried and didn't do much but rattle us. Our trail truck was rendered immobile, and we had to drive back through the kill zone to get them.

Another IED blew up on our truck, this time it was late and lightly lifted the ass end of the truck.

We hooked up the other truck and towed it into Patrol Base Uvani. As we rounded the corner, another IED buried in a trash pile blew up on our trail truck, knocking the tow chains off and almost breaching the ballistic window on the truck commander's side.

Then the bullets rained down on our position.

We made it into the Patrol Base, only one man was slightly injured with shrapnel to the face. As we sat waiting to leave, explosions went off out in the city. The guys on the roof were engaging the enemy. We, for some reason, naivety maybe, decided to self-recover back to FOB Danger in Tikrit. This hour drive would now take us almost three hours, limping an immobile truck back to the FOB.

While we were in the patrol base, and I was listening to the explosions out in the city, the fear started to creep into me. For a moment, I was scared.

There is no way we are getting out of here alive, I thought.

That was it. The fear washed over me and was gone. What will be, will be. Have a good time while it lasts.

I left the fear in Iraq. In the sand. In those IED holes. I would go on to deploy two more times in support of the war on terror. The fear stayed in the sand. The fear stayed with the war. I left the fear, and I went home. To family, cable TV, and fast food. The war stayed there, in the news. The war was there. It wasn't coming to me, to my kids, to my parents, to Walmart. The war stayed there, tucked away safely in the cradle of civilization.

Until…

The second day of the new year 2024. The air raid alarm had gone off in Odesa. Shaheds were heading towards the city, but they wouldn't be there for a few hours. I had time to walk my tiny five-month-old baby girl through Victory Park. We walked there every day. I felt safe there. There was no infrastructure to blow up, no building to target. I enjoyed my daughter bundled up and staring up at me from her bassinet.

My wife messaged me to pick something up from the pharmacy. We made our way out of the park. I walked into the pharmacy and bought the medicine, then headed east towards the sea and to home. I was completely wrapped up in the moment. The cool air, walking my baby in this beautiful city, speaking my fledgling Ukrainian to the pharmacist.

RAAAAAAUUUUUUUUUUUUUGGGGHHHHHHH

An air defense missile ripped through the sky above my head, spurning towards the sea, followed by an explosion that made its way back up the street I was walking down, shaking windows and kissing my cheeks on its way out.

I heard the drones overhead. The Shahed sounds like a moped with a busted muffler or 1000 angry wasps, and when it's close, it sounds like 100,000 wasps who just had their nest kicked in.

I fucked up.

I had forgotten the alarm. Instead of going home, I went to the drug store as if there wasn't a war raging in the country I called home.

Stupid, stupid, stupid.

People ducked off the sidewalks. I stood there with white knuckled grip on the stroller.

Where the fuck do I go?

The baby slept.

I stood against the side of a building.

The fear came.

How the hell are we getting out of this one?

I wondered what she would be, what she would miss out on because I had been so god damned complacent. Who would she be? No school, no sports, her first Christmas being her last. What will her voice sound like? Would she enter and get out of this world without having a voice? A first word.

I lay over the stroller. I kissed her red nose.

You will not be alone. I will be with you.

I pulled the stroller back onto the sidewalk. I ran as gently as I could the two blocks to our apartment as the wasps swarmed overhead and the bullets and flak launched into the sky. The security guy saw me coming and motioned me towards the parking garage. He had opened it for us, and I ran inside.

I left the fear out in the street. Not all of it. Most of it.

But I keep a little bit with me.

A few more explosions echoed out in the city.

The war is here with me now. It's here with my daughter, my wife, our son, and our friends. It's in our parks, apartment buildings, our zoos, science museums, our beaches, our hospitals, our schools.

How the hell are we getting out of this one?